AN HISTORIAN'S
APPROACH
TO RELIGION

AN HISTORIAN'S APPROACH TO RELIGION

ARNOLD TOYNBEE

Second edition

Oxford   London   Toronto   New York

OXFORD UNIVERSITY PRESS

1979

Oxford University Press, Walton Street, Oxford OX2 6DP

OXFORD LONDON GLASGOW
NEW YORK TORONTO MELBOURNE WELLINGTON
KUALA LUMPUR SINGAPORE JAKARTA HONG KONG TOKYO
DELHI BOMBAY CALCUTTA MADRAS KARACHI
IBADAN NAIROBI DAR ES SALAAM CAPE TOWN

First edition 1956
Second edition 1979

British Library Cataloguing in Publication Data

Toynbee, Arnold, b.1889
  An historian's approach to religion.–2nd ed.

  1. Religion
  I. Title
  200   BL48   78–40535
  ISBN 0–19–215260–2

*Printed in Great Britain
by Whitstable Litho Ltd*

Preface to the First Edition

THIS book originated in two courses of Gifford Lectures
delivered at the University of Edinburgh in the years 1952 and
1953. When the University did me the honour of inviting me to
be one of their Gifford Lecturers, and asked me to propose a
subject, I suggested that I should talk about the glimpse that
we get of the Universe when we look at it from an historian's
point of view. I found myself intimidated by this subject when
I offered it, and still more when I learnt that it had been
accepted. I offered it because, in my own life, I had reached a
point at which the question 'What is our attitude towards
Religion?' was calling for an answer too insistently for me to be
able to ignore it any longer. I might, perhaps, have gone on
trying to ignore it if I could have persuaded myself that the
question was no more than a personal one; for then it would
have been of no great importance or interest to other people.
I believe, however, that, in finding myself pursued by this
question, I am having one of the characteristic experiences of
the living generation in the Western World. We have been
reminded of Religion by the quickening touch of Adversity;
and this common experience is a serious call for a candid inquiry
into the meaning of the glimpse of Reality that each of us
obtains in the course of following this or that walk of life.

The famous title of Sir Thomas Browne's book *Religio
Medici* shows that I could have described my subject in the two
words *Religio Historici*, instead of the present five, if Latin titles
for books in English were still tolerated by readers.

An Historian's Approach to Religion necessarily re-traverses
some of the ground covered in *A Study of History*. The present
book is on a far smaller scale; so, in chapters dealing with topics
already discussed in the other book, I have given references to
this, for the convenience of any reader who may care to go
into greater detail. In the present summary treatment, I have
not been able to repeat my explanations of the terms that I
use, or to support the points that I make by illustrations and
arguments. I have had to state my theses rather baldly, and
this might perhaps give the impression that I have mistaken
personal views of mine for *choses jugées*. I know very well that,

in both books, I have been presenting merely one view among many possible alternatives. My object in writing is to ask questions, not to coin dogmas. If any passages in the present book seem dogmatic, this is an effect of compression in the writing, not of illusions in the writer's mind.

While I have been writing this book I have had the pleasure of being constantly reminded of two happy visits to the Institute for Advanced Study at Princeton, during which I was able to prepare the lectures, thanks to the hospitality of the Institute and the generosity of the Rockefeller Foundation, and of two happy months which my wife and I spent in Edinburgh while the lectures were being delivered. Above all, I think, with gratitude, of the friendships which we made, thanks to the kindness with which we were received. It would take many lines to mention all our friends in Edinburgh, but I cannot leave unmentioned Sir Edward and Lady Appleton and Dr. and Mrs. Baillie. Though our time in Edinburgh passed all too quickly, our memory of it will be a lasting possession for the rest of our lives.

In revising chapters 19 and 20 for the press, I have had the benefit of comments and criticisms from the Reverend Dr. Henry P. van Dusen, President of Union Theological Seminary, and the Reverend E. H. Robertson, Assistant Head of Religious Broadcasting in the B.B.C. Neither of these kind critics bears any responsibility for the final version of these chapters, but I am very conscious of the help that they have given me, and very grateful for their goodness in finding the time to read these chapters in draft.

This book, as well as *A Study of History*, has been typed by Miss Bridget Reddin with her usual care and accuracy in deciphering a heavily corrected manuscript.

My wife has done a great service to the reader, as well as to me, in making an index that is a key to topics and ideas, and not just to names. At every stage in the writing of the book, she has also helped me in countless other ways.

ARNOLD TOYNBEE

December 1955

Preface to the Second Edition

THE major part of this book is a reprint of *An Historian's Approach to Religion*, first published in 1956, and based on the Gifford Lectures which my late husband, Arnold Toynbee, gave in Edinburgh in 1952 and 1953. By the wish of the founder of the Gifford Lectures, the lecturer was barred from basing what he had to say on any form of 'revealed religion'. It has therefore seemed not inappropriate to add as an appendix to this new edition my husband's hitherto unpublished paper 'Gropings in the Dark', in which Arnold explained his personal religious beliefs. He wrote this paper in September 1973, just after he had finished writing his posthumously published book *Mankind and Mother Earth*. It was therefore his last attempt to put into words his ideas about the mysteries of the universe and the nature of what he liked to call Ultimate Spiritual Reality.

As the title of the paper shows, Arnold did not think that he had arrived at a solution to these mysteries, but, being the man that he was, he felt entitled, indeed bound, to make his speculations known to other people. His approach to religious problems was an intellectual one. He could not make the final leap into the unverifiable act of faith which would have enabled him to accept, as his own belief and code of practice, Christianity or any of the other higher religions in which he was always interested and about which he wrote a good deal in many different books and articles.

Arnold's parents were (he presumed) orthodox Christians of moderate views. However, another member of the household was a great-uncle, a retired Merchant Navy captain, whose religious views were by no means moderate, but were so extremely Evangelical that he really seemed to his great-nephew to regard the Pope and the Devil as being virtually the same. Arnold was taken regularly to church as a child, and became thoroughly familiar with the Bible and with the Anglican liturgy. He often told me that he was glad to have had this background; as he wrote in 'Gropings in the Dark', he was 'steeped in the Christian tradition'. Yet he also told me (and wrote in the most autobiographical of his books, *Experiences*, when he was nearing 80) that, even as a child, he never believed in the Virgin Birth. By the time he was an undergraduate he had taken to calling himself an agnostic (never an atheist). This remained his position to the end of his life, and in *Experiences* he was at pains to explain that, whatever might happen on his deathbed, agnosticism was his considered view on religion during the whole of his adult life. But whatever he chose to call himself, it is clear that he was a deeply religious-minded man, whose attitude was summed up in the statement which Arnold was fond of quoting, made by the Roman Senator Q. Aurelius Symmachus in the course of a debate with Saint Ambrose: 'The heart of so great a mystery can never be approached by one road only.' All the same, I think he envied people who could accept one of the 'higher religions' as their own. He came near to accepting Roman Catholicism after his first wife, Rosalind Murray, became a convert to that faith; his son Lawrence followed his mother, and was sent to school at Ampleforth College. Arnold made friends with several of the monks at Ampleforth and they remained his friends after it had become clear that he could not stifle his doubts and become a Catholic. (I suspect that his great uncle Harry's influence on him as a child may have had something to do with this; and I think the same influence may have been responsible for his apparent belief that other people were as sensitive to the pricks of conscience as he was himself.) During the fourteen months that he spent in the Purey Cust Nursing Home at York, between the time of his stroke in August 1974 and his death, I think he was sometimes still trying to understand the mystery of the Universe, though difficulties in speech and inability to write legibly made it hard for him to communicate his thoughts and feelings. It was noticeable that during this period he always recognized and showed his pleasure at seeing any of his Catholic friends who came to visit him; but I do not think that this meant that he was any nearer to a deathbed conversion than he was when writing *Experiences* several years earlier. He was always pleased also to see the chaplain at the Purey Cust, a retired Anglican bishop, and indeed made greater efforts to communicate with him than with any of his other visitors.

Many of the ideas which he put forward in this paper 'Gropings in the Dark' had already been discussed in *An*

Historian's Approach to Religion, and in the chapter 'Religion: what I believe and what I disbelieve' in *Experiences*. In later works (for instance in *Surviving the Future*), he sometimes expressed the opinion that every human being has a religion, whether he admits it or not; and in all his writings on religious subjects he made it clear that he thought love to be the most important fact of life—indeed, its *raison d'être*. In his chapter on religion in *Experiences*, he showed an inclination to find the Marcionite version of Christianity more acceptable than the orthodox version. By the time he was writing *Mankind and Mother Earth* he had come to regard as unacceptable the concept of an omnipotent and loving super-personal god, and to assume that other people in the 'post-Christian' world agreed with him about this. He argues the case for this view in 'Gropings in the Dark'.

Though much of 'Gropings in the Dark' is thus a repetition of things that he said elsewhere, he does air some new ideas, and also makes some admissions about himself which I do not think that he had made before.

The paper is divided into four sections of unequal length. In the first section, headed 'Self', he wrote that his concentration on work, which made him so unusually productive, could be explained by his preference for keeping his mind occupied by creative activities such as writing, or taking notes in preparation for writing, rather than the concentration on meditation which might have been expected of him at the age of 84 if he had been, say, a Hindu. He attributed this preference to a desire to avoid further 'communion with Ultimate Spiritual Reality' after having had three experiences of this kind in the course of his life (he described two of these in *Experiences*). In this, he seemed to share Samuel Johnson's feeling that 'it is an awful thing to fall into the hands of the living God', to his own surprise when he was thinking rationally. He also admitted that concentration on work was no less childish a way of keeping his mind occupied than watching television—a practice that he had always 'arrogantly despised'.

In the second, and longer, section of 'Gropings in the Dark', under the heading 'Existence', he put forward some new ideas about the presence in the biosphere of life, consciousness, and love, which he thought may have seized opportunities successively to 'invade' the biosphere. At the end of this section he wrote that 'a scientist may be able to prove that I speak as a fool. Nevertheless, at my peril, I do venture to speak . . . because the problem of existence concerns all human beings, not only the scientifically competent minority.'

The remaining two sections of the paper, headed 'Evil' and 'Ultimate Reality' contain few, if any, ideas that he had not put forward before, but the argument is cogent, and supported by references to, and quotations from, the Bible and from the 'Scriptures' of other religions.

A short explanation is perhaps needed of what my husband meant when he was writing about the consciousness of men and of animals, and the distinction that he drew between the two. This was primarily that man was, and animals were not, conscious of their own mortality. But consciousness in man also seems to have meant to him the freedom of choice which is not evident, at any rate to the same extent, in animals. He dates the beginning of his own consciousness from the age of about two years, and I think this date is explained by his memory of an episode that took place during the summer following his second birthday, when he was staying with his parents at a seaside place in Wales. One day he deliberately ran away from his nurse straight into the sea, and his conscience told him (later on, if not at the time) that this was not the right choice to have made, since it greatly distressed his nurse.

My husband was never much interested in animals, though he always tried to avoid killing even an insect. His relative ignorance of animals and their behaviour perhaps explains why, in 'Gropings in the Dark', he describes predatory animals such as tigers and sharks as evil, though not wicked, as men are when they become predators. This reference to predatory animals as evil seems to ignore the 'balance of nature' and the consequences of overpopulation that would follow if animals did not prey on each other as well as on plants and vegetation. I do not know whether his eyes were closed to these consequences, but I think it is more likely that he believed the existence and behaviour of predatory animals to be one of those innate evils of the Universe which finally led him to the conclusion that the concept of an omnipotent but loving creator-god was impossible to accept.

VERONICA TOYNBEE

May 1978

Table of Contents

PART I

THE DAWN OF THE HIGHER RELIGIONS

PART II

RELIGION IN A WESTERNIZING WORLD

APPENDIX
GROPINGS IN THE DARK

PART I

The Dawn of the Higher Religions

I

THE HISTORIAN'S POINT OF VIEW

WHEN a human being looks at the Universe, his view of the mystery cannot be more than a glimpse, and even this may be delusive. The human observer has to take his bearings from the point in Space and moment in Time at which he finds himself; and he is bound to be self-centred; for this is part of the price of being a living creature. So his view will inevitably be partial and subjective; and, if all human beings were exact replicas of one standard pattern, like the standardized parts of some mass-produced machine, Mankind's view of Reality would be rather narrowly limited. Fortunately, our human plight is not so bad as that, because the uniformity of Human Nature is relieved by the variety of human personalities. Each personality has something in it that is unique, and each walk of life has its peculiar experience, outlook, and approach. There is, for instance, the doctor's approach to the mystery of the Universe (*religio medici*); and there is the mathematician's, the sailor's, the farmer's, the miner's, the business man's, the shepherd's, the carpenter's, and a host of others, among which the historian's (*religio historici*) is one. By comparing notes and putting individual and professional experiences together, the Collective Human Intellect can widen Man's view a little, for the benefit of each and all. Any note of any point of view may be an aid to this collective endeavour, and the present book is an attempt to describe, not the personal religion of the author, but the glimpse of the Universe that his fellow-historians and he are able to catch from the point of view at which they arrive through following the historian's professional path. No doubt, every historian has his own personal angle of vision, and there are also different schools of historical thought which have their characteristically different sectarian outlooks. We must examine these differences between one school of historians and another; but it may be best to start by considering what it is that all historians, in virtue simply of being historians, will be found to have in common.

The historian's profession, whatever he makes of it, is an attempt to correct a self-centredness that is one of the intrinsic limitations and imperfections, not merely of human life, but of all life on the face of the Earth. The historian arrives at his professional point of view by consciously and deliberately trying to shift his angle of vision away from the initial self-centred standpoint that is natural to him as a living creature.

The role of self-centredness in Life on Earth is an ambivalent one. On the one hand, self-centredness is evidently of the essence of Terrestrial Life. A living creature might, indeed, be defined as a minor and subordinate piece of the Universe which, by a *tour de force*, has partially disengaged itself from the rest and has set itself up as an autonomous power that strives, up to the limits of its capacity, to make the rest of the Universe minister to its selfish purposes. In other words, every living creature is striving to make itself into a centre of the Universe, and, in the act, is entering into rivalry with every other living creature, with the Universe itself, and with the Power that creates and sustains the Universe and that is the Reality underlying the fleeting phenomena. For every living creature, this self-centredness is one of the necessities of life, because it is indispensable for the creature's existence. A complete renunciation of self-centredness would bring with it, for any living creature, a complete extinction of that particular local and temporary vehicle of Life (even though this might not mean an extinction of Life itself); and an insight into this psychological truth is the intellectual starting-point of Buddhism.

With the ceasing of craving, grasping ceases; with the ceasing of grasping, coming into existence ceases.[1]

Self-centredness is thus a necessity of Life, but this necessity is also a sin. Self-centredness is an intellectual error, because

---

[1] *Upādāna-Sutta*, ii, 84, quoted in Thomas, E. J., *The History of Buddhist Thought* (London 1933, Kegan Paul), p. 62.

no living creature is in truth the centre of the Universe; and it is also a moral error, because no living creature has a right to act as if it were the centre of the Universe. It has no right to treat its fellow-creatures, the Universe, and God or Reality as if they existed simply in order to minister to one self-centred living creature's demands. To hold this mistaken belief and to act on it is the sin of *hybris* (as it is called in the language of Hellenic psychology); and this *hybris* is the inordinate, criminal, and suicidal pride which brings Lucifer to his fall (as the tragedy of Life is presented in the Christian myth).

Since self-centredness is thus both a necessity of life and at the same time a sin that entails a nemesis, every living creature finds itself in a life-long quandary. A living creature can keep itself alive only in so far, and for so long, as it can contrive to steer clear both of suicide through self-assertion and of euthanasia through self-renunciation. The middle path is as narrow as a razor's edge, and the traveller has to keep his balance under the perpetual high tension of two pulls towards two abysses between which he has to pick his way.

The problem set to a living creature by its self-centredness is thus a matter of life and death; it is a problem that continually besets every human being; and the historian's point of view is one of several mental tools with which human beings have equipped themselves for trying to respond to this formidable challenge.

The historian's point of view is one of Mankind's more recent acquisitions. It is inaccessible to Primitive Man, because it cannot be attained without the help of an instrument which Primitive Man does not possess. The historian's point of view presupposes the taking and keeping of records that can make the life of other people in other generations and at other places revive in the historian's imagination so vividly that he will be able to recognize that this alien life has had the same objective reality, and the same moral claims, as the life of the historian and his contemporaries has here and now. Primitive Man lacks this instrument, because the invention of techniques for the taking and keeping of records has been one of the accompaniments of the recent rise of the civilizations within the last 6,000 years out of the 600,000 or 1,000,000 years of Mankind's existence on Earth up to date. Primitive Man has no means of re-evoking the Past farther back in Time than the time-span of tradition. Before the invention of written records, it is true, the faculty of memory develops a potency that it does not maintain in the sequel; but its span, even in the primitive human psyche, is relatively short, except for the recollection of the bare names in a genealogy. Behind this close-drawn mental horizon, the whole past is confounded in an undifferentiated and nebulous 'Age of the Ancestors'. Within this short vista of unaided memory, Primitive Man has neither the mental room nor the intellectual means for jumping clear of Man's innate self-centredness. For Primitive Man, the Past—and therefore also the Future, which the human mind can imagine only by analogy with an already imagined Past—is simply the narrow, close-clipped penumbra of his Present.

By contrast, the art of taking and keeping records enables Man in Process of Civilization to see people who have lived in other times and places, not simply as a background to his own here and now, but as his counterparts and peers—his 'psychological contemporaries', so to speak. He is able to recognize that, for these other people in their different time and place, their own life seemed to be the centre of the Universe, as his generation's life seems to be to his generation here and now.

Moreover, when Man in Process of Civilization makes it his profession to be an historian, he not only understands intellectually an earlier generation's sense of its own importance in its own right; he also enters sympathetically into his predecessors' feelings. He can do this because the impulse that moves an historian to study the records of the Past is a disinterested curiosity—a curiosity that extends farther than the limits within which every living creature is constrained to feel some curiosity about its environment for the sake of its own self-preservation. In New York in A.D. 1956, for example, an historian will not live to do his work unless he shares his neighbours' self-regarding curiosity about the high-powered contemporary traffic on the roads; but the historian will be distinguished from his fellow-pedestrians in 1956 by being also interested in 'historic' horse-drawn vehicles, once plying in the same streets, in spite of these extinct conveyances' present impotence to take the historian unawares and run over him.

This margin of curiosity that is superfluous from a utilitarian point of view seems to be one of the characteristics that distinguish, not only historians, but all human beings from most other living creatures. It is this specifically human psychic faculty that inspires Man in Process of Civilization to take advantage of the opportunity, opened up for him by his accumulation of records, for partially extricating himself on the intellectual plane from the innate self-centredness of a living creature. Human Nature's surplus margin of curiosity, which the historian turns to professional account, is also perhaps an indication that this feat of breaking out of an inherited self-centredness is part of the birthright and the mission of Human Nature itself. However that may be, it is evident that the Human Spirit is, in fact, in a position to break out of its self-centredness as soon as it interests itself in the lives of other people in other times and places for their own sake. For, when once a human being has recognized that these other human beings, in their time and place, had as *much* right as his own generation has, here and now, to behave as if they were the centre of the Universe, he must also recognize that his own generation has as *little* right as these other generations had to maintain this self-centred attitude. When a number of claimants, standing at different points in Time and Space, make the identical claim that each claimant's own particular point in Time-Space is the central one, common sense suggests that, if Time-Space does have any central point at all, this is not to be found in the local and temporary standpoint of any generation of any parochial human community.

Considering the inadequacy of human means of communication before the industrial revolution that broke out in the West less than two centuries ago, it would seem probable that the accumulation of records enabled historians to transcend self-centredness in the Time-dimension before they were able to transcend it in the Space-dimension. A Sumerian priest, studying records in the temple of a god personifying the priest's own parochial city-state, could become aware of previous generations of his own community as real people, on a psychological par with the living generation, some thousands of years before a Modern Western archaeologist, excavating a site at Tall-al-'Amārnah in Egypt, could become aware, in the same sense, of the reality of the Emperor Ikhnaton's generation in a society which had had a différent geographical locus from the excavator's own, and which had been buried in oblivion for perhaps as long as 1,600 years before being disinterred by the curiosity of Modern Western Man. The disinterment of Ikhnaton is a classic feat of the historian's art of bringing the dead back to life, since this controversial figure has aroused in his re-discoverers some of the feeling that he evoked in his contemporaries. A twentieth-century Western historian who finds himself moved to take sides for or against this revolutionary Egyptian philosopher-king has undoubtedly broken out of the prison-house of self-centredness; but this feat of breaking out into the realm of spiritual freedom is hard and rare even on the intellectual plane, on which it is relatively easy to achieve; and, even when it is carried on to the plane of feeling, it is, at best, never more than very imperfect.

The Modern Western philosopher Croce has said that all history is contemporary history and that no history can be anything but this.[1] His meaning is that even a comparatively sophisticated Man in Process of Civilization is still, like Primitive Man, the prisoner of his own time and place. He is, indeed, their prisoner in two senses.

He is their prisoner in the objective sense that his only standing-ground for viewing the upper reaches of the river of History is the constantly moving locus of the mast-head of the little boat in which the observer himself is travelling all the time down a lower reach of the same ever-rolling stream. This is the reason why each successive generation of historians in the Modern Age of Western history has been impelled to write its own history of the Graeco-Roman Civilization. Each successive generation sees this identical episode of past history in a new perspective imposed by the transit to this generation's historical position from the position of its predecessors. This new perspective brings the familiar features of an old landscape into a new relation with one another; it changes their relative prominence; and it even brings previously invisible features to light and at the same time screens previous landmarks.

[1] Croce, Benedetto, *Teoria e Storia della Storiografia*, 2nd edition (Bari 1920, Laterza), p. 4: 'Ogni vera storia è storia contemporanea'; p. 5: 'La contemporaneità non è carattere di una classe di storie . . . ma carattere intrinseco di ogni storia.'

The historian is also the prisoner of his own time and place in a subjective sense. We have just observed that our Modern Western historians have been so successful in bringing the Egyptian emperor Ikhnaton back to life that they too, like his Egyptian contemporaries, are moved to feel strongly about him. Yet they do not feel about him in the same way as his Egyptian contemporaries felt. Their feelings about this reanimated Egyptian figure who was so controversial a character in his own lifetime find their fuel, not in the philosophical, religious, and political controversies that were rife in the New Empire of Egypt in the fourteenth century B.C., but in controversial current issues in the life of the historians' own society in their own day. They have written about Ikhnaton with something of the same animus, for him or against him, which they would have shown if they had been writing about Lenin or Hitler or Churchill or Franklin D. Roosevelt. In other words, they have imported into their feelings about Ikhnaton something of their feelings about controversial contemporaries of their own; and, in so far as they have done this, they have drawn Ikhnaton out of his own social milieu into theirs.

Even the most highly gifted historians will be found, on examination, to have remained prisoners to some extent—as can be seen in the case of Gibbon, who, in writing *The History of the Decline and Fall of the Roman Empire*, might seem, at first sight, to have chosen a subject that was sharply detached from the life of the historian's own prosperous and confident generation in his own Western Society. Yet Gibbon was a prisoner of his own time and place in at least three ways. He was inspired to choose his subject by a personal experience which linked the Roman Empire in the Age of the Antonines with the Rome of A.D. 1764; he was able to enter imaginatively into the life of the Roman Empire in the Antonine Age because he felt an affinity between this and the life of his own generation in a Modern Western Society; and he was concerned to inquire whether his own society could ever be overtaken by the disaster that had actually overtaken another society whose affinity with his own he had recognized.

Thus the historian's transcendence of self-centredness is never more than partial and imperfect; and even contemporaries who have been brought up in different cultural milieux find it difficult to appreciate one another's mutually alien cultural heritages now that a Modern Western technology has given them the means of meeting one another. In the world of A.D. 1956 the greatest cultural gulf was not the rift between a Judaic Western Liberalism and a Judaic Western Communism; it was the chasm between the whole Judaic group of ideologies and religions—Communism, Liberalism, Christianity, Islam, and their parent Judaism itself —on the one hand and the Buddhaic group of philosophies and religions—post-Buddhaic Hinduism, the Mahāyāna, and the Hīnayāna—on the other hand. In the bridging of this chasm the contemporary historian has a part to play which is as difficult as it is important. The self-correction through self-transcendence, which is the essence of his profession, no doubt always falls short of its objective; yet, even so, it is something to the good; for to some extent it does succeed in shifting the mental standpoint, and widening the mental horizon, of an innately self-centred living creature.

This transcendence of self-centredness to some degree— though, no doubt, imperfectly, at best—is therefore an achievement that is common to all historians of all schools. But the slightly widened horizon which the historian's angle of vision opens up has displayed different pictures of the Universe to historians of different schools. So far, there have been two fundamental alternative views.

One of these two views sees the rhythm of the Universe as a cyclic movement governed by an Impersonal Law. On this view the apparent rhythm of the stellar cosmos—the day-and-night cycle and the annual cycle of the seasons—is assumed to be the fundamental rhythm of the Universe as a whole. This astronomical view of History provides a radical correction of the bias towards self-centredness that is innate in every living creature; but it corrects self-centredness at the price of taking the significance out of History—and, indeed, out of the Universe itself. From this astronomical standpoint it is impossible for an historian to believe that his own here and now has any special importance; but it is equally difficult for him to believe that any other human being's here and now has ever had, or will ever have, any special importance either. In the words of an Hellenic philosopher-king,

The rational soul ranges over the whole cosmos and the surrounding void and explores the scheme of things. It reaches into the abyss of boundless Time and not only comprehends, but studies the significance of, the periodic new birth of the Universe. These studies bring the rational soul to a realization of the truth that there will be nothing new to be seen by those who come after us, and that, by the same token, those that have gone before us have not seen anything, either, that is beyond *our* ken. In this sense it would be true to say that any man of forty who is endowed with moderate intelligence has seen—in the light of the uniformity of Nature—the entire Past and Future.[1]

Hence, in the Graeco-Roman World and in the Indian World, in both of which this view was prevalent, History was rated at a low value. In the words of an Hellenic philosopher-scientist,

The poet and the historian differ not by writing in verse or in prose. The work of Herodotus might be put into verse, and it would still be a species of History, *with* metre no less than without it. The true difference is that one relates what has happened, the other what *may* happen. Poetry, therefore, is a more philosophical and a higher (σπουδαιότερον) thing than History; for Poetry tends to express the universal, History the particular. By the universal I mean how a person of a certain type will on occasion speak or act, according to the law of probability or necessity. . . . The particular is—for example—what Alcibiades did or suffered.[2]

The Indians, being more whole-hearted than the Greeks in living up to this Greek and Indian philosophy, disdained to write history. The Greeks, though their theoretical contempt for History was as great as the Indians' contempt for it was, were moved by their keen curiosity to study History, and by their fine aesthetic sense to embody the results in great works of literary art. Yet, in spite of the production of these monuments of Greek historical writing, Aristotle's low estimate of History was the considered verdict on History that would have been given by most Greeks in most ages of Hellenic history, as well as by almost all Indians at all times.

[1] Marcus Aurelius Antoninus, *Meditations*, Book XI, chap. 1.
[2] Aristotle, *Poetics*, chap. 9 (1451 B), translated by Butcher, S. H., in *Aristotle's Theory of Poetry and Fine Art* (London 1902, Macmillan).

The other fundamental view sees the rhythm of the Universe as a non-recurrent movement governed by Intellect and Will. The play of Intellect and Will is the only movement known to Man that appears to be unquestionably non-recurrent; and on this view the fundamental rhythm of the Universe as a whole is assumed to be identical with the rhythm in the career of an individual human being. It is assumed to be a drama that has a beginning and an end, that is punctuated by crises and by decisive events, that is animated by challenges and responses, and that unfolds a plot like the plot of a play. This volitional view of History gives History the maximum of significance, in contrast to the cyclic impersonal view; but it does this at the risk of tempting the historian to relapse into the self-centredness —innate in every creature—which it is the historian's mission to transcend.

This is the view of History that was prevalent in Israel and that has been inherited from Israel, through Jewry and through Jewry's congener the Zoroastrian Church, by Christianity and Islam. In the Judaic societies, History has been rated at a high value at the cost of a relapse into a sense of self-importance which a sense of History ought to correct.

It is true that the intellect and will whose plan and purpose are deemed, on this view, to govern History are those, not of any human beings, acting either severally or collectively, but of a transcendent and omnipotent One True God; and, à priori, a sense of the greatness of God might be expected to be as effective a cure for the self-centredness of one of God's creatures as a sense of the inexorability of laws of Nature. But the Judaic societies have re-opened the door to self-centredness by casting themselves, in rivalry with one another and ignoring the rest of Mankind, for the privileged role of being God's 'Chosen People', who, in virtue of God's choice of them, have a key-part to play in History—in contrast to a heathen majority of Mankind who are worshippers of false gods. A soi-disant 'Chosen People's' attitude towards the rest of their fellow human beings is a corollary and counterpart of the attitude towards other gods which they ascribe to the God by whom they believe themselves to have been singled out. The One True God is conceived of as being a jealous god. He is not merely the One True God in fact; He is intolerant of the worship wrongly paid to spurious divinities. The affirmation that 'there is no god but God' is deemed, by the adherents of the Judaic religions, to entail the commandment: 'Thou shalt have none other gods but Me'; and what God is believed to feel about false gods sets the standard for what God's 'Chosen People' believe themselves entitled to feel about heathen human beings.

Thus, in the Judaic societies, Human Nature's innate self-centredness is consecrated by being given the blessing of a God who is held to be not only almighty but also all-wise and all-righteous. This formidable enhancement of self-centredness is an evil that is inherent in the belief that there is a 'Chosen People' and that I and my fellow-tribesmen are It. And this evil is not exorcised by rising, as the Prophets have risen, to a sublimely austere conception of the mission to which the 'Chosen People' have been called. They may accept the hard doctrine that they have been called, not to enjoy unique power, wealth, and glory, but to bear unique burdens and to suffer unique tribulations for the fulfilment of God's purposes;[1] but, even then, their abiding belief in their own uniqueness still orients them towards a centre that lies in themselves and not in the God from whose fiat their uniqueness derives. This is the moral effect, *a fortiori*, of those latterday Western ideologies, such as Communism and National Socialism, in which the Judaic belief in being a 'Chosen People' has been retained while the complementary Judaic belief in the existence of an Almighty God has been discarded.

Thus the Judaeo-Zoroastrian view of History, like the Indo-Hellenic view, offers us an escape from one evil at the price of involving us in another. The picture of a cyclic Universe governed by impersonal laws of Nature promises to cure Human Nature of its self-centredness at the cost of robbing History of its significance; the picture of a non-repetitive Universe governed by a personal God promises to give History a maximum of significance at the cost of tempting holders of this view to relapse into self-centredness and to allow themselves to run to extremes of it with an untroubled conscience. Confronted with a choice between these two alternatives, we

---

[1] See Wright, G. E., *The Old Testament against its Environment* (London 1950, Student Christian Movement Press); Rowley, H. H., *The Biblical Doctrine of Election* (London 1950, Lutterworth Press).

may find ourselves shrinking from choosing either of them when
we have observed the sinister side of each. Yet these are the
two fundamental alternative views that have been accessible
to human souls so far; and today a majority of Mankind holds
either one of these two views or the other. The dilemma
presented by the choice between them will haunt us throughout
our inquiry. At the same time there have been other views in
the field; and two, at least, of these have been important
enough in the history of Man in Process of Civilization to
deserve some notice.

One of these two views sees in History a structure like that of
a Modern Western piece of music—though, in origin, this
view is not Western but is Chinese. In this Chinese view,
History is a series of variations on a theme enunciated at the
start; and this view cuts across both the Judaeo-Zoroastrian
view and the Indo-Hellenic, which are complementary to
each other besides being mutually exclusive.

The Chinese view is akin to the Hellenic both in seeing the
rhythm of History as being repetitive and in not being self-
centred. My generation, here and now, is felt to have no worth
by comparison with a Classical Past whose example is believed
to provide an absolute standard of conduct for all subsequent
ages in all conceivable circumstances. The best that we, in our
generation, can do to make ourselves less unworthy of our
forebears is to model our conduct on theirs, as recorded in a
classical literature, as faithfully as we can. On the other hand
the Chinese view is akin to the Judaeo-Zoroastrian in seeing
History in terms of personality and in seeing it as being full of
significance. The repetition of classical precedents is not an
automatic result of the operation of an Impersonal Law; it is a
conscious and deliberate act which is inspired by admiration
and is achieved by moral effort. There is a sense—self-evident,
no doubt, to Chinese minds when they come across the Judaic
and Indian views and compare these with their own view—
in which this Chinese view gets the best of both the Indian and
the Jewish World and so eludes our Indo-Jewish dilemma by a
characteristically Chinese feat of deftness and tact. This
Chinese view, like the Greek, has inspired notable works of
historical literature, and, under a recent exotic top-dressing of
Communism, it was perhaps still reigning, in A.D. 1956, in the

psychic underworld of nearly a quarter of the human race. The weakness of the Chinese view is that, in contrast to both the Jewish and the Indian, it is archaistic, epimethean, and static.

The other of the two secondary views sees the movement of the Universe as a chaotic, disorderly, fortuitous flux, in which there is no rhythm or pattern of any kind to be discerned. This has been the prevalent view of one school of Western historians in a post-Christian age of Western history. It will not bear comparison with either the Indian view or the Jewish; for, when confronted with either of these, it stands convicted of failing to go to the root of the question—'What is the nature of the Universe?'—that all historians ought to be trying to answer.

This Late Modern Western answer to a fundamental question is a superficial answer because it is content to accept the concept of Chance uncritically as being a sufficient explanation of the nature of the Universe, without taking cognizance of the philosophers' analysis of it. Yet Bergson, among other contemporary Western philosophers, has pointed out[1] that the notion of Chance, Disorder, and Chaos is merely a relative and not an absolute one.

If, at a venture, I select a volume in my library, I may replace it on the shelves, after taking a glance at it, with the remark 'This isn't verse'. But is this really what I perceived when I was turning the pages? Clearly not. I did not see, and I never shall see, an absence of verse. What I did see was prose. But, as it is poetry that I am wanting, I express what I find in terms of what I am looking for; and, instead of saying 'Here is some prose', I say 'This isn't verse'. Inversely, if it takes my fancy to read some prose and I stumble on a volume of verse, I shall exclaim 'This isn't prose'; and in using these words I shall be translating the data of my perception, which shows me verse, into the language of my expectation and my interest, which are set upon the idea of prose and therefore will not hear of anything else.

As Bergson lucidly explains, the appearance of Chance, Disorder, or Chaos is nothing but a negative finding disguised in an illusorily positive form of expression. The order that we fail to find in a particular situation is not Order in the absolute

[1] In *L'Évolution Créatrice*, 24th edition (Paris 1921, Alcan), pp. 239-58.

but merely one order, out of a number of alternative possible orders, for which we happen to have been looking. In finding a chaos, all that we have discovered is that we have stumbled upon some order which is not the particular order that we are seeking. Our investigation will not be complete till we have verified what this unsought and unexpected order is; and, when we have identified it, we shall have under our eyes an order and not a chaos.

On this showing, perhaps all that is meant by historians of this antinomian Late Modern Western school, when they declare that History is an unintelligible chaos, is that they do not find in it either of the two forms of order that are most familiar to them. They do not find in History either the Jewish rule of a living God or the Greek rule of an Impersonal Law. But they have still to elucidate for themselves the third alternative form of order that, is not finding either of those other two, they are bound to find in History *ex hypothesi*; and we may be sure that, in the meantime, they do see some order, pattern, and shape in History at some level of the Psyche; for, if they saw no shape in History, they could have no vision of it. When they protest that they see no shape, what they are really doing is to refuse to bring a latent picture of the Universe up and out into the light of consciousness; and, in making this refusal, they are allowing their historical thought to be governed by some pattern embedded in their minds at the subconscious level. This subconscious pattern will be holding their conscious thought at its mercy because they are deliberately leaving it out of conscious control; and a mental pattern that is not consciously criticized is likely to be archaic, infantile, and crude.

The crudeness of the pattern that some Late Modern historians are subconsciously following is indicated by the crudeness of the fragments of it that rise to the level of their consciousness like the flotsam that rises to the surface of the sea from a hulk that has gone to the bottom. Samples of these uncritically accepted intellectual *clichés* are the conventional terms 'Europe'; 'the European heritage from Israel, Greece, and Rome'; 'a cycle of Cathay' (perhaps, after all, not worse than a recent 'fifty years of Europe' that Tennyson did not live to experience); and 'Oriental' as a standing epithet for the pejorative abstract

nouns decadence, stagnation, corruption, despotism, fanaticism, superstition, and irrationality.

Such shreds and tatters of foundered and forgotten patterns
are bound to govern the thinking of historians for whom it is a
dogma that, in History, no pattern of any kind is to be found;
for, in truth, every thought and every word is a pattern found
by the Mind in Reality; and a complete renunciation of all
patterns, if this could really be achieved, would reduce the
Mind's picture of the Universe to the 'perfect and absolute
blank' that was the beauty of the Bellman's marine chart.[1]
An antinomian historian who still had the courage of his
convictions when he had grasped their philosophical consequences would find himself having to renounce not only
Marcus Aurelius's pattern and Saint Augustine's and Confucius's, and not only those scraps of patterns—'Europe',
'Oriental' and the rest—which professedly antinomian historians have usually allowed themselves without realizing that this
was inconsistent with their own doctrine. The uncompromising
antinomian would have also to renounce the patterns inherent
in the proper nouns 'Nicaragua' and 'Napoleon' and in the
common nouns 'country', 'king', and 'man'. He would have,
in fact, to achieve that suspension of all discursive thought
which is part of a mystic's *yoga* for extricating himself from the
world of phenomena; and, since this is, of course, just the
opposite of the antinomian historian's intended objective, it is a
consequence that would seem to reduce his doctrine *ad absurdum*.

Meanwhile, pending a settlement of accounts between the
antinomian historians and the philosophers, we shall perhaps
be justified in seeing in the chaotic view of the nature of the
Universe, not a distinct positive view, on a par with the cyclic
view and with the volitional view, but simply a useful reminder
that neither of these two fundamental views is more than a
hypothesis that is open to challenge.

[1] See Carroll, Lewis, *The Hunting of the Snark*.

2

THE WORSHIP OF NATURE

IF we set out to make a survey of the religions that have been practised at different times and places by the numerous human societies and communities of whom we have some knowledge, our first impression will be one of a bewilderingly infinite variety. Yet, on consideration and analysis, this apparent variety resolves itself into variations on Man's worship or quest of no more than three objects or objectives: namely, Nature; Man himself; and an Absolute Reality that is not either Nature or Man but is in them and at the same time beyond them.

Anyone who has been brought up in the tradition of one of the Judaic religions will have been predisposed by his spiritual heritage to approach Reality in Its personal aspect as God—the One True God of Judaism, Christianity, and Islam; and this approach to Reality may be called an act of worship as aptly as the act of worshipping Man or worshipping Nature. But Muslim, Christian, and Jewish mystics pass on from this worship of Reality as a personality to a union with Reality in which the distinction between personalities fades away; and this vision of Reality as a unitive, undifferentiated, and impersonal state of Being—a vision which is hard to attain for a traveller along the Judaic path—is the first glimpse of Reality which the same traveller would have been predisposed to catch if the accident of birth had endowed him with an Indian spiritual background instead of a Judaic one. A Buddhist or a Hindu will approach Reality in its impersonal aspect as Nirvāna (a state attained through the extinction of Desire) or as Brahma[1] (undifferentiated, and therefore ineffable, Being); and his spiritual activity will not be an act of worship. If he is a Buddhist, it will be a process of purgation, in which the state of Nirvāna will be reached when Desire has burnt itself out. If he is a Hindu, it will be a process of union with Reality which

---

[1] A neuter substantive, to be distinguished from the masculine substantive Brahmā, which is the Sanskrit name for the same Absolute Reality in Its aspect as a person.

it might be more accurate to describe as an intuition that the apparent distinction between his own personality and the Absolute is illusory.

Thus, though the first approaches of the Indian and the Judaic religions are made from different angles along different paths, the Indian vision of Reality as an impersonal state of Being is not unknown to the Judaic religions; and, conversely, the personal aspect of Reality, which is to the fore in the Judaic religions, is not unknown to the Indian religions. The Hinayanian Buddhist gospel of self-liberation through self-extinction has not been able to dispense with the spiritual support of a human saviour in the person of the Buddha Gautama. The Mahāyāna's line of approach to Reality lies through the human wayfarer's relation with a bodhisattva who, in all but name, is a personal saviour-god. In post-Buddhaic Hinduism, the Mahayanian bodhisattvas have their counterparts in saviours who are personal and divine avowedly.

Thus the difference between the Indian and the Judaic vision of Reality proves, on examination, to be, not a difference in view, but one of emphasis. In both visions, Reality reveals itself in two aspects, as a personal God and as a unitive state of spiritual Being; neither of these aspects is eliminated in either vision; and, whether we are thinking primarily in Indian or primarily in Judaic terms, we cannot think of Reality as being either Brahma-Nirvāna or God exclusively. Throughout this inquiry, we shall have to try to think in terms of both the personal and the impersonal aspect of Reality at once; and this comprehensive way of thinking is hard to achieve and no less hard to express. The personal form of expression will be likely to predominate in a book written primarily for Christian or ex-Christian readers by a writer brought up in a Christian milieu. But, wherever the present writer drops into this Christian Judaic usage, the reader must construe his Judaic language as a shorthand script for referring to Reality in both of those two, out of its perhaps innumerable, facets that have revealed themselves, so far, to human seekers.

If we are right in concluding that all the higher religions have an identical object of their worship, or objective of their quest, in a Reality that is one and the same behind its diverse aspects or facets, we shall be confirmed in our finding that the alternative objects or objectives of Religion are only three; and we shall then find that the history of Man's choice between these three alternatives is a drama that, in our time, is not yet in its last act. We can already, perhaps, make out the elements of the plot, but we do not yet know the dénouement. Man begins by worshipping Nature; when he ceases to worship Nature, he is left with a spiritual vacuum which he is impelled to fill; and he is then confronted with the choice of substituting for the worship of Nature either a worship of himself or an approach to Absolute Reality through the worship of God or quest for Brahma or for Nirvāna. This religious issue was raised by the recent rise of the civilizations, and it has not yet been decided. In a twentieth-century world in which the whole living generation of Mankind is being knit together into a single society within a framework built by Western technology, this is the fundamental issue underlying all current economic, political, and ideological controversies. Shall Man worship Man or shall he worship God and seek Brahma-Nirvāna?

Of these three religions or spiritual paths that have been in competition for Man's allegiance during the Age of the Civilizations, the worship of Nature is by far the oldest and the most deeply rooted. What Man's original religion may have been is a question that was still under debate in A.D. 1956. The evidence existing at that date did not seem to warrant either the rejection or the adoption of Father W. Schmidt's theory based on his observation of common elements in the religions of the most primitive surviving peoples, now scattered in holes and corners at opposite extremities of the inhabited surface of the Earth. Father Schmidt's conclusion is that the worship of God which has been brought into the field by the latterday higher religions is a revival, not an innovation, and is, in fact, a revival of the earliest religion of Mankind.[1] It is, indeed, conceivable that Man did not begin to worship Nature until he had begun to be able to manipulate her for his own purposes; for it would perhaps be difficult to worship a power which one had no hope of being able to influence. The worship of Nature will have had its *floruit* in the long age during which Man felt himself to be neither wholly impotent in the face of Nature (so

---

[1] See Schmidt, Father W., *The Origin and Growth of Religion*, English translation by Rose, H. J. (London 1921, Methuen).

that it was now no longer quite useless for him to try to influence her) nor wholly master of her (so that to try to influence her was still worth his while). This period, which will have begun when Man began to pass out of a purely passive food-gathering stage of winning his livelihood into a comparatively active hunting and fishing stage, must have lasted for hundreds of thousands of years. This is a long spell of time by comparison with the 3,000 years or thereabouts during which Man— having reached a stage in his history at which he is no longer willing to worship Nature because he fancies that he has sub-jugated her—has been torn between Man himself and God as the object of his worship (or between human power or happi-ness and Brahma-Nirvāna as his spiritual objective).

Man did achieve the subjugation of Non-Human Nature in the Upper Palaeolithic Age a few tens of thousands of years ago—at a date, that is to say, which is very recent on the Time-scale of the age of the Human Race, but is a considerable time ago on the Time-scale of the age of the civilizations. Since that date there has been no possibility of any other creature's challenging Man's supremacy on Earth, and no possibility of Man's losing his battle with Inanimate Nature so long as the climate of the Earth's surface remains within the range within which it has oscillated since this planet first gave harbour to Life. Before the close of the Upper Palaeolithic Age, all Man's subsequent technological triumphs that have been achieved within these last few tens of thousands of years—down to the discovery of the techniques for combating or fostering disease-germs and for splitting the atom—were already virtually assured. They could have been predicted, no doubt, at any stage, by a twentieth-century man of science if he could have been carried back into the past by some Wellsian 'time-machine'.

Yet, in spite of this apparently decisive and definitive victory of Man over Non-Human Nature, the worship of Nature is still to be seen embedded in the living higher religions. Its presence is very evident in current Hinduism (e.g. in the worship of the *lingam* as a symbol of the self-reproductive power of Life). It is also to be seen in the Mahāyāna (e.g. in the charting of the structure of the Subconscious Psyche in the *mandala*) and in Christianity (e.g. in the cult of the Mother and Child and in the

sacrament of the Bread and the Wine). The worship of
Nature is to be found even in Islam, which is the most rational
of all the living Judaic higher religions, and which is a match
for Judaism itself in the severity of its monotheism and in the
clearness of its apprehension of the transcendent aspect of God.
The Black Stone fetish embedded in the wall of the Ka'bah
at Mecca may serve as a symbol of the survival of elements of
Nature-worship, not only in Islam itself, but in all the living
higher religions.

Moreover, these elements of Nature-worship embedded in
living higher religions are something more than the fossilized
remains of a dead primitive religion; they are indications that,
below the surface of the Psyche, the worship of Nature is still
alive. It is alive because the Non-Human Nature over which
Man won his decisive victory in the Upper Palaeolithic Age
is only one half—and this the less formidable half—of the
Nature with which Man is confronted. The other half of
Nature, with which Man still has to cope, is Nature as he finds
her within himself.

Non-Human Nature can be subjugated by Man by main
force. It is true that, on the face of the Earth in A.D. 1956, there
were some striking exhibits—for instance, the 'dust-bowls' in
the basins of the Yellow River and the Mississippi—of the
posthumous revenge that even Non-Human Nature has
sometimes succeeded in taking on her high-handed human
conqueror. On the whole, however, she has yielded to Man like
a docile sheep, whereas Human Nature has shown itself as
refractory, and as recalcitrant to human control, as a goat or a
camel or a mule. When Man tries to coerce Human Nature, he
defeats his own purpose; for, so far from cowing it, coercion
merely stimulates its obstinacy, rebelliousness, and animosity.
It was Human Nature that Horace had in mind when he wrote
that Nature will always keep on coming back at you, even if
you drive her out with a pitchfork;[1] and, in the Subconscious
Psyche's repertory of 'primordial images', this Nature that is
Man's inseparable and intractable companion is expressively
portrayed as a bull. This creature, far stronger physically than
Man, which Man has precariously subjugated by the exercise

[1] Naturam expellas furcâ, tamen usque recurret.'—Horace, *Epistulae* I,
x, 24.

of his Intellect and his Will, is an apt symbol for those subconscious principalities and powers in the Psyche which are so
much more difficult for the Intellect and the Will to cope with
than any veritably non-human living creature is.

Two antithetical alternative policies for coping with this
psychic bull are commended in two significant myths. In the
Mithraic myth a hero slays the monster and staggers forward
with his victim's inseparable carcase weighing on his shoulders.
In the Zen Mahayanian Buddhist myth a boy-herdsman makes
friends with the great ox and comes home riding on the
monster's back to the music of the rider's flute. The boy's deft
diplomacy is a more effective way of dealing with Man's
problem than the hero's crude resort to force; for the force
which sometimes recoils upon its user, even when Non-Human
Nature is its target, is a wholly inappropriate instrument for
dealing with the psychic bull. The contrast between these two
antithetical policies lies at the heart of a problem which was
exercising the people of the United States in the sequel to the
Second World War. In a previous chapter of their history, in
which they had been breaking in the physical continent of
North America, the people of the United States had disposed
of the historic bison on the Great Plains in Mithras' way: they
had just set upon him and exterminated him. But now they
were having to cope with a psychic bison incarnate in the
Russians, in the peoples of Asia and Africa and Indian America,
in the Americans' own European kinsmen, and, most awkward
of all, in the Americans themselves; and this could not be done
by the drastic methods that had proved so effective in dealing
with forests, wild animals, and human savages who could be
treated as part of their continent's fauna. In A.D. 1956 the
Americans were being pushed, by the sudden transformation of
the *dramatis personae* on their stage, into changing over from the
Mithraic tactics to the Zen Buddhist tactics at short notice, and
this task of psychic re-adaptation was imposing on them a
severe nervous strain.

The abiding untamed power of the great subconscious abyss
of Human Nature has been underestimated by Man in Process
of Civilization since the discovery of the Intellect and the
Will by the philosophers, though the philosophers have not
gone to the same lengths of *hybris* in all societies. In China the

uncompromisingly rationalistic Legist school of philosophy was eventually driven off the field by a Confucian school which tempered its Rationalism with a conservative respect for a pre-rationalist tradition. In India the Hinayanian Buddhist school of philosophy recognized that the demonic sub-rational elements in Human Nature could not be conquered without an arduous struggle, and it was concerned to conserve psychic energy for employment on the Will's formidable ethical enter-prise by discouraging the Intellect from exploring the bound-less realm of Metaphysics.[1] Yet the Hīnayāna underestimated the difficulty of the task that it was setting itself; for it believed that Desire could be extinguished by the Intellect and the Will through their own unaided efforts. In Greece the rationalism of the philosophers was still more overweening. It was in-clined to ignore the existence of the subconscious abyss of the Psyche altogether; to treat the Intellect and the Will as if they were the whole of Human Nature; and to deify them as if they were masters of the situation.

When the Intellect and the Will thus ignore the subconscious abyss of the Psyche, they do so at their peril; for, so far from being the whole of Human Nature, they are merely a spirit moving upon the face of the waters[2]—a feeble light cast by a wick that draws its faint luminosity from the opaque oil in the bowl of the lamp on whose surface the wick is floating. 'The light shineth in the darkness, and the darkness comprehendeth it not.'[3]

At a time when this question of the relation between the Will and Intellect and the Subconscious Psyche was much on the writer's mind, he found himself in Southern California among the green lawns of Los Angeles. The city is so extensive when measured by the standard of mobility even of the driver of an automobile that the pedestrian visitor is prone to forget that, on the map of the continent as seen by a traveller in an aero-plane, this garden-city which, on the ground, seems boundless, is merely a tiny patch of verdure marooned in the midst of a vast desert. Moreover, the green is so perpetual that the spectator is also prone to forget that it is kept in existence only by a likewise perpetual *tour de force*. Though on every lawn he sees the sprinklers twisting and turning all day long, he soon comes

---

[1] See further Chapter 5, p. 62, below.   [2] Gen. i. 2.   [3] John i. 5.

to take the lawns for granted, as if they had been natural products of a non-existent rainfall. So it gives him a shock when on some vacant lot—kept vacant, perhaps, by a speculator in the hope of rising prices—he sees the savage desert sage-brush bristling up out of a parched and dusty ground. He then realizes that, under the artificial green lawns, the same savage Nature that has here broken its way to the surface is all the time eagerly waiting for an opportunity thus to come into its own again. This is the precarious position of the Intellect and Will. At any moment they may be impaled on the bristles of the sprouting sage-brush, be tossed on the horns of the goring bull, or be blown up from the crater of the erupting volcano.

In spite of his pride of Intellect and Will, Man has, for his self-preservation, to find some way of coping with a Nature that, in the Human Psyche, is still untamed and that, in this psychic field, cannot be tamed by force. Man has met this need by unavowedly retaining the worship of Nature in an age in which his official object of worship is either himself or God. The relics of a once official Nature-worship that are visibly embedded in the living religions are only a small fraction of the Nature-worship that still survives, as the Pyramids and other visible remains of dead civilizations are small compared with the wealth of the relics that the archaeologists disinter from below the ground, and as the peak of an iceberg that protrudes above the surface of the sea is small compared with the mass of the iceberg's submerged base.

The new Western science of Psychology, which has come into action in the lifetime of the living generation, has begun to reveal the vast subterranean temple of Nature-worship in the Psyche's subconscious abyss; and it has already demonstrated that this worship—long since repudiated on the rational surface of Life—has survived at these lower levels because, at these depths, Human Nature is still as wild as ever it was. The Intellect and Will may have gained a decisive victory over External Physical Nature perhaps as long as 30,000 years ago; and, perhaps as long as 3,000 years ago, they may have staked out a claim to be the only elements in Human Nature that are of any account. Yet they are only just beginning, in our day, to discover, explore, and so perhaps master, step by step, the actually still untamed Inner Psychic Nature of Man himself.

The Nature that Man is still worshipping unavowedly in the subconscious depths of his psyche is Janus-faced.

The first aspect in which Nature presents herself to Man's intellect and will is as a monster who is creating and destroying perpetually, prodigally, aimlessly, senselessly, ruthlessly, and immorally—or, it might be more accurate to say 'unmorally', since this bestial Nature does not seem even to be aware of there being any difference between right and wrong. This is the seamy side of the picture of the Universe that has its respectable side in the Indo-Hellenic vision of a cyclic movement governed by an Impersonal Law. Whereas the astronomical side of the picture deadens Human Life to insignificance, the demonic side livens the Universe into a nightmare of lust and of bloodthirstiness. In the external, physical dimension, this nightmare was seen at close quarters by the crew of the *Kon-Tiki*, who, in sailing across the Pacific on a raft awash, found themselves in direct contact with the only considerable province of an External Physical Nature which post-Palaeolithic Man had not tamed by A.D. 1947. The Behemoth and Leviathan of *The Book of Job* are symbols of this demonic aspect of Nature in the psychic dimension as well as the physical. 'Canst thou draw out Leviathan with an hook? . . . He is a king over all the children of pride.'[1]

This monstrously creative-destructive epiphany of Nature has been deified as Vishnu-Shiva, Durga-Kali, Cybele-Hecate; and the human worshippers of this Protean Janus-faced power have sought to win its co-operation with their human purposes by pandering to Nature's lust and bloodthirstiness in such practices as ritual prostitution and as the sacrifice of living creatures on an ascending scale of agony in which the most efficacious victim of all is the sacrificer's only child. Classical arenas of this hideous worship of Nature the monster have been Mexico, West Africa, India, and, above all, Canaan.

Since there cannot be lust and cruelty without suffering, and since a cosmic monster has no other target than herself on which the suffering can be inflicted, Nature the monster necessarily has another aspect in which she presents herself as Nature the victim, sacrificing herself to herself for the sake of preserving her existence, making her progress, and fulfilling

[1] Job xli. 1 and 34.

her mission. This is the tragic side of the picture of the Universe that has its triumphant side in the Judaeo-Zoroastrian vision of an irreversible movement governed by Intellect and Will; and this other aspect of Nature was also seen at close quarters, in the external, physical dimension, by the crew of the *Kon-Tiki*. A symbol of this tragic aspect of Nature in the psychic dimension, as well as the physical, is the dragon Ti'āmat, out of whose slaughtered body the matricidal gods fashioned the Universe according to the Sumerian myth. This efficaciously suffering aspect of Nature has been deified in the tableau of the victim-child and the grief-stricken parent: Tammuz and Ishtar; Persephone and Demeter; Rachel weeping for her children because they are not;[1] the mother through whose soul a sword shall pierce as she watches her son being crucified.[2] The human worshippers of Nature in this tragic aspect have sought to place themselves in sympathy with her by acts of self-sacrifice, and Canaan has been one of the principal scenes of this tragic form of Nature-worship too.

The identity of Nature the victim with Nature the monster looks paradoxical at first sight; for these two aspects of one power seem to stand at opposite poles of the moral gamut. Yet, when we read the Sumerian Epic of the Creation in the Babylonian version of it that our Modern Western archaeologists have retrieved, we find our sympathies veering round as we watch the transfiguration of Ti'āmat from the monster of a fairy-tale into the heroine of a tragedy. The odious dragon-mother of the Universe who has turned against her own off-spring and has set out to destroy them begins to excite pity when, in the last fifty lines of Tablet IV, she meets her fate at the hands of Marduk, the champion of the gods of the younger generation.

> With his unsparing mace he crushed her skull. . . .
> Then the Lord paused to view her dead body,
> That he might divide the monster and do artful works.
> He split her, like a shellfish, in two parts.[3]

The poem's climax and close is the transformation of a blind

---

[1] Jer. xxxi. 15; Matt. ii. 18.   [2] Luke ii. 35.

[3] *Enūma Eliš*, Tablet IV, lines 130 and 135-7, English translation in *Ancient Near Eastern Texts*, ed. by Pritchard, J. B. (Princeton 1950, University Press), p. 67.

destructive force into a means of creation; and this transformation comes about through the transfiguration of the principal
character in the drama from a monster into a victim.

This metamorphosis of the goddess has its counterpart in a
corresponding change in the spiritual significance of the
worshipper's act of sacrifice. Mesha's accepted sacrifice of his
eldest son and heir to Chemosh,[1] Abraham's arrested sacrifice
of Isaac to Yahweh,[2] and God the Son's accepted sacrifice of
Himself to God the Father are all ritually the same act, yet the
first and the third of these three performances of it are spiritually
at opposite poles. Mesha's son, though an efficacious victim, is
an unwilling one, sacrificed to a monster god, whereas Christ is
God voluntarily sacrificing Himself. Abraham's arrested
sacrifice of an unresisting Isaac is the middle term linking these
two morally antithetical extremes. An Attis' physical self-
mutilation and a Christian monk's spiritual self-dedication are
likewise ritually the same act and likewise spiritually at
opposite poles; and the middle term linking these is the passage
in the Gospel[3] commending those who mutilate themselves for
Christ's sake—a text on which Origen is said to have acted as
if the words had been meant to be taken literally.

This polarization of the worship of Nature opens the way for
the worships of Man and God. The worship of Nature the
monster leads on to Man's suicidal worship of Man himself.
The worship of Nature the victim leads on to Man's redeeming
worship of a God who sets His worshippers a divine example
by sacrificing Himself for their sake.

[1] 2 Kings iii. 27.   [2] Gen. xxii. 1-19.   [3] Matt. xix. 12.

3
MAN-WORSHIP: THE IDOLIZATION OF PAROCHIAL COMMUNITIES[1]

MOST of the societies that have embarked on the enterprise of Civilization so far have started life on the political plane as mosaics of parochial states. This has been the regular original structure of the civilizations of the third generation, which have arisen since the beginning of the Christian Era and whose early history is sufficiently well documented for us to be able to trace their institutions back to their origins. Since we find the same dispensation prevalent in the civilizations of the first and second generations, at the dates when the curtain rises on their histories, we may infer that, in these too, the mosaic of parochial states is an original feature. This political structure of the civilizations in their early days has its counterpart on the religious plane. In the civilizations of all three generations, at the earliest dates to which their surviving records take us back, the parochial communities into which a society is articulated in its first phase are not only the predominant political institutions; they are also the predominant objects of worship.

This worship of one's own collective human power, as embodied in a parochial community and organized in a parochial state, has been in truth the master religion in the civilizations of the third generation, as well as in those of the first and second. But in the civilizations of the third generation the worshippers of parochial communities have shrunk from avowing that their allegiance to these gods in collective human form (France, Britannia, and the like) is paramount over their allegiance to one of the higher religions, because the civilizations of the third generation are younger than the higher religions and have each started life under the aegis of one or other of them. On the other hand the civilizations of the first two generations, to which we shall be confining our attention in the First Part of this book, all arose before any of the higher

[1] The subject of this chapter has been dealt with in greater detail by the writer in *A Study of History*, vol. iv, pp. 156-90, 206-22, 263-91, 303-20; vol. ix, pp. 7-8, 234-87.

religions had made their appearance. Here too, the worship of
parochial communities had to win its way at the expense of
another religion that had previously held the field, but the
traditional religion in this case was Nature-worship; and
Man-worship was able to establish its ascendancy over Nature-
worship without having to pay tribute to the subordinated
religion by camouflaging itself. In this earlier religious
revolution, there was no feeling that the old religion and the
new religion were incompatible, and there was therefore no
awareness that a revolution was taking place. Accordingly, in
the civilizations of the first and second generations, at the
earliest dates to which we can trace their histories back, we
find Primitive Man's legacy of Nature-worship not only co-
existing with, but associated with, an undisguised worship of
the parochial communities into which the nascent civilization
has articulated itself.

In Egypt, for example, we find the worships of the Sun, the
Corn, and the Nile surviving side by side with the self-worship
of the cantons.[1] In Sumer and Akkad we find the worship of
Tammuz and Ishtar surviving side by side with the self-worship
of the city-states. In China we find an annual agricultural
liturgy embedded in the Confucian Classics, and an annual
agricultural ritual, in which the prince communes with Heaven
and ploughs the first furrow of the new agricultural year,
surviving side by side with the self-worship of the Contending
States and of the oecumenical empire by which they were
superseded. In Canaan we find the worship of fertility-gods,
the ba'als and the ashtoroths, and the agricultural rites embedded in the Pentateuch, surviving side by side with the self-
worship of the city-states and cantons. In Hellas we find—
for example, at Athens—the annual agricultural festivals—
Thesmophoria, Anthesteria, Dionysia and the rest—surviving
side by side with the self-worship of the local city-state which,
at Athens, is projected on to the goddess Athene.

In this gradual, peaceful, and imperceptible religious revolution, the new religion has not only imposed itself on the old one;
in many cases it has actually commandeered one of the old

---

[1] Usually called 'nomes' by Modern Western archaeologists, because
'nomós' was the Greek word into which the Ancient Egyptian word had
been translated.

Nature-gods to serve also as the representative of the new worship of parochial collective human power. There are, it is true, some deifications of parochial communities—for instance, Asshur and Romulus—in which the community-god bears the community's name and has therefore presumably never had any previous other function, but has been called into existence expressly in order to play his political role. Such artificially fabricated community-gods seem, however, to be exceptional. Most of the historic parochial community-gods bear marks of having been in existence already as Nature-gods before they were given the additional role of serving as gods representing human communities.

In Attica, Athene continued to be the patroness of olive-cultivation after she had been turned into Athena Polias—the deification of a parochial human community that took its name from her (for the names 'Athens' and 'Athenians' are derived from the name 'Athene'; it is not the goddess that is named after them). Yahweh, on the evidence of the traditional account of the making of the Covenant between Yahweh and Israel on Sinai, would appear to have been a volcano-god or a weather-god before he was adopted to serve as the war-god of a confederacy of nomad tribes. Amon-Re, who came to be a deification of the Thebaid and consequently of an Egyptian oecumenical empire, was a combination of the Sun-god, Re, with Amon, 'the Breath of Life',[1] whose generative power was symbolized in the portrayal of him as a ram. The gods representing the cantons out of which the Egyptian United Kingdom and the Egyptian Empire were successively built up seem originally to have been totems representing aspects of Nature on which their worshippers had once depended for their livelihood. This conscription of Nature-gods to serve also as community-gods put their worshippers at their ease by ensuring that Nature and Society should work in harmony; and the maintenance of this harmony seems to have been the principal objective of religious institutions and rites in Egypt and Sumer, the two civilizations of the first generation of which we have the least imperfect knowledge.[2]

[1] See Frankfort, H., *Kingship and the Gods* (Chicago 1948, University of Chicago Press), p. 160.
[2] See Frankfort, op. cit., *passim*.

The process by which parochial-community-worship has been imposed on a previously established religion may thus have been different in the histories of civilizations of different generations, but one unhappy consequence has been the same. In all cases, the victory of parochial-community-worship has worked havoc. In the earlier of the two occurrences of the religious revolution, in which the subordinated religion was some form of an ancient Nature-worship, the havoc-making effect of the victory of parochial-community-worship was to turn Polytheism into a destructively explosive force.

Nature-worship is a polytheistic religion *ex hypothesi*, because Man worships Nature on account of her still being intractable to him, and she is this only so long as he has not yet detected the fundamental unity and simplicity and regularity underlying her superficial diversity and multiplicity and capriciousness. But in an agricultural society a polytheistic worship of Nature does not drive the worshippers of different Nature-gods into war with one another. A fratricidal strife does arise, it is true, between farmer Cain, the worshipper of Nature the giver of crops, shepherd Abel the worshipper of Nature the giver of flocks, and huntsman Nimrod the worshipper of Nature the giver of game. Recent incidents in this warfare have been the corralling of the Eurasian Nomads by the Muscovite and Manchu champions of Sedentary Civilization in the eighteenth century of the Christian Era, and the North American farmer's successive wars of extermination, in the nineteenth century, against the Indian hunter and the Texan cattleman. But this strife between the worshippers of Nature in these different aspects of her bountifulness to Man has been no more than a minor theme in the history of Man in Process of Civilization. This is because no civilization has subsisted by hunting and only one has subsisted by stock-breeding; all the others have subsisted by agriculture; and, in an agricultural society, there is no inevitable conflict between the worshippers of an olive-goddess, a corn-goddess, and a wine-god. The same husband-man will worship all three agricultural divinities because he will be cultivating all three crops.

There is no inevitable conflict, either, between the worshippers of the same agricultural divinities in different parochial communities. So far from setting them at variance, their common agricultural religion is a bond between them. Though the crops and the technique for coaxing them out of the Earth will vary from place to place according to the differences in the local soil and climate, there will everywhere be the same annually recurrent experience of hope and anxiety regarding the outcome of the husbandman's activity. This activity is the cult of a divinity as well as the cultivation of a plant, because the success that is indispensable for *Homo Agricola's* survival is dependent only partly on what is done by the husbandman himself, and depends, for the rest, upon Nature's mysterious activities. The common religion answering to this common experience will draw together all worshippers of Demeter and Dionysus everywhere. A Mexican peasant would have felt himself at home at an Attic festival in honour of the wheat-goddess, and an Attic peasant at a Mexican festival in honour of the maize-god; and neither of them would have felt himself a stranger even in the rice-eating half of the World, where loaves and tortillas are unknown.

Unhappily, Polytheism begins to produce new and pernicious social effects when its domain is extended from the realm of Nature-worship to a province of the realm of Man-worship in which the object of worship is parochial collective human power. Local worships of deified parochial communities inevitably drive their respective devotees into war with one another. Whereas Demeter our common Mother Earth is the same goddess in Attica and in Laconia, the Athene Polias of Athens and the Athana Chalcioecus of Sparta, who are the respective deifications of these two parochial communities, are bound to be rival goddesses in spite of their bearing the same name. The worship of Nature tends to unite the members of different communities because it is not self-centred; it is the worship of a power in whose presence all human beings have the identical experience of being made aware of their own human weakness. On the other hand the worship of parochial communities tends to set their respective members at variance because this religion is an expression of self-centredness; because self-centredness is the source of all strife; and because the collective ego is a more dangerous object of worship than the individual ego is.

The collective ego is more dangerous because it is more

powerful, more demonic, and less patently unworthy of devotion. The collective ego combines the puny individual power of each of its devotees into the collective power of Leviathan. This collective power is at the mercy of sub-conscious passions because it escapes the control of the Intellect and Will that put some restraint on the individual ego. And bad behaviour that would be condemned unhesitatingly by the conscience in an individual culprit is apt to be condoned when it is perpetrated by Leviathan, under the illusion that the first person is absolved from self-centredness by being transposed from the singular number into the plural. This is, however, just the opposite of the truth; for, when an individual projects his self-centredness on to a community, he is able, with less sense of sin, to carry his egotism to greater lengths of enormity. 'Patriotism is the last refuge of a scoundrel';[1] and the callous-ness of committees testifies still more eloquently than the fury of mobs that, in collective action, the ego is capable of descending to depths to which it does not fall when it is acting on its individual responsiblity.

The warfare to which parochial-community-worship leads is apt to rankle, sooner or later, into war to the death; and this self-inflicted doom is insidious, because the ultimately fatal effects of this religion are slow to reveal themselves and do not become unmistakably clear till the mischief has become mortally grave.

In its first phase the warfare between deified parochial states is usually waged in a temperate spirit and is confined within moderate limits. In this first phase the worshippers of each parochial god recognize in some degree that each neighbour parochial god is the legitimate sovereign in his own territory. Each local god will be deemed to have both the right and the power to punish alien human trespassers on his domain who commit a grievous wrong against him by committing it against his people; and this consideration counsels caution and restraint in waging war on foreign soil. It tends to prevent war from becoming total. The bashful invader will refrain, not only from desecrating the enemy's temples, but from poisoning his wells and from cutting down his fruit trees. The Romans, when they had made up their minds to go to all

[1] Dr. Johnson on the 7th April, 1775 (Boswell's *Life*).

lengths in warring down an enemy community, used to take the preliminary precautions of inviting the enemy gods to evacuate the doomed city and of tempting them to change sides by offering them, in exchange, honourable places in the Roman pantheon. When a local community has been exterminated or deported in defiance of the local divinity and without regard to his sovereign prerogatives, the outraged parochial god may bring the usurpers of his domain and scorners of his majesty to heel by making the place too hot to hold them except on his terms. The colonists planted by the Assyrian Government on territory that had been cleared of its previous human occupants by the deportation of the Children of Israel soon found, to their cost, that Israel's undeported god Yahweh had lost none of his local potency; and they had no peace till they took to worshipping this very present local god instead of the gods that they had brought with them from their homelands.[1]

Thus the conduct of war between parochial states is kept within bounds, at the start, by a common belief in the equality of sovereign parochial gods, each within his own domain. But this belief is apt to break down, and, with it, the restraint that is imposed by it. They break down because the self-worship of a parochial community is essentially incompatible with the moderation commended in such maxims as 'Live and let live' and 'Do as you would be done by'. Every form of Man-worship is a religious expression of self-centredness, and is consequently infected with the intellectual mistake and the moral sin of treating a part of the Universe as if it were the whole—of trying to wrest the Universe round into centring on something in it that is not and ought not to be anything more than a subordinate part of it. Since self-centredness is innate in every living creature, it wins allegiance for any religion that ministers to it. It also inhibits any living creature that fails to break away from it from loving its neighbour as itself, and a total failure to achieve this arduous moral feat has a disastrous effect on social relations.

A further reason why it is difficult to keep the warfare between parochial states at a low psychological temperature is because parochial-community-worship wins devotion not only

[1] See 2 Kings xvii. 24-41.

by ministering disastrously to self-centredness. It wins it also by giving a beneficent stimulus to Man's nobler activities in the first chapter of the story. In the histories of most civilizations in their first chapters, parochial states have done more to enrich their members' lives by fostering the arts than they have done to impoverish them by taking a toll of blood and treasure. For example, the rise of the Athenian city-state made life richer for its citizens by creating the Attic drama out of a primitive fertility-ritual before life was made intolerable for them by a series of ever more devastating wars between Athens and her rivals. The earlier Athens that had been 'the education of Hellas'[1] won and held the allegiance of Athenian men and women, over whom she had cast her spell, for the benefit of the later Athens that was 'a tyrant power';[2] and, though these two arrogant phrases were coined to describe Athens' effect on the lives of the citizens of other Hellenic city-states, they describe her effect on the lives of her own citizens no less aptly. This is the tragic theme of Thucydides' history of the Great Atheno-Peloponnesian War, and there have been many other performances of the same tragedy that have not found their Thucydides.

The strength of the devotion that parochial-community-worship thus evokes holds its devotees in bondage to it even when it is carrying them to self-destruction; and so the warfare between contending parochial states tends to grow more intense and more devastating in a crescendo movement. Respect for one's neighbours' gods and consideration for these alien gods' human protégés are wasting assets. All parochial-community-worship ends in a worship of Moloch, and this 'horrid king'[3] exacts more cruel sacrifices than the Golden Calf. War to the death between parochial states has been the immediate external cause of the breakdowns and disintegrations of almost all, if not all, the civilizations that have committed suicide up to date. The decline and fall of the First Mayan Civilization is perhaps the only doubtful case.

The devotion to the worship of Moloch is apt to persist until it is too late to save the life of the civilization that is being

---

[1] Thucydides, Book II, chap. 41.   [2] Thucydides, Book III, chap. 37.
[3] Milton, *Paradise Lost*, Book I. See also the Annexe to the present chapter on pp. 37-40, below.

destroyed by it. It does break down at last, but not until a stage of social disintegration has been reached at which the blood-tax exacted by the waging of ever more intensive, ferocious, and devastating warfare has come palpably to outweigh any cultural and spiritual benefits that the contending parochial states may once have conferred on their citizens. At this stage there is apt to be a revulsion from an infatuation with parochialism to a horror of it. The ruin that their civilization has now unmistakably brought upon itself by parochial-community-worship disgusts the members of the afflicted society with Polytheism of all kinds, and men's and women's hearts are now ready to transfer their religious allegiance to some object of worship that will give them peace by uniting them, and that will unite them in virtue of being, itself, unitary and universal. But the rejection of discredited parochial gods does not decide the question what monistic religion shall be adopted, in place of them, from among three alternatives that offer themselves.

After Nature-worship has been overlaid by parochial-community-worship, and after this has been found by experience to be materially disastrous and morally evil, the radical alternative is to renounce, not only Nature-worship, but also Man-worship in any form, and to turn towards an Absolute Reality that is beyond, as well as in, both Man and Nature. The possibility of such a new spiritual departure is opened up by the epiphany of the higher religions, which arise, as we shall see, in times of troubles precipitated by breakdowns and disintegrations of civilizations through the intensification of the warfare between idolized parochial states. But these higher religions make their entry into Society from below upwards, and the dominant minority—even in adversity and even after it has come to be disillusioned with its own ancestral institutions—is either unaware of these new religious movements in the ranks of the proletariat or, if vaguely aware of them, is hostile to them. It is prejudiced against them by their proletarian source and by their exotic appearance; and, at a deeper level of feeling, it is repelled by their acceptance of suffering as an opportunity and a means for bringing good out of evil. Rather than turn to the nascent higher religions, the dominant minority tries to fill the spiritual vacuum, left by the discrediting of parochial-community-worship, with some other form of Man-worship; and two alternative forms of this present themselves.

The line of least resistance for disillusioned ex-devotees of parochial-community-worship is to replace their fallen idols by another idol of the same genus but a different species, namely, an oecumenical community under whose all-embracing aegis Mankind can look forward to living in peace and concord as a single family. This alternative collective form of Man-worship now lies ready to hand, because the political result of the destruction of the parochial states by one another, and of their forfeiture of the devotion of their citizens, is to leave a single oecumenical empire master of the field. This oecumenical empire can claim the allegiance that the parochial states have lost, because it has brought to Mankind the universal peace for which everyone has been longing throughout the generations or centuries during which the now shattered and discredited parochial states have been bringing, not peace, but the sword.

The oecumenical empires that have risen and fallen hitherto have none of them been literally world-wide. The Chinese Empire and the Roman Empire, for example, lived side by side for more than two centuries without ever coming into direct contact with one another. A literally oecumenical state was not a practical possibility before 'the annihilation of distance' by Modern Western technology. But the Chinese Empire, the Roman Empire, and their kind have been oecumenical in a psychological sense. They have embraced within their borders the whole of a society which had previously been parcelled out among a number of parochial states perpetually at war with one another. In bringing unity and, with unity, peace to an entire society, the Roman Empire and the Chinese Empire have been states of a new sort, and they may prove to have been forerunners of a future world-state covering the whole habitable and traversable surface of the planet.

Besides the worship of an oecumenical state, there is a second form of Man-worship which may be adopted as a substitute for the worship of a parochial community, and this is the worship of Man, not in any collective form at all, but in the individual form of the spiritually self-sufficient philosopher—the hero who has found spiritual strength to stand alone, out in the cold, when the parochial state that has housed his ancestors for so many generations has fallen, in fearful ruin, about his and his contemporaries' ears.

These two alternative forms of Man-worship need to be examined before we go on to observe the epiphany of the higher religions.

3 ANNEXE

'MOLOCH' AND MOLK

'MOLOCH' or 'MOLECH'—taken to mean 'God worshipped as king'—is a household word for Jews and Christians who are familiar with either the original or a translation of the Hebrew Scriptures in what has come to be their canonical recension.

First Moloch, horrid king, besmeared with blood
Of human sacrifice and parents' tears,
Though, for the noise of drums and timbrels loud,
Their children's cries unheard, that passed through fire
To his grim idol.

Thus, in Jewry and Christendom, 'Moloch-worship' is an apt symbol for the parochial-community-worship that exacts from its worshippers an ever increasing toll of blood.

The rite of sacrificing one's first-born son by burning him alive was, in truth, practised both in Canaan and in the Canaanite colonies overseas in North-West Africa. There is literary evidence of the practice for Israel, Moab, Judah, and Carthage; and for Carthage there is archaeological evidence as well.

For Israel, we have the saga of Jephthah's sacrifice of his daughter (Judges xi. 29-40) and the account of the rebuilding of Jericho by King Ahab's officer Hiel, who 'laid the foundations thereof in Abiram his firstborn and set up the gates thereof in his youngest son Segub' (1 Kings xvi. 34). When Moab was being hard pressed by the united forces of Israel, Judah, and Edom, Mesha King of Moab 'took his eldest son that should have reigned in his stead, and offered him for a burnt offering upon the wall' (2 Kings iii. 27). In Judah, King Ahaz (reigned *circa* 741-725 B.C.) and King Manasseh (reigned *circa* 696-641 B.C.) are recorded each to have 'made his son pass through the fire' (2 Kings xvi. 3 and xxi. 6).

In Judah, from at least as early as the eighth century B.C., the rite seems to have become controversial. According to Isa. xxx. 33, the sacrificial pyre at Tophet, in the valley of Hinnom, just outside the walls of Jerusalem, is kindled by the breath of the Lord 'like a stream of brimstone'. But the rite is denounced by Amos (v. 26); and Jeremiah, in three passages (vii. 31; xix. 5; xxxii. 35), makes Yahweh expressly reject the imputation that He had commanded it. Before Jeremiah's day, the rite had been abolished, and the sanctuary at Tophet had been desecrated, by King Josiah (reigned *circa* 639-608 B.C.). The rite is forbidden in Lev. xviii. 21 and xx. 2-5. It is denounced in Ezek. xvi. 20-1 and in Deut.-Isa. lvii. 5; and in Ezek. xx. 25-6 it is cited as one of the 'statutes that were not good' which Yahweh had given to His people because they had despised the statutes which He had given them previously. An unanswerable verdict on the rite is given in a passage appended to the Book of the Prophet Micah: 'Shall I give my first-born for my transgression? The fruit of my body for the sin of my soul?' (Mic. vi. 7).

At Carthage, the local tophet has been discovered by modern Western archaeologists. It stretches in a narrow belt, several hundred yards in length, along the shore of the harbour;[1] and its location and stratification suggest that it dates from the foundation of the city. Among the literary records of the practice of the rite at Carthage are the saga of the tyrant Malchus's sacrifice of his son Carthalon, the priest of Melqart,[2] and the account of the sacrifice of 200 children, levied from the leading families of the Carthaginian oligarchy in 310 B.C.,[3] when Carthage was as gravely menaced by Agathocles' invasion as Moab had been, in Mesha's day, by Jehoram's.

[1] Charles-Picard, G., *Les Religions de l'Afrique Antique* (Paris 1954, Plon), pp. 28-9, with the plans on pp. 48-51. Cp. Dussaud, R., 'La Religion des Phéniciens', in '*Mana*': *Introduction a l'Histoire des Religions, I: Les Anciennes Religions Orientales*, ii (Paris 1949, Presses Universaires de France), pp. 383-4.

[2] Justin, *Epitoma Historiarum Philippicarum Pompei Trogi*, Book xviii, chap. 7 (the name Malchus is an emendation of the Maleus and Maceus of the MSS.).

[3] Diodorus of Agyrium, *A Library of History*, Book II, chap. 14.

The two earliest inscriptions so far discovered in the tophet at Carthage run *nesib molk Ba'al*, and this formula has been interpreted as meaning 'stele (commemoration) of a sacrifice to Ba'al (Hammon)'. If this interpretation of the word *molk* as meaning a sacrifice (of one's own child) is correct, it is possible that Moloch or Molech—'God the King'—who figures in certain passages of what is now the canonical re-cension of the Bible (e.g., in Lev. xviii. 21 and xx. 2, and in 1 Kings xi. 5 and 7, and in 2 Kings xxiii. 10), may be the product of an error in the pointing of the word *molk* in the massoretic text. However that may be, it seems certain that the sacrifice of one's own child by burning alive, or, as in the Malchus saga, by crucifixion, was a Canaanite practice; that such human sacrifices were made to the gods Yahweh of Israel and Judah, Chemosh of Moab, and Ba'al Hammon of Carthage; and that the rite itself was called *molk*.

The child that was sacrificed by its father was perhaps a substitute for the father himself; for a Carthaginian instance of self-sacrifice is recorded by Herodotus (Book VII, chaps. 166-7), in his account of the battle between the Carthaginians and the Siceliot Greeks at Himera in 480 B.C. When the battle went against the Carthaginians, their commander, Hamilcar, is reported to have thrown himself into the flames of the pyre on which he had been sacrificing less precious victims. Whether or no the child-victim was a substitute for its father, there is conclusive evidence that, in both Israel and Carthage, the practice eventually arose of reprieving the child-victim by the substitution of an animal. In the religious history of Israel we have an echo of this innovation in the myth of the substitution of the ram for Isaac (Gen. xxii. 1-19). In the religious history of Carthage, *molk omor*, the sacrifice of a lamb in lieu of a child, is known to have been practised before the destruction of Carthage in 146 B.C. and to have become common form under the subsequent Roman régime. In the upper levels of the tophet at Carthage, many of the urns contain the remains of animals, not of children, and figures of animals—presumably representing the victims—appear on the stelae.[1] Yet human sacrifice, which was abolished as early as the seventh century B.C. in Judah, lingered on in the North-African Canaan

[1] Charles-Picard, op. cit., pp. 49-50.

overseas till at least as late as the reign of the Emperor
Tiberius, and perhaps till as late as the third century of the
Christian Era.[1]

A rite which is practised by human beings is often attributed
by them to the gods whom they worship; and in the Phoenician
mythology we find one of the sons of the god El being sacrificed
by El himself to his father the sky god (according to Philo of
Byblos) and another of El's sons, Mot, being sacrificed, in the
form of a corn spirit, by the goddess 'Anat (according to the
mythological poems discovered at Ras-ash-Shamrah).[2] This
Canaanite picture of the divine economy re-emerges, perhaps
from a Galilaean source, in Christian theology. God the Son,
whose body is bread and whose blood is wine, sacrifices Himself to God the Father as a lamb whose death redeems Mankind.

[1] The dating depends on the interpretation of an ambiguous passage in
Tertullian's *Apologeticus*, chap. 9.
[2] See Charles-Picard, op. cit., p. 43.

4

MAN-WORSHIP: THE IDOLIZATION OF AN OECUMENICAL COMMUNITY[1]

THE idolatrous worship of collective human power on an oecumenical scale has a number of advantages over the parochial form of Man-worship.

Its most obvious advantage is its timeliness at a stage in the history of a disintegrating civilization when life under the old parochial dispensation has become intolerable. Aristotle's retrospective appreciation of the old régime may be true to the historical facts. The once idolized parochial community may originally have come into existence, as he suggests, as one of the necessities of life, and, after that, it may have justified its existence, for a time, by serving as an institutional instrument for enabling individual human beings to live a good life[2] through finding scope for their creative powers. Yet in Aristotle's world by Aristotle's day it was no less evident— though the philosopher is silent about this, if not blind to it— that an idolized institution which, for a time, had been a stimulus had now turned into a scourge. At a stage at which constant fratricidal warfare between contending idolized parochial states has brought a society to the verge of dissolution, the alternative idolatrous worship of an oecumenical empire becomes one of the necessities of life in its turn, because it offers the only immediately effective means now of saving the self-lacerated society from committing social suicide.

The worship of an oecumenical empire has a second advantage which is intrinsic. The temper in which the worship of parochial communities is embraced by its devotees is juvenile in the shortness of its view. It is a naïvely optimistic response to a temporary stimulus, without any foreboding of the next chapter in the story, in which the same idolization of the same institution is going to bring grievous loss instead of

[1] The subject of this chapter has been dealt with in greater detail by the writer in *A Study of History*, vol. v, pp. 38-9, 47-56; vol. vi, pp. 185-96, 332-8; vol. vii, pp. 1-52.

[2] See Aristotle, *Politics*, Book I, chap. ii, § 8 (1252 B).

gratifying gain. By contrast, the temper in which the worship of an oecumenical empire is embraced is comparatively adult. It is a response to a long-drawn-out experience of suffering, and consequently it is disciplined by a more sober appreciation of the limits of the beneficial results that can be expected from any human institution.

A third advantage is that the ideals of co-operation, concord, and peace, for which the worship of an oecumenical community stands, are in fact more likely to promote human welfare, because they are more far-sighted and less narrowly self-centred, than the ideals of competition, strife, and war, which are countenanced, and indeed positively fostered, by the worship of parochial states. A classic exposition of this point has been made by a Greek man of letters in a eulogy of the Roman Empire in the Age of the Antonines:

At a moment when the states of the World were already laid out on the funeral pyre as the victims of their own fratricidal strife and turmoil, they were all at once presented with the [Roman] dominion and straightway came to life again.[1]

Universal states have a fourth advantage in the personalities of their founders. These great men have all been more effective and impressive, and most of them also more beneficent and benevolent, than the leading soldiers and statesmen of the contending states which a universal state supersedes. In the veneration paid to their memories by Posterity, the founders of universal states have been surpassed only by the founders of the philosophies and the higher religions.

Providence has . . . [sent] him to us and to Posterity as a saviour whose mission has been to put an end to War and to set the Universe in order.[2]

The feelings expressed in this contemporary encomium of the Emperor Augustus were, no doubt, also felt by as many millions of grateful subjects of the Achaemenian Emperors

---

[1] Aristeides, P. Aelius, *In Romam* (Or. XXVI), §§ 68-70.
[2] Decree passed, probably in 9 B.C., by the *Koinon* of the Roman Province of Asia, printed in Dittenberger, W., *Orientis Graecae Inscriptiones Selectae*, vol. ii (Leipzig 1905, Hirzel), pp. 48-60.

Cyrus and Darius, the Chinese Emperor Han Liu Pang, and the Ottoman Emperors Murād I and Mehmed II.

The greatest achievement of the greatest of these founders of oecumenical empires has been to leave behind them a school of public servants, civil and military, to carry on their work: a hereditary aristocracy like the Persian Megistanes and the Inca Orejones; or a professional public service like that of the Chinese Empire, the Roman Empire, and the Indian Empire under a British régime; or a lay monastic order, like the Ottoman Emperor's slave-household.

This combination of advantages is a strong one, and, in virtue of it, an oecumenical empire, after having originally won acceptance by performing the negative service of saving Society from imminent self-destruction, is apt to win increasing positive respect and affection with the passage of time. The moral hold that it has won is demonstrated after it has fallen into adversity.

After an oecumenical empire has gone into decline to the point of becoming practically impotent, its *fainéant* emperors still continue for generations and centuries to be the indispensable founts of legitimization for the usurpers who have carved out successor-states at their expense. An act of investiture at the hands of the legitimate emperor is required in order to secure the subjects' acquiescence in the usurper's rule; and this apparent formality is a matter of such practical importance that the most hard-headed usurpers take the greatest pains to obtain it, and make the greatest parade of it thereafter. An Odovacer, a Theodoric, and a Clovis ruled stolen western provinces of the Roman Empire as vicegerents of the Roman Imperial Government surviving at Constantinople; the Hindu Marāthās and the Christian British East India Company ruled in India as vicegerents of *fainéant* Muslim 'Great Moguls' at Delhi; and most of the Christian successor-states of the Ottoman Empire were content to start life as autonomous principalities under the Padishah's suzerainty before venturing to claim sovereign independence for themselves.

Moreover, even after a moribund oecumenical empire has at last received its long delayed *coup de grâce*, there may be attempts, and even repeated attempts, to resuscitate it. Classical examples of such renaissances are the resuscitation of the Ts'in and Han Empire in China by the Sui and T'ang dynasties; the resuscitation of the Roman Empire in Orthodox Christendom, first as the Byzantine Empire and then as 'Moscow the Third Rome'; the three avatars of the Roman Empire in Western Christendom that were conjured up successively by Charlemagne, by Otto I, and by the Hapsburgs; and the Ottoman Empire's attempt, from the end of the eighteenth century of the Christian Era onwards, to revive its drooping prestige by posing as an avatar of the Arab Caliphate.

An oecumenical empire's hold over its worshippers' hearts is thus both strong and well deserved; and yet even an oecumenical empire is an unsatisfying object of worship, whether it offers itself for adoration in an institution or in a person. The institutional representation of the idol will be too remote, impersonal, and aloof to win sufficient affection, while the personal incarnation of it will be too familiar and unworthy to inspire sufficient respect.

The impersonalness of an oecumenical empire as an institution makes itself felt in the remoteness of its metropolis from the daily life of the great majority of its subjects. Now that Rome's citizens are deployed as far afield as Cadiz, Bayrut, and Cologne, and now that Rome has no need to call them to arms for her defence against neighbouring rival Powers, Dea Roma can no longer inspire, even in their hearts, the same love and devotion as when every Roman citizen lived and worked within a day's march of the Capitol and might be called upon, in any campaigning season, to fight for Rome against Clusium or Samnium. *A fortiori*, a subject of the Roman Empire who is a citizen of Sparta or Athens, or some other once sovereign independent city-state of glorious as well as shameful memory, will not be able to worship Dea Roma with anything like the conviction and enthusiasm with which he has once worshipped Athana Chalcioecus or Athene Polias. The thrill which he then felt can be recaptured by a Modern Western pilgrim when he stands on the acropolis of Athens at the spot where Pheidias' statue of the Attic Athene once stood, and stares at the peak of Aegina and the pinnacle of Acrocorinthus a stone's throw away, just across the Saronic Gulf. As he gazes, the figures of a Corinthian Poseidon and an Aeginetan Athana Aphaia rise up, before his inward eye, to bid defiance to the queen of Athens. The parochial goddess was a very present help against her rival over there, before Dea Roma's long arm put them both down from their seats. Dea Roma, the ubiquitous policewoman, cannot mean anything like as much as this to her Athenian clients, even when they have eventually been granted Roman citizenship, or even when the value of Rome's service to their Hellenic Civilization has been brought home to them in the third century of the Christian Era by a recurrence of the danger of social collapse.

Nor can the subjects of an oecumenical empire be moved to feel much enthusiasm for the imperial public services of which they are the beneficiaries—though these services are more substantial than those provided by any parochial state ever have been or could be. Under the new oecumenical régime a more or less efficiently and justly managed imperial police, administration, and law give to any subject a guarantee that he can count on enjoying peace, security, and justice wherever he goes. Yet a régime which thus confers on him the freedom of the whole Inhabited World does not have the effect of making him feel at home in it. A public service on this oecumenical scale is too impersonal to inspire great affection or even great gratitude.

It is impersonal even in oecumenical empires in which the founders, and the public servants who carry on the founders' work, come from the interior of their world—as they did, for example, in Ur-Nammu's Sumero-Akkadian 'Empire of the Four Quarters' and in the empire, equated with 'All that is under Heaven', into which the Chinese World was re-united by Han Liu Pang. In this, however, those two empires were exceptional. Most oecumenical empires have been founded and maintained, not by sons of the household from their own interior, but either by marchmen or by aliens. Examples of marchmen empire-builders are the Amorite rulers of Hammurabi's reconstituted 'Empire of Sumer and Akkad'; the Roman rulers of an Hellenic oecumenical empire; the successive Persian and Arab rulers of a South-West Asian oecumenical empire; the Theban founders of both the Middle and the New Empire of Egypt; the still more southerly founders of the Old Empire; and the Ts'in founders of a Chinese oecumenical empire that was afterwards salvaged and re-founded by Han Liu Pang. Examples of alien empire-builders are the successive

Mughal and British rulers of an oecumenical empire in India and the 'Osmanli rulers of one in Eastern Orthodox Christendom.

Where the rulers are aliens or marchmen, there is a ready-made psychological gulf between them and their subjects; yet neither the British in India nor the 'Osmanlis in the Near East were content till they had artificially widened this natural barrier. After having fraternized with their Indian subjects in the eighteenth century, the British rulers of India deliberately held aloof from them in the nineteenth. The 'Osmanlis went to the length of keeping the free Muslim *conquistadores* of Eastern Orthodox Christendom at arm's length from the administration of their own empire. They placed this in the hands of a lay monastic corporation, recruited from the Empire's Christian population, who were aloof from the Emperor's Muslim and Christian subjects alike because their voluntary conversion to Islam detached them from their ancestral Christian social milieu without assimilating them to their new co-religionists who were Muslims and freemen by birth. It is even more significant that in the Chinese Empire, which was administered by civil servants drawn from the interior of the Chinese World and sedulously educated in an ancestral Chinese tradition, one of the *arcana imperii* was the rule that an official must never be posted in his home province.

It was, of course, no accident that the Chinese, Ottoman, and British Indian imperial governments all took pains to secure an identical result by these diverse means. Their common concern to make sure that their civil servants should be aloof from their subjects was not perverse. It was inspired by a conviction, founded on experience, that familiarity was inimical to impartiality and efficiency. An aloofness cultivated on this calculation was not to their discredit; but it inevitably set limits to the gratitude and love which they could expect to evoke in the hearts of their subjects.

The alternative focus for the loyalty of an oecumenical empire's subjects is a deified ruler in lieu of a deified institution; and the worship of a Roman Empire as Divus Caesar does not suffer from the remoteness, impersonalness, and aloofness that are the weaknesses of its worship as Dea Roma. While few subjects of the Roman Empire can ever visit Rome, Caesar can travel everywhere; he can stay for whatever length of time he chooses wherever he finds the most urgent work to do; and Caesar, Augustus, and Hadrian each did, in fact, spend a large part of his working life on the road and in the camp. Divus Caesar has the advantage over Dea Roma again in being a god who is a human being of like passions with his subjects; and, since he is also an exceptionally potent human being, on whose fiat the lives and fortunes of all his subjects depend, he will excite strong feelings of hope or fear, veneration or contempt, love or hate. But this palpable human nature of Divus Caesar's, which is the strength of his relation with his subjects, is also the weakness of it; for no man is really God or anything like God. Even the least ungodlike human being who has been cast for this superhuman part of playing Divus Caesar will fail egregiously to live up to it (as witness Caesar himself at Alexandria), while the failure of the least exemplary of these deified human beings will be scandalous. The prestige of a Caesar's or an Augustus's genius may enable a Tiberius or a Claudius to 'get by', but there is a limit to its vicarious efficacity. It cannot save the reputation of a Gaius or a Nero; nor can the prestige of a Marcus Aurelius's virtue save the reputation of a Commodus, whom his father ought never to have designated as his successor.

There is also a weakness that Divus Caesar and Dea Roma have in common. In either form, the worship of an oecumenical empire is an artificial product, instead of being the spontaneous growth that the previous worship of parochial states is. It is invented and promoted for *raison d'état*, and is propagated by political action; and, though it does respond to a yearning for political unity that is genuine and is very widely felt, its artificiality nevertheless debars it from winning the hearts of its beneficiaries.

For these reasons, the managers of an oecumenical empire find it less and less easy, as time goes on, to secure sufficient devotion from their subjects for the empire as an object of worship in itself, whether in the chillingly impersonal form of a deified institution or in the unedifying personal form of a deified emperor; and this depreciation of the political value of the deification of the empire finds its reflection in a change of policy. A tendency sets in to 'play down' the doctrine of the

Emperor's divinity or even to renounce it altogether, and to seek political compensation for the loss that is thus being written off by trying to find a new religious sanction for the empire in something outside it and above it.

The divinity of the Emperor was, for example, 'played down' progressively in Egypt at successive stages of the long history of the Egyptian Empire. Pharaoh 'the Great God' in his own right becomes the Pharaoh who is a god in virtue of his being the son of the Sun-god Re; and this divinely begotten god incarnate is a more human figure in the New Empire than in the Middle Empire, and in the Middle Empire than in the Old Empire. From the age of the Middle Empire onwards he is 'the Good God'.[1] In the New Empire the heretic emperor Ikhnaton goes to the length of having himself represented, in realistic visual art, as a life-like human being in the bosom of his family; and, though he allows himself to be worshipped as a god by his Court, he presents himself to the World as the human servant and expositor of a god, manifesting Himself in the Sun-disk, who is transcendent and unique.

In the Sumero-Akkadian World, divinity was claimed by human rulers only exceptionally, and then only half-heartedly. The Akkadian militarist Naramsin allowed his name to be written with the determinative character signifying a god, and his person to be portrayed wearing a god's horned crown.[2] The successors of Ur-Nammu, the founder of the Empire of Sumer and Akkad, went to the further length of having themselves worshipped as gods, in temples dedicated to them by name, in the city-states which they had brought under the dominion of their imperial city Ur. But 'even the King of Ur was not worshipped in a temple in his own city. He might be a god at Eshnunna; but at Ur he was the servant of the city's owner, the moon-god Nanna';[3] and, when Hammurabi, King of Babylon, re-established the Empire of Sumer and Akkad after an interregnum, he did not revive the pretension to rule as a god incarnate, but reverted to the original Sumerian practice of ruling as a god's vicegerent. Hammurabi's conception of his own position and credentials is proclaimed in his

---

[1] See Frankfort, H., *Kingship and the Gods* (Chicago 1948, University of Chicago Press), p. 39.
[2] See Frankfort, H., op. cit., pp. 224-5.   [3] Frankfort, op. cit., p. 302.

name, if this is correctly interpreted as meaning 'The Uncle [i.e. the god Marduk] is [or 'be'] exalted'. Such personal names of human beings in the form of a sentence, in which a god is the subject of a statement or a prayer, were common in Babylonia and Assyria, as they were afterwards in Israel and in Islam; and, wherever they are current, they indicate that the bearer looks upon himself as being a transcendent god's servant, and not as being, himself, a god incarnate.

The precedent set by Hammurabi, in making no claim to divinity for himself, was, in fact, followed by all subsequent rulers of universal states in South-West Asia. Hammurabi ruled as the human servant of Marduk—the city-god of Babylon, whose dominion had become oecumenical *pari passu* with his human vicegerent's. The Achaemenidae ruled as human servants of Ahuramazda (and perhaps also, locally, as servants of the gods of their subject peoples). The Umayyads, and, more explicitly, the 'Abbasids, ruled as human servants of Allah. The precedent that the Babylonian Emperor had set was also followed, no doubt unawares, by the Roman Emperor Aurelian, when he chose to rule, not as the god that each of his predecessors had been for their subjects in the eastern provinces, but as the chosen vicegerent of a transcendent god—Sol Invictus, 'the Unconquered Sun'—who had once been the god of Ikhnaton.

The purpose of this transfer of divinity from the human ruler to a transcendent god on whose behalf he acts is divulged in a saying attributed to Aurelian by a Greek historian; the ineffectiveness of the policy is registered in its failure to save Aurelian from meeting the fate of his deified predecessors.

Aurelian used to say that the soldiers deluded themselves in supposing that the destinies of the Emperors lay in their hands. For he used to aver that it was God who had bestowed the purple and . . . had decided the period of his reign.[1]

Evidently, when once the soldiers have broken through any inhibition that they may ever have felt against murdering a god incarnate in an emperor, it becomes less dangerous for the wearer of the imperial crown to be, not a god himself, but the human vicegerent of a transcendent god whom the murderers

[1] *Auctor Anonymus post Dionem*, Dindorf's edition, p. 229.

cannot liquidate because he is not flesh and blood. Dead gods do not fulminate. A god who can be liquidated will be debarred, in the act, from all possibility of being able to inflict posthumous punishment for the crime successfully committed against him. But a transcendent god, who survives his murdered human servant's death, will live on to punish the murderers— as Yahweh lived on in the land of Israel, after the deportation of his people, to settle accounts with the deportees' supplanters.

This reasoning, which makes the transfer of divinity seem politic, is psychologically cogent on one condition that is all-important. The ruler's purpose in seeking a religious sanction for his rule outside himself is to find one that will have an effective hold upon the imagination and the feelings of his subjects at a stage at which, *ex hypothesi*, their veneration for a god incarnate in an emperor has worn too thin to serve any longer as a prophylactic against assassination. The weakness of Aurelian's position *vis-à-vis* the soldiers—who did eventually murder him in his turn—was that the soldiers did not seriously believe in the transcendent god whose unconscious agents Aurelian declares them to have been, any more than they had seriously believed in the divinity of the human gods Gaius, Nero, and Commodus. The human emperor's transcendent divine protector must be a god in whom the Emperor's subjects do believe, genuinely and spontaneously, if this god's protection is to be effective.

Here the Hammurabis and Aurelians find themselves in a dilemma; for they will be chary of putting themselves in the hands of any divine patron who is not also their own creature, or at least their own nominee. If the imperial god is no longer to be the Emperor himself, political prudence will counsel that he must be under his human protégé's control in the sense of being a divinity of the Emperor's choice, served by a priesthood who are the Emperor's appointees, and worshipped with a ritual which the Emperor has approved, if he has not actually devised it himself. Here, however, the Emperor of the *bas empire* has set himself an insoluble problem; for the very conditions of appointment that make a tutelary god *persona grata* to the Emperor himself make him a nonentity in the eyes of the Emperor's subjects whom the puppet divinity has been commissioned to overawe.

Attempts to impose, by political authority, a religion that has been artificially manufactured for *raison d'état* seem, indeed, always to have failed to win the necessary allegiance from the subjects of a ruler who has sought to obtain a sanction of this artificial kind for his tottering political authority. Inability to win sufficient devotion is, as we have seen, one of the weaknesses of the worship of the oecumenical empire itself, and there will be the same fatal weakness in any artificial substitute.

In an age of Egyptian history in which the divinity of Pharaoh was on the wane, Ikhnaton failed to replace the traditional god incarnate by an abstract transcendent god, symbolized by the Sun-disk. The Aton had been designed by his human creator to serve, in an Egyptian oecumenical empire, as a common object of worship for the whole Human Race, in the empire's Syrian and Nubian fringes, as well as in its Egyptian core. But Ikhnaton's Egyptian subjects, at any rate, could not be persuaded to believe in this new artificial god imposed on them from above by political authority. They could not feel for the Aton what their ancestors had felt for the very present god incarnate whose divine father, Amon-Re, immortalized, in a theological union between a Theban Life-god and a Deltaic Sun-god, the political unification of the two components of the Egyptian World. This lack of popular response made it impossible for the Aton to provide an effective religious sanction for his creator-vicegerent's régime; and this artificial religion lasted no longer than Ikhnaton's own life and reign.

In a later age of Egyptian history, Ptolemy I failed, like Ikhnaton before him, to make an artificial religion produce the result that was his objective. This Macedonian Greek founder of an Egyptian successor-state of the Achaemenian Empire wanted to create a bond of feeling between the intrusive Greek and the indigenous Egyptian element in the population of his usurped dominions.[1] He sought to achieve this politically desirable effect by Hellenizing the Egyptian god Osiris-Apis, in whose temple at Memphis, the ancient national capital of Egypt, the successive bull-incarnations of Apis were buried. This Memphite Egyptian god was given a new temple in

[1] This is the motive for the establishment of the cult of Osiris that has been attributed to Ptolemy by most Modern Western students of his policy, but there are some dissentient opinions (see Nilsson, M.P., *Geschichte der Griechischen Religion*, vol. ii (Munich 1950, Beck), p. 148).

Rhacôtis, the Egyptian quarter of Ptolemy's new Greek capital Alexandria, and here he was installed under the name Serapis, in a Hellenized visual form in which he would be an acceptable object of worship for Greeks both in Ptolemy's dominions and beyond them. Since, by Ptolemy's day, the Greeks were beginning to be addicted to the religiosity to which the Egyptians had long since succumbed, this new Hellenic version of an old Egyptian cult did duly strike root. But, if this successful religious innovation of Ptolemy's was really inspired by the ulterior political purpose of promoting a rapprochement between Greeks and Egyptians, then his policy was a failure. The old Egyptian cult of a Memphite Osiris-Apis and the new Greek cult of an Alexandrian Serapis lived on side by side for centuries without ever coalescing; so that the naturalization of an Egyptian god in the Hellenic World did nothing to bring together this common god's respective Greek and Egyptian worshippers.

This failure of the cult of Serapis to bridge the gulf between Greeks and Egyptians in the generation of the Macedonian conquest of the Achaemenian Empire contrasts significantly with the success of the cult of the Virgin of Guadalupe— inaugurated in the generation of the Castilian conquest of Mexico—in bridging the gulf between Spaniards and Indians; and the reason for the difference in the outcome is clear. The Virgin who was to become the patroness of a new nation, in which Indians and Creoles were to be merged, made her epiphany in the guise of an Indian goddess to an Indian peasant, and the peasant's tale of his visions was doubted by the Spanish authorities till it was vindicated by a miracle. The conquerors found it hardly credible that the Queen of Heaven should have chosen to manifest herself as an Indian to an Indian convert. But this epiphany as an Indian to an Indian, which was a stumbling-block for the Virgin's hereditary Spanish worshippers, won the Indians' devotion for a goddess, imported by the conquerors, who had signified so graciously that she had taken the conquered to her heart; and thus the Great Mother of the Old World was adopted, as the Virgin of Guadalupe, by conquered natives of the New World without forfeiting her immigrant worshippers' allegiance. In the light of the history of Ptolemy I's unsuccessful attempt to make

Religion serve a political purpose, we may surmise that the shrine at Guadalupe would never have played the key-part that it has played in the life of Mexico since the conquest if its founder had been, not the Indian peasant Juan Diego, but the Spanish empire-builder Hernan Cortés.

Ptolemy's I's failure to fuse his Greek and Egyptian subjects together into a single community by winning their hearts for a common religious cult did not have the explosive consequences of the Seleucid Emperor Antiochus IV's unsuccessful attempt, a century and a half later, to achieve a cultural *Gleichschaltung* by a similar religious innovation. Antiochus hoped to create among his multifarious subjects a common feeling of imperial patriotism by identifying the old parochial god of each of the local communities in his empire with a new imperial god Zeus Ouranios. But when the Emperor attempted to transfigure Yahweh of Jerusalem into the new imperial god's standard likeness, the result was a religious explosion that has affected the whole subsequent course of the World's history.

Four centuries after Antiochus IV's day, a minor explosion was produced by the Roman Emperor Elagabalus when he made the converse attempt to transfigure the local god of his own Syrian native city into an oecumenical god for all the peoples under Roman rule. The Romans were no more willing to adopt a black stone fetish from Emesa as the supreme tutelary god of the Roman Empire than the Jews had been willing to adopt a standard statue of the Seleucid imperial god Zeus Ouranios as the image of their local god Yahweh. Aurelian, in succession to Elagabalus, failed to win allegiance for the Sun-god, incongruously embodied in Elagabalus's black stone, by presenting him in the less shocking abstract form of Sol Invictus.

Thereafter, Maximinus Daia and Julian each in turn sought to build up an artificial religion for the Roman Empire on a broader basis by cementing together all the current religions except Christianity with mortar made of the Neoplatonic philosophy. But Maximinus's and Julian's problem was no longer the same as Elagabalus's and Aurelian's. In renewing their predecessors' attempts to manufacture an artificial religion, the two later emperors were concerned, not so much to secure a new religious sanction for their rule, as to

forestall the occupation of the religious vacuum in their subjects' hearts by a living religion. This was one which, so far from
having been manufactured and imposed by any Roman
emperor, had made its epiphany in a social underworld and
had won its way in defiance of the Roman Imperial Government's will. And, before Julian had re-embarked on Maximinus Daia's forlorn hope of opposing Christianity by staging
an artificial pagan counter-church, Constantine the Great had
shown a deeper understanding of the reasons for Aurelian's
failure when he had transferred his allegiance from a tame and
therefore impotent Sol Invictus to the Almighty God worshipped by the Christians—a god who was potent in virtue of
being intractable.

Constantine had, indeed, divined that a new departure was
called for by the successive bankruptcies of the worship of a
god incarnate in the Emperor and the worship of a transcendent god who, though officially the Emperor's patron, was
in truth the Emperor's puppet and was consequently incapable
of winning the hearts of the Emperor's subjects. When artificial religions have thus failed to provide the imperial régime
with the effective religious sanction that it needs, there is only
one alternative left to an Imperial Government. It must place
itself under the aegis of some living religion that has arisen
spontaneously and that cannot be discounted by the Imperial
Government's subjects as being a cult manufactured by the
imperial authorities for raison d'état. In the Roman Empire
both these necessary conditions were fulfilled conspicuously by
Christianity, whose spiritual independence of the imperial
authorities was attested by a long record of martyrdoms,
beginning with the Crucifixion of its Founder. In placing the
Roman Empire under the aegis of Christianity, Constantine
was following unawares a South-West Asian precedent, as
Aurelian had been following one in proclaiming himself vicegerent of Sol Invictus. Aurelian had been anticipated by
Hammurabi the vicegerent of Marduk the god of Babylon, and
Constantine by Cyrus and Darius the vicegerents of Ahuramazda the god of the Prophet Zarathustra. The Achaemenidae
had placed themselves under the aegis of a higher religion
which, like Christianity, was an independent spiritual power,
and this Persian example was followed by Arab Caliphs—

political 'successors' of the Prophet Muhammad—who ruled as 'commanders of the faithful' adherents of Islam.

The step taken by Constantine was revolutionary in the sense that he was purchasing an effective religious sanction for the Roman Empire at the price of submitting to the spiritual authority of a Christian Church that was not under the Imperial Government's control and that had so far always proved unamenable to it. Was not the emperor-convert placing himself at the victorious church's mercy? The impotence of an emperor to dethrone an officially established higher religion is illustrated, not only by Julian's failure, but also by Akbar's and by Hākim's. Akbar was defeated in an attempt to replace Islam by an artificial Dīn Ilāhī that was to have served the same purpose as Ptolemy I's artificial cult of Serapis and as Antiochus IV's artificial cult of Zeus Ouranios. Hākim was defeated in an attempt to revert from the worship of the God of Islam, Christianity, and Judaism to the pagan worship of a god incarnate in the Emperor himself. In A.D. 1956 Hākim's artificial religion had only a tiny band of adherents in the Druses of the Lebanon and Syria, while Akbar's artificial religion had no surviving adherents at all.

'It is', in truth, 'a fearful thing to fall into the hands of the living God';[1] and so, even when the proven sterility of all manufactured religions drives rulers in search of a religious sanction to turn towards some living religion that is untainted by *raison d'état*, Human Nature will still seek for an alternative to the dread ordeal of making an approach to Absolute Reality. In this situation, souls that have been disillusioned with the worship of collective human power, both parochial and oecumenical, are apt to turn, first, to a form of man-worship which is distinguished from other forms of it by being neither collective nor artificial. The deified self-sufficient philosopher shares with the deified parochial community the merit of being an idol that has not been manufactured in cold blood, while he shares with the deified oecumenical ruler the merit of being a person and not an institution. The worship of Man as a self-sufficient philosopher has therefore also to be tried and found wanting before the field can become clear for occupation by the higher religions.

[1] Heb. x. 31.

5

MAN-WORSHIP: THE IDOLIZATION OF A SELF-SUFFICIENT PHILOSOPHER[1]

WE have seen that the impersonal worship of a universal state as a deified institution has an alternative in the personal worship of it as a deified ruler. In the deified philosopher, Man, idolized as an individual, jumps clear of the deified ruler's dependence on the worship of collective human power and stands upright, without a crutch, as an idol exclusively in his own individual right.

This idolized self-sufficient philosopher is the final product of the liberation of the individual in a parochial community in the first phase of a civilization's history. In this phase, as we have noticed, the parochial communities into which a nascent civilization articulates itself win the devotion of their members by enabling them, not only to have Life, but to have it more abundantly.[2] In primitive societies, self-centredness is in the first person plural. Like the ant in the ant-heap and the bee in the beehive, the primitive human being is a social animal and little more. A progressive transposition of self-centredness from the first person plural into the first person singular through a progressive liberation of the individual is the chief stimulus given to human life by the parochial communities of a society in process of civilization in these communities' early days. No doubt Man, like the Ant and the Bee, is a social animal by nature, and would be going against his own nature if he were to refuse to express himself in social action. Indeed, any act of self-expression is bound to be a social act as well, since there can be no self-expression without an audience. All the same, the self-expression of an individual who is aware of having a consciousness and a will of his own is a far more stimulating form of social activity than the action of a human being who is under such overwhelming pressure from the society of which

[1] The subject of this chapter has been dealt with in greater detail by the writer in *A Study of History*, vol. v, pp. 39-40, 56-8; vol. vi, pp. 132-48, 242-59, 366.
[2] John x. 10.

he is a member that his sociality holds his individuality down below the level of consciousness. The liberation of the individual in the sense of setting him free, not to repudiate his innate and inalienable sociality, but to fulfil his social nature consciously and deliberately, is the boon that is brought to Man —or at least to some outstanding men—in a parochial community in the first phase of a civilization's history.

In this chapter of history we can watch the individual emerging by progressive stages. He makes his first appearance as a bare name in a list of annual office-holders whose individual names are recorded for the public purpose of giving distinctive labels to otherwise indistinguishable years in the community's life—as, for example, in the Assyrian list of holders of the office of *limmu*, the Attic list of eponymous archons, and the Roman list of consuls. Except for the one point that they are inscribed and not merely committed to memory, these archaic lists of annual office-holders do not carry the individual much farther along the road towards recognition than the primitive lists of ancestors; and a decisive new departure is made only when the individual is entered in the record as the author of an historical achievement.

At this stage the picture preserved in the record becomes stereoscopic. It shows us the individual following some particular career, and this with varying results that may be either good or bad for himself and for the society in whose life he is playing his individual part. He may have recorded his own activities as a builder, like the Assyrian kings who address us in the earliest of the Assyrian inscriptions so far retrieved by Modern Western archaeologists. He may have expounded his policy and have recorded his own successes and failures as a lawgiver and a statesman, as Solon has done in the poems that still circulate under his name. He may be celebrated, like Pheidias, as an artist who has made individual works of art out of the public works that the community has commissioned him to carry out. He may be celebrated, like Aeschylus, as a poet who has made individual works of art out of public celebrations of an annually recurrent religious rite which was originally just repetitive and therefore anonymous. And he may be undeservedly illustrious or deservedly infamous as a conqueror who has won individual renown and power for himself in the warfare between his own parochial community and its neighbours. Classic monuments of this sinister military notoriety are the records of victorious aggressive campaigns which made their appearance in the Assyrian kings' inscriptions, first as prefaces to innocent building-records, and then as the principal narrative, to which the building-record is now attached perfunctorily as a mere conventional appendage.

The emergence of the individual as a war-lord foreshadows the opening of a breach between liberated individuals and militarized parochial communities. We have seen that the warfare between parochial communities rankles, sooner or later, into war to the death. This disastrous intensification of the violence with which inter-parochial wars are waged is partly due to the scope that these wars give to individuals who make their mark as conquerors. The individuals whose self-expression takes this form find the opportunity for achieving their individual ambitions expanding with each increase in the toll taken by War from Society. But the individuality of the militarists makes these anti-social gains at the cost of the war-lords' fellow-individuals whose fields of activity lie in other directions; and so, in the experience of a majority of the individual members of a militarized parochial community, the process of militarization changes the relation between the community and them. An institution that, in a past chapter of history, has enriched their lives by giving them the opening for a liberation of their individuality, now impoverishes their lives by exacting from them heavier and heavier sacrifices. Yahweh 'the man of war'[1] has revealed himself to be Moloch the 'horrid king'; and this appalling new epiphany of the old parochial god leads to a parting of the ways in the attitudes of individuals towards their parochial state, along lines corresponding to the differences in their fields of activity.

At this parting of the ways, the war-lords become more devoted than ever to the worship of parochial collective human power that gives such scope for the achievement of military ambitions. In the age of the civilizations of the second generation they stand self-condemned in the gloating war-communiqués inscribed by Assyrian kings in the style of Asshur-nasir-pal II and in the still more damning style of

[1] Exod. xv. 3.

Tiglath-pileser III. In the age of the civilizations of the first generation, they stand self-condemned in the grim visual records carved on Naramsin's stele and on Narmer's palette. The stele is a monument of Akkadian militarism in action against the highlanders of Gutium during the fight to the death between the contending states of the Sumero-Akkadian World; the palette is a monument of Egyptian militarism at the moment of the fight's culmination and close through the annihilation of all belligerents except one single victorious survivor.

On the other side of the picture we see the war-lords' victims revolting against the blood-tax. The repeated revolts of the Assyrian people against the sacrifices exacted from them by their militarist kings were too flagrant to allow even the historiographer-royal to ignore these shocking incidents entirely. The reluctance of the Spartans to continue to make the sacrifices required of them for the reconquest of Messene in the Second Spartano-Messenian War is commemorated in the verses of the poet Tyrtaeus, who was commissioned by the Spartan Government of the day to rally the Spartan warriors' faltering *moral*. Tyrtaeus's success showed that a poet, as well as a king, could become a war-profiteer. While Tyrtaeus's martial poetry is said to have cajoled the Spartan rank and file into continuing to sacrifice their lives, the poet himself won fame as well as a fee. Another Greek poet, however, won equal fame, not by commending the military virtues, but by repudiating them when he was called upon to pay the blood-tax in his own person.

Archilochus had to fight for his city-state Paros in a colonial war of conquest on the island of Thasos which was as unjust as Sparta's war to reconquer her Hellenic neighbour Messene. The Parian poet-conscript saved his life by a flagrant breach of the conventional code of military honour, and then aggravated his offence by publishing, in defiance of contemporary Hellenic public opinion, a poem impudently advertising his contempt for the citizen's traditional obligation to give his life for his country.

> My shield is now the pride and joy
> Of some pugnacious Saïan boy.

> I dropped it by a briar-patch—
> As good as new; inside, no scratch.
> A pity? Yes, but here am I
> Alive. And what's left if we die?
> Old shield, go hang! I'll buy a new
> Replacement quite as good as you.

The fact that this provocative poem is still in circulation shows that, when Archilochus published it, he knew what he was about. He must have reckoned that, in the movement of Hellenic public opinion, the revolt against the blood-tax was now sufficiently wide-spread, whatever Spartan mothers might still say, for a Parian poet to be able to boast of his common-sense cowardice with impunity.

In Hellenic history, this poem of Archilochus's is a landmark, because he was the first individual member of the Hellenic Society who had the audacity publicly to flout the fiat of his parochial community. But Archilochus had debarred himself from winning a following or starting a movement by choosing to be no hero. His disobedience to his community had taken the uninspiring form of shirking a personal challenge to him to perform a traditional social duty at the risk of his life. In Hellenic history the hero who could and did become the pattern for a new ideal of spiritual self-sufficiency was Socrates, a citizen-philosopher who, in honourable contrast to Archi-lochus, had scrupulously and cheerfully done his traditional duty by his community in duly risking his life on active military service. This untarnished civic record put Socrates in a strong moral position when, eventually, he deliberately laid his life down in disobeying his community, and voluntarily suffering martyrdom at its hands, because he was unwilling to carry out the state's orders that he should act against the dictates of his conscience.

Socrates chose to lose his life in order to save it; and, in his encounter with Athens, his conduct was so noble, and hers so invidious, that his martyrdom dealt parochial-community-worship, not only at Athens, but throughout the Hellenic World, a blow from which it was never afterwards able to recover. Since almost every post-Socratic school of Hellenic philosophy looked back, and up, to Socrates as its patriarch, the echoes of the judicial murder committed at Athens in 399

B.C. reverberated down all subsequent centuries of Hellenic history and shook the prestige of city-state sovereignty as severely as the prestige of the royal power in the parochial kingdoms of Medieval Western Christendom was shaken by the echoes of the assassination of Thomas Becket. No doubt, Socrates did not intend or foresee the immense and continuing moral effect that his death was to have. In bringing discredit upon idolized parochial communities, Socrates opened the way in the Hellenic World for the discovery of worthier alternative objects of worship. He became the historic exemplar of a new ideal of a human god—a god incarnate, not in a community, but in an individual human being.

In thus taking the martyrdom of Socrates as the inspiration for a new form of Man-worship—the idolization of a self-sufficient philosopher—the post-Socratic votaries of this new Hellenic faith were misconstruing Socrates' beliefs and were doing Socrates himself an injustice. In choosing to be made a martyr rather than carry out the state's orders against his conscience, Socrates was not convicting himself of being one of 'certain which trusted in themselves that they were righteous and despised others'.[1] He believed himself to be following the guidance of a spiritual presence, other than himself, which he called his supernatural monitor, using the Greek word in its diminutive form *daimonion* to signify the intimacy of his personal relation with this 'still small voice'. In thus sacrificing his life at the instance of a divine guide that was neither one of the forces of Nature nor the human community of which Socrates was a member, but was also not Socrates himself, Socrates was in truth the precursor, not of the philosophers, Hellenic, Indian, or Chinese—most of whom died peacefully in their beds—but of the Jewish and Christian martyrs.

In the un-Socratic pursuit of spiritual self-sufficiency, the philosophers sought to fill the spiritual vacuum created by the failure of parochial-community-worship; and, in the Hellenic World, India, and China alike, they came near enough to reaching their goal to demonstrate that the individual human soul was capable of rising to spiritual heights that were beyond the reach of any collective projection of the Self. But the Indians alone commanded sufficient intellectual clarity to be

[1] Luke xviii. 9.

able to think out the problem to ultimate conclusions in theory, and sufficient moral courage to be able to follow out these conclusions to their goal in practice; and they too, like their Greek and Chinese confrères, were caught out by weaknesses in their common ideal that were both intrinsic and radical.

The Indian philosophers of the Hinayanian Buddhist school grasped, and acted on, the paradoxical truth that, for human beings, the logically inevitable objective of the pursuit of self-sufficiency is self-extinction. Complete spiritual self-sufficiency is unattainable by any living creature so long as it continues to be a self; and this is so because of the contradiction that lies at the very heart of life incarnate—and thereby 'incarcerate'—in living creatures in their unredeemed state of nature on Earth. Every living creature is trying, as we have observed, to make itself into the centre of the Universe. But the fuel that feeds the flame of the creature's self-assertion is Desire, and Desire is a bond that binds the individual creature to the rest of Creation and so makes it the slave of the Universe instead of its master. This inner contradiction means that ordinary life is a tension for which another name is Suffering. Without a complete liberation from this painful tension there can be no complete self-sufficiency, and therefore a complete self-sufficiency can be attained only by burning away the spiritual fuel—Desire—that is both the nutriment of self-centredness and the impediment to the achievement of its objective. It is only in Nirvāna—a state of being in which the flame of Desire has been blown out and, in the act, the Self has been completely extinguished—that the tension of ordinary mundane life is resolved.

Nirvāna, which means, literally, 'being blown out', is a negative form of expression; and the Buddha is recorded to have parried His disciples' requests for a positive definition of it in the language of metaphysics, because He was on the watch to keep His sheep from turning aside into the agreeable field of unprofitable speculation out of the hard road of arduous action along which He was shepherding them.[1] In the metaphysical terms of contemporary non-Buddhist Indian thought, the blowing out of the flame of Desire might, perhaps, be equated with the act of seeing through Maya—the veil cast over the

[1] See Chapter 2, p. 22, above.

face of Reality by the illusory world of phenomena—and the attainment of Nirvāna be equated with a consequent intuition that the Self (the Ātman) is identical with Absolute Reality (Brahma): 'Thou art that'. The Buddha, for His part, if ever He had allowed himself to be drawn on to this metaphysical ground, might perhaps have pronounced that His non-Buddhist Indian contemporaries' spiritual objective was in truth the same as His own. He might have agreed that Nirvāna and Brahma were merely two different names for the same Absolute Reality, and might not have denied that He and His contemporaries were also of one mind in thinking that, at the level of Absolute Reality—and only at this level—the incompatibility between Self and self-sufficiency disappears. But He would assuredly have gone on to insist that the common objective could be attained only by the exertion of the Will, and never merely by the play of the Intellect. For the practical attainment of Brahma-Nirvāna, a mere intuition of the Self's identity with this Absolute Reality would not avail, since the reason why Absolute Reality alone is capable of being self-sufficient is because Absolute Reality alone is not a Self. Self is another name for Maya, the illusory world of phenomena; and therefore the only way in which the intuition of the Self's identity with Absolute Reality can be translated into an act of union is by an act of Will through which the Self burns itself out till nothing but Absolute Reality is left.[1]

In India in the days of the Buddha Siddhārtha Gautama and His disciples of the primitive Hinayanian school, as in the Hellenic World in the days of Socrates and his successors Zeno and Epicurus, the warfare between parochial states had reached an intolerable pitch of intensity. Both the Buddhist and the Hellenic philosophers detached themselves from the parochial communities into which they happened to have been born; but the Buddhists went much farther than this. They sought to detach themselves from every form of mundane society and, beyond that, from the lusts of mundane life itself; and the very sincerity and resoluteness with which these Hinayanian Buddhist philosophers pursued their spiritual quest raise two questions: Is absolute detachment an attainable

---

[1] See further Chapter 6, p. 83, below, for the relation between the Buddha's attitude and the standpoint of contemporary Indian thinkers.

objective? And, supposing it to be attainable, is the pursuit of it a good activity?[1]

Absolute detachment looks as if it might be intrinsically unattainable, because it is hard to see how the intensely arduous spiritual effort to detach oneself from all other desires can be achieved without attaching oneself to the single master-desire of extinguishing every desire save this. Is the extinction of the desire to desire nothing but the extinction of desire a psychological possibility? Evidently the fathers of the Hīnayāna school were aware of this psychological crux in their path, for, in the traditional formulation of the second of their Four Holy Truths, the 'craving for extinction' is enumerated, as well as the 'craving to perpetuate oneself' and the 'craving for sensuous experience', as one of the forms taken by the craving that is the origination of Ill because it is a craving that leads to rebirth.

The second question is whether the pursuit of absolute detachment, if feasible, is also good. If the Buddha was right, as He surely was, in holding that absolute detachment can be achieved only through the extinction of all desire whatsoever, then the Hīnayāna must require not only the suppression of desires that are ordinarily regarded as being selfish, such as those for personal pleasure, prosperity, and power for oneself, but also the suppression of desires that are ordinarily regarded as being altruistic, such as Love and Pity for one's fellow sentient beings. For a philosopher whose objective is to free himself from all bonds of feeling, an altruistic Love and Pity are no less compromising than a ruthless pursuit of selfish lusts. If this impartial suppression of all desires, bad and good alike, was thus a logical consequence of the Hinayanian Buddhist doctrine, the Buddha Himself was guilty of a sublime inconsistency. For He resisted the temptation to make the immediate exit into Nirvāna that His Enlightenment had brought within His reach, and chose, instead, to postpone His own release from suffering in order to teach the way of release to His fellows. Followers of the latterday Mahayanian school of Buddhism could fairly claim that, on the evidence of a legend included in the Hinayanian canon of Buddhist scripture, the Buddha had practised,

[1] These questions are taken up again in Chapter 19, pp. 274-5, and Chapter 20, pp. 289-94, below.

not the Hīnayāna, but the Mahāyāna in His own life. But these same Mahayanian Buddhists also accused their Hinayanian predecessors and opponents of having, unlike their common master, been selfishly consistent in following the path of absolute and undiscriminating detachment that the Buddha had prescribed in His teaching. The Mahayanian Buddhist's verdict on the Hinayanian philosopher can be summed up in an inversion of the Scribes' and Pharisees' jibe at Christ on the Cross. 'He saved himself; others he cannot save.'[1]

Whether or not this verdict was justly passed on the Buddhist philosophers of the Hinayanian school, it would certainly have been applicable to the Hellenic philosophers of the Stoic and Epicurean schools; for these were conspicuously inferior to the Hinayanian Buddhist Indian philosophers both intellectually and morally. In their parallel quest of 'imperturbability' and 'invulnerability', they did not lay the axe to the root of the tree, as the Hinayanian philosophers did in setting themselves the target of extinguishing their selves. On the other hand, the Hellenic philosophers went to greater lengths than the Hinayanian philosophers went in deliberately extinguishing their unselfish feelings of Love and Pity for their suffering fellow creatures.

Pity is a mental illness induced by the spectacle of other people's miseries. . . . The sage does not succumb to mental diseases of that sort.[2]

If you are kissing a child of yours—or a brother, or a friend—never put your imagination unreservedly into the act and never give your emotion free rein, but curb it and check it.[3]

These passages from the works of two of the leading exponents of Stoicism in the oecumenical age of Hellenic history are fair samples of Stoic doctrine and damning evidences of Stoicism's failure. In seeking to make themselves into gods by detaching themselves from their fellow human beings, the Stoics and Epicureans were not raising themselves to the divine level that they aspired to reach. They were depressing themselves to a sub-human level; and the self-defeat to which they

[1] See Matt. xxvii. 42; Mark xv. 31; Luke xxiii. 35.
[2] Seneca, De Clementiâ, Book II, chap. 5, § 4.
[3] Epictetus, Dissertationes, Book III, chap. 24, § 85.

brought themselves was the inevitable nemesis of the *hybris* which they had committed. In truth, Man is not God and cannot make himself into God; and therefore the philosophers' overweening attempt to attain to a godlike self-sufficiency brings upon them an ironical nemesis by constraining them to contract their godlike human faculties of Love and Pity to sub-human dimensions instead of expanding them to divine dimensions. God alone can be absolutely loving and compassionate as well as absolutely self-sufficient. Man had better hold fast to the measure of Love and Pity that is within his compass, at the price of letting the quest for self-sufficiency go by the board. Even when he has lowered himself to a sub-human level of casting out Love and Pity to the best of his ability, Man is still incapable of self-sufficiency on this side of Nirvāna.

The Chinese philosophers of the Confucian school avoided the half-hearted Hellenic philosophers' fate of falling between two stools because they did not attempt to cultivate the detachment which was the common objective of the Stoics and the Hinayanian Buddhists. The Confucians were content to leave themselves exposed to pain and frustration by setting themselves the traditional workaday moral targets of being good sons and good civil servants. Confucius's life-work, like the Buddha's, was the foundation of a school of practical philosophy; and, like the Buddha's, again, it was a *pis aller* from a self-regarding point of view. But, when we go on to consider what course each of them would have taken if he had followed his bent, the outward resemblance between their careers discloses an inward antithesis. The Buddha founded His school at the price of voluntarily postponing His exit into Nirvāna; Confucius founded his in consequence of failing to achieve his ambition to be employed by some parochial prince as his minister of state. Between the unemployed potential civil-servant and the self-deferred potential arhat there is a great gulf fixed.

It will be seen that the Confucian philosophy did not commit its followers to that conflict with the innate sociality of Human Nature to which the Buddhist and Stoic philosophers were committed by their effort to extinguish Desire. In the Indian and the Greek philosophers' practice, this conflict was partially resolved by a compromise with sociality at the cost of the self-sufficiency which was the philosophers' objective; and this compromise involved them in intellectual inconsistency, while it did not absolve them from emotional tension. These unhappy experiences were consequences of the sin of *hybris* which the Indian and the Greek philosophers were committing in setting themselves to attain a godlike self-sufficiency that is not in truth attainable by Man either individually or collectively. The Chinese philosophers were able to avoid these spiritual pitfalls, and to keep their feet on the ground, because they were not too proud to find their targets in traditional human social virtues; and it is assuredly no accident that Confucianism has achieved a solid practical success that puts the practical achievements of Stoicism, Epicureanism, and the Hīnayāna in the shade.

In A.D. 1956 it could be surmised that, under a veneer of Communism, Confucianism was still decisively moulding the lives of a Chinese people who, at that date, amounted to something between a fifth and a quarter of the whole living generation of Mankind. From the second century B.C. until after the turn of the nineteenth and twentieth centuries of the Christian Era, Confucianism had retained the abiding allegiance of an intellectual élite in this populous Chinese Society. In spite of the occasional inroads of alien and theoretically incompatible ways of life—as, for instance, the Mahayanian form of Buddhism—Confucianism had always hitherto eventually recaptured its hold on the masses, even when these had temporarily wavered away from it. In the same year A.D. 1956 there was not one of the Hellenic philosophies that still had any surviving adherents in any corner of the World; and perhaps the reason why these Hellenic schools had died out was because, in their practical compromise with Society, they had shown the same half-heartedness as in their pursuit of their objective of Self-Sufficiency.

The Hinayanian Buddhist philosophers had shown a greater genius for action in showing a greater contempt for logic. These Indians had pushed their compromise with sociality, as well as their pursuit of self-sufficiency, to lengths to which the Greeks had never gone; and this wholeheartedness at the price of consistency had brought with it a practical reward.

In A.D. 1956 the Hinayanian Buddhist philosophy was the dominant way of life in Ceylon, Burma, Siam, and Cambodia; and in that year a Hinayanian Buddhist oecumenical council was in session at Rangoon, sitting placidly within a stone's throw of the tense borderline between a Communist-dominated and a Western-dominated hemisphere. This serenity was an heroic example of a spirit that was also in evidence in ordinary life in the Hinayanian Buddhist countries. Many Western observers, including Westerners who were still Christians, were impressed by the strength, pervasiveness, and beneficence of the Hīnayāna's influence on the êthos of the people at large, beyond the small circle of professed philosopher-monks. If philosophers, as well as prophets, are to be known by their fruits,[1] the Hinayanian Buddhist philosophers need not fear comparison with their Mahayanian critics. Yet the local survival of the Hīnayāna in South-Eastern Asia was no more than a modest practical success by comparison with the tenacity of Confucianism; and elsewhere the Hīnayāna, like the Hellenic philosophies, had been superseded by other faiths. In its Indian homeland it had been evicted by a post-Buddhaic Hinduism; and, on the threshold of a vast mission-field in China, Korea, and Japan, the adherents of an advancing Buddhism had fallen away from a Hinayanian philosophy to a Mahayanian religion, in which the social demands of Love and Pity had been given patent precedence over the pursuit of self-sufficiency through self-extinction.

The would-be self-sufficient philosopher's compromise with Sociality is as inevitable as it is illogical; for Man is intrinsically a social animal. His sociality is so much of the essence of his nature that the philosopher's attempt to eradicate a disastrous idolization of Society by repudiating Society itself is an impossible enterprise for any human being to carry out in practice.

This truth is admitted, rather grudgingly and ungraciously, by Plato in his simile of the Prisoners in the Cave.[2] Plato concedes that those few human beings who have escaped from the darkness and the bondage of ordinary human life by struggling up and out into the sunlight of Philosophy must constrain themselves, out of a sense of social duty, to re-descend into the cave in shifts, turn and turn about, in order to give the

[1] Matt. vii. 16 and 20.   [2] *Republic*, 514 A—521 C.

unfortunate permanent denizens of the Underworld the benefit of the philosophers' own exceptional enlightenment. Plato is making the same concession on more generous terms when he declares[1] that the only hope for a cessation of evils for the parochial states of the Hellenic World, and indeed for all Mankind, is that either philosophers should become kings or kings should take to Philosophy. The hope of being able to help the despot Dionysius II of Syracuse to take to Philosophy did move Plato himself to come out of his academic retreat and implicate himself in the politics of an arbitrarily-governed parochial state.

Plato's attempt to serve as Dionysius II's philosopher-adviser was a failure; but less eminent later Hellenic philosophers were more successful in performing this social service for more reputable Hellenic princes. Bion the Borysthenite performed it for King Antigonus Gonatas of Macedon, and Sphaerus the Borysthenite or Bosporan for King Cleomenes III of Sparta. But the historic instance of a philosopher's success in the role of helping a prince to take to philosophy is Confucius's posthumous influence, at a time-range of more than 2,000 years away, on the Manchu world-rulers K'ang Hsi and Ch'ien Lung. This remote philosophical control, which had so much greater a political effect than any that Confucius could have achieved in the service of one of the parochial princes of his own day, could not have been exerted if Confucius had not been a *philosophe malgré lui* as a consequence of being an unemployed candidate for the public service in which he would so much rather have spent his life.

The princes, just cited, who had the grace to take advantage of the services of philosopher-mentors, living or dead, all remained princes first and foremost, with a tincture of Philosophy tempering and mellowing their statesmanship. Princes who have been philosophers first and foremost and have subordinated—or tried to subordinate—*raison d'état* to Philosophy have been fewer and farther between. The philosophic crank Alexarchus, who, in a post-Alexandrine Hellenic World, was able to found an ephemeral 'Uranopolis' ('Commonwealth of Heaven') on the neck of the Athos Peninsula, thanks to the accident of his happening to be the brother of the criminal

[1] In *Republic*, 473 D, 499 B, 501 E.

Macedonian war-lord Cassander, may be mentioned as a curiosity. But Marcus Aurelius, who had become a post-humous disciple of Zeno before ascending the throne, and Açoka, who, when already on the throne, became a post-humous disciple of the Buddha, were, each of them, the ruler of an oecumenical empire; and *a priori* they might, each of them, have been expected to realize Plato's hopes on a scale beyond Plato's dreams. The degree in which Marcus fell short of Açoka in taking effective steps to turn this appar-ently golden opportunity to account gives the measure, not of the Roman prince's inferiority in spiritual stature to the Magadhan prince, but of the Stoic philosophy's inferiority to the Hīnayāna. But the failure of Açoka, as well as Marcus, to produce decisive and lasting spiritual effects gives the measure of Philosophy's spiritual ineffectiveness even in the hands of an emperor who is, at heart, a philosopher first and foremost, and is not just seeking to make Philosophy serve as a spiritual sanction for his régime, in the place of a discredited deification of Rome and Caesar.

Marcus—to judge by his candid self-revelation in his *journal intime*—felt as one of Plato's spiritually emancipated philosophers would have felt if he had found himself con-demned to return to the cave, not for an occasional shift, but for life. In Marcus's experience, the burden of his imperial office was the common burden of life at its maximum weight, and Philosophy's service to the imperial colporteur, though invaluable, was limited. It was not a way of release from sentient existence for himself and for all his fellow sentient beings; it was a means of easing the incidence of a personal load that might otherwise have proved too heavy for the Soul to carry to the end of the journey of life.

Human life! Its duration is momentary, its substance in per-petual flux, its senses dim, its physical organism perishable, its consciousness a vortex, its destiny dark, its repute uncertain—in fact, the material element is a rolling stream, the spiritual element dreams and vapour, life a war and a sojourning in a far country, fame oblivion. What can see us through? One thing and one only —Philosophy; and that means keeping the spirit within us un-spoiled and undishonoured, not giving way to pleasure or pain, never acting unthinkingly or deceitfully or insincerely, and never being dependent on the moral support of others. It also means taking what comes contentedly as all part of the process to which we owe our own being; and, above all, it means facing Death calmly —taking it simply as a dissolution of the atoms of which every living organism is composed. Their perpetual transformation does not hurt the atoms, so why should one mind the whole organism being transformed and dissolved? It is a law of Nature, and Natural Law can never be wrong.[1]

This tribute of Marcus's to Philosophy bears the stamp of a noble spirit; yet, for Açoka, Philosophy meant much more than this. It was not just a private citadel into which he could occasionally withdraw to recuperate from a world-ruler's life-long spiritual travail; it was an enlightenment that transfigured, for him, the conventional conception of the uses to which a ruler should put his power. Açoka was converted to Buddhism by his horror at the suffering caused by a victorious war of aggression. He had waged this war for the immoral purpose of making his empire conterminous with his world by force; and, during the rest of his reign, he pursued his original aim of world-conquest on a different plane. He now used his power for the purpose of communicating to his fellow human beings the enlightenment that had transformed his own outlook; and the means that he now employed was not coercive military action, which manifestly would have been ineffective for this purpose, but persuasive missionary work. His monuments are the inscriptions in which he has expounded and commended the Hīnayāna to his subjects and has recorded the despatch of missions abroad to the Macedonian successor-states of the Achaemenian Empire.

In voluntarily staying at his post in order to proclaim the good tidings of release to his fellows, Açoka was faithfully following the example of his master Siddhārtha Gautama. For the distinctive feature in the Buddha's life, experience, and activity is not His intuition that the only way to escape Pain is to extinguish Desire; it is the accompanying conviction, on which He acted for the rest of His life, that the intuition of the liberating truth has laid upon the enlightened spirit a moral obligation to remain in existence in order to teach to others the way of self-release from Suffering. Gautama, like Jesus,

---

[1] Marcus Aurelius Antoninus, *Meditations*, Book II, *ad fin.*

dedicated Himself to His mission in the World by victoriously resisting a temptation to take a short cut. At the crisis of His life, Gautama was tempted to use His newly attained spiritual power for the purpose of making His own immediate exit into Nirvāna instead of showing others the way; Jesus was tempted to use it for the purpose of imposing the Kingdom of Heaven on Earth instead of preaching it. Both victories over the temptation were deliberate acts of self-sacrifice. Both required a revulsion from a self-regarding personal asceticism to a life of familiar intercourse with ordinary people in order to bring them spiritual aid. And in both cases the victor-missionary's commerce with the World caused scandal among the professional practitioners of a conventional religion. The Buddha's life after the temptation shocked the Yogis, as Christ's life after the temptation shocked the Scribes and Pharisees.

This parallel indicates that, though the Buddha, unlike Christ, set out to teach a philosophy, the spirit in which He acted destined Him also to become the founder of a religion. The Mahāyāna can fairly claim Him as her founder on the evidence of the Hīnayāna's scriptures. And it is through His love and pity, much more than through His insight into the means of release from the suffering by which His pity and love were evoked, that the Buddha is still alive and at work in the World to-day. If the prescription of spiritual exercises for the attainment of self-sufficiency through self-extinction had been the end, as well as the beginning, of the Buddha's work, we may guess that His philosophy would have died the death of Zeno's and Epicurus's. For a philosophy that is not transfigured into a religion is likely to prove ineffective for several reasons. Philosophy fails to touch the hearts of ordinary people because it is handed down to them from above by an intellectual élite; because it is conveyed to them in the scientific language of the Intellect and not in the poetic language of the Heart; and because it is preached out of a half-reluctant sense of duty, not from a whole-hearted impulse of love. The missionary-philosopher is bound, as a philosopher, to be half-hearted as a missionary. While his illogical sense of social duty requires him to spread enlightenment among his fellow-beings, his self-regarding quest for personal self-sufficiency is counselling him, all the time, not to let himself be diverted from his personal goal by allowing himself to succumb to Love and Pity.

Thus Philosophy fails to fill the spiritual vacuum created by the successive failures of parochial-community-worship and oecumenical-community-worship; and this final failure of Man-worship in the form of the idolization of individual self-sufficiency shows that Man-worship of any kind is unable to satisfy Man's spiritual needs. The one school of philosophy that has succeeded in satisfying them is Siddhārtha Gautama's; and it has achieved this by quickening the letter of its doctrine with the spirit of its Founder's sublimely illogical practice.

6

THE EPIPHANY OF THE HIGHER RELIGIONS [1]

In all forms of Man-worship there are two errors which are sins, besides being mistakes. It is an error to worship Man at all, because Man is not God, even though Man may be rather less ungodlike individually than he is collectively; and it is an error to worship human power—either collective and physical or individual and psychic—because the worship of human power prevents the worshipper from finding the right attitude towards Suffering.

In human life, Suffering is the antithesis of Power, and it is also a more characteristic and more fundamental element in Life than Power is. We have already seen that Suffering is of the essence of Life, because it is the inevitable product of an unresolvable tension between a living creature's essential impulse to try to make itself into the centre of the Universe and its essential dependence on the rest of Creation and on the Absolute Reality in which all creatures live and move and have their being.[2] On the other hand, human power, in all its forms, is limited and, in the last resort, illusory. Therefore any attitude towards Life that idolizes human power is bound to be a wrong attitude towards Suffering and, in consequence, a wrong attitude towards Life itself. The idolatrous worship of parochial states leads their war-lords to inflict Suffering pitilessly in the pursuit of Power. The idolatrous worship of an oecumenical state leads to a policy of keeping Suffering within bounds by force, and so to the paradox of inflicting Suffering for the purpose of limiting it. Since an oecumenical state is the most estimable kind of state that Man has succeeded in creating so far, the moral paradox inherent in an oecumenical state is a verdict on states of all kinds: in its worse and its better

[1] The subject of this chapter has been dealt with in greater detail by the writer in *A Study of History*, vol. v, pp. 58-194, 581-90; vol. vi, pp. 1-175, 259-78, 376-439; vol. vii, pp. 158-63, 381-568, 692-768; vol. ix, pp. 395-405, 604-41.

[2] Acts xvii. 28.

varieties alike, the state is the nemesis of Original Sin. Finally, the idolatrous worship of an individual human self-sufficiency leads to a repression of the Pity for Suffering, and of the Love for the sufferer, that are natural to Man because he is a social animal.

The failure of both the idolization of the self-sufficient philosopher and the idolization of the oecumenical community to meet the challenge presented by the failure of parochial-community-worship opens the way for a rejection of the worship of human power in all forms; and this disillusionment with discredited human idols opens the way, further, for a change of heart through a change of attitude towards Suffering. The converted soul abandons an unconverted Human Nature's effort to escape Suffering for oneself by the acquisition and exercise of some kind of Power—whether collective and physical or individual and psychic. It adopts, instead, the opposite attitude of accepting Suffering for oneself and trying to turn one's own suffering to positive account by acting, at the cost of suffering, on one's feelings of Pity and Love for one's fellow-creatures. This change of heart in Man opens his eyes to a new vision of God. It gives him a glimpse of a God who is Love as well as Power, and who is not a deification either of Human or of Non-Human Nature, but is the deliverer of these and all His creatures from the evil of self-centredness to which every creature is prone. The new religions in which this change of heart expresses itself may be called 'higher religions', because they rise above Man-worship as well as above Nature-worship.

An historian's first approach to the higher religions will be by way of the social milieu in which they make their epiphany. They are not the product of their social milieu; the events that produce them are encounters between human beings and the Absolute Reality that is in, and at the same time beyond, all the phenomena of Existence, Life, and History; and any soul may meet God at any time and place in any historical circumstances. Nevertheless, an examination of the social milieu will help us to understand the nature, as well as the rise, of religions in which this experience of meeting God is communicated and commended to Mankind as the inspiration for a new way of life.

The deification of human power in the two forms of an oecumenical community and a self-sufficient philosopher has usually been instituted by members of the remnant of a dominant minority in a society that is disintegrating. This is obviously the social origin of the founders of oecumenical empires, and the founders of schools of philosophy have also come from the same social source. They have, most of them, been sophisticated men, born into the middle, or even the upper, class of Society. Confucius was an unemployed civil servant; Plato was a disillusioned aristocrat; Siddhārtha Gautama was the son of a parochial prince. By contrast, the founders of the higher religions have mostly arisen in the ranks of the vast majority of the members of a disintegrating society whose normal human sufferings have been intensified to an abnormal degree by the social breakdown and disintegration resulting from the failure of parochial-community-worship. In the successive degrees of this abnormal suffering the last turn of the screw, short of physical extermination, is the experience of being uprooted from one's home and becoming a refugee, exile, or deportee who has been wrenched out of his ancestral framework. The infliction of such extreme suffering on the grand scale is a self-indictment of the society in which these atrocities are committed, and in the Westernizing World of the twentieth century of the Christian Era there was a subconscious self-defensive conspiracy to minimize the painfulness of deracination by the euphemism of calling the sufferers 'displaced persons'. In the Hellenic World of the fifth century B.C., Herodotus did not flinch from calling them *déracinés* outright.

This has been the human seed from which the higher religions have sprung. The origin of the Buddhist religion is only an apparent exception to this rule; for, though the Buddha was a prince who became a philosopher, Siddhārtha Gautama's first step on His quest for enlightenment was to slip out of His father's palace in order to live voluntarily in 'the homeless state' for the rest of His life. The enlightenment that He sought was primarily intellectual, but He did not yield, when He had found it, to the temptation to take the logically consequent step of immediately making His own exit into Nirvāna. Instead, He chose inconsequently to stay in the World in order to impart His intellectual illumination to His fellow sentient beings and to instruct them how to take the path that He had blazed by bringing the Will as well as the Intellect into play. Thus the Buddha was an illogical evangelist, besides being a voluntary *déraciné*, and it was no accident that the founder of a philosophy who had taken these self-sacrificing turnings at two decisive moments in His life should posthumously have become also the founder of a higher religion.

This transfiguration of the philosophy of the Hīnayāna into the religion of the Mahāyāna, which had been fore-shadowed in the example set by the Buddha in His own life, did not begin to declare itself among His disciples till some three hundred years had passed since their Master's death. The first glimmer of the slow dawn of the Mahāyāna appeared among people who had been uprooted in the second century B.C. by a Greek and a subsequent Central Asian Nomad invasion of India; and the nascent higher religion spread from a Hellenized Indian World across a Hellenized South-West Asian World into an East Asian World in an age when Eastern Asia, South-Western Asia, and India were each passing through a time of troubles. In the South-West Asian, Egyptian, and Hellenic worlds, this same time of troubles also saw the rise of another higher religion—Christianity—among people who had been uprooted by Macedonian and Roman militarism and by a consequent social revolution. In an earlier age the time of troubles precipitated by the breakdown of the Babylonian and Syrian civilizations had seen the rise of two older higher religions—Judaism and Zoroastrianism—among people who had been uprooted in the eighth and seventh centuries B.C. by Assyrian militarism and by a subsequent *Völkerwanderung* of Central Asian Nomads.

The epiphany of these new higher religions in the souls of the *déracinés* was neither quick nor easy. The breakdown and dis-integration of Society and the victims' consequent loss of their ancestral heritage, including the physical home in which their lives had had their roots, was a challenge of unusual severity. A majority of those who were overtaken by it completely failed to respond and were spiritually crushed by the experience. The Lost Ten Tribes of Israel are the classic symbol of the multitude that has thus passed into oblivion without leaving any spiritual memorial. Some of the victims responded to the challenge by trying to use against their oppressors the physical violence that these oppressors had used against them. These Spartacists took the sword and perished with it.[1] Others responded by replying to violence, not with violence, but with gentleness, and, among these, some created new societies of new kinds. But, of these new societies, some merely aimed at, and succeeded in, preserving a remnant of one or other of the shattered parochial communities associated with an outlived parochial past. This parochial past had shattered itself by its own sins and was rightly discredited; and, among the *déracinés* who made the gentle response, only those who resolutely turned their faces away from this fallen idol succeeded in founding higher religions which had a mission to all Mankind and whose message was a revelation of some means of coping with the fundamental problems of human life.

These diverse responses to an identical challenge may be illustrated briefly by citing a few classic examples.

Among the would-be saviours by violence we can distinguish archaists, futurists, and archaists who involuntarily turn into futurists and so defeat their own original purpose under the stress of their struggle to achieve it. Classic examples of pure archaists—people who have learnt nothing and forgotten nothing—are the parochial nationalists in South-West Asia who, in 522-521 B.C., tried, by force of arms, to prevent Darius the son of Hystaspes from maintaining a Persian world-empire which had brought peace to South-West Asia after its devastation by the Assyrians and the Nomads. The archaist-futurists start by trying forcibly to restore the *ancien régime* in some disintegrating parochial community, but are led on unintentionally into making a revolution that sweeps away the last remnants of the treasured Past and inaugurates a new régime in its stead. A classic example is King Cleomenes III's revolution at Sparta in the third century B.C. Cleomenes' intention was to restore an *ancien régime* in which the Spartiates had been a dominant minority ruling over serfs and satellites. Since the dominance of the Spartiates was now imperilled by a decline in their numbers, Cleomenes set out to check and reverse this tendency; but he ended by inaugurating a political

[1] Matt. xxvi. 52.

and social revolution in which the citizens of the satellite
communities were given the Spartiate franchise and the
Spartiate lands were redistributed among citizens of both the
naturalized and the Spartiate-born class. Gaius Gracchus's
revolution in the Roman Commonwealth in the second
century B.C. ran the same unintended course. Gaius's intention
was to restore an *ancien régime* in which the Roman public
land had been at the Roman State's disposal for distribution
into homesteads for landless citizens. He ended by letting loose
a social revolution in which the satellite communities of the
Commonwealth acquired the Roman franchise and the Roman
oligarchy was deprived of its virtual monopoly of political
power by a military dictatorship representing the unprivileged
majority in the body politic.

The transformation of the post-Exilic Jewish concept of the
Messiah is a classic example of a similar revolution in the realm
of unrealized political aspirations. The Messiah was thought of
originally as a nationalist leader who would attain for Jewry the
goal that Darius I's opponents were seeking to attain in 522-521
B.C. The Messiah was to re-establish the Davidic parochial
kingdom of Judah and Israel. But, in a world in which parochial states had come to be anachronisms, and in which the
only practical choice now was between alternative oecumenical
empires, the Messiah subsequently came to be thought of as a
Jewish empire-builder who was to emulate and supersede the
work of a Persian Cyrus and Darius or a Roman Caesar and
Augustus. The Messiah was now to be the founder of an
oecumenical empire in which the Jews were to take the
Persians' or the Romans' place as the World's imperial people.

The futurists are revolutionaries who consciously and
deliberately set out to break with a disintegrating social past
in order to create a new society. The new society, however,
that the futurist is trying to make has two fundamental characteristics in common with the old society that the archaist is
trying to save. Both are this-worldly and both are the children
of force. The futurist is therefore apt, like the archaist, to
produce results that run ironically counter to his intentions.
The futurist becomes an archaist *malgré lui*, as the archaist
becomes *malgré lui* a futurist. One classic exemplar of the type
is Aristonicus of Pergamum, the revolutionary founder, in the

second century B.C., of an abortive utopia in Western Anatolia. Aristonicus called the insurgent slaves and peasants who joined his standard 'the citizens of the Commonwealth of the Sun'. His god, like Ikhnaton's and Aurelian's, was the heavenly body that is the symbol and the vindicator of Justice because he sheds his light and warmth impartially on all men, oppressed and oppressors alike. But the result of a liberation of under-dog by force would be, not to inaugurate a new régime founded upon Justice, but simply to perpetuate the old unjust régime with no change except a reversal of roles. 'The last shall be first, and the first last',[1] not in the spiritual hierarchy of a new Kingdom of Heaven, but in the economic and political hierarchy of the old Kingdom of This World. This alloy of Archaism in Futurism partly accounts for the failures of Aristonicus in a Roman Asia and of his contemporaries the insurgent Syrian slave-kings Eunus, Cleon, and Athenio in a Roman Sicily.

When we turn to the would-be saviours who make a gentle response to the challenge of violence, we find archaists here too, but also founders of a genuinely new kind of society.

Classic examples in Hellenic history of gentle archaists are Agis the forerunner of Cleomenes and Tiberius the forerunner of Gaius Gracchus. Both were martyrs to their gentleness, and both gave their lives for it in vain, since, in both cases, the moral drawn from the martyr's fate by the martyr's successor was the Machiavellian one that a would-be reformer must not be too proud to fight. In Jewish history the classic gentle archaist is Rabbi Johanan ben Zakkai. The Jewish community in Palestine had been brought to the brink of its second historic catastrophe by an archaist-futurist Messianism that believed passionately in retorting to violence by violence. At that moment, Johanan ben Zakkai became, without suffering martyrdom, the founder of a Jewish diasporà that was to be held together by a zeal, not for establishing a Jewish oecumenical empire by force of arms, but for keeping the Mosaic Law in the prophetic spirit.

During the siege, Johanan b. Zakkai escaped out of Jerusalem and obtained permission from Titus to retire to the village of

---

[1] Matt. xx. 16.

Jabne or Jamnia, and teach there openly. When the news of the fall of Jerusalem came to Jamnia, Johanan's disciple Joshua b. Hanania cried out 'Woe to us, because the place is destroyed where they make propitiation for the sins of Israel!' But Johanan answered 'My Son, let it not grieve thee; we have yet one propitiation equal to it, and what is that but the bestowal of kindnesses? —even as it is written *I desired kindness and not sacrifice*'.[1]

Johanan ben Zakkai's inspiration has enabled Judaism to survive in diasporà in the western quarter of the Old World for more than eighteen centuries since the third historic catastrophe of Judaism in Palestine in the reign of the Roman Emperor Hadrian. The same spirit has enabled Zoroastrianism to survive likewise in diasporà on the west coast of India since the overthrow, in the seventh century of the Christian Era, by force of Arab arms, of a Sasanian Empire in which Zoroastrianism had been the established religion. This change of heart in Zoroastrianism, like the change in Judaism, from violence to gentleness, was a response to the experience of an overwhelming military and political disaster. In the history of Zoroastrianism, this change was indeed remarkable, since, in the Sasanian Empire, Zoroastrianism had actually attained, over a period of four hundred years, the objective which a latterday oecumenical Jewish Messianism had merely dreamed of attaining. During those four centuries ending in the Arab conquest, the Sasanian Empire had successfully played the part of a counter-world-power which had been able to deal with the Roman Empire on equal terms and to take 'Irāq, as well as Iran, out of the Hellenic Civilization's orbit.

The survival of the Zoroastrian and Jewish diasporàs in formidably adverse circumstances is a testimony to the effectiveness of Archaism as a social cement when it is compounded with the spirit of gentleness; but the spiritual price of this social *tour de force* has been exorbitantly high. Each of these two communities has succeeded in preserving its identity in diasporà at the cost of subjecting itself to the meticulous observance of an archaic ritual law. Since this law is the only fragment of the community's shattered social fabric that has not perished, long ago, at the time of the extinction of the state

[1] Burkitt, F. C., *Jewish and Christian Apocalypses* (London 1914, Milford), p. 8, note 1.

and the dispersal of the people, ritual-law-worship is evidently the only form in which collective self-worship could have weathered these catastrophes. Yet it is an untoward achievement to have kept up, by this *tour de force*, a form of Man-worship that has been found to be a bad religion by the general experience of Mankind; and, in any religion, a concentration of attention and effort on formalities is spiritually sterilizing.

If non-violent Archaism has thus proved to be a blind ally, the acceptance of Suffering as the price of following the promptings of Pity and Love has proved to open up an approach towards Absolute Reality. This approach has been made along two separate roads, on each of which the spiritual traveller has been offered an ideal figure to follow as his exemplar and his guide. On the Indian road the ideal figure is the bodhisattva; on the Palestinian road it is the Suffering Servant. The two roads run parallel towards a meeting-point at Infinity that is their common objective; for both roads are approaches to the same Absolute Reality. But, though their goal is thus identical, the roads themselves are separate; and, though the traveller along each of them comes to see the same Absolute Reality through a glass darkly,[1] there is a difference between the Indian and the Palestinian lens. For these two semi-translucent windows, which give a glimpse of Absolute Reality through a medium that obscures it and distorts it, have been fashioned out of different patches of the veil of phenomena—the illusory mirage of Maya—by which Man's spiritual vision is bounded.

No doubt the incorporeal light that is radiated into the phenomenal world by Absolute Reality does infuse all phenomena, even the most opaque, as physical sunlight penetrates a terrestrial living creature through the skin as well as through the eye. If Maya were not even a faint and warped reflexion of Reality, it would not be visible and could not conjure up the illusion of being a thing in itself with an independent existence of its own. Yet, when the divers members of a living body are considered as so many means of communication between the organism and the heavenly body by whose light and warmth the organism is kept alive, there can be no comparison between the skin's conductive power and the eye's. And, when we go

[1] I Cor. xiii. 12.

on to consider the genesis of the eye, we find it marvellous that an organ of vision, however imperfect, should have been fashioned out of two patches of a skin which, over all the rest of its surface, has remained crassly incapable of affording to the body even the faintest glimmer of sight. In the non-corporeal universe of spiritual life, it is no less marvellous that two lenses, through which a human soul can catch a partial glimpse of Absolute Reality, should have been fashioned out of such apparently unpromising rudiments of religious intuition as those which are the historical origins of Buddhism and Christianity. It is also, no doubt, a mercy that neither of these two dark glasses has ever become fully translucent; 'for there shall no man see Me and live'.[1] A naked vision of Absolute Reality, wholly unveiled, would be more than any terrestrial soul could bear. For the epiphany of Reality is not just a discovery made by the Soul nor even just a revelation given by Reality; it is an encounter between two spiritual presences that are infinitely unequal in power. This encounter discharges creative action; and the lightning would blast the frail human participant if some non-conductive residue of Maya did not still intervene to shield him at the price of dimming his vision.

We have already observed[2] that the two lenses through which Buddhism and Christianity give the Soul a glimpse of an identical Reality have been fashioned out of very diverse materials. Buddhism has attained its vision of Reality by looking inwards into the Human Soul; Christianity by looking outwards towards a god.

Pre-Buddhist Indian thinkers who had looked into the Soul had been so deeply impressed by the vastness and the potency of this inner spiritual universe that they had jumped to the conclusion that the Self was identical with Absolute Reality: 'Thou are That'. The Buddha found Reality in a state of Nirvāna, in which the faggot of desires labelled 'Self' had all been burnt away.[3] The Mahayanian school of Buddhists came to see that the Buddha Himself had acted in accordance with a further truth that had not been given recognition in the Hinayanian philosophy, though many Hinayanian philosophers may have acted on it in following their Master. The

---

[1] Exod. xxxiii. 20.   [2] In Chapter 2, pp. 16-17, above.
[3] See Chapter 5, pp. 62-3, above.

Buddha had taught, by the example of His own life, that the attainment of Nirvāna by oneself and for oneself is not enough. In order to become the perfect bodhisattva, the potentially perfect philosopher must make the sacrifice of postponing his own exit into Nirvāna in order to guide the feet of his suffering fellow-beings along the road over which he has already found his own way.

The bodhisattva is a being who has followed the Buddha's personal example by being faithful to the Buddha's practice instead of carrying out the Buddha's instructions to their logical consequences. A Hinayanian Buddhist philosopher who yielded to the logic of these instructions would find himself constrained to aim at attaining self-sufficiency through self-extinction, and to pursue this aim single-mindedly for himself and by himself. The bodhisattva of the Mahayanian mythology is a candidate for Buddha-hood who, like the Buddha at His Enlightenment, has reached the threshold of Nirvāna and now has it in his power at any moment to take the last step on the course of his exit. But, like the Buddha at His temptation, the bodhisattva holds back, at this point, from expiring into his rest. He holds back, not just for the Buddha's brief forty-years' pause, but for a period of aeons upon aeons. In making this choice he deliberately sentences himself to an age-long penal servitude which he has it in his power to avoid; and he makes this sacrifice from the same motive that impelled the Buddha to make it. 'He saved others; himself he *will* not save',[1] is the praise of this good shepherd that is constantly on the lips of the grateful sheep that he is tending at so great a cost to himself.

The bodhisattva's sovereign motive and distinguishing mark is thus a feeling for his fellow-beings which, for the Hinayanian philosopher, is an irrational impediment to his concentration on his objective of self-release. The difference in their attitude towards Suffering is what differentiates the philosopher from the bodhisattva. For the arhat, as the Hinayanian philosopher is called in the Buddhist terminology, Suffering is the worst of evils and the pursuit of self-release from Suffering has the first claim on the sufferer's spiritual energies. For the bodhisattva, Suffering is the inevitable price of acting on the promptings

---

[1] 'He saved others; himself he *can*not save'.—Matt. xxvii. 42.

of Love and Pity, and this self-sacrificing action has the first claim on him.

The Mahayanian Buddhist vision of Reality as Pity and Love, as well as Power, has been reached by Christianity from a quite different starting-point. Christianity sees Reality as a God who is both almighty and all-loving. This Christian vision of God is a heritage from Israel. The god of Israel was Yahweh; and, before Yahweh became the parochial god of a community of Nomads when they were in the act of breaking out of the North Arabian Steppe into the Palestinian province of 'the New Empire' of Egypt, he would appear to have been a god embodying one of the forces of Nature. Perhaps he was a volcano or perhaps the weather, to judge by the traditional account, in the Pentateuch, of the sights and sounds that proclaimed Yahweh's presence at the making of his covenant with Israel at Mount Sinai. A god who had thus identified himself with a human tribe, and had led his 'Chosen People' in an aggressive war of expropriation and extermination against the inhabitants of a country that had been neither Israel's to take nor Yahweh's to give, might not seem to have been a promising medium for an approach to Reality. Yet the sufferings inflicted on Israel and Judah by Assyrian and Babylonian hands during a time of troubles that dragged on from the eighth into the sixth century B.C., inspired the Prophets to see, through the wraith of Yahweh the parochial war-god, another Yahweh who had more in common with the god in the Sun who was worshipped by Ikhnaton, Aristonicus, and Aurelian.

This Atonian Yahweh was Justice and Mercy as well as Power, and his Power and Justice were not circumscribed within the narrow frontiers of a pair of Palestinian communities, but were omnipotent, ubiquitous, and impartial. In the Prophets' piercing vision the barrier between the Human Soul and Reality was thus transfigured from a veil into a lens. But the vision had still to be clarified by the further insight that the God Almighty who was Justice and Mercy was also Pity and Love; and, though the greatest of the Prophets beheld Pity and Love incarnate in a Suffering Servant, it was a stumbling-block to the Jews[1] when Christianity identified this human

[1] 1 Cor. i. 23.

figure with the sublime God who had made His epiphany through Yahweh's forbidding lineaments. In Deutero-Isaiah's vision, the saving sufferer is a human sufferer who seems in some passages to be a collective Israel and in others to be an individual Israelite leader or prophet. In the Christian development of this Jewish concept, the suffering saviour is not a man but is God Himself, who has 'emptied Himself' by incarnating Himself as a human being in order to save His human creatures at the cost of voluntarily subjecting Himself to an extreme experience of the Suffering that is of the essence of Human Life.

The spirit that should be in you is the spirit that was in Christ Jesus. Finding Himself existing in God's form and on an equality with God, He did not think of this as a prize to be clutched. No, He emptied Himself by taking a menial's form—for this is what He did in assimilating Himself to human beings. Exposing Himself thus in human guise, He showed His humility in His obedience. He was obedient even to the point of submitting to die—and this by a death on the Cross.[1]

It will be seen that the Mahāyāna and Christianity have two intuitions in common. Instead of kicking against the pricks of Suffering, they both accept Suffering as an opportunity for acting on the promptings of Love and Pity. And they both believe that this ideal is practicable for Man because the trail has been blazed for Man by a Supreme Being who has demonstrated his own devotion to the ideal by subjecting himself to the Suffering that is the necessary price of acting on it. In a society in which the divine participant is a self-sacrificing saviour,[2] a new way of life is opened up for the human participants. This way is a new one in the sense that it brings with it a prospect of reconciling elements in Human Life that have seemed irreconcilable under previous dispensations. It is a

---

[1] Phil. ii. 5-8.

[2] All societies of all species have included, among their members, gods, as well as human beings, animals, and plants. What differentiates them is not the presence or absence of a divine member, but the invariably present divine member's character. A Canaanite community whose god is Yahweh will differ from one whose god is Chemosh or Ba'al Hammon. A Christian Church whose godhead includes the person of a suffering saviour god incarnate, and a Mahāyāna whose bodhisattva is an Avalokita or an Amitabha, will differ from a Jewish diasporà whose god is the God of the Prophets.

way in which a living being can transcend its innate self-centredness by other means than the self-extinction that is the way of the Hīnayāna.

'Whosoever will lose his life for My sake shall find it.'[1] If the Self submits to Suffering for the sake of service, it can transcend itself by devoting itself, at the cost of Suffering, to acts of Love and Pity; and in these acts it will be attaining, without seeking it, the self-fulfilment which an innately social being can never attain through self-centredness. Self-fulfilment comes only when it is unsought, like those blessings that were bestowed on Solomon, in his dream, just because he had resisted the temptation to ask for them and had prayed, instead, for the gift that would make him a good servant of God to the benefit of his people.[2] The Christian-Mahayanian way of life also surmounts another previously unsurmountable dilemma. It makes it possible for the Universe to have significance without at the same time making it necessary for this significance to depend upon the Universe's centring round the Self. On the Christian-Mahayanian road the significance can be found in self-sacrifice for the sake of other living beings and for the love of a Supreme Being who is the centre of the Universe because He is Love as well as Power.

At the epiphany of the higher religions the light shineth in the darkness; but the darkness has still to comprehend it;[3] and the history of the higher religions during the disintegration of the civilizations of the second generation is an illustration of the Parable of the Sower. In the last four chapters of this first part of the book we shall be watching the seed, sown during this episode of mundane history, withstanding one of the possibilities of frustration that are described in the Parable, but succumbing to each of the other two, and also to a third mishap which is not mentioned by the writer of the Gospel according to Saint Matthew because it is beyond his social horizon.

This miscarriage of so much of the seed at its first sowing will not appear either surprising or discouraging when it is looked at from the historian's angle of vision. Life on Earth, as the historian sees it, is a process in Time, and no action can ever have an instantaneous effect. A span of 1,956 years or 2,500 years is a very short time in the historian's perspective, in

[1] Matt. xvi. 25. [2] See 1 Kings iii. 5-14; 2 Chron. i. 7-12. [3] John i. 5.

which it is measured on the Time-scale of the duration of Mankind's existence up to date. And, even within the brief period that has elapsed since the first epiphany of a higher religion on Earth, the lives of the Saints bear witness that some of the seed has already fallen on good ground.

He that received seed into the good ground is he that heareth the Word and understandeth it; which also beareth fruit and bringeth forth, some an hundred-fold, some sixty, some thirty.[1]

This scripture has already been fulfilled in such lives as those of John Wesley and Saint Francis de Sales and, *in excelsis*, Saint Francis of Assisi.

[1] Matt. xiii. 23.

7

ENCOUNTERS BETWEEN HIGHER RELIGIONS AND IDOLIZED OECUMENICAL EMPIRES[1]

He that received the seed into stony places, the same is he that heareth the Word and anon with joy receiveth it; yet hath he not root in himself, but dureth for a while; for, when tribulation or persecution ariseth because of the Word, by and by he is offended.—Matt. xiii. 20-1.

OF all the challenges that are encountered by the sower of the seed, the challenge of persecution is the one to which the followers of the higher religions have succeeded in responding with the greatest measure of success. Though, in all persecutions, there are, no doubt, always many weaker vessels who do fail to stand the ordeal, the followers of the higher religions have been conspicuous, on the whole, for their steadfastness and courage when put to the test.

The Christian Church was put to this test by the Roman Empire; the Mahāyāna by the Chinese Empire in its avatar in the age of the T'ang Dynasty. Both churches responded by producing martyrs; but the Christians in the Roman Empire seem to have been more steadfast than the Mahayanian Buddhists in China in standing a more severe ordeal; and this apparent pre-eminence of the Christians in a common heroism is, indeed, what was to be expected. We should expect both the Mahāyāna and Christianity to shine in facing persecution, since the distinguishing mark of the higher religions is, as we have seen, their voluntary acceptance of Suffering as an opportunity for active service. At the same time we should expect the persecution itself to be sharper, and the endurance of it more heroic, in the western than in the eastern half of the Old World because the temper of life in South-West Asia and in the Graeco-Roman Society was more tragic and more intransigent than the temper in either India or China. In

[1] The subject of this chapter has been dealt with in greater detail by the writer in *A Study of History*, vol. v, pp. 581-7, 646-712; vol. vii, pp. 95-108, 158-63, 188-93, 237-9, 338-44, 692-700.

appraising both the comparative mildness of the T'ang imperial government and the comparative softness of its Buddhist victims, we must make due allowance for this general difference in psychological climate. It would be unwarrantable to assume that the T'ang régime was more virtuous than the Roman régime was, or that the Buddhist martyrs were less heroic than the Christian martyrs were.

The same difference in temper between the two halves of the Old World comes out in other historical parallels as well. For example, Christianity and Buddhism were, each, expelled from its homeland by a rival younger religion which had derived its inspiration from the older religion that it was opposing and evicting. Christianity was expelled from South-West Asia by Islam; Buddhism was expelled from India by a post-Buddhaic Hinduism whose philosophy bears indelible marks of its Buddhist origin. But the advance of Hinduism at Buddhism's expense in India in the age of the Gupta Dynasty was accomplished as peacefully as the previous advance of Buddhism at the expense of a pre-Buddhist Indian paganism in the age of the Maurya Emperor Açoka. By contrast with this Indian record, the supplanting of Christianity by Islam in South-West Asia and Egypt in the age of the Arab Caliphate was a story of pressure and penalization—though, by contrast with the treatment of subject Jews and Muslims in Christendom, the treatment of subject 'People of the Book' in Dār-al-Islām has been honourably distinguished by its comparative tolerance.

When a higher religion of either family—the Judaic or the Buddhaic—comes into collision with an oecumenical empire, the conflict is of momentous importance. In an oecumenical empire, a higher religion is meeting its most formidable adversary—Man's worship of collective human power—in its least maleficent and least unedifying form. As an object of worship, an idolized oecumenical empire shines out against the foil of its fallen predecessors the parochial states in an antecedent time of troubles. In contrast to these fallen idols, as well as to a nascent Judaic higher religion, an oecumenical empire brings, not the sword, but peace.[1] It is a régime under which, on the whole, the best elements of a dominant minority

[1] An inversion of Matt. x. 34.

are in command; for the public spirit of its professional civil service and professional army counts for much more, in its effect on the lives of its subjects, than the personal unworthiness of individual emperors. In the third place an oecumenical empire is the antithesis of the fallen parochial states and the forerunner of the nascent higher religions in standing for the ideal of the unity and brotherhood of all Mankind. This remote oecumenical collective human idol may not be capable of evoking such warm positive devotion as the familiar parochial idols—a Sparta or an Athens, a Judah or a Tyre, an Assyria or a Babylonia, a Ts'i or a Ch'u; but, nevertheless, any threat to an oecumenical empire's stability, security, and survival will arouse alarm and opposition, not only among the dominant minority, but among the masses as well.

An intuition that Christianity did threaten the stability of the Roman Empire does not, perhaps, account for the original persecution of Christianity by Nero, since Nero was manifestly seeking a scapegoat for personal odium incurred through personal misconduct. But it does account for the subsequent retention of this proscription on the statute book, through the reigns of 'the virtuous emperors' from Nerva to Marcus inclusive, until its repeal in A.D. 313 by Constantine I and Licinius in Constantine's Edict of Milan. The Roman authorities would have felt that they had been justified in acting on their intuition regarding Christianity if they had been acquainted with two passages in the Christian Church's scriptures —Matt. x. 34-7 and Luke xii. 49-53—in which the Founder of the Church is represented as saying that He has come to bring, not peace and unity, but strife and discord. On the Christian side there was an intuition that Man-worship in its oecumenical collective form was the most imposing, attractive, and specious idolatry still in the field, and that therefore the Christian was called upon to show the utmost stalwartness and intransigence in resisting it.

This conflict between the Roman Empire and Christianity, and the feelings animating the two parties to the conflict, are particularly interesting for us in our Western World in the twentieth century of the Christian Era, because a recurrence of the same social and spiritual situation would appear to be one of the alternative possibilities ahead of us in the future course of our own history. In any conceivable event, a rapid political unification of our world, in its turn, seems to be foreshadowed by 'the annihilation of distance' and the concomitant increase in the potency of weapons of war which are two closely related achievements of the West's fast accelerating progress in technology. Our world may be unified, not in a new way, by the agreement for which we hope, but in the old way by the force by which the Graeco-Roman World and most other worlds have, in fact, been unified in the past. In that event, the sufferings that we have experienced in our lifetime would be trifles by comparison with the sufferings, still untasted, which would then overtake us. If a literally world-wide counterpart of a Roman or a Chinese oecumenical empire had to be purchased by us at this traditional enormous price, the cost in suffering would be increased, beyond all past experience, by the unprecedented destructiveness of our latterday weapons of war. We can imagine what our feelings would be if an oecumenical peace and order which had been established at this fearful cost were to be threatened with disruption—a threat to plunge us back into that awful agony which had almost been the end of us—by the rise, in our midst, of some apparently subversive religion. How, for example, would the Christian texts Matt. x. 34-7 and Luke xii. 49-53 strike us if the Communists were to quote them as slogans for the Marxian 'class war', taking a leaf out of the book of those Christian propagandists in the Roman Empire who used to quote Greek poets as witnesses to the truth of Christian beliefs and to the righteousness of Christian ideals?

The religious issue between the Christian Church and the Roman Empire, like that between Socrates and Athens, was sharply defined—and this for the same reason. Like Socrates, the Christians behaved as good citizens in fulfilling all civic duties that were not vetoed by their conscience. Notwithstanding the Roman imperial authorities' standing proscription of Christianity, and notwithstanding the inclusion in the Gospels of revolutionary texts like those cited, the Christians were, in practice, law-abiding subjects of the oecumenical empire in all ordinary matters of everyday life. In this normal practice they were acting on other texts in the Gospels which went to great lengths in inculcating obedience to the established political régime. 'Render unto Caesar the things that are Caesar's'[1] is an injunction to pay taxes; and in Saint Paul's Epistle to the Romans[2] there is an injunction to obey the law in all things, and this on three grounds: 'There is no power but of God; the powers that be are ordained of God; whosoever, therefore, resisteth the power, resisteth the ordinance of God.'

If the Roman imperial authorities had been aware of this passage in a letter from a far-ranging Christian missionary to his converts in the metropolis, their feelings would have been mixed. They would have felt that their Christian subjects' private code of conduct told them to do the right thing for the wrong reason. It was right, of course, to tell them to obey the Government, but wrong to give them this directive on the ground that 'the powers that be are ordained of God.' For, if the ultimate authority is a god who is not the Oecumenical Community itself and is not even the Oecumenical Government's nominee, but is the freely chosen god of a private society, then this paramount God who tells His worshippers today to obey the Government may tell them tomorrow to disobey it. The right reason for obeying the Government is because the State is, not ordained of God, but identical with God or alternatively master of Him.

This issue did not arise over conflicting attitudes towards military service, though there was a potential occasion for conflict here. There had never been any explicit remission of the duty to serve which had been incumbent on all citizens in the parochial Roman State out of which the oecumenical Roman Empire had arisen, and on the other hand the Christian had a conscientious objection to shedding blood in war and therefore to serving in the Army. This tension between conscience and civic duty had not entered into the issue between Athens and Socrates, since Socrates had had no conscientious objection to military service and had, in fact, performed his own service manfully. In practice, however, this potential occasion for conflict between the Roman Empire and the Christian Church caused little trouble, because in practice the post-Augustan Roman Army, in contrast to the pre-Marian Roman Army, was a professional force recruited by voluntary enlistment, and the recruiting-grounds of the Army and the

---

[1] Matt. xxii. 21.　　　[2] Rom. xiii. 1-7.

Church lay in different quarters. The Army recruited mainly from the ex-barbarian peasantry in the frontier provinces of the Empire, the Church mainly from the urban population in the cities of the interior. There were contemporary higher religions that, unlike Christianity, did find their mission-field in the Army's main recruiting-ground, but the two that won most converts there were the worships of Mithras and of Juppiter Dolichênus, and neither of these was opposed in principle to the use of force.

Considering that the Christian code of conduct prescribed obedience to the State, and that the Roman Imperial Government did not, in practice, impose compulsory military service on its citizens, we can see that there was no inevitable occasion for conflict between Church and State on the plane of practical life. The issue over which they did fall into grave conflict with one another was one of principle. The two parties were in accord in feeling that this point of principle was supremely important, and in this consensus they were surely right. The question was whether Caesar himself was God, or whether Caesar was merely the human vicegerent of a One True God whom Caesar had not nominated and did not and could not control. This question whether Man in one or other of his less ungodlike forms is God, or whether the True God is to be found neither in Man or in Non-Human Nature, was, and still is, one of the great issues confronting human souls.

In the tragedy of the conflict between the Christian Church and the Roman Empire there were four *dramatis personae*: the Dominant Minority of the Graeco-Roman Society; the Roman Imperial Army; the Masses; and the Higher Religions, of which Christianity—the eventual victor—was one.

Under the imperial Roman régime the more respectable elements in the Dominant Minority were, as we have noticed, now in command—in contrast to the situation during the foregoing time of troubles, in which the militarists and profiteers had had a free hand. Those licensed criminals had now been replaced by dutiful civil servants, but these carried out their duties in the unenthusiastic spirit displayed by Seneca's brother Gallio when he did justice to Saint Paul at Corinth.[1] Since the liquidation or subordination of the former parochial states

[1] See Acts xviii. 17.

of the Graeco-Roman World, after these had discredited themselves by becoming Molochs, life had lost its savour for the remnant of the former governing class; and, if it had lost it even for Roman oecumenical civil servants, with their immense opportunities (which they did not neglect) for doing constructive work, it must have lost it, *a fortiori*, for Roman barristers, for Asian men of letters, and even for Athenian artists and for Alexandrian scholars.

Superficially the Roman Empire in the age of the Principate might look like the Hellenic philosophers' utopia transposed from a parochial to an oecumenical scale. The Empire was a world-wide federation of city-states, in which every cultivated member of the middle class was a citizen of a parochial as well as an oecumenical community. Down to the eve of the visible collapse in A.D. 235 the number of the city-states within the framework of the Empire was still growing, and even the youngest and the most provincial of them were still being embellished with magnificent public buildings. Yet, long before the system revealed its unsoundness by visibly breaking down, this superstructure of urban life had come to weigh upon the peasantry as an incubus without continuing to benefit the bourgeoisie. It was no longer giving them the stimulus that they had received from the parochial communities in the age before the first breakdown of the Graeco-Roman Civilization in the fifth century B.C. The bourgeoisie, and, above all, the followers of the liberal professions, found life under the Principate dull.

Meanwhile, the Army was, as we have noticed, being recruited in a higher and higher proportion from the ex-barbarian peasantry in the most seriously threatened of the frontier provinces, particularly the Illyrian provinces and Thrace. The Army provided an avenue along which the Graeco-Roman Society could be entered by proselytes whose level of cultivation was still too low for them to be able to enter by acquiring citizenship in even a provincial city-state. These military candidates for civilization were volunteers, and they had a naïve *esprit de corps* which declared itself in a loyalty to their unit, to the Army as a whole, and eventually to the Graeco-Roman Society itself when, in the third century, they were required to sacrifice themselves in saving the Empire and Society from destruction.

Till the Christian martyrs stepped into the arena, these professional soldiers were distinguished among the population of the Empire by being the only people in it who might be called upon at any moment to lay down their lives in a cause that they felt to be worthy of this supreme personal sacrifice. This staking of their lives on their life-work gave the soldiers a zest for life which was enjoyed by no one else in the Empire till the Christian martyrs made their appearance.

Under the unitary, orderly, and humane oecumenical régime of the *Pax Romana*, the masses were no longer oppressed to the intolerable degree at which they had broken into their repeated revolts during the foregoing time of troubles. Moreover, the cessation of inter-parochial wars had dried up one of the sources of supply for the slave-trade. Yet, though no longer goaded into insurrection, the masses were still a proletariat in the sense of being *in* Society without being *of* it; and, even for the urban proletariat which enjoyed a dole of 'bread and shows', the city-state culture was an incubus which cost a high price without giving any proportionate return. The masses were sheep without a shepherd, and their attitude towards the existing state of Society was one of neutrality: they were neither up in arms against it any longer nor loyal to it yet. They were thus a potential recruiting-ground for a new society, if one should present itself as an alternative to the established order. The silent yet menacing presence of this vast enigmatic underworld gave the dominant minority in the Roman Empire a feeling of insecurity and uneasiness such as the underworld in the United States was giving to the dominant minority there in A.D. 1956; and this was one of the grounds of the Imperial Government's nervousness about Christianity and the other higher religions which were seeping through the population of the Empire from below upwards.

The higher religions were alternative and competitive endeavours to fill the spiritual vacuum which the dullness of life in the Empire had created in the souls of a great majority of its inhabitants. The philosophies (including Astrology) appealed to the sophisticated middle class because they based their practical precepts on intellectual propositions. The worships of Mithras and Juppiter Dolichênus appealed to the Army because these gods stood for the promotion of virtue by militancy. The worships of Isis, Cybele, and other avatars of the Great Mother appealed to the women. Christianity appealed to the masses, and this for three reasons: it treated them, not as proletarians, but as human souls; it showed its consideration for them in a practical way by taking care of the widows and orphans, the sick and the aged, for whom neither the municipal governments of the city-states nor the oecumenical government of the Empire performed any comparable services;[1] and it did all this disinterestedly, under the inspiration of Christian ideals, and not with the ulterior aim of recruiting supporters. The most convincing tribute to these works of Christian charity has been paid by Christianity's thirteenth-hour opponent, the ex-Christian Roman Emperor Julian, in a letter to one of the prelates of his abortive pagan counter-church:

Are we refusing to face the fact that Atheism[2] owes its success above all to its philanthropy towards strangers and to its provision for funerals and to its parade of a high puritanical morality? . . . It is a disgrace to us that our own people should be notoriously going short of assistance from us when in the Jewish community there is not a single beggar, while the impious Galilaeans are supporting not only their own poor but ours as well.

This passage in a letter of Julian's to Arsaces, the pagan Chief Priest of Galatia, testifies that Christian charity has won pagan hearts. At the same time it exposes the forlornness of

[1] The Imperial Government did have to its credit, in the Alimenta Italiae, one social service which was a monument of enlightened, constructive, and skilfully planned administration (see Hirschfeld, O., *Die Kaiserlichen Verwaltungsbeamten* (Berlin 1905, Weidman), pp. 212-24). These appear to have been initiated by Nerva, launched by Trajan, and multiplied by Trajan's successors down to Marcus inclusive. Capital derived from funds at the Emperor's disposal was lent at low rates of interest to Italian farmers, and the interest was spent on financing the marriages of young people who were too poor to be able to set up house without financial assistance. The institution thus served the double purpose of fostering agriculture and promoting the increase of population. The Alimenta seem, however, to have been confined to Italy, and, in the recurrence of troubles after the death of Marcus, they were wiped out by the great inflation in the third century of the Christian Era.

[2] i.e. Christianity, which Julian calls by this reproachful name in allusion to Christianity's rejection of the gods of the Graeco-Roman pantheon.

the anti-Christian Emperor's hope of being able to counteract the moral effect of this expression of the Christian spirit by a forced pagan imitation of spontaneous Christian practice.

Julian was, in fact, setting himself the unpromising task of trying to re-open an issue that had, in truth, been settled already before ever he was raised on the shield at Paris. By that time, Christianity had already won decisive victories on two fronts: over all the other higher religions that were in competition with it in the western half of the Hellenic World[1] and over the Roman Imperial Government. In so far as this double victory can be accounted for by the effect that Christianity made upon the hearts and minds of the men and women to whom it was addressing itself, it can be ascribed to two causes which have been mentioned already. The Christian Church won the hearts of the masses because it did more for the masses than was done for them by any of the rival higher religions or by either the imperial or the municipal public authorities; and the Christians were the only people in the Roman Empire, except the professional soldiers, who were prepared to lay down their lives for the sake of an ideal.

The affinity, on this crucial point, between the Christian spirit and the military spirit was recognized and proclaimed by the early leaders of the Christian Church in exhortations to their followers in which they commended to them the Roman military virtues. For, though they had a conscientious objection to the shedding of blood, to which, in the Army, these virtues were dedicated, they admired the reverse side of the soldier's professional performance: his readiness to sacrifice his own life in the act of taking his adversary's life, and the discipline and devotion through which he prepared himself for rising to this height of self-abnegation. The note struck in the Epistle to the Ephesians, vi. 10-17, was followed up by the Early Fathers of the Church from Clement and Ignatius to Tertullian inclusive.

We ought to take to heart the discipline and the self-surrender with which the soldiers in the service of our rulers carry out their instructions. They cannot all be legates, tribunes, centurions,

---

[1] In the eastern half of the Hellenic World the victor in Hindustan and the Oxus-Jaxartes Basin was the Mahāyāna, while the victor in Iran was Zoroastrianism.

optiones, or officers of other grades, but each of them in his own appointed post carries out the orders of the Emperor and the rulers.[1]

Take care to give satisfaction to the sovereign whose soldiers you are, and from whom you draw your pay. . . . Take care that none of you shall be convicted of being a deserter. . . . Think of your works as being your deposits, and then you will exert yourselves to see that the receipts that you draw against these shall be on the scale that you would wish.[2]

The Roman Army's code of military honour thus played its part in the inspiration of the Christian martyrs; but the martyr's self-sacrifice made a greater impression than the soldier's, and this for several reasons. In the first place, the soldiers performed their heroic actions on remote frontiers where there was no public to see them, while the Christians performed theirs in the full light of publicity in the amphitheatres of the principal cities in the interior of the Graeco-Roman World. In the second place, the soldiers were recruited from still warlike ex-barbarian rural populations, whose old-fashioned bravery was taken for granted, whereas the Christians were recruited from urban populations that had long since become maturely civilized and were no longer warlike. The unconverted members of this class were not at all prone to display either courage or idealism; so the moral effect of conversion, as demonstrated in the Christian martyrs, was something startling. In the third place the soldiers' heroism, while genuine, was at the same time virtually obligatory. Their enlistment in the Army was their last voluntary act. When once they had enlisted, they had no choice as to how they should behave. It they had flinched from giving their lives on the battlefield, they would have been condemned to death by court-martial, after having been execrated by their companions in arms, for having failed to do their military duty. Thus they would have forfeited their lives all the same, but have lost them in disgrace instead of giving them with honour. By contrast, the Christians were usually offered, by the civil magistrates, the maximum opportunity of avoiding the death-sentence with a minimum loss of face.

[1] The First Epistle of Clement to the Corinthians, 37.
[2] Ignatius's Epistle to Polycarp, 6.

Policy, as well as humanity, moved the magistrate to save the life of the Christian prisoner before his tribunal if he could persuade the prisoner to co-operate with him to the extent required; for the magistrate was as well aware as the prisoner was that the martyr's blood was seed.[1] But, if, perhaps just for this reason, the prisoner was determined to become a martyr, he had it in his power to force the magistrate's hand, since the magistrate's attitude was as illogical as it was politic and humane. It was, as we have observed, the common view of the two parties that a point of principle, and this one of capital importance, was at stake in the question whether the Christians should or should not acknowledge the divinity of Rome and of Caesar. Therefore, in the last resort, the Roman magistrate was bound to pass sentence of death on any Christian who refused to make this acknowledgment by performing a symbolic outward visible act of worship. The magistrate's usual tactics were to press the prisoner to clear himself by performing the rite, on the ground that this was only a formality; and it was here that the magistrate was not on strong ground. For, if the rite was really no more than a formality after all, why should not the State waive its demand for the performance of it, instead of insisting on punishing a refusal with death? Though the Imperial Government had taken the offensive against the Christian Church in its general proscription of Christianity from the reign of Nero onwards, in the prosecutions of individual Christians the prisoners seem to have taken the offensive more often than the magistrates. Would-be martyrs insisted on forcing the issue and deliberately made it impossible for the magistrate to avoid imposing the death-penalty.

Among the innumerable human beings who have laid down their lives in a cause, the martyrs to a belief in the truth and value of the higher religions are the only people, so far, who have made this sacrifice for the sake of a god who has not been some form of collective human power, either oecumenical or parochial. Most voluntary acts of self-sacrifice have been made on the battlefield on behalf of some deified state; but the Christian martyrs under the Roman Empire were neither the first nor the last of their kind. The first, perhaps, were the Jewish martyrs who suffered under the Seleucid Monarchy in

[1] 'Semen est sanguis Christianorum'—Tertullian, *Apologeticus*, chap. 50.

167 B.C.; and, since the repeal of the proscription of Christianity in the Roman Empire in A.D. 313, there have been other Christian martyrs—for example, those Roman Catholic Christian missionaries and their converts who suffered in Japan and in China in the Early Modern Age of Western history. The Jews have continued to suffer martyrdom at many times and places, and the Muslims have suffered it under a Mongol world-empire, as well as the Chinese Mahayanian Buddhists under the T'ang Dynasty. The voluntary laying-down of life, not in the service of an idolized state, but for the sake of the God or Absolute Reality that is revealed in the higher religions, has, in fact, never died out since it first began.

This epiphany of the martyrs is a portent. Considering the innate savagery of Human Nature and the perpetual proneness of Original Sin to break out of the control under which we strive half-heartedly to bring it, we cannot foresee a time when human beings will no longer be challenged to give their lives in a cause. But we can, perhaps, foresee a time when Mankind will have rid itself of the institution of War, as it has already rid itself of the institution of Slavery; and, if and when self-sacrifice on the battlefield thus ceases to be a possibility, then martyrdom may come to be the only way in which it will still be open to men and women to offer their lives up. Thus the situation in the Roman Empire from A.D. 63 to A.D. 313, and in the Chinese Empire at times during the ninth century of the Christian Era, might be prophetic of a future that, in A.D. 1956, was still beyond Mankind's horizon.

7 ANNEXE

CHRISTIAN MARTYRS AGAINST ROMAN MILITARY SERVICE

The uncommon case of a Christian civilian becoming a martyr through refusing to submit to being conscripted into the Army has to be distinguished from the slightly less rare cases of Christian soldiers becoming martyrs through finding that their religious scruples clashed with their military duty. In this second category we have to distinguish, again, between soldiers converted to Christianity after enlistment and Christians who had already been members of the Church before they had voluntarily joined the Army.

The conscript-martyr Maximilianus of Theveste was called up for compulsory enrolment in the Army because he was in the exceptional position of being the son of a veteran. Maximilianus's father, Fabius Victor, was also a Christian; but we do not know whether he had already been one while in the Army or had been converted after his discharge.

In the consulate of Tuscus and Anulinus, on the 12th March [A.D. 295], at Theveste, Fabius Victor, together with Maximilianus, was brought into court. Pompeianus, Advocate of the Fisc, was called. Pompeianus said: 'Fabius Victor is employed in the commutation office of the provincial administration at Caesarea. Victor is present with the fit recruit Maximilianus, Victor's son. Maximilianus is a qualified recruit, so I ask the court to have him measured.' *Dion, the Proconsul, to Maximilianus:* 'What is your name?' *Maximilianus:* 'Now, why do you want to know my name? I have a conscientious objection to military service: I am a Christian.' *The Proconsul:* 'Equip him.' While he was being equipped, Maximilianus answered: 'I can't serve; I can't sin against my conscience; I am a Christian.' *The Proconsul:* 'Take his measure.' His measure was taken and was reported by the sergeant-at-arms as being five foot, ten inches. *The Proconsul to the Sergeant-at-arms:* 'Have him sealed.' Maximilianus offered resistance, and answered: 'I won't do it; I can't serve.' *The Proconsul:* 'Serve, or you will lose your life.' *Maximilianus:* 'I won't serve. You may behead me, but I won't serve the powers of This World; I *will* serve my God.' (Original Latin text in Knopf, D. R., and Krüger, G., *Ausgewälte Martyrerakten*, 3rd edition (Tübingen 1929, Mohr), pp. 86-7; Harnack, A., *Militia Christi* (Tübingen 1905, Mohr), pp. 114-17. The case of Maximilianus is discussed in Harnack, op. cit., pp. 84-5.)

The following are examples of martyrs who suffered, not for refusing to serve, but for refusing, when already in the service, to perform some military duty that they could not reconcile with their Christian conscience.

Tertullian's *De Coronâ* deals with the case of a Christian soldier who was martyred for refusing to wear, at a parade, a laurel crown which was part of the regulation dress for this occasion, but which, in the Christian soldier's eyes, was a badge of paganism which he could not assume without being untrue to his Christian faith (see Harnack, op. cit., pp. 61-9).

The Christian centurion Marcellus was martyred for

refusing to perform his military duty of playing his part in the celebration of the Emperor's birthday (text of his *acta* in Knopf and Krüger, op. cit., pp. 87-9; Harnack, op. cit., pp. 117-19).

The Christian soldier Dasius was martyred on the 23rd November 303, at Durostorum, for refusing to play the part, for which he had been designated, of mock king in a Saturnalia play that was to be performed by soldiers of his unit (text of his *acta* in Knopf and Krüger, op. cit., pp. 91-5).

8

THE DIVERSION OF HIGHER RELIGIONS FROM THEIR SPIRITUAL MISSION TO MUNDANE TASKS[1]

And these are they which are sown among thorns: such as hear the Word, and the cares of This World and the deceitfulness of riches and the lusts of other things, entering in, choke the Word, and it becometh unfruitful.—Mark vi. 18-19.

WHAT is to be the higher religions' relation to the old order? This is a question that is bound to present itself. The higher religions make their epiphany in the World with a spiritual mission of their own—the mission of preaching to every creature a new gospel[2] by which Man is inducted into a new attitude towards Suffering through a new revelation of the character of God. But, though the higher religions' Gospel is thus a new kind of spiritual seed, their mission-field is not virgin soil. In the very nature of the case, it could not have been, since the spiritual education that has made the first recipients of the new gospel capable of receiving it has been the work of long and painful experience. The epiphany of the higher religions could have taken place only on ground that had been prepared for it by the rise, breakdown, and disintegration of civilizations of the second generation. The epiphany thus presupposes the presence of an old order in the field; and, even if this old order has been a failure and has fallen into discredit, its debris, at any rate, will still be cumbering the ground, and, even in ruins, it will still be a power to be reckoned with.

The relation between this old order and the new gospel is bound to be one of conflict, open or latent, because these two dispensations are fundamentally irreconcilable. The old order is founded on a belief that Man is God, overlying an older belief that Non-Human Nature is God. Man-worship refuses to acknowledge and act upon the truth that Suffering is of the

[1] The subject of this chapter has been dealt with in greater detail by the writer in *A Study of History*, vol. i, pp. 40-1, 56-7, 90-2, 347-402; vol. v, pp. 646-712; vol. vii, pp. 392-423, 526-50.

[2] Mark xvi. 15; Col. i. 23.

essence of Life. It tries either to suppress Suffering through the mobilization of collective human power or to evade it individually through a self-extinction of which the half-measure is a self-detachment from the ties knit by Pity and Love. The new gospel is founded on a belief that Absolute Reality is neither Man nor Nature, but is beyond and above them both. It recognizes the truth that Suffering is of the essence of Life; and, instead of trying to get rid of Suffering, it tries to use it as an opportunity for acting on feelings of Pity and Love which it believes to be divine as well as human. It believes that this way of acting expresses the nature and purpose of Life more truly, and therefore more creatively, than self-assertion expresses them. In following the lead of Love, Man will be exposing himself to Suffering, because he will be swimming against the current of self-centredness. But the new gospel tells him that, in exposing himself to Suffering for Love's sake, he will be swimming, not against, but with, the main current of the Universe, because an Absolute Reality which, in one of its aspects, is the True God is a Love which has expressed itself in self-sacrifice, besides being a Power which has created the Universe and is sustaining it. God is the centre of the Universe, not through a self-centred self-assertion that would defeat itself because it would be repellent, but through a self-sacrifice that evokes an answering love and an answering self-sacrifice in God's creatures. The fundamental irreconcilibility of these two beliefs and objectives is the ground for the saying, attributed to Jesus, that he is come to bring, not peace, but strife.[1]

The question what the higher religions' relation to the old order is to be remains simple and easy so long as the old order is proscribing and persecuting them; it becomes complicated and difficult if and when the old order offers to come to terms.

Blessed are ye when men shall hate you and when they shall separate you from their company and shall reproach you and cast out your name as evil for the Son of Man's sake. . . . Woe unto you when all men shall speak well of you! For so did their fathers to the false prophets.[2]

So long as a Church is proscribed and is exposed to the peril of being persecuted at any moment, its membership is likely to be

[1] Matt. x. 34-7; Luke xii. 49-52.   [2] Luke vi. 22 and 26.

limited to a spiritual élite who are both disinterested and courageous. As soon as it is taken into partnership by the powers that be, its moral quality is likely to be diluted through mass-conversions of time-servers eager to jump on to the victor's band-waggon. So long as a church is proscribed, it can build up a new society at its own peril without being implicated in the old society's weaknesses and sins. When it has been taken into partnership with the old society, it will be involved in its failures and be led astray into serving its purposes instead of continuing to serve its own incompatible purpose single-mindedly. Therefore the negotiation of a concordat with any of the institutions embodying the old order is likely to blunt a church's edge for the execution of its own spiritual mission, and even to divert it from this mission into the old order's service. Yet, since a church's mission is to preach the gospel to every creature, a church would be acting at variance with its own purpose if it were to rebuff offers of reconciliation proposed by former opponents, even if these offers are suspect of being insincere and of being inspired, at least subconsciously, by an intention to carry the old struggle on by means of a new, more subtle, and more effective strategy.

Conversely, the old order stands to gain by proposing terms for a concordat. It is losing nothing further by making a public acknowledgment that it has tried and failed to suppress the preachers of the new gospel by physical force. It is merely acknowledging an already patent fact; and, in making this concession, it is purchasing cheaply for itself a chance of carrying on the struggle by a new strategy. It can now try to defeat its adversary by mobilizing, for its own purposes, the strength which has enabled this adversary to withstand victoriously all forcible attempts to suppress him. This strength resides in two elements: the new gospel's spiritual appeal to human souls in virtue of its truth and rightness; and the new institution—the church—which the preachers of the new gospel will have had to build up as a necessary means for carrying out their spiritual aim. The construction of a church is unavoidable, since institutions of some sort—Devil's work though all institutions may be[1]—are the only instruments that Mankind has yet devised for giving human relations a wider range than can be

[1] 'God created Man, but the Devil invented Man's institutions.'

attained through direct personal intercourse.[1] Cannot the hold which the Church has secured over people's minds and hearts by disseminating a new gospel with a strong appeal be turned to account for the benefit of the old order? The answer is that the Church can be captured and converted into an instrument for the furtherance of the old order's interests if the manœuvre is not advertised or avowed.

A classic example of this stratagem is the Roman Empire's change of policy, though not of aim, in its dealings with the Christian Church after the failure of a persecution—launched, at Galerius's instance, by Diocletian against his own better judgement—which had been the most ineffective, as well as the most cold-blooded, systematic, and cruel, in the whole series. The Roman Empire's paramount aim in now offering terms was that of every state—and, indeed, every institution—at all times from the beginning to the end of its existence. Its aim was to keep itself in being; and an overture to Christianity was the logical next step in the pursuit of an unchanging objective.

We have noticed already that, before offering a concordat to the Christian Church, the Roman Imperial Government had already tried, and found wanting, two successive devices for mobilizing Religion in its support. First it had instituted a worship of itself; then it had set up another artificial god to provide a professedly external religious sanction for itself: the Sol Invictus worshipped by Aurelian, inherited from Constantius Chlorus by his son Constantine the Great, and entrenched in the Neoplatonic counter-church that was organized by Maximinus Daia and was afterwards revived by Julian. By the time when Constantine was raised on the shield at York, the successive failures of both these devices had made it evident that the only alternative left to the Empire was to find a religious sanction for itself that would be external to it genuinely and not merely in pretence. A sanction conferred by the Christian Church would be indisputably one of this kind, considering that the Christian Church had arisen spontaneously and had withstood victoriously the Imperial Government's utmost efforts to suppress it. The Empire had nothing more to lose by trying, as a last resort, to capture the Church's power for the Empire's purpose.

[1] See Chapter 19, pp. 265-6, below.

These were some of the considerations underlying the change of policy that was carried out by Constantine in the light of his predecessors' trials and errors; but neither he nor they were consciously or deliberately Machiavellian. The would-be conservative, as well as the guardedly radical, emperors in this series, from a rustic Aurelian to a superficially cultivated Julian inclusive, were, all alike, ex-barbarian *novi homines* of the first, the second, or, at the farthest remove, the third generation; and they all ran true to type in being naïvely unintrospective and therefore naïvely sincere. There was no hypocrisy, though there may have been much unconscious calculation, in Aurelian's conversion to the worship of Sol Invictus or in Constantine's conversion from this to the worship of Christ. Constantine was moved to capitulate to Christ by the experience that was to move the Scandinavian vikings to capitulate to Him seven or eight hundred years later. The attribute of Christ that took an ex-barbarian Constantine captive was not Christ's self-sacrificing love but Christ's invincible power. What moved him to transfer his allegiance to Christ from Sol Invictus was his conviction that, in Christ, Sol had met a god who was stronger than Sol himself.

Constantine's slowness in advertising his change of religious allegiance in the images and superscriptions on his coins is an indication that he was aware of the hazardousness of his radical new departure. A concordat between two parties with incompatible purposes is a wager. Either party is buying a chance of being able to make the other serve his purpose at the risk of the other's proving the winner in playing the same game. For the Roman Empire, Constantine's policy of securing the Christian Church's sanction for the Empire at the price of the Emperor's conversion to Christianity was evidently riskier than Aurelian's policy of placing the Empire under the protection of the Emperor's own nominee and creature Sol Invictus, or than Augustus's policy of equating the Empire itself with God by instituting the worships of Dea Roma and Divus Caesar. At the same time, the Christian Church was incurring a greater risk in being forced, by Constantine's offer, into becoming official instead of continuing to be proscribed. The Church was, in truth, making with the Empire the wager that Faust made with Mephistopheles.

Christianity is not, of course, the only religion that has been captured by a mundane power to serve some non-religious purpose. A brief survey of instances of the diversion of higher religions to the pursuit of these alien objectives may enable us to see what the result is apt to be; and we may then go on to look at instances in which such attempts at capture have been resisted. For political purposes, we find higher religions being captured by oecumenical empires, their successors, and their avatars, by parochial states, and even posthumously by states of one kind or another that are already extinct by the time when they manage to win this purchase on the future. We also find higher religions being captured to serve mundane purposes that are, not political, but cultural.

The capture of the Christian Church by the Roman Empire has parallels in the eastern half of the Hellenic World in the capture of the Mahāyāna by the contemporary Kushan Empire in the Oxus-Jaxartes Basin and Hindustan and the capture of the Zoroastrian Church by the Later Arsacid, followed by the Sasanian, counter-empire that held 'Irāq and Iran against Roman attempts to re-conquer for Hellenism these lost dominions of Alexander's Macedonian successors. Islam, likewise, was captured by the Umayyad Dynasty—to the indignation of sincerely religious Muslims—to serve the political turn of a South-West Asian oecumenical empire that the Umayyads were reconstituting out of one of the Roman Empire's barbarian successor-states. A post-Buddhaic Hinduism proved a more pliant instrument in the service of the Indian oecumenical empire that was established by the Gupta Dynasty. The Christian Church, first in its Arian and then in its Catholic shape, was subsequently taken into the service of the North European barbarian successor-states of the Roman Empire in the west. Islam was used by its own founder as an instrument for establishing the nucleus of an Arab barbarian successor-state of the Roman Empire in the east before it was diverted by the Umayyads to serve the more ambitious enterprise of re-establishing the Achaemenian Empire in the shape of an Arab Caliphate. The Mahāyāna, after making its long trek from the Kushan Empire to Eastern Asia, was taken into the service of the Eurasian Nomad barbarian successor-states of the Chinese Empire in the north. Hinduism was used in the same way by the Eurasian Nomad barbarian successor-states of the Gupta Empire; the Sikh Church by a Panjābī successor-state of the Mughal Empire in India; the Jewish Church by a Maccabaean successor-state of the Seleucid successor-state of the Achaemenian Empire.

While it is manifest in the cases of Judaism, Christianity, and the Mahāyāna that a higher religion was being diverted from its own mission in being exploited politically, this is not less true, though it may perhaps be less obvious, in the cases of Islam and Sikhism. Islam originated as a version, made for Arab pagan barbarians on the fringe of the Graeco-Roman World, of the new vision of God that had been attained in Judaism and Christianity. The Prophet Muhammad had faithfully carried out an authentically religious mission at Mecca for twelve discouraging years, during which he had made few converts and had suffered much persecution, before he succumbed to the temptation to move from Mecca to Medina. His *hijrah* was not only a geographical migration but was also at the same time the counter-transfiguration of a prophet without honour in his own country into the successful president, by invitation, of a rival oasis-state. It was as if Jesus, at His temptation in the wilderness, had allowed Himself to fall into the fatal error of accepting just one little principality —some diminutive Andorra or San Marino—out of all the kingdoms of This World that were being offered to Him by Satan. Sikhism, again, originated as a concordance of Hinduism with Islam, and it fell from this religious height into a political trough because the Sikh gurus Har Govind and Govind Singh, and their eventual political successor the Sikh war-lord Ranjīt Singh, succumbed, like the Prophet Muhammad, to the temptation to use force.

Higher religions have also been captured by avatars of universal states. The Eastern Orthodox Christian Church, for example, has lent itself to the purposes of the East Roman Empire, the Ottoman Empire, and Moscow 'the Third Rome'. In all these avatars of the Roman Empire the Church has been made into the department of state that Constantine had intended it to become and that it would duly have become in the Roman Empire itself if the Roman Empire had not gone to pieces in the fifth, sixth, and seventh centuries of the Christian

Era. The defeat, by sheer force, at Constantinople, in the early years of the fifth century, of Saint John Chrysostom's intrepid reassertion of the Church's spiritual independence was a portent of what would have happened in the Roman Empire and an anticipation of what did happen in the East Roman Empire after its rehabilitation in the eighth century.

A classic example of the capture of a higher religion by parochial states is the domination of the Western Christian Church by the modern successor-states of a medieval Western Christian Papal Commonwealth. Protestantism was exploited politically in Luther's lifetime and with his collusion, as Islam had been in Muhammad's and with his. It is more significant that the Roman Catholic fraction of a fissile Western Church, which formally preserved its oecumenical range and its independence of parochial governments, was captured, *de facto*, by the Spanish, Danubian Hapsburg, and French monarchies, no less effectively than the Protestant fragments were captured by parochial principalities in Germany, Scandinavia, and Britain. In the Islamic World, where the ancient schism between the Sunnah and the Shi'ah became virulent again in the same generation that saw the fission of the Church in Western Christendom, Imāmī Shi'ism was captured and exploited overtly by the Safawī Dynasty, while the Sunnah was made to serve the Ottoman Dynasty, as Roman Catholicism was made to serve the Hapsburgs, *de facto*.

The strangest of all these captures of higher religions for political purposes are those that have been made by states posthumously. Communities that have not only been deprived of their political independence but have been uprooted and been dispersed abroad among alien majorities have, as we have already noticed, succeeded in a few cases in retaining their corporate identity even in these utterly adverse circumstances. They have achieved this *tour de force* by diverting some higher religion from its true mission of preaching the new gospel to all men to the alien task of keeping in existence an uprooted community's diasporà. The Jewish Church was thus dedicated to keeping in existence a diasporà of the Maccabaean successor-state of the Seleucid successor-state of the Achaemenian Empire; the Zoroastrian Church to keeping in existence a diasporà of a Sasanian Empire that had been the Roman Empire's peer and rival; the Gregorian Monophysite Christian Church to keeping in existence the diasporà of the Roman and Sasanian Empires' Armenian buffer-state. The Coptic Monophysite Christian Church was dedicated to keeping in existence the diasporà of a Pharaonic United Kingdom of Upper and Lower Egypt which had been taken over intact by successive alien conquerors, down to the Romans, till it had been dissolved at last in the re-organization of the Roman Empire by Diocletian. The oecumenical Patriarchate of the Eastern Orthodox Christian Church was dedicated to keeping in existence the Greek diasporà of an East Roman Empire which had been broken up by Frankish and Turkish assailants.

On the cultural plane there is a classic example of the exploitation of higher religions for mundane purposes in the history of the encounter between the Graeco-Roman Civilization and its contemporaries in South-West Asia and Egypt. The Nestorian and Monophysite versions of Christianity had originated in theological disputes that had arisen over the translation of the Christian gospel into terms of Greek metaphysics; but both these schools of Christian theology were conscripted for the non-religious service of a cultural counter-offensive, in an Oriental underworld, against a long dominant Hellenism. These are two clear instances of a cultural exploitation of Christianity; and there was also a cultural as well as a political side to the exploitation of Judaism by the Maccabees, of Zoroastrianism by the Sasanidae, and of Islam by the Umayyad Caliphs. For, in their military conflicts with the Seleucid Monarchy and with the Roman Empire, these South-West Asian political powers were also waging a cultural war against the Graeco-Roman Civilization. In the parallel encounter between the Graeco-Roman Civilization and the contemporary civilization of India, the Tantric version of the Mahāyāna in Bengal (still extant in Tibet) played the part that Nestorianism and Monophysitism played in South-West Asia and Egypt, while Hinduism played the part that was played there by Islam. In the encounter between the Islamic and the Hindu civilizations, Sikhism, which had been founded to transcend the division between Hindus and Muslims by preaching the gospel of the higher religions to all men in terms that all men could accept, was diverted—under provocation from a

Mughal Empire that grew more intolerant as it became more decrepit—into serving as the instrument of a militant Hindu reaction against the militancy of Islam.

The effect of this capture of higher religions for alien mundane purposes has been doubly disastrous. On the one hand the captured higher religions have been diverted from their true mission of preaching to all men a new gospel in which God is revealed as being Love, and Suffering as being the price and opportunity for following Love's lead. The diversion of Hinduism and Islam, at early stages in their histories, from their religious mission to mundane tasks is perhaps one reason why these churches seem—at least in the eyes of an historian brought up in a Western Christian environment—to have been, so far, less illuminating exponents of the new gospel than either Christianity or Buddhism. On the other hand the effect on the mundane movements in whose service the higher religions have been enlisted has been to import into them a whole-heartedness which the new gospel alone can inspire; and this effect has been untoward. Whole-heartedness can rise to sainthood when it is directed to the religious purpose that is its true end, but it is apt to descend to a demonic savagery when it is prostituted to the service of mundane causes. Man-worship, unreinforced by a captured higher religion, is not capable of evoking more than a limited response, even when it is presented in its least unworthy form—as the cults of Dea Roma and Divus Caesar have demonstrated by falling flat. But Man-worship is much more formidable, as we shall remind ourselves in the second part of this book, when it is keyed up through being perversely inspired by the new gospel's glowing spirit.

Though the miscarriage of the higher religions through their diversion to mundane purposes has been a frequently repeated tragedy in their short history up to date, resistance movements have never been altogether in abeyance. Perhaps the most notable of these, so far, has been the attempt, in Medieval Western Christendom, to create a commonwealth under Papal auspices. In this Commonwealth it was intended that a church, embodying one of the higher religions, should not be captured by, but capture, the entire body social of a civilization and also the bodies politic into which this society was articulating itself. In Early Medieval Western Christendom the conditions were unusually favourable for this ecclesiastical experiment, owing to the unusual barbarousness of the lay elements in the society. The North European barbarian successor-states of the Roman Empire had been more incompetent than its Arab successor-state and than the Eurasian Nomad successor-states of the Chinese Empire; and thereafter the attempt to revive the Roman Empire had been a fiasco in Western Christendom, whereas it had been a success in Eastern Orthodox Christendom, as the corresponding attempt to revive the Chinese Empire had been in Eastern Asia. Thus the Early Medieval Western Christian Church had an unusually favourable chance of influencing its social milieu; and it rose to the occasion in the ambitiously idealistic policy of a Pope Gregory VII and a Pope Innocent III. The miscarriage of this Medieval Western Respublica Christiana through the human shortcomings of ecclesiastical statesmen is the most tragic of all the disasters that the Western Society has brought upon itself so far.

The lamentable failure of this promising attempt to create a Western Christian Commonwealth was followed by a revival in Western Christendom, at the beginning of the Modern Age, of the idolatrous worship of parochial states that had been the principal religion of a pagan Graeco-Roman Society before its breakdown. Yet the Western Christian Church did not submit, without resistance, to being enslaved in the service of this renascent form of Man-worship. The Roman Catholic Church has never acquiesced in being turned into a department of this or that parochial Western state, even where it has been virtually reduced to this subordinate position *de facto*; and, in states in which a Protestant church has acquiesced in such enslavement as the purchase-price of the privilege of being officially established, free non-conformist Protestant churches have sprung up.

Free non-conformist churches sprang up in Russia likewise, in protest against the Eastern Orthodox Church's subservience to the resurgence, in Russia, of an idolized oecumenical state, even before a fourteenth-century Muscovite avatar of the Roman Empire had been reinforced, in the eighteenth century, by the importation of a Modern Western 'enlightened autocracy'. Similarly the capture of the Early Christian Church by the Roman Imperial Government in the fourth century was resisted by the militantly sectarian Donatists, and the exploitation of Islam for the Umayyad Dynasty's political purposes by the militant Khārijites,[1] as well as by the non-violent, yet not less single-minded, doctors of the Islamic Law at Medina.

These smouldering religious resistance movements are auguries that the choking of the Word by the cares of the World and the lusts of other things is not going to be the end of the higher religions, notwithstanding the thorns' effectiveness in preventing the seed from coming to harvest hitherto. 'The smoking flax shall he not quench.'[2]

---

[1] The word *khārijī*, like the word *pharisee*, means someone who separates himself (from the *profanum vulgus*).

[2] Isa. xlii. 3, quoted in Matt. xii. 20.

9

ENCOUNTERS BETWEEN HIGHER RELIGIONS AND PHILOSOPHIES[1]

And some seeds fell upon a conveyor-belt and were carried into a factory, where they were processed, refrigerated, and sterilized.

IN order to describe, in the imagery of the Parable of the Sower, the miscarriage that has overtaken the new gospel of the higher religions through their encounter with the philosophies, a post-Hellenic historian has to improvise and interpolate a verse, since this was not one of the miscarriages foreseen by the poet in whose imagination this parable was conceived, though a writer in the first century of the Christian Era was writing in a Hellenizing world. It is, indeed, rather surprising that something equivalent to this spurious verse should not have found its way into the parable by the time when the Gospels were in circulation in the Greek language. By that time, Saint Paul's epistles had already been dictated by him in the same Greek language, which was his and his Gentile converts' common mother-tongue; and, when once the New Testament was current in Greek and was winning Greek-speaking converts, it was surely evident that, sooner or later, the Christian Scripture would catch the attention of a philosophically educated dominant minority of the Graeco-Roman public and would be challenged by them to prove itself intelligible and credible in terms of their philosophy. Indeed, was it not also evident that, before the eventual delivery of this challenge from outside the Christian fold, it would already have been more than half met by educated Greek-speaking exponents of the Christian gospel who would have expounded this gospel in Hellenic philosophical terms spontaneously and unselfconsciously because these terms were their own ancestral intellectual idiom? Not much more than fifty years after the publication of the latest of the Gospels, and more than 150

---

[1] The subject of this chapter has been dealt with in greater detail by the writer in *A Study of History*, vol. vii, pp. 465-506.

years before the drafting of the earliest of the Creeds, Christianity was, in fact, presented in semi-philosophical terms to a pagan public by Christian apologists writing in the Age of the Antonines.

The translation of the gospel of Christianity, and, after it, the gospel of Islam, into terms of Hellenic metaphysics was, indeed, unavoidable. Christianity and Islam made their epiphanies in a Hellenizing World in which they could no more avoid an encounter with Hellenic philosophy than they could avoid one with the Roman Imperial Government. We have seen that, in its encounter with the Roman Imperial Government, Christianity was notably successful so long as it was being proscribed and persecuted, but was notably unsuccessful in coping with the Roman Empire and its successors when they adroitly took the Church into partnership with themselves. The story of the Christian Church's encounter with Hellenic philosophy has the same plot. So long as Christianity was ignored or ridiculed by the philosophically educated middle and upper class of the Graeco-Roman Society, its relation w'th representatives of this class did not involve it in any great intellectual difficulties or embarrassments. Christianity's intellectual troubles began when this philosophically educated class reconsidered its attitude and took Christianity seriously and sympathetically enough to demand a presentation of Christianity in Hellenic philosophical terminology.

The Church could not afford to rebuff an overture for an intellectual rapprochement with the philosophically educated upper class, any more than it could afford to reject an offer for a political rapprochement with the Imperial Government —and this for the same reason: the Church's mission was to convert the World, not to hide her light under a bushel.[1] So, at her peril, the Church must embrace any opportunities for conversion that might offer themselves; and the conversion of the professional philosophers called for special efforts, because these were the most difficult of all elements in the Graeco-Roman Society for the Christian Church to win. Unlike the rest of the pagan majority of the population of the Roman Empire, the philosophers were too proud to jump on to the Church's band-waggon just because the Emperor

[1] Matt. v. 15; Mark iv. 21; Luke xi. 33.

Constantine I had patronized Christianity and because the Emperor Theodosius I had penalized Paganism. The philosophers' ideal was self-sufficiency, intellectual as well as moral; they had worked out an intellectual as well as a moral system of their own, and they believed that they could live by it. If Christianity was to have any prospect of converting the professors at the universities of Athens and Alexandria or the magnates of the senatorial aristocracy at Rome, the Church must be prepared to come on to the philosophers' intellectual ground by translating her gospel into their terms.

Possibly the Church could have afforded to ignore these intransigent professorial and aristocratic côteries if they had been the only representatives of the Hellenic philosophical attitude of mind. Actually, this attitude of mind was more widespread and more pervasive. It was to be found, in some degree, in anyone with any pretensions to having had an Hellenic education, and it survived, as we have already noticed, in Hellenically educated converts to Christianity. It would have been difficult to put the Christian gospel into writing in Greek prose without putting it into Greek philosophical language to some extent. Hence the Christian vision of Reality was gradually, unconsciously, and unintentionally translated into terms that came to be more and more Hellenic, and more and more professionally philosophical, as the process of conversion to Christianity gradually spread upwards in the social scale.

This explains why the Christian Church did eventually translate its gospel into terms of Hellenic philosophy deliberately and systematically—thereby precipitating a theology—after it had become first the official religion of the Roman Imperial Government and then the sole religion tolerated in the Roman Empire. It also explains why Islam likewise translated its gospel into the same Hellenic intellectual terms after the Arab Caliphate had become the successor-state of the Roman Empire in the Empire's partially Hellenized eastern provinces. In the history of the relations of the Mahāyāna and of a post-Buddhaic Hinduism to Indian philosophy—particularly to the Hinayanian Buddhist school—the order of events was the reverse of their order in the history of the relations of Christianity and Islam with the Hellenic philosophy. So far from arising outside the orbit of Philosophy and subsequently colliding and coming to terms with her, the Mahāyāna and the post-Buddhaic Hinduism arose within the bosom of Philosophy and subsequently elicited from the philosophers' intellectual approach to the problem of Life two higher religions which sent their roots down below the intellectual surface to the subconscious depths of Human Nature. In their metamorphosis from philosophies into religions, Buddhism and Hinduism did trail clouds of Indian philosophy behind them; but the process of transfiguring a philosophy into higher religions seems to have left the resultant Buddhaic religions freer from cramping and warping intellectual trammels than Christianity and Islam were left by the opposite process of translating these two Judaic higher religions into terms of a philosophy.

The translation of the gospels of Christianity and Islam into terms of Hellenic metaphysics has had awkward consequences because it has ignored the distinction between two facets of Truth which cannot be focussed into unity by the imperfectly unified faculties of the Human Mind. In the Human Psyche there are two organs: a conscious volitional surface and a sub-conscious emotional abyss. Each of these two organs has its own way of looking at, and peering through, the dark glass that screens Reality from Man's inward eye and, in screening it, dimly reveals it; and therefore either mode of imperfect apprehension legitimately calls its findings 'the Truth'. But the qualities of these two visible facets of a latent unitary Truth are as different as the nature of the two organs of the human psyche that receive these 'broken lights'. If we assume, against the evidence of our experience, that these two facets of Truth are identical, and that something that is true in one of the two senses must therefore also be true in the other sense as well, just because the two facets of Truth have been legitimately labelled with the same name, we shall put ourselves in danger of losing our hold on both the aspects in which Truth presents itself to our mental vision.

'Truth' is not the only common word that the Intellect and the Subconscious Psyche jointly own and severally use in different meanings. One reason why it is possible to confuse one of the two facets of Truth with the other is because they have in common, not just one word, but their whole vocabulary. They have to share it because this is the sole vocabulary with which *Homo sapiens* has managed, so far, to equip himself for these two or for any other purposes.[1] In ordinary commonsense human intercourse, this double usage of a single vocabulary does not lead to a confusion between the two different kinds of meaning. According to the context, we take the same word, phrase, sentence, or narrative either in the Subconscious Psyche's sense or in the Intellect's sense without either mistaking one of the two for the other or deliberately identifying them.

We do not, for instance, take in an identical sense an account of a battle in Palestine in this morning's newspaper and an account of a battle in Heaven in *Paradise Lost*; and, if anyone were to suggest that either account was 'untrue' because it was not meant in the same sense as the other account, we should answer: 'Why, the author never intended it in that other sense; so how can you suggest that he is departing from the Truth when he is using those words in his own sense?' There have, however, been attempts to translate one of the two kinds of Truth into the other. For example, the Intellect's dry record of the sordid behaviour of barbarian war-lords has been run away with by the Subconscious and been translated by it into heroic poetry. Conversely, heroic poetry has been pinned down by the Intellect and been translated into prosy chronicles; and the pinning-down of the Christian gospel in creeds, in which the words are used in the sense attaching to them in Greek metaphysics, is another instance of the attempt to translate the Truth of the Subconscious Psyche into terms of the Truth of the Intellect.

[1] The single vocabulary that has to serve Man for all his purposes includes music that is older than words, and feelings that are older than music.

'The emotions are the track on which the experience runs. Sex feeling runs on some of the same tracks as religious feeling; both express themselves by fear, anger, wonder, joy, silence, speech; but it does not mean that they are identical experiences because they use the same tracks. The power of a woman over a man is not identical with that of God, but many of its emotional responses are the same, for the simple reason that a man is not equipped with two sorts of tears and two sorts of laughter, one for God and the other for a woman. Sacred and secular music use the same notes, but with different results.'—Rattenbury, J. E., *Wesley's Legacy to the World* (London 1928, Epworth Press), p. 72.

In all these translations either from the Truth of the Sub-conscious into the Truth of the Intellect or *vice versa*, the original is apt to be changed out of all recognition, and, in the process of being transformed, to be denatured, through being taken as if it were Truth in the other sense of the word from the sense originally intended.[1] The Truth apprehended by the Subconscious Psyche finds its natural expression in Poetry; the Truth apprehended by the Intellect finds its natural expression in Science. Poetry and Science have, as we have observed, to use the same vocabulary, because Man has only one vocabulary, and this has therefore to serve all Man's purposes.

> Words strain,
> crack, and sometime break, under the burden.[2]

But to assume that identical words must have identical mean-ings in scientific and poetic contexts is to be blind to the differ-ence between Poetry and Science themselves.

Poetry comes to light in individual flashes of intuitive insight shooting up out of the Subconscious. One flash will differ from another in degree of brightness, but there is no Time-relation between successive flashes. When we place two poems of different dates side by side, we may become aware of a differ-ence between them in degrees of genius; but we shall not have been able to tell *a priori* whether the earlier or the later poem is

---

[1] In the Medieval Western allegory of Love, we can watch the trans-formation taking place by stages, the first of which is 'a twelfth century *jeu d'esprit* called the *Concilium in Monte Romarici*'.

'The whole poem illustrates the influence of Ovid, and the religion of Love, very well; but it is by no means an instance of "Ovid misunder-stood". The worship of the god Amor had been a mock-religion in Ovid's *Art of Love*. The French poet has taken over this conception of an erotic religion with a full understanding of its flippancy, and proceeded to elaborate the joke in terms of the only religion he knows—medieval Christianity. . . . The love religion often begins as a parody of the real religion. This does not mean that it may not soon become something more serious than a parody. . . . The distance between "the lord of terrible aspect" in the *Vita Nuova* and the god of lovers in *The Council of Remiremont* is a measure of the tradition's width and complexity.'—Lewis, C. S., *The Allegory of Love: A study in Medieval Tradition* (Oxford 1936, Clarendon Press), pp. 20-1. See the whole passage, pp. 18-23, and also pp. 5-8.

[2] Eliot, T. S., *Four Quartets*, 'Burnt Norton', V.

going to strike us as being the greater piece of poetry. In fact, the Time-relation between them is irrelevant and without significance for any purposes of comparison; for a later poem cannot be brought into a relation with an earlier poem in which it will abrogate the earlier poem or be abrogated by it, or will modify it or be modified by it, or will add to it or be added to by it. In the realm of Poetry, comparison does not lead on to combination. The explanation of this relation of mutual independence between one poem and another seems to be that each poem springs separately from a common source, and that this common source of all poems is timeless. Each poem is like a bucketful of water drawn up from a well in which the water is 'the same yesterday and to-day and for ever.'[1] At the sub-conscious level, from which Poetry rises, Human Nature seems to be the same always and everywhere—the same in Primitive Man as in Man in Process of Civilization; the same in different societies in process of civilization; the same in different individuals beneath their different conscious and volitional personalities.

By contrast, the Intellect progressively improves its comprehension of the Universe in the course of Time; and Science is a cumulative charting of this continually changing picture of the Universe on the Psyche's conscious surface. So in Science, in contrast to Poetry, there is a Time-relation between successive reports of facts. A comparison of new reports with old reports does lead to a combination in which the reports modify one another until they fit together, for the moment, into a single self-consistent whole; and this will be re-organized, in its turn, in the light of further reports. Thus the Intellect's scientific chart of the Universe is perpetually changing because it is perpetually growing. Any state of the chart, in any particular time and place, will be only provisional, because, at any time or place, a new piece of information may transform the whole pattern of the chart. For instance, it has been transformed in our lifetime by the discoveries of the principle of Relativity, of the structure of the Atom, and of the existence of the Subconscious Abyss of the Human Psyche. Thus any presentation, whether particular or general, of scientific truth is always precarious and temporary. The difference in

[1] Heb. xiii. 8.

character between scientific truth and poetic truth may be summed up as follows: poetic truth is absolute because it is static in the Time-dimension; scientific truth is relative because it is cumulative in the Time-dimension.

In either mode of apprehending the Truth, however, there can be either a vision of some particular feature or aspect of the Truth or a vision of the whole of it. On the poetic level of the Subconscious Psyche, the comprehensive vision is Prophecy;[1] on the scientific level of the Intellect it is Metaphysics. If our foregoing analysis of the difference between Poetry and Science is correct, it will follow that Prophetic Vision's attempt to present a comprehensive view of poetic truth must, in the very nature of the two modes of apprehension, be more feasible than the attempt made by Metaphysics to present a comprehensive view of scientific truth. No doubt, even the most illuminating prophetic utterance will fall infinitely far short of expressing poetic truth in its plenitude; 'for My thoughts are not your thoughts, neither are your ways My ways, saith the Lord. For, as the Heavens are higher than the Earth, so are My ways higher than your ways, and My thoughts than your thoughts.'[2] Nevertheless, a prophetic utterance may be, as far as it goes, an expression of absolute poetic truth. And this will be an expression of unique value, standing by itself, and not subject to abrogation, addition, or subtraction when confronted with other expressions, perhaps differing from it in the degree of their illumination, that have been uttered in other times and places. By contrast, the attempt made by Metaphysics to present a comprehensive view of scientific truth can never and nowhere be more than an interim provisional report on the general progress of Science up to date.

This modest view of the capacity and the function of Metaphysics was taken, in the history of the Hellenic philosophy, by some of the greatest of its practitioners. Plato, for example, was a practical exemplar of a personal union between a metaphysician and a prophet. He was also sharply aware of

---

[1] 'Prophecy' in the original and authentic sense in which the word means, not a forecast of the future, but the revelation of a mystery that is out of the Intellect's reach. The literal meaning of 'prophecy' is the 'utterance' of Truth from a hidden source from which Truth cannot be extracted by intellectual processes.

[2] [Deutero-] Isa. lv. 8-9.

the distinction between scientific truth and poetic truth; and, wherever in his metaphysical thinking he reaches the limits beyond which Logic will not carry him on the plane of Science, he deliberately and avowedly ascends to the plane of Poetry and abandons Logic for Myth. In Plato's legacy, it is the poetry and the prophetic vision that have had a perennial message for other souls, whereas his science and his metaphysics have 'dated'. Epicurus and Zeno, again, presented their metaphysics as the minimum provisional intellectual framework required for their ethics; and the Buddha always flatly refused to discuss Metaphysics at all. He was concerned with practice, not with theory; His practical programme for His disciples was exacting; and He was on His guard against giving them an intellectual opening for turning aside from their arduous moral quest. In taking this practical view, Hinayanian Buddhism, Epicureanism, and Stoicism were setting their feet on the road which Confucius followed out to the end.

Confucianism was, however, as we have noticed, exceptional among the philosophies in frankly accepting the traditional social targets of conduct. For the Indian and Hellenic schools of philosophy, the paramount objective was self-sufficiency for the individual; and the Hellenic philosophers pursued their quest for self-sufficiency in the province of Thought as well as in the province of Conduct. The philosophically educated élite of the Graeco-Roman public wished to believe that it possessed, in its metaphysics, a complete and final blue-print of scientific truth —a demand on Metaphysics that was incompatible with the nature of scientific truth, since this, as we have seen, is cumulative and therefore relative and provisional. In fact, a philosophically educated Graeco-Roman public opinion demanded that Metaphysics should do for scientific truth something that, if it could be done at all in any field, could be done only for poetic truth, and this not by Metaphysics, but only by Prophetic Vision. It was this impracticable demand among a philosophically educated public—including converts to Christianity and Islam from the upper strata of Society—that constrained Christians and Muslims to translate their gospels out of the prophet's poetic medium of expression into the philosopher's scientific medium. This attempt to translate the poetic truth revealed in Christianity and Islam into scientific

truth has had consequences that have been adverse to the fulfilment of the higher religions' authentic mission.

The Prophetic Vision that has made its epiphany in the
higher religions—pre-eminently, perhaps, in Christianity and
in the Mahāyāna—consists, if we are right, of two intuitions.
The first of these is that Suffering is something to be accepted
as the price of acting on the promptings of Love, and indeed to
be embraced as an opportunity for thus following Love's lead.
The second intuition is that this attitude towards Suffering is
practicable. The ideal has been put into practice by a Supreme
Being; and this means that a human being who tries to do
the same will be swimming with the current of Absolute
Reality while swimming against the current of his own self-
centredness.

The meaning and value of these intuitions lie in their apprehension of timeless truths and values: the truth that Suffering is the price of Life, and that therefore Life and Suffering
are inseparable; the truth that, through self-sacrifice, Suffering can be made to serve the cause of Love; the value of Love
as being worth its cost in Suffering; the truth and value of
the conviction that this truth about Suffering and this value
of Love are not just an illusory truth and a fictitious value that
Man has invented for himself, but are stamped as authentic by
positive acts of love and self-sacrifice performed by a Supreme
Being; and the value of the mutual love of a self-sacrificing
Good Shepherd for His human sheep and of his human sheep
for Him. So long as Prophetic Vision is expressing itself
spontaneously in the poetry that is its natural medium, we can
concentrate our attention and our efforts on these illuminating
and saving truths and values which the vision reveals. But, as
soon as we try to translate these intuitions into terms of scientific
truth, our first concern has to be the irrelevant and trivial and
never finally answerable question: Do these statements—
which are now to be taken as if they were statements of scientific
fact—fit in, or do they not fit in, with the interim edition of the
scientific chart of the Universe that I have before me on my
study table here and now?

Thus the attempt to translate Prophetic Vision, expressed in
the language of poetic truth, into a metaphysical blue-print,
expressed in the language of scientific truth, has two untoward

effects. It forces us to direct our attention from what is essential and momentous in the poetic truth of Prophetic Vision to the trivial and intrinsically insoluble question of its relation to scientific truth; and it substitutes a provisional report for a timeless intuition. Even if we could succeed in translating poetic truth into scientific truth at the risk of robbing it of its meaning and value, our scientific formula would no sooner have been drafted than it would be already obsolete.

This is what has happened to Christianity and Islam as a consequence of the attempts to translate them into terms of Hellenic metaphysics. This intellectual 'processing' took the life out of them even for the small minority of philosophically educated people in the Graeco-Roman World who thought in the particular terms of Hellenic metaphysics; and these Hellenic terms have become a greater and greater stumbling-block as the progress of Science has travelled farther and farther away from the local and temporary formulation of scientific truth in the blue-print of Hellenic metaphysics. This 'dating' of the translation of a Prophetic Vision into the scientific language of Metaphysics has been inevitable; but the 'dating' of a translation that is bound to have been a mistranslation does not impugn the original, since the mistranslated gospel is, in its original poetry, a kind of truth that is timeless.

If this reasoning is right, then the stumbling block that has been placed at the feet of Posterity by the mistranslation of the Christian and Islamic gospels into terms of Hellenic metaphysics is an unnecessary one. It is there merely because of the historical accident that, during the first four or five centuries of the Christian Era, the Christian Church had to try to talk to a philosophically educated Hellenic public in that public's own metaphysical terms. This past episode of history is surely no reason why, in a twentieth-century Western and Westernizing World, this forced translation into the language of a now superseded metaphysics—a translation made in another time and place to meet a local and temporary requirement—should be taken by us as a shibboleth. It would be no remedy, however, to replace this old translation into the metaphysics of the Hellenic World of the fourth and fifth centuries of the Christian Era by a new translation into the metaphysics of the Western World of the twentieth century;

for this more recent blue-print is likewise bound to be super-seded in its turn by the continuance of the cumulative con-struction of the scientific chart of the Universe.

Strip the Christian and Islamic gospels of their incongruous and outworn Greek scientific dress; resist the temptation to put them into an alternative scientific dress of a Western cut which will also be incongruous and ephemeral; and take the truth that they express in the non-scientific poetical sense that is the natural sense in this context: if we were to give ourselves these instructions and could bring ourselves to carry them out, perhaps we should find that we had cleared the way for getting to grips with the question: What is Truth? But, of course, we should not yet have answered the question. We should still have to ask ourselves: In what sense did Christians, in those very early days before the statement of Christian beliefs began to be Hellenized, mean that Jesus was the Son of God, that He rose from the dead, that He ascended into Heaven? Can we hold these beliefs in the original Christian meaning of them, whatever this may appear to have been, in our world in our age? If we can and do hold these beliefs in a different meaning, have we, or have we not, as much right to our meaning as the original Christians had to theirs? If two ways of taking the meaning of a belief in the realm of poetic truth turn out to be different, does it necessarily follow, on this poetic plane, that one or other of the two ways must be false? These questions will meet us again in the second part of this book.

10

THE IDOLIZATION OF RELIGIOUS INSTITUTIONS

When anyone heareth the Word of the Kingdom and understandeth it not, then cometh the Wicked One and catcheth away that which was sown in his heart.—Matt. xiii. 19.

IN the two preceding chapters we have seen that a religion may be diverted from its path, with unfortunate consequences, by an encounter with some institution of another species. Yet a wrong turning taken as the result of an encounter with some external force or power can never be either so perverse or so fatal as one taken through allowing ourselves to be 'betrayed by what is false within'.[1] In any living creature, the worst of all sins is the idolization of itself or of its own handiwork. This sin is the worst of all because it is the greatest moral and intellectual rebellion that a creature can make against its true state of subordination to God the Absolute Reality, and also because it opens the door to all other sins. This arch-sin is committed by the followers of a higher religion when they idolize their own religious institutions; and self-idolizing claims to uniqueness and finality have been made, in authoritarian terms that forbid dissent and even discussion, by all the higher religions, and particularly by those of Israelite origin.

Among the small number of human beings who have been venerated and adored by Posterity within the 5,000 or 6,000 years during which this has been possible thanks to the keeping and preservation of records, by far the longest and widest fame has been won by the founders of higher religions and philosophies. Among their posthumous adherents there has been a strong tendency to canonize them as unique and final authorities, and to justify this canonization by an apotheosis. The apotheosis of founders of philosophies is particularly remarkable, because the philosophies have been apt to arise in cultivated, sophisticated, rationalistic, critical-minded, disillusioned social milieux that might have been expected, *a*

[1] Meredith, G., *Modern Love*, xliii.

priori, to be unpropitious to, and immune against, extravagance and superstition. Yet both Siddhārtha Gautama and Epicurus —perhaps because each of them presented his message in negative terms that were in tune with the temper of his public —were virtually deified by their followers. Epicurus was styled 'saviour' and is called 'a god' outright by Lucretius.[1] Gautama was styled 'the Buddha' ('the Enlightened Being'); and His followers' feeling that He was a superhuman presence was expressed in a set of birth-stories—presenting the birth as a miraculous event of cosmic significance—that has likewise attached itself to Plato, to Augustus, and to Jesus in two of the four Gospels. If the founders of philosophies underwent this posthumous transfiguration in the crucible of their followers' memories, it is no wonder that the same transfiguration should also have overtaken the founders of higher religions. For the higher religions, in contrast to the philosophies, have been apt to arise in social milieux in which the prevalent psychic atmosphere has been that of Poetry and Prophetic Vision, not Science and Metaphysics, and in which there has therefore been no inhibition upon feelings of veneration and adoration.

Even the most recent of the prophets, Muhammad, who lived in the full light of History and who never claimed to be superhuman, did claim for himself, not merely that he was the latest of the prophets, but that he was the last of them that there was ever to be. He also claimed that he had received revelations from God through the Archangel Gabriel and that, on the Night of Power, he had ascended into Heaven and, in the Seventh Heaven, had been admitted into God's presence. Zarathustra—who, like Muhammad, never claimed for himself to be more than a man—was transfigured retrospectively by his followers when they had come to believe that from Zarathustra's seed a superhuman saviour, the Saoshyant was to be begotten at the end of Time. Jesus of Nazareth was identified by His followers with the Messiah (in Greek 'the Christ' and in English 'the [Lord's] Anointed [King]') who was expected by the Jews to be begotten at the end of Time from the seed of David. Other leaders in Jewry, both before and after Jesus, were identified by their followers with the Messiah as Jesus was—for example, Simon Maccabaeus in the

[1] Lucretius, *De Rerum Naturâ*, Book V, ll. 7-12.

second century B.C. and Bar Kokhba ('the Son of a star') in the second century of the Christian Era. The Jews had conceived of the Messiah as being a human king who, like an Achaemenian Emperor, would be commissioned and inspired by God without being God himself. The Christians saw in Jesus, not only the vicegerent, but the Son, of God, and went on to pronounce Him to be co-equal, as one of three persons in a triune godhead, with God the Father and God the Holy Spirit. 'In thus deifying your founder you are deifying your church and ultimately yourselves' is the comment that Christians might hear from the lips of Jews and Muslims. The critics would, however, be implicitly passing a censure on their own religions as well. For, whether the founder of a higher religion is or is not deemed to be God Himself, he is credited with a superhuman authority; and this authority is deemed to have been bequeathed and transmitted by him, after his departure from This World, to some perennial depository of his legacy.

This perennial authority may be invested in a living corporation or in a canonical holy scripture; and, if in a living corporation, in one of this or that alternative type. It may be an unorganized body like the doctors of the Jewish and the Islamic Law, who are recruited by apprenticeship and co-option, or like the Brahmans, who are qualified by birth for the efficacious performance of religious rites. Or it may be an organized priesthood, like the hereditary Israelite priests and Levites and the hereditary Median magi who took possession of Zarathustra's religious heritage. These two types of living corporation may also be combined, as they are in the Roman Catholic Christian Church, in which the priesthood, like the Jewish and the Zoroastrian priesthood, is an organized hierarchy (though it differs from them both in being non-hereditary), while the highest source of authority is the head of the hierarchy acting in unison with an oecumenical council of fathers whose powers correspond to those of the Jewish and Islamic doctors.

The alternative is for the perennial authority to be invested in a canonical holy scripture. All the higher religions made their epiphany in literate societies; all of them have therefore had sacred books purporting to be authentic records of their founder's words and acts; and so, when the adherents of a higher religion have revolted against the authority of a living corporation, they have been apt to appeal to the authority of Holy Scripture as an alternative depository of the founder's legacy. They have taken the line that Holy Scripture, not the priesthood or the doctors, is the ultimate perennial authority representing the founder, and that each individual member of the Church has a right, at his peril, to interpret this written oracle for himself. Protestant Western Christianity is perhaps, among all the higher religions, the one in which the attribution of authority to a book instead of to a priesthood has been the most conscious and deliberate. Sikhism—in which the Granth is virtually deified—is perhaps the religion in which the idolization of a book has been carried to the farthest lengths.

There is no higher religion in which both the alternative depositories of authority are not to be found side by side, though their relative importance has varied greatly as between one religion and another. Protestant Western Christianity and Islam have not succeeded in doing without professional ministers of religion, while, on the other hand, Roman Catholic Western Christianity and Hinduism have not ever gone so far as officially to abrogate the authority of Holy Scripture, however wide the latitude that they may have given to the priesthood for interpreting the Scriptures to the laity. The histories of Judaism and Christianity indicate that the authority invested in Holy Scripture is apt to outlive the authority vested in a living corporation. An authoritarian scripture suffers, however, from a weakness from which an authoritarian corporation is exempt. The possibility of re-interpreting a written text to meet a changeless Human Nature's ever-changing situation is more narrowly circumscribed than the possibility of re-interpreting the unwritten lore of a hierarchy or of a body of doctors or fathers claiming to be inspired by a Holy Spirit which, like the wind, 'bloweth where it listeth'.[1]

The authority of Holy Scripture or of a living corporation or of both kinds of depository of the founder's legacy has been the higher religions' sanction for their self-centred claims to uniqueness and finality, but these claims are exposed to challenge. One challenge to them is the historian's point of

[1] John iii. 8.

view; another is the interpretation of the rhythm of the Universe as a cyclic movement governed by an Impersonal Law; another is the interpretation of it as a non-recurrent movement governed by Intellect and Will; another is the persistent survival of a number of competing claimants to the necessarily exclusive privilege of being the recipients and vehicles of a unique and final revelation. These divers challenges bring the higher religions' self-idolizing claims under a formidable convergent fire, and each gun in the battery is worth inspecting.

The historian's point of view is the product of a conscious and deliberate endeavour to break out of the self-centredness that is innate in every living creature. The pursuit of this endeavour is common to historians of all schools, and it would be impossible to be an historian of any school if one were utterly incapable of performing this self-transcending feat of detachment and reorientation. In an historian's eyes, therefore, the higher religions' claims to uniqueness and finality will look like almost impious proclamations of a deliberate reversion to the self-centredness that is the hall-mark of 'Original Sin'.

The historian's point of view is not incompatible with the belief that God has revealed Himself to Man for the purpose of helping Man to gain spiritual salvation that would be unattainable by Man's unaided efforts; but the historian will be suspicious, *a priori*, of any presentation of this thesis that goes on to assert that a *unique* and *final* revelation has been given by God to *my* people in *my* time on *my* satellite of *my* sun in *my* galaxy. In this self-centred application of the thesis that God reveals Himself to His creatures, the historian will espy the Devil's cloven hoof. For there is no logically necessary connexion between the belief that God reveals Himself to His creatures and the belief that God has chosen out, to be the recipient of His revelation, one creature that happens to be precisely *I myself*, and that this revelation, given exclusively to *me*, is a *unique* and a *final* one.

There is nothing in logic to debar a Jew from believing, in accordance with the theory of probability, that, if there is any 'Chosen People', it is not Israel, but, say, the Chinese, or to debar any human inhabitant of the Earth from believing that, if there is any 'Chosen People', it is not *Homo Terricola* but the

Martians. If an historian ever did come across any such rationally unself-centred applications of the belief that God has chosen some particular people to be the recipient of His revelation, the disinterestedness of these findings would be a strong ground for investigating them very sympathetically and seriously. But, though there is no necessary logical connexion, there is, of course, a very compelling psychological connexion, between the proposition 'God has revealed Himself' and the proposition 'God has revealed himself exclusively to *me*'. Indeed, it might be difficult to put one's finger on any actual presentation of the belief that God reveals Himself to His creatures that did not at the same time cast for the role of being God's 'Chosen People' the members of the particular church that subscribes to this particular presentation of the general thesis.

The interpretation of the rhythm of the Universe as a cyclic movement governed by an Impersonal Law admits of an endless series of successive avatars of God, bringing revelation and salvation to His creatures in successive cycles; but the possibility of recurrence is incompatible with the dogma that there has been, or will be, an incarnation of God that has been, or will be, unique and final. The doctrine of avatars is characteristic of both Mahayanian Buddhism and post-Buddhaic Hinduism. In the Mahāyāna, the Buddha has been transfigured into a being who is not only superhuman but is also super-divine. But Siddhārtha Gautama, the historical founder of the Hinayanian school of Indian philosophy *circa* 500 B.C., has had to pay for being thus raised higher than the gods by forfeiting His human uniqueness. In the Mahāyāna He has been reduced to being one avatar—and this neither the most significant nor the most potent one—in a series of avatars of Buddhahood in successive 'worlds on worlds' that are

> rolling ever
> From creation to decay,
> Like the bubbles on a river,
> Sparkling, bursting, borne away.[1]

This cyclic interpretation of the rhythm of the Universe is incompatible with the Judaic belief in a peak in Time-Space at

[1] Shelley, *Hellas*, 11. 197-200.

which God is going to give (according to non-Zionist Judaism),
or has already given (according to Zionist Judaism, Christianity, and Islam), a unique and final dispensation to His 'Chosen
People'. In an Indian or an Hellenic philosopher's eyes, the
non-Zionist Jewish version of this belief would probably seem
the least preposterous, because this version relegates the advent
of the Messiah and his inauguration of the Millennium to a
future date which, for all that any human being can tell, might
be postponed to an infinitely distant future. But what is the
philosopher to make of the Christian-Muslim-Zionist version
of the Judaic belief, in which the unique and final peak in
Space-Time is deemed to be already in the Past: Muhammad
the *last* of the prophets; Jesus the *sole* incarnation of God; the
return of Israel to Eretz Israel a *fait accompli*?

Those schools of Judaism which have believed, like Judaism's
Christian and Muslim pupils, that the peak has already been
attained have impugned the Judaic belief by a *reductio* of it *ad
absurdum*. If the significance and the consummation of History
are to be found in the advent of the Messiah, then those Jews
who acknowledged Simon Maccabaeus's claim to be the
Messiah would have had to see the peak in the inauguration,
in 142 B.C., in the hill country of Judaea, of a short-lived
Hasmonaean successor-state of the Seleucid successor-state of
the Achaemenian Empire. If the significance and the consummation of History are to be found in the return of Israel to
Eretz Israel, Zionists would have to see the peak in the carving-
out of a state of Israel, once again by force of arms and this
time in Philistia, after the end of the Second World War. Yet
who could seriously see in either of these two turbulent and controversial political events the *raison d'être* of the Universe? It is
true that a less mundane and more ethereal view of God's design
has been taken by Christianity and by Islam; but, since the
Christian-Muslim claim to uniqueness and finality is derived
from the Jewish, a *reductio ad absurdum* of the Jewish claim im-
pugns the Christian-Muslim claim as well.

The interpretation of the rhythm of the Universe as a non-
recurrent movement governed by Intellect and Will is the most
searching of all the challenges to the Judaic claim to uniqueness
and finality, because it is a challenge to this Judaic claim from
the Judaic *Weltanschauung* itself. It is true that an Almighty

God who was planning to reveal Himself to His creatures and to place the means of salvation within their reach would have it in His power to carry out His plan by performing a unique and final act at a single point in Space-Time and by picking out a single human community—Israel or Judah or the Zoroastrian or the Christian or the Islamic Church—to be the special recipient of His grace and special vehicle of His means of salvation. So this monotheistic *Weltanschauung*, unlike the cyclic one, is not incompatible *a priori* with a claim to uniqueness and finality. Yet, if the claim is not actually irreconcilable with the theology, it is decidedly incongruous with it; for, if one believes that God has this power, it is difficult to believe simultaneously that He also has the will to use this power in this way.

It is, in fact, difficult to imagine that a God whose mind and will govern the whole course of the Universe would compromise the conduct of His government by acting on a caprice. It would seem highly improbable that He would pick out just *me* and *my* tribe to be His prophet and His 'Chosen People'. Any such idea of mine would seem less likely to be the Truth than to be an hallucination conjured up by my innate self-centredness. And it would seem hardly more probable that God would choose out any other particular prophet or particular people to be the unique and final instruments of His purpose. Any such idea would seem incongruous with the concept of a God whose thoughts and plans are, *ex hypothesi*, infinitely greater than the whole of His creation, and *a fortiori*, greater than any single creature and than any single point in Space-Time. Does not any creature stand convicted of megalomania if he allows himself to imagine that God can have committed Himself in an annunciation to one or more of His creatures, or, still more preposterous, in a covenant with one or more of them, at a particular point in Space-Time, to making this particular encounter of theirs with Him into the supreme moment in the history of His creation?

The persistent survival of a number of competing claimants to the privilege of being the recipients and vehicles of a unique and final revelation is a challenge to all the competing claims alike; for the privilege, if it has ever been granted, is necessarily exclusive. Only one of these absolute claims can be valid if there is any validity in any one of them. The rest of them must be false in any case when made in these absolute terms. The first test of the valid claim, if there were a valid one, might be expected to be that it should win a universal recognition and acceptance from all Mankind in competition with its rivals, and that these rivals' false claims should all be confuted and rejected; and some of the claimants that were once in the field have, in fact, fallen out. Of all the philosophies thrown up by all the civilizations up to date, only two—Confucianism and the Hinayanian school of Buddhism—are still in the field today. Epicureanism, Stoicism, and the Legist and Mohist schools of Chinese philosophy are now extinct, and the Hīnayāna might not have survived if it had not gone far towards transforming itself, like the Mahāyāna, from a philosophy into a religion. Of all the higher religions that were once in competition in the Hellenic World, only six are still in the field today. Zoroastrianism, Judaism, Christianity, Islam, the Mahāyāna, and Hinduism are still there; but the worships of Mithras, Cybele, Isis, and Juppiter Dolichenus are now extinct, except in so far as they have been unavowedly taken up into Christianity. Yet here we have two philosophies and six higher religions —eight faiths and ways of life in all—still in the field some 2,500 years after the date at which the earliest of the philosophies made their epiphany.

No doubt, 2,500 years is not a very long time on any Timescale. It is less than half the Age of the Civilizations up to date, and is only a 240th, or perhaps only a 400th, part of the Age of the Human Race up to date. Two thousand five hundred years is, nevertheless, an appreciable length of time compared with th e life-spans of those philosophies and higher religions that have already fallen out of the race. On that standard, all eight surviving faiths have shown considerable stayingpower; and, on this reckoning, there would seem to be a presumption in favour of the likelihood that these eight survivors will continue to exist in the same *Oikoumenê* side by side. But, the longer they do continue to exist side by side, the more convincingly will the fact of their co-existence militate against any acceptance of the exclusive claim to uniqueness and finality that is made by each of them in contradiction with the identical claim made by each of its seven contemporaries.

Considering how numerous and how formidable the objections to this claim have proved to be, how are we to explain the persistence of each of the surviving higher religions in asserting the claim on its own behalf as well as in refuting its contemporaries' assertion of it by surviving? The explanation of both the assertion and the survival seems to be partly sociological and partly psychological.

The sociological explanation of the assertion of the claim is perhaps to be found in the human circumstances in which the higher religions made their epiphanies. They made them in social milieux in which disillusionment and suffering had evoked a yearning for some new hope of salvation; in which the failure of the worship of parochial human communities had left a spiritual vacuum; in which the artificially promoted alternative worship of an oecumenical human community had left its subjects' hearts cold; and in which the competition between the higher religions themselves for the prize of filling the spiritual vacuum was very severe. Higher religions competing with one another in this arena were inevitably tempted to pitch their rival claims high.

As for the psychological explanation of the assertion of the claim, this is perhaps to be found in a human craving to escape from the burdensome responsibility of having to take decisions for oneself. It may look as if this burden can be escaped by submitting one's own intellect and will to some authority to which one can feel it proper to submit because one has recognized its claims as being unique and final. This craving to escape responsibility can be reconciled with an unexorcized self-centredness by the belief that, in submitting to the authority of the Church, one becomes a member of the 'Chosen People'. This craving for an authority that will lift the burden of responsibility from one's shoulders is, no doubt, at its strongest in social situations in which Society is in disintegration; but it is an innate and perennial craving which, in every soul everywhere and always, is on the wait for an opportunity to break out.

The sociological explanation of the survival of half a dozen competing faiths, each making an exclusive claim for itself, is perhaps to be found in the lack, until our own day, of adequate means of physical communication on an oecumenical scale.

This would explain why each of the eight surviving rival faiths has fallen so far short, as it has fallen, of making good its claim that its destiny is to become the exclusive faith of all Mankind throughout the *Oikoumenê*; it would also explain why each of them has, on the other hand, succeeded in entrenching itself in some particular region of the Earth's surface, side by side with its rivals entrenched in other regions. Even the Jewish and Zoroastrian diasporàs have their regional limits. There are few Jews beyond the bounds of Dār-al-Islām and Christendom, and few Parsees beyond the bounds of India and Iran.

There is also a possible psychological explanation of the survival of eight faiths on one planet. It is possible that each of the surviving faiths may prove to have an affinity with one of the diverse alternative possible organizations and orientations of the Human Psyche. For the present, this psychological explanation can be offered only tentatively, because the study of psychological types, initiated by C. G. Jung, is still in the exploratory stage. But it is conceivable that an affinity between some one of these psychological types and some one of the surviving faiths might prove to be the explanation of this particular faith's survival in contrast to the fate of its now extinct former competitors, and it is not inconceivable that the survival of all the surviving faiths might eventually be accounted for, at least partially, on these lines.[1]

If each of the surviving faiths does, in truth, have an affinity with one particular psychological type, we can tentatively forecast some of the effects, on the religious plane, of 'the annihilation of distance' and the social unification of the *Oikoumenê* that are being achieved in our day through a sudden vast improvement in physical means of communication. This technological revolution may be expected to break the regional monopolies, but not—at least, not in the first chapter of the next episode in Mankind's spiritual history—to result in any single faith's converting a regional monopoly into an oecumenical one by driving all its rivals off the whole of the field. In the next chapter we may expect to see all the now surviving faiths continue to hold the field side by side and continue to

[1] This question has been discussed in greater detail by the writer in *A Study of History*, vol. vii, pp. 716-36.

divide the allegiance of Mankind between them. But we may also expect to see the individual's adherence to a particular faith determined, in an ever larger number of instances, not by the geographical accident of the locality of his birth-place, but by a deliberate choice of the faith with which he feels the closest personal affinity—a feeling that will, presumably, be determined by the type of his psychological organization and orientation. The adherents of each religion thus seem likely, in the next chapter, to come gradually to be distributed all over the *Oikoumenê*, but it may also be expected that, in the process, they will come to be intermingled everywhere with adherents of all the other faiths, as the Jews are already intermingled with Muslims and Christians and the Parsees with Muslims and Hindus. As a result, the appearance of the religious map of the *Oikoumenê* may be expected to change from the pattern of a patchwork quilt to the texture of a piece of shot silk.

The higher religions' identical and therefore incompatible claims to be unique and final revelations arouse passionate feelings in the hearts of their respective partisans and opponents, and there may be long and bitter controversy before an oecumenical verdict is delivered. But, whatever may be the eventual verdict on the claims of the higher religions, it is evident already that the epiphany of these religions has been a decisive and significant new departure in History. Our Human Reason cannot allow us to accept as the Truth the self-centred view of the Universe that is innate in every living creature. But our Human Conscience, which has a claim to be heard as well, cannot allow us alternatively to accept as the Truth a view of History that is meaningless. This meaningless view is a necessary corollary of the belief that the Universe is governed by inexorable laws of Nature, and is also a possible corollary of the alternative belief that the Universe is governed by the will of an Almighty God—supposing that we were to think of God as being, not self-sacrificing Love, but a capricious tyrant.

In the history of the Universe, in so far as human insight has been able to probe the mystery of it so far, we can see events that have been decisive and therefore significant: the successive geneses of our galaxy, our sun, and our planet; the epiphany of Life on this planet; the epiphanies of the Vertebrates, of the

Mammals, of Man. These are all instances in which a particular creature has, in fact, served as the instrument or vehicle for a decisive event at a particular point in Space-Time. If it is not incredible that the Earth may have been singled out *circa* 2,000,000,000 B.C. for becoming a home of Physical Life, it is neither more nor less incredible that Abraham may have been singled out *circa* 1700 B.C. at Ur, or Israel *circa* 1200 B.C. at the foot of Mount Sinai, for becoming a vehicle of God's grace to God's creatures. If it is not incredible that the First Adam may have been created, *circa* 1,000,000 or 600,000 B.C., at some point, not yet located by pre-historians, on the land-surface of this planet, it would be neither more nor less incredible that a Second Adam may have become incarnate in Galilee at the beginning of the Christian Era. There are also events that are decisive, and therefore significant, in the life-history, in This World, of every individual human being. And, if God, at least in one of His infinitely numerous and diverse aspects, faculties, and potencies, is a spirit expressing Itself in an intellect and a will which it would not be altogether misleading to think of in anthropomorphic terms, then there will be events that will be significant, because decisive, in God's working out of His divine plan. The acceptance of a belief that there have been, and of an expectation that there will continue to be, decisive new departures does not, however, require the acceptance of a belief that any one of these new departures has been, or will be, not only decisive, but unique and final. The two beliefs are, indeed, incompatible.

The Human Spirit that dwells in each one of us cannot refrain from seeking for an explanation of the Universe in which we find ourselves, and it insists that our *Weltanschauung* shall give the Universe significance without making the Universe centre round the Self. In logic it may be impossible to reconcile these two requirements. Yet, even in the teeth of logic, the Human Spirit will not consent to abandon its search for an explanation of the mystery; and the new gospel revealed in the higher religions does seem to offer a reconciliation in its intuition that the meaning of Life, Existence, and Reality is Love. If God is self-sacrificing Love, and if God has taught Man, not merely by precept but by example, that the right attitude towards Suffering is to embrace it in order to make it serve the cause of Love, we can catch, in this vision, a glimpse of Reality that will satisfy both the Heart and the Head.

If this is the Truth, and if the revelation of it is the gospel of the higher religions, then we must hold fast to this inestimably precious spiritual possession. We must not allow ourselves to be alienated from it by our conscience's just condemnation of the sinful claim to uniqueness and finality for each particular claimant's particular faith. We must not allow ourselves, either, to be disconcerted by premonitions of the metamorphoses which the outward forms of all our ancestral faiths may have to undergo in the course of the aeons during which Mankind may continue to survive on the face of the Earth.

For I am persuaded that neither death nor life nor angels nor principalities nor powers, nor things present nor things to come, nor height nor depth nor any other creature, shall be able to separate us from the love of God which is in Christ Jesus our Lord.[1]

[1] Rom. viii. 38-9.

PART II

Religion in a Westernizing World

I I

THE ASCENDANCY OF THE MODERN WESTERN CIVILIZATION

THE spread of the Modern Western Civilization over the face of the planet has been the most prominent single feature in the history of Mankind during the last four or five centuries.

The expansion of one society into the domains of its contemporaries was something that had happened already, more than once, in the Age of the Civilizations. For example, the two societies of an earlier generation to which the Western Civilization was affiliated had both expanded in their day to opposite extremities of the Old World and beyond. The Canaanite Civilization still lives on in a Jewish diasporà that has crossed the Atlantic and seeded itself in the Americas. The same civilization's eastward trek across the breadth of the Continent is commemorated, in the Temple of Heaven at Peking, in the letters of the Aramaic Alphabet—here written vertically instead of horizontally—in which the Manchu and Mongol versions of the trilingual inscriptions are recorded side by side with the Chinese. As for the Graeco-Roman Civilization, it was carried eastwards as far as Japan in the Greek style of visual art that had been adopted by the Mahāyāna in North-Western India, while it was carried westwards as far as Hadrian's Wall by Roman arms. The civilization of the pastoral nomads, again, spread all over the Eurasian Steppe, as is attested by the uniformity of 'the Animal Style' of Scythian art in the great western bay of the Steppe and in the great northern loop of the Yellow River, while its penetration into the adjoining domains of the sedentary civilizations is attested by the uniformity of the Sarmatian style of military equipment as this is portrayed in Chinese terra-cotta figurines of the T'ang Age and on the Bayeux Tapestry.

The expansion of the Modern Western Civilization has been unique, not in being far-flung, but in being literally world-wide. The Eurasian nomads conquered all but the outer rind of the Old World by ranging on horseback over grasslands and deserts that were as conductive as rivers and seas. Within seventy-one years of Chingis Khan's first eruption from the Steppe in A.D. 1209, the Mongols had conquered China, the Oxus-Jaxartes Basin, Persia, and 'Irāq; imposed their suzerainty on Burma and Russia; and raided Japan, India, Syria, Silesia, and Hungary. In the thirteenth century of the Christian Era the steppe-borne nomad Mongol cavalry had indeed a wide range; yet they were outranged by the sedentary Westerners when these, from the fifteenth century onwards, mastered the still more conductive medium of the Ocean through their invention of a new type of sailing-ship that was able to keep the sea continuously for months on end.[1] This Ocean-faring Modern Western four-masted or three-masted square-rigged sailing-ship made the expansion of the Modern Western Civilization literally ubiquitous, because it gave Western mariners access to all coasts, including those of the Americas and the Antipodes. The steppe-borne horse had conveyed its nomad rider to the back doors of all the civiliza-tions of the Old World; the Ocean-borne ship conveyed its Western navigator to the front doors of all the civilizations on the face of the planet.

The Modern Western sailing-ship was the instrument and the symbol of the West's ascendancy in the World during a Modern Age of Western history that came to an end between about A.D. 1860 and A.D. 1890. In its independence of the land, this sailing-ship was superior to its land-bound supplanter the post-Modern Western steamship; and in A.D. 1956 the Ocean on which the Western sailing-ship and the Western steamship had been successively launched had not been put out of use by the post-Modern Western conquest of the Air, as the Steppe had been put out of use by the Modern Western conquest of the Ocean. Aircraft could not perform the ship's function of carrying staple goods in bulk at a price that the traffic could bear; and, since the Industrial Revolution, this ponderous traffic had come to be one of the necessities of a Westernizing

[1] See *A Study of History*, vol. ix, pp. 364-8.

World's economic life. The Modern Western sailing-ship was the vehicle that had created the possibility of world-unity in the literal sense of uniting the whole Human Race, throughout the habitable area of the planet's surface, into a single society; and in our day, when we have seen the nineteenth-century clipper disappear from off the face of the seas, we have also seen the possibility created by its fifteenth-century prototype become a certainty. In A.D. 1956 it was already unquestionable that the social unification of Mankind was going to come to pass. The question that still remained open was not what was going to happen but merely how an inevitable consummation was going to be reached.

In the fifteenth century of the Christian Era, when the Western Civilization, equipped with its new instrument the Modern Western sailing-ship, set out on its world-wide career of expansion, it was still a civilization of the same type as its contemporaries in other parts of the Old World: an Eastern Orthodox Christendom in South-East Europe and Anatolia; a branch of this same Eastern Orthodox Christendom in Russia; a Turco-Persian Islamic Civilization stretching from South-East Europe to India; an Arabic Islamic Civilization stretching from Morocco to Indonesia; a Hindu Civilization in India and Indonesia; an East Asian Civilization in China; and a branch of this same East Asian Civilization in Korea and Japan. Every one of these Old-World civilizations of the third generation, including the Western, had taken shape within a social 'chrysalis' provided by a society of a different species— a higher religion—and in the fifteenth century of the Christian Era all of them, again including the Western, were still living within an inherited traditional religious framework, both social and spiritual. In this typical feature, which was manifestly an important one, Western Christendom was a civilization of the same character as its sister civilizations in the Old World at the time when the West made its first impact, over the Ocean, on all other living civilizations in both the Old World and the New. At this stage the West was peculiar only in its mobility, in which it had now surpassed even the Eurasian nomads.

This common characteristic of being set in the framework of a higher religion made fifteenth-century and sixteenth-century Western Christendom familiar to its contemporaries in the

Old World and at the same time repulsive to them. It was familiar because of its traditional religious setting. It was repulsive because Western Christianity was a different religion —and, being a Judaic religion, was also a militantly rival one —to Eastern Orthodox Christianity, Islam, Hinduism, and Buddhism, which were the religious frameworks of the other living civilizations in the Old World.

In the seventeenth century of the Christian Era, however, when the West's mastery of the Ocean was now firmly established, and when consequently the West had already become the potential master of the World, the West went through a revolution that had been by far the greatest in its history down to A.D. 1956. In the seventeenth century the Western Civilization broke out of its traditional Western Christian chrysalis and abstracted from it a new secular version of itself, in which Religion was replaced by Technology as Western Man's paramount interest and pursuit. This domestic spiritual revolution in the West quickly precipitated a corresponding revolution in the other civilizations' attitude towards the alien Western Civilization that was pressing hard upon them. These two seventeenth-century revolutions are examined more closely in the thirteenth, fourteenth, and fifteenth chapters of this book. The purpose of the present chapter is simply to outline the plot of the historical drama with which the whole of this second part of the book is concerned. At this point we have merely to note that the effect of the seventeenth-century secularization of the Western Civilization on the attitude of the non-Western civilizations was to remove the previous obstacle to a reception of the Western Civilization by them. In consequence, the whole of the non-Western World had become deeply committed to the Late Modern secularized version of the Western Civilization by the middle of the twentieth century; and so, when a secularized Western Society was overtaken, rather suddenly and unexpectedly, by a spiritual crisis, this Western malaise made an impact on a technologically Westernizing World.

There is one salient feature of the Late Modern Western Civilization that has already begun to look strange to us in the current early chapter of our post-Modern Age of Western history, and this strange salient feature is Late Modern

Western Man's supreme self-assurance. From the later decades of the seventeenth century of the Christian Era down to August 1914, Late Modern Western Man assumed that the secularized version of his ancestral civilization which he had now abstracted from its traditional Western Christian religious chrysalis was the last word in Civilization in two senses. He assumed that this was the mature and perfect form of Civilized Society: Civilization with a capital 'C' (for he now dismissed the other living civilizations as being 'semi-civilized', and the original unsecularized version of his own Western Civilization as being 'medieval'). He also assumed that his latterday secularized Western Civilization was definitive in the sense of being, not merely perfect, but permanent. 'A lily of a day'[1] may be perfect without being permanent, but 'Civilization' was credited by its Western exponents with both these attributes of divinity: it was deemed to have come to stay for ever and to be immune against the destruction that had overtaken so many primitive and semi-civilized cultures in the past.

The abuses of tyranny are restrained by the mutual influence of fear and shame; republics have acquired order and stability; monarchies have imbibed the principles of freedom, or, at least, of moderation; and some sense of honour and justice is introduced into the most defective constitutions by the general manners of the times. In peace, the progress of knowledge and industry is accelerated by the emulation of so many active rivals; in war, the European forces are exercised by temperate and indecisive contests.[2]

Gibbon's assurance was amazing to Westerners reading this passage in A.D. 1956; yet readers who had already been grown-up in August 1914 could remember in 1956 that, down to 1914, they themselves had still seen the Western Civilization's prospects with Gibbon's eyes—in disregard of warnings that had been uttered, before Gibbon's day and long before theirs, by the sceptical-minded seventeenth-century Western heralds of a self-confident Late Modern Western Age.[3]

[1] Ben Jonson.
[2] Gibbon, Edward, *The History of the Decline and Fall of the Roman Empire* chap. xxxviii, ad fin.: 'General Observations on the Fall of the Roman Empire in the West'—written, probably in A.D. 1781 (the year of Cornwallis's capitulation at Yorktown), by a British subject who fancied himself to be an arch-sceptic.
[3] See Chapter 11, Annexe, below.

Since A.D. 1914 we have come to realize that our Late Modern Western secularized civilization has not, after all, distinguished itself from all its predecessors by having achieved perfection, and therefore has also not distinguished itself from them by having achieved immunity against destruction. We have realized that, in discarding, in the seventeenth century, the doctrine of Original Sin together with the rest of the West's Christian religious heritage, Western Man did not slough off Original Sin itself. Mr. Lightheart merely steamed off the label from a packet that still stayed strapped as fast as ever to his shoulders; and the sequel to this facile operation has shown how little warrant Lightheart had for feeling himself superior to that old-fashioned pilgrim, Christian. In removing the label from the load, Lightheart fancied that he had dispensed himself from Christian's *corvée*; and so, when Christian's long travail was rewarded at last by his release from his burden, Lightheart was still left carrying his burden unawares.

This persistence of Original Sin in a secularized Western Society was dumbly attested by the everyday private experience of every Western man and woman in every generation. Yet it has required the public atrocities committed by children of our Western Civilization in our lifetime to extort from us the recognition that Original Sin is still alive in Western Man. The pioneer explorations made by our post-Modern Western psychologists into the subconscious depths of the Human Psyche have now begun to make us aware again, as our forefathers were aware down to the earlier decades of the seventeenth century, how strong and how formidable Man's Original Sin is.

This addition of a psychic dimension to our scientific knowledge, following on the heels of appalling unforeseen public events, has compelled us to address ourselves again to one of Mankind's major perennial tasks—the struggle with Original Sin—which we have ignored and neglected for more than 300 years; and we have had to resume the struggle in circumstances which, in one important point, are more formidable than any with which the children of the Western or any other civilization have ever been faced in the past. Down to the outbreak of the Western Industrial Revolution in the eighteenth century of the Christian Era, the narrowness of the limits of Man's command over Non-Human Nature set correspondingly narrow limits to the force of the 'drive' that Man was able to put into his acts, either for good or for evil. But now, as a double-edged reward for our transference of our treasure from Religion to Technology, we have made such unprecedented technological progress during these last 200 years that our actions have come to have the 'drive' of atomic energy behind them. Our wickedness is not more wicked, and our goodness not more good, than the conduct of our pre-industrial forefathers was. But the practical consequences of our actions, whether bad or good, are now far more serious. No doubt it was always true that 'the wages of Sin is Death';[1] but today, when we find ourselves once again forced by events to face, and grapple with, Sin, the truth of St. Paul's warning cannot be ignored. This manifest deadliness of our evil acts in an Atomic Age is a ground both for fear and for hope: for fear, because we may bring destruction on ourselves; for hope, because we cannot now blind ourselves to this possibility, and may therefore be moved, by our awareness of our danger, to repent and to mend our ways.

This twentieth-century spiritual crisis in the West would have been momentous in itself, even if it had merely been a local domestic Western affair. Its momentousness is magnified tenfold by a consequence of the literally world-wide expansion of the Western Civilization and of its progressive reception, in its secularized form, by the non-Western majority of the Human Race. The West's present spiritual crisis is also the World's. During the last quarter of a millennium, one non-Western civilization after another has received our secularized Western Civilization. Most of them have received it reluctantly, in spite of finding it repellent; and the consideration that has overcome their distaste has been the supposition that this disagreeable alien way of life to which they were painfully adapting themselves really was what it purported to be: a Civilization that was definitive in the sense of being both perfect and permanent, as our Western Civilization looked to Gibbon and still looked to us in our time down to A.D. 1914. Yet the non-Western civilizations had no sooner discarded their own cultural heritages, with their traditional religious frameworks, and adopted our secularized Western Civilization

[1] Rom. vi. 23.

instead, than they found that this adopted civilization was not, after all, the definitive way of life that they had credulously believed it to be on the strength of the contemporary West's own naïve belief in itself.

Thus the non-Western majority of Mankind, after having put itself through one spiritual revolution—the process of conversion from its hereditary civilizations to a secularized Western Civilization—has now immediately found itself plunged into a second spiritual revolution of which it had had no foreboding. It has adopted the secularized Western Civilization just in time to find itself involved in the West's unexpected twentieth-century spiritual crisis. Thus the West has played on the World, in all good faith, an unintentional trick. It has sold to the World a civilization that has turned out not to be what either the seller or the buyers believed it to be at the time of the sale. This mishap seems likely to make the twentieth-century spiritual crisis even more distressing to the Westernizing majority of Mankind than it is to the Western minority; and this distress may generate bitterness.

At the same time, these non-Western converts to the Western Civilization bring with them hope as well as fear; for they come trailing some still undiscarded clouds of glory from their own religious heritages, which they have abandoned a shorter time ago than the West has abandoned its Christian religious heritage. These undiscarded elements in the religious heritages of the non-Western majority of Mankind have now been brought, by the process of Westernization, into the World's common stock of spiritual treasure; and perhaps they may work together with the surviving remnant of Western Christianity to re-introduce the discarded religious element into a Western Civilization that has now become the common civilization of all Mankind, for better or for worse.

This hope kindled into a flame in the writer's heart on the 13th October 1953, when, on the eve of a Round Table Conference convened by the Council of Europe in Rome, he was making a long-meditated pilgrimage to the Sacro Speco: the cave on the rocky flank of a ravine, beyond Subiaco, where Saint Benedict is traditionally believed to have spent his years of spiritual travail as an anchorite before receiving and accepting his call to Monte Cassino. Here was the primal germ-cell

of Western Christendom; and, as the pilgrim read the moving
Latin inscription in which Pope Pius IX had recorded the
names of all the lands, stretching away to the ends of the Earth,
that had been evangelized by a spiritual impetus issuing from
this hallowed spot, he prayed that the spirit which had once
created a Western Christian Civilization out of the chaos of the
Dark Age might return to re-consecrate a latterday Westernizing World.

II ANNEXE

SEVENTEENTH-CENTURY FOREBODINGS OF THE
SPIRITUAL PRICE OF THE SEVENTEENTH-CENTURY
REVULSION FROM RELIGIOUS FANATICISM

The spiritual vacuum that was to be the price of the seventeenth-century revulsion from religious fanaticism was foreseen
and deplored in the seventh decade of the seventeenth century
by a clergyman of the Episcopalian Established Church of
England who was the first secretary of the Royal Society, and
in the last decade of the same century by a French Huguenot
refugee in Amsterdam who was the forerunner of Voltaire and
the Encyclopaedists.

The fierceness of violent inspirations is in good measure departed:
the remains of it will be soon chac'd out of the World by the re-
membrance of the terrible footsteps it has everywhere left behind it.
And, though the Church of Rome still preserves its pomp, yet the
real authority of that too is apparently decaying. . . . This is the
present state of Christendom. It is now impossible to spread the
same clouds over the World again: the universal disposition of this
age is bent upon a rational religion. . . .
    Let it be a true observation that many modern naturalists have
bin negligent in the worship of God; yet perhaps they have bin
driven on this profaneness by the late extravagant excesses of enthusiasm. The infinit pretences to inspiration, and immediat
communion with God, that have abounded in this age, have
carry'd several men of wit so far as to reject the whole matter—
who would not have bin so exorbitant if the others had kept within
more moderate bounds. . . . From hence it may be gather'd that
the way to reduce a real and sober sense of religion is, not by in-
deavoring to cast a veil of darkness again over the minds of men, but
chiefly by allaying the violence of spiritual madness, and that the

one extreme will decreas proportionably to the less'ning of the other.

It is apparent to all that the influence which Christianity once obtain'd on mens minds is prodigiously decay'd. The generality of Christendom is now well-nigh arriv'd at that fatal condition which did immediatly precede the destruction of the worships of the Ancient World, when the face of Religion in their public assemblies was quite different from that apprehension which men had concerning it in privat: in public they observ'd its rules with much solemnity, but in privat regarded it not at all. It is difficult to declare by what means and degrees we are come to this dangerous point; but this is certain, that the spiritual vices of this age have well-nigh contributed as much towards it as the carnal; and, for these, the most efficacious remedy that Man of himself can use is not so much the sublime part of divinity as its intelligible and natural and practicable doctrines.[1]

There is a very widespread feeling that the same people who, in our age, have dispersed the darkness that the Schoolmen had spread all over Europe have multiplied the number of the 'tough-minded' spirits (*les esprits forts*) and have opened the door to Atheism or to Scepticism or to a disbelief in the crucial mysteries of Christianity. The study of philosophy is not held solely responsible for the growth of irreligion; literature shares the blame; for it is contended that Atheism did not begin to declare itself in France before the reign of Francis I, and that it began to make its appearance in Italy at the time of the *floruit* of the Humanists.[2]

The seventeenth-century Western advocates of tolerant-mindedness were aware that the overthrow of a theology imposed by authority would bring to light the limitations of the powers of the human reason. No doubt, they are sometimes inwardly rejoicing in revolutionary changes which they are affecting to deplore. In an age in which the free expression of sceptical opinions in matters of religion had not yet quite ceased to be dangerous, *eironeia*, in the Socratic sense of a use of words with an innuendo running counter to their ostensible meaning, was a convenient intellectual weapon to use in the cause of enlightenment, and Bayle was a pre-Gibbonian adept in this Gibbonian art. But a series of passages in Bayle's *Dictionaire*, in which the price of enlightenment is pointed out, seem to

[1] Sprat, Tho., *The History of the Royal Society for the Improving of Natural Knowledge* (London 1667, Martyn), pp. 366-76.
[2] Bayle, P., *Dictionaire*, 3rd ed., iv. 2688a, s.v. Takiddin.

reveal an oscillation between irony and earnestness in the spirit in which Bayle is making this point.

In the following passages the spirit of irony is manifestly predominant.

Since the mysteries of the Gospel are of a supernatural order, they cannot and must not be subjected to the rules of natural light. They are not made for being exposed to the test of philosophical disputations. Their greatness and sublimity forbid them to undergo this ordeal. It would be contrary to the nature of things that they should come out from such a combat as the victors. Their essential character is to be an object of Faith, not an object of Scientific Knowledge.[1]

Roman Catholics and Protestants make war on one another over innumerable articles of religion, but they agree on the point of holding [with one accord] that the mysteries of the Gospel are above Reason. . . . From this it necessarily follows that it is impossible to solve the difficulties raised by the philosophers, and consequently that a disputation conducted exclusively in the light of our natural human intelligence will always end unfavourably for the theologians, and that these will find themselves compelled to give ground and to take shelter under the canon of supernatural light. It is evident that the Reason would never be capable of attaining something that is above it. So it must be admitted that the Reason cannot supply answers to its own objections, and accordingly that these objections will hold the field so long as we do not have recourse to the authority of God and do not bow to the necessity of surrendering our understandings to an obedience to [the dictates of] the Faith.[2]

This is how those who want to make Theology subject to Philosophy ought to be instructed in their proper duty. They should be shown the absurdity of the consequences to which their method leads, and by this road they should be led back to one of the principles of Christian humility, namely, that metaphysical notions ought not to be taken as our rule for judging the conduct of God, instead of our conforming our views, as we ought, to the oracles of Scripture.[3]

On the other hand, in the following passages in which the same point is made, Bayle would appear to be at any rate more than half in earnest.

[1] Ibid., iv. 2991, II Éclaircissement.
[2] Ibid., iv. 2990, II Éclaircissement.
[3] Ibid., iii. 2128 a, s.v. Origène.

Our Reason is capable of nothing but the creation of a universal confusion and universal doubt: it has no sooner built up a system than it shows you the means of knocking it down. It is a veritable Penelope, who unpicks during the night the tapestry that she has woven during the day. Accordingly, the best use that one can make of philosophical studies is to recognise that it is a way that leads astray, and that we ought to look for another guide, which we shall find in the light of Revelation.[1]

Man's lot is so unfortunately placed that those lights which deliver him from one evil precipitate him into another. Cast out ignorance and barbarism, and you will overthrow superstition. . . . But, in the act of illuminating men's minds in regard to these [mental] disorders, you will be inspiring them with a passion for examining everything, they will apply the fine tooth-comb, and they will go into such subtleties that they will find nothing that will content their wretched Reason.[2]

[1] Ibid., i. 700 b, s.v. Bunel.   [2] Ibid., iv. 2688 b, s.v. Takiddin.

12

THE WORLD'S REJECTION OF EARLY MODERN WESTERN CHRISTIANITY

THE Portuguese and Spaniards, who were the first wave of Western conquerors of the World, were impelled, not only by a quest for wealth and power, but also by an eagerness to propagate the conquerors' ancestral Western form of Christianity. Their zeal for the propagation of Christianity was fanatical, in the sense of being hostile—or perhaps, rather, blind—to those elements in the essence of the other living higher religions that were either identical with, or complementary to, the essence of the religion of Western Christendom. Resemblances to Western Christian practice that were too striking to be ignored—as, for example, the similarity of the Mahayanian Buddhist to the Western Christian liturgy—were credited to the foresight and resourcefulness of the Devil. Foreseeing the eventual advent of Western Christian missionaries to give light to them that sit in darkness,[1] he had sought to render the heathen immune against salvation by inoculating them in advance, on homeopathic principles, with a counterfeit likeness of the true religion. The Portuguese and Spanish pioneers' minds were closed, but their missionary zeal was sincere and disinterested—as they demonstrated by continuing to proselytize even when this was manifestly detrimental to their economic and political interests. In this point the Portuguese and Spanish first wave of Western conquerors presents a contrast to the Dutch and British contingents in the second wave, which did not impinge forcefully upon the living non-Western civilizations of the Old World until after the secularizing revolution in the West in the seventeenth century of the Christian Era. The Protestant Christian Western empire-builders of the second wave deliberately subordinated religious missionary work to commercial and political considerations. They discouraged and discountenanced their own missionaries when these created

[1] Luke i. 79.

embarrassments for the Western trader and the Western administrator.

On the other hand the Early Modern Roman Catholic Western Christian missionaries gave a further proof of their sincerity in the lengths to which they went in translating Christianity into terms of their prospective converts' art, philosophy, and êthos. They recognized that, in coming on to these prospective converts' ground, they would be improving the chances of success for their own mission, and, in this cause they showed themselves ready to waive their natural human prejudice in favour of their ancestral Western manners and customs and to discard anything in Western Christianity that, as they saw it, was merely one of Christianity's accidental Western trappings and was not of the essence of Christianity itself.

This was not, of course, the first occasion on which Christian missionaries had been moved to practise a discriminating liberalism by their single-minded pursuit of their aim of preaching the Gospel to every creature.[1] In converting the Graeco-Roman Society in the course of the first five centuries of the Christian Era, the Early Christian Church had smoothed the convert's path by transferring local cults and festivals from pagan gods to Christian saints and by translating Christian beliefs into terms of Greek philosophy.[2] The sixteenth-century Jesuit Western Christian missionaries in India and Eastern Asia were following in Clement of Alexandria's footsteps, and were not striking out a new line without precedent in the Church's history. At the same time, their liberal attitude was not characteristic of the contemporary Roman Church as a whole, and was not even consistently maintained by the Jesuits themselves in all their mission-fields. Opposition on the part of the Franciscans and Dominicans finally ruined the Jesuits' work, and, with it, Christianity's prospects, first in Japan and then in China; and, in their dealings with non-Western Christians who were members of other churches— for example, the Monophysites in Abyssinia and the Nestorians in Southern India—the Jesuits were as intransigent as any of their fellow Roman Catholic missionaries in trying to coerce independent heterodox Christians into union with the Roman Church. Nevertheless, the vein of liberalism in the Early

[1] Mark xvi. 15.   [2] See Chapter 9, pp. 116-18, above.

Modern Western Roman Catholic missionaries' outlook and policy is noteworthy, both in itself and for its bearing on the future; for the shipwreck of this promising endeavour in the seventeenth century does not rule out the possibility that it might be repeated in the twentieth century with better success in the light of chastening experience.

In the realm of language, this liberal spirit declared itself in the Spanish dominions in the Americas and in the Philippines. The Roman Catholic Christian missionaries here disregarded the Spanish secular authorities' injunction to impose the Castilian language on the Indians as the medium of religious instruction. In their single-minded concern to preach the Gospel, the missionaries refused to be diverted by *raison d'état* from taking the shortest way to reach the Indians' hearts. Even in the Philippines, where there was no pre-Castilian *lingua franca*, they learnt, and preached in, the local languages; and they went much farther in the Viceroyalty of Peru, where a native *lingua franca* had already been put into currency by the Spanish conquerors' Inca predecessors. The missionaries in Peru reduced this Quichua *lingua franca* to writing in the Latin Alphabet; in A.D. 1576 a chair of Quichua was founded at the University of Lima, where it was maintained until A.D. 1770; and in 1680 a knowledge of Quichua was made an obligatory qualification for any candidate for ordination in Peru to the Roman Catholic Christian priesthood.

In the realm of Art, Christian iconography was translated into the Hindu style in India and into the East Asian style in China and Japan, while in Mexico the spirit of a benignant vein in Meso-American visual art that had always been subordinate and had latterly been almost entirely submerged under the savagery of an Aztec ascendancy was reproduced, and given predominance, in a cheerfully extravagant version of the Early Modern Western baroque style. In the ultra-Baroque village churches of the Puebla district the writer found himself in the presence of the aesthetic and emotional equivalent of a pre-Columbian fresco, depicting the merry paradise of the usually grim Mexican rain-god Tlaloc, which he had seen a few days before at Teotihuacán; and the sixteenth-century missionaries' success in divining and meeting their Indian peasant converts' spiritual needs was attested in A.D. 1953 by the loving care that the converts' descendants were still lavishing on these magnificent works of an exotic architecture and art that had been bequeathed to them by the Spanish friars who had arrived in the wake of the *conquistadores*.

In the realm of philosophy, the sixteenth-century Roman Catholic missionaries had translated Christian doctrine into Hindu and Confucian terms, as it had been translated into Hellenic terms by the second-century Alexandrian fathers; and there were Western philosopher-missionaries who had schooled themselves to write, dress, eat, and live like Hindu sanyasis or like Confucian litterati. A symbol of this liberalism, and an earnest of the success that it promised to achieve, was to be seen in the shrine of the Virgin of Guadalupe, on the outskirts of Mexico City, which has been mentioned in a previous context.[1]

It is all the more significant that even this liberally adapted version of Western Christianity was rejected wherever the non-Western party to the encounter had the power. It was perhaps not surprising that in Abyssinia, where a long-established Monophysite Christianity was not treated by the Roman Catholic missionaries with the considerateness that they showed to non-Christian philosophies in Eastern Asia and India, both the missionaries and all other Portuguese nationals should have been ejected within less than 100 years after they had been welcomed as providential liberators of Abyssinia from her Somali Muslim invaders. But it is remarkable that, in the same decade, and after just about the same number of years of probation, the Roman Catholic missionaries and their lay fellow-Westerners should have been ejected likewise from Japan, and eventually have been ejected also from China and from Independent India, and should have held their ground only in Portuguese India and in the Spanish Empire, where the missionaries had the backing of irresistible political and, in the last resort, military force.

The ostensible reason for this rejection of Western Christianity by non-Western peoples in the seventeenth century was the association of the missionaries' work with Western military and political aggression. Hideyoshi and his Tokugawa successors proscribed Roman Catholic Western Christianity in Japan because they feared that the Japanese converts to it might be made to serve as 'a fifth column' whose support would enable

[1] See Chapter 4, pp. 52-3, above.

the United Kingdom of Portugal and Spain to conquer Japan, while they felt confident that Japan would be impregnable against the assaults of even the most formidable concentration of Western power if the assailants had no collaborators inside Japan's defences. Thereafter the Bakufu tolerated the presence in Japan of Dutch Protestant Western Christians only on the two conditions that they should submit to being interned on an islet and that they should refrain from attempting to win any Japanese converts for their own version of Christianity. Roman Catholic Western Christianity was subsequently proscribed in China because the Pope and his representatives in Eastern Asia, in their anxiety to make sure that the Jesuits' liberalism should not compromise the Church's theism, had been so tactless as to lay down the law to the Emperor in regard to the meaning of some hallowed terms in the classical Chinese vocabulary. A deeper reason for the rejection of Western Christianity was the intrinsic difficulty and painfulness of any conversion from one way of life to another. It remained painful and difficult even when the missionaries had met the converts nearly half way by translating as much of Christianity as possible into the converts' own terms.

Nevertheless, the wholeheartedness of the conversion of at least a nucleus of the converts to Roman Catholic Christianity in Japan was attested by the survival of a 'faithful remnant' underground for 231 years (A.D. 1637-1868) during which the penalty for detection was death. In Mexico, again, the Indians, though they had been converted to Christianity by force and had never been given freedom to reject it, displayed their voluntary attachment to it, 300 years later, in their resistance to the militant anti-clericalism which was in the ascendant during one stage of the long revolution that started in Mexico in A.D. 1910. In A.D. 1953 the Indian peasants were once more free to show their pride in their village churches and their zest for the Roman Catholic Christian liturgy. In the same year, however, the writer found a different spirit prevailing among the Chamulas—a highland people on the remote Las Casas plateau, in the south-western corner of the Mexican Republic, where Spanish military and political power had been so near to the end of their tether that the local tribesmen had been able to hold their own.

Even in 1953 the city of Las Casas, inhabited by Ladino descendants of sixteenth-century Spanish and Tlascalec colonists, felt like an island of Western Civilization set in an alien sea; and the short drive from this insulated Western city to the village capital of the unassimilated Chamula tribe carried the visitor into another world. Among the buildings round the village green, the most prominent was a fine Baroque church; but there was no tabernacle on the altar; the priest from Las Casas ventured to come to officiate there on sufferance not more than once or twice a year, so it was said; and the church was in the hands of shamans who, for decency's sake, were called 'sacristans'. The effigies of the Christian saints on their litters had been transfigured into representations of pre-Christian gods in the eyes of their Chamula worshippers, who, squatting on the rush-covered floor, were making weird music on outlandish-looking instruments. The crosses planted in the open had turned into living presences that were aniconic embodiments of the rain-god. In short, in Chamula the West's sixteenth-century assault in the form of a Roman Catholic Christian mission had been successfully repelled, and it remained to be seen what would be the outcome of the West's twentieth-century return to the charge. This post-Christian Western assault upon the Chamula had been mounted in the brand-new co-operative store and brand-new clinic by which the de-Christianized church was now flanked. Would Western medicine and Western business organization prove more effective than Western religion as engines for capturing this obstinately pagan fastness?

In the Hispanicized regions of Asia and the New World, such stubborn pockets of resistance as Chamula were rare by the year A.D. 1956; and, wherever Spanish and Portuguese rule had been made effective, as it had been at Goa as well as in most parts of the Spanish Empire of the Indies, the Indians had not been given the option of rejecting either Roman Catholic Christianity or the secular elements in the Early Modern version of the Western Civilization. They had been compelled to take them both, and to take them at one bite; and the difference in the sequel here and elsewhere suggests that, if one is going to have to receive an alien civilization at all, it is less damaging to receive it all at once than to be dosed with it in successive instalments. The forcibly and abruptly converted Asian and American subjects of the Portuguese and Spanish crowns took their compulsory new religion to their hearts and made something of their own out of it; and one consequence was that the original barrier between conquerors and conquered was overcome. Community of religion opened the way for inter-marriage, and the two societies merged into one, in which the social and cultural framework was Western, but in which a good deal of Indian wine had been poured into the Western bottles.

The sequel was different, and less happy, as we shall see, in those non-Western societies that came under French, Dutch, and British rule or influence after the secularization of Western life in the seventeenth century. Here there was no attempt either to impart or to receive any more of the Western Civilization than its secular side, and, even of this, the recipients usually sought, at the outset, to take no more than the military technique. This half-heartedness condemned the partial converts to a post-Christian Western Civilization to go through a protracted involuntary revolution in which they found themselves compelled to follow up their initial reception of the West's military technique by adopting one more element of a secularized Western Civilization after another—and this without its leading to a union between the two societies. The recipients gradually became estranged from their own ancestral culture without ever coming to feel that the progressively adopted Western culture had become wholly theirs. The results were a schism in Society and a schism in the Soul that have remained unhealed so far.

12 ANNEXE

TWO SEVENTEENTH-CENTURY WESTERN OBSERVERS' VIEWS OF WESTERN CHRISTIANITY AS AN INSTRUMENT OF WESTERN IMPERIALISM

The extent to which Locke and Bayle had detached themselves from the religious fanaticism that had been common to Protestant and Catholic Western Christians in the Early Modern Age of Western history is revealed in their ability to place themselves imaginatively in the position of the contemporary non-Western societies and governments and to look through their eyes at the West's impact upon them.

Without taking the liberty of researching into the reasons that may actuate God, in His wisdom, in permitting at one time what He does not permit at another, it can be said that the Christianity of the sixteenth century had no right to hope for the same favour or the same protection from God as the Christianity of the first three centuries. This was a benign, gentle, patient religion that recommended subjects to be submissive to their princes and that did not aspire to raise itself to the throne by means of rebellions. But the Christianity that was preached to the Infidels in the sixteenth century was no longer like that: it was a sanguinary, murderous religion, which had been hardened to the shedding of blood for some five or six centuries past. It had contracted a very long-ingrained habit of maintaining itself, and of seeking aggrandisement, by putting to the sword anything that offered to resist it. Faggots, executioners, the frightful tribunal of the Inquisition, the Crusades, papal bulls inciting subjects to rebel, seditious preachers, conspiracies, assassinations of princes—these were the regular means that this sixteenth-century Christianity employed against all who would not submit to its orders. Had it, then, any right to count on receiving the blessing that Heaven had granted to the Primitive Church, to the Gospel of peace, patience, and gentleness?

No doubt, the best course that the Japanese could have followed would have been to become converts to the true God; but, since they had not sufficient spiritual lights to lead them to renounce their own false religion, there was no alternative left to them but the choice between either persecuting or else being persecuted. They could not preserve their established government or their established religious cult unless they could get rid of the Christians; for, sooner or later, the Christians would have brought both the one and the other to ruin. They would have armed all their neophytes; they would have introduced into the country the armed assistance and the inhuman principles of the Spaniards; and, by main force of killing and hanging, as they had done in America, they would have brought the whole of Japan under their yoke. So, when one looks at the situation from a purely political point of view, one has to admit that the persecution which the Christians suffered in that country was a legitimate application of the means enjoined by prudence for forestalling the overthrow of the monarchy and the rape of a commonwealth.[1]

---

[1] Bayle, P., *Dictionaire*, 3rd ed., ii. 1533 a and b, s.v. Japon.

An inconsiderable and weak number of Christians, destitute of everything, arrive in a Pagan country; these foreigners beseech the inhabitants, by the bowels of humanity, that they would succour them with the necessaries of life; those necessaries are given them, habitations are granted, and they all join together and grow up into one body of people. The Christian religion by this means takes root in that country and spreads itself, but does not suddenly grow the strongest. While things are in this condition, peace, friendship, faith, and equal justice are preserved amongst them. At length the magistrate becomes a Christian, and by that means their party becomes the most powerful. Then immediately all compacts are to be broken, all civil rights to be violated, that idolatry may be extirpated; and, unless these innocent Pagans, strict observers of the rules of equity and the law of Nature, and no ways offending against the laws of the society—I say, unless they will forsake their ancient religion and embrace a new and strange one, they are to be turned out of the lands and possessions of their forefathers, and perhaps deprived of life itself. Then, at last, it appears what zeal for the Church, joined with the desire of dominion, is capable to produce, and how easily the pretence of religion, and of the care of souls, serves for a cloak to covetousness, rapine, and ambition.[1]

What could be better calculated to make the Christian religion odious in the eyes of all the peoples of the World than the spectacle of Christians first insinuating themselves on the footing of people who ask for nothing beyond the liberty to propound their doctrine and then having the hardihood to pull down the temples of the native religion of the country and to refuse to rebuild them when the Government gives the order. Will not this give the Infidels ground for saying: 'At the beginning, these people ask for nothing except bare toleration; but, in a little while, they will be wanting to participate with us in public office and employment, and then to become our masters. At the beginning, they consider themselves very happy if we do not burn them alive, then very ill-used if they enjoy fewer privileges than other people, and then, again, very ill-used if they do not enjoy a monopoly of dominion. For a time they are like Caesar, who wanted merely to be under no master; and then they become like Pompey, who wanted to have no equals'. . . . These are the inevitable inconveniences to which people expose themselves when they hotly maintain that the power of the secular arm ought to be used for the establishment of orthodoxy.[2]

[1] Locke, John, *A Letter concerning Toleration* (first published in A.D. 1689).
[2] Bayle, op. cit., i. 10 b, s.v. Abdas.

The most extreme advocates of toleration . . . do not know how to reconcile the Emperor of China's edict with the sagacity with which the Emperor is credited. I am speaking of the Edict of Toleration which the Emperor has made for the benefit of the Christians and of which so good an account has been given by one of the Jesuit fathers. The advocates of toleration believe that a sagacious prince would not have granted to the Pope's missionaries and to their neophytes a title to enjoy freedom of conscience without having first informed himself about their principles of conversion and about the way in which these principles have been applied by their predecessors. If, on this point, he had taken steps to obtain all the clarifications that were demanded by sound policy, he would never have allowed to the missionaries what he has granted to them in fact; he would have known that these are gentry who maintain that Jesus Christ commands them to 'compel to come in'— that is to say, to banish, imprison, torture, kill, and dragoon all who refuse to become converts to the Gospel, and to dethrone princes who oppose their progress. It is impossible to see how the Emperor of China could have cleared himself of the charge of having shown an inexcusable imprudence if, knowing this, he had granted the Edict all the same. So we must save his honour by supposing that he knew nothing about it—though even this defence leaves him culpable for having so signally failed to inform himself sufficiently of something that it was very necessary for him to know. As far as can be seen, he will not live long enough to have occasion to rue his negligence; but it would be rash to guarantee that his descendants will not execrate his memory, for possibly they may find themselves obliged, unexpectedly soon, to resist dangerous seditions stirred up by the adherents of the new religion, and to cut their throats as the only alternative to having their own throats cut by them. Possibly it will be a case of playing the game of Greek meeting Greek (*jouer au plus fin*), as it was the other day in Japan.[1]

[1] Bayle, op. cit., iii. 1991 a and b, s.v. Milton.

13

THE BREAKDOWN OF THE WESTERN CHRISTIAN WAY OF LIFE AND THE SEVENTEENTH-CENTURY WESTERN REACTION AGAINST THE WEST'S CHRISTIAN HERITAGE

THE distinctive Medieval Western Christian way of life began to break down under the pontificate of Pope Innocent III (*fungebatur* A.D. 1198-1216), after a period of growth which had gone forward for about a century and a half. A post-Modern Westerner, looking back at the Western Middle Ages in their flower from the morrow of a Modern Age that deemed itself to be superior and ended in worse confusion and disappointment, may be in danger, at this remove, of seeing the medieval Western scene in an ideal light that would have surprised a contemporary viewing this scene prosaically at close quarters. Yet, when due allowance has been made for this possibility of undue idealization, the Medieval Western Christian way of life still looks like one of Mankind's rarer achievements; and its genius seems to have been a delicate but creative balance between authority and liberty. On the social plane this was a balance between the moral authority of the Apostle at Rome and the political liberty of parochial princes and city-states. That supple constitution endowed the Medieval Western Christian Commonwealth with a social diversity in unity which a contemporary Eastern Orthodox Christendom failed to attain—and, in failing, condemned itself to have to choose between the two grim alternatives of life-in-death under a totalitarian oecumenical empire and a war to the death between totalitarian parochial states. On the intellectual plane the Western Respublica Christiana was a balance between the theological authority of established Western Christian dogma and the philosophical liberty, within this theological framework, for schoolmen to cultivate Aristotelian philosophy and science, not only in secular studies, but even within the domain of Theology itself.

This promising medieval Western way of life was broken up

by successive shocks to a faith in these religious institutions on which their survival depended. The first of these shocks was administered by the thirteenth-century conflict between the Papacy and the Emperor Frederick II; for this conflict revealed the Papacy to Western eyes in the new and distressing light of a self-centred institution, fighting nakedly for supremacy in a struggle for power and falling into the Antichristian sins of implacability and *hybris* in its malign persecution of Frederick's hapless heirs. The second shock was administered by the fourteenth-century 'Babylonish Captivity', at Avignon, in which the Papacy sought compensation for the political fall which had been the nemesis of its spiritual pride by building up an unedifying mercenary-minded financial organization on an oecumenical scale. The third shock was administered by 'the Great Schism', in which the Papacy came to stand for the antithesis of that unity of Western Christendom for which it had not ceased to stand, even when it had been translated from Rome, where it had fought and finally defeated the Hohenstaufen Power, to Avignon, where it had lain under the shadow of the French Crown. Avignon had, indeed, been a geographically more convenient seat than Rome for a Papacy that had not yet come to be divided against itself, since the Rhône Valley was much nearer than the Tiber Valley was to the centre of the Western Christendom of the fourteenth century; and, though the Papacy's prestige had been raised by the Pope's re-migration from Avignon to Rome in A.D. 1376, this moral gain was far more than offset by the scandal of the outbreak of the schism in A.D. 1378.

The fourth shock was administered by the fifteenth-century conflict between the Papacy and a Conciliar Movement in which the local representatives of the Western Christian Church in the parochial states of the Western Christian Commonwealth sought to restore the ecclesiastical unity of the West which the Great Schism had shattered. The remedy proposed by the fathers of the Western Church in successive oecumenical councils was to underpin a reunified Papal Monarchy by giving it a new constitutional foundation on a parliamentary representative basis, for which there were living Western models in the oecumenical representative government of some of the religious orders and in the parochial representative government of the parliamentary secular kingdoms. But this movement for saving the essence of the Papal Church of Gregory VII and Innocent III was defeated by a fifteenth-century Papacy's determination to convert its shaken moral presidency of a Western Christian Commonwealth into an oecumenical ecclesiastical autocracy on the model of the parochial secular North Italian autocracies of the day. Since these were successful copies, on a miniature scale, of the Emperor Frederick II's abortive re-evocation, in the West, of a Diocletianic secular autocracy on the grand scale, the fifteenth-century Papacy was re-minting itself, at one remove, in the image of the thirteenth-century Papacy's arch-enemy.

The nemesis of the defeat of the Conciliar Movement was the Protestant Reformation, and the outbreak of this administered a fifth shock to Western souls which was the death of the Unitary Western Christian Church. The Great Schism, shocking though it was, had been a temporary personal struggle between two or three rival claimants to a Papal throne that was recognized, by all concerned, as being unitary in principle. But the Reformation resulted in a permanent break-up of the Western Christian Church into a Tridentine Roman Catholic Church and a number of Protestant churches that was as numerous as the number of the parochial states in which these churches were respectively established. In the Roman Catholic parochial states, to a hardly lesser degree *de facto* than in their Protestant neighbours, the secular sovereign now made himself master in his own house on the ecclesiastical as well as on the secular plane. The nemesis of the Reformation was the bout of Western wars of religion, and these fratricidal wars administered a sixth shock. They exhibited Catholics and Protestants in France, the Netherlands, Germany, and Ireland, and rival sects of Protestants in England and Scotland, in the brutal act of trying to suppress one another by force of arms. It was a still more lamentable spectacle to see Religion being used as a tool for the furtherance of mundane military and political purposes, and to recognize that this was a consequence of Religion's own unprincipled attempt to use War and Politics as weapons in ecclesiastical struggles for supremacy.

A simultaneous shock was administered by the renaissance of Hellenism in the West. The resuscitated ghost of Hellenism was accepted, in a still authoritarian-minded Early Modern Age of Western history, as an authority independent of, and therefore necessarily in rivalry with, the authority of the Western Christian Church. In the Middle Ages the Western Church had managed to harness to her own chariot the re-suscitated ghost of Aristotle and to exorcise the resuscitated ghost of the Roman Empire; but in the Early Modern Age she was worsted by the pagan spirit of a classical Latin and Greek literature and an Hellenic parochial state. This political ghost of the dynamic Hellenism of a pre-Alexandrine Age rose up first in Northern and Central Italy and then, from the close of the fifteenth century onwards, in Transalpine and Trans-marine Western Europe; and, it has been the most malignant of all the Hellenic *numina* by which the Hellenistic Christian Civilization of the West has been haunted. For, in the realm of Politics, the renaissance of Hellenism has been more persistent than it has been in the realms of Literature and the Visual Arts. In the realm of Literature the ghost which fifteenth-century popes and cardinals had failed to reconcile with a traditional Western Christianity was laid before the end of the seventeenth century, in 'the Battle of the Books', by Trans-alpine prophets of Technology. In the realm of the Visual Arts it was laid at the turn of the eighteenth and nineteenth centuries in the Romantic Movement. But, in the realm of Politics, it haunts us still; and we do not yet know whether two world wars have been enough to quench this baleful *revenant's* thirst for blood.

This, in outline, is the historical background of the moral and intellectual discredit into which the West's Christian heritage has fallen in the West's own estimation since the seventeenth century. The grounds of this revulsion were partly moral and partly intellectual. The moral reason for it was that the West's religious dissensions had bred devastating, yet inconclusive, political and military strife in a spirit of hatred, malice, and all uncharitableness, and this in unavowed pursuit of sordid worldly objectives that were in scandalous contradic-tion with Christianity's high spiritual professions. The in-tellectual reason was that the traditional Western Christian panorama of the Universe, which had been built up out of an amalgam of Christian myth, Jewish scripture, and Greek philosophy and science by a series of great composers, from St. Paul to St. Thomas Aquinas inclusive, had ceased to command unquestioning assent in Western minds.

This intellectual revulsion against a traditional Western Christianity potently reinforced the moral revulsion's effect. But it may be doubted whether intellectual misgivings alone would have availed to alienate Western souls from the Western Christian tradition so rapidly and decisively. The outburst of moral indignation at the iniquity of the Wars of Religion was the explosion that blew the irreparable breach in the massive fortifications of the Medieval Western Christian *Weltanschauung*. One practical expression of this moral revolt was a deliberate transference of seventeenth-century Western Man's spiritual treasure from an incurably polemical Theology to an apparently non-controversial Natural Science; and the consequent progressive demolition of the intellectual structure of Medieval Western Christianity was thus an after-effect of a previous revolt against its moral pretensions.

13 ANNEXE

CONTEMPORARY EXPRESSIONS OF THE SEVENTEENTH-CENTURY WEST'S REACTION AGAINST THE WEST'S CHRISTIAN HERITAGE

A. MORAL INDIGNATION

(i) *The Devastating Effects of the Wars of Religion*

'Tis zeal for opinions that hath fill'd our Hemispheer with smoke and darkness, and by a dear experience we know the fury of those flames it hath kindled. Had not Heaven prevented, they had turn'd our Paradise into a Desert. . . . If our Returning Lord shall scarce find faith on Earth, where will he look for charity? . . . The union of a sect within it self is a pitiful charity: it's no concord of Christians, but a conspiracy against Christ. . . . What eagerness in the profession of disciplinarian uncertainties, when the love of God and our neighbour, those Evangelical unquestionables, want that fervent ardor.[1]

Rulers ought to employ a page to repeat to them every morning: 'See that you do not torment anyone on account of his religious opinions, and that you do not extend the power of the sword to

[1] Glanvill, J., *The Vanity of Dogmatising* (London 1661, Eversden), pp. 229-31.

touch the conscience. Look at what Charles IX and his successor gained by doing that; it is a real miracle that the French Monarchy did not perish on the altar of their Catholicism. Such miracles will not happen every day; pray don't put your trust in that. They would not let the January Edict alone, and then, after more than thirty years of devastation, after thousands and thousands of torrents of blood had been poured out, and thousands and thousands of acts of treachery and incendiarism had been perpetrated, they had to grant an edict that was still more favourable.'

Those responsible for the conduct of ecclesiastical affairs are the second class of people who ought to cultivate a lively memory of the sixteenth century. When one talks to them of toleration, they fancy that what they are hearing is the most frightful and most monstrous of all conceivable dogmas; and, in order to interest the secular arm in their passions, they exclaim that it would mean depriving the public authorities of the fairest ornament in their crown if they were not to be allowed at least to inflict the pains of imprisonment and banishment on heretics. If, though, they examined carefully the consequences that are to be feared from a war of religion, they would be more moderate. 'So you do not want,' one might say to them, 'to see this sect worshipping God after its own fashion and preaching its own views; but take care: if it comes to drawing swords instead of just speaking and writing against your dogmas, take care that this sect does not overthrow your temples and put you in jeopardy of your very lives. What did you gain in France and in Holland in pressing for persecution? Put no trust in your superiority in numbers. Your princes have neighbours, and consequently your sectaries will not lack either protectors or assistance, even if they be Turks.'

Finally, I would beg those restless theologians that take such pleasure in innovations to keep on casting their eyes back to the wars of religion of the sixteenth century. Of these, the Reformers were the innocent cause: no consideration must give them pause, because, according to their principles, there was no middle way: all Papists had either to be abandoned to eternal damnation or else to be converted to Protestantism. But, when people who are persuaded that an error is not damning still refuse to respect the *uti possidetis* and prefer disturbing the public peace to keeping their private notions to themselves, such conduct is detestable beyond words. They ought to consider the consequences of their novelties and of their assault upon established custom. If they can bring themselves to embark on this course without being constrained to it by absolute necessity, they must have the heart of a tiger.[1]

[1] Bayle, P., *Dictionaire*, 3rd ed., iii. 1845 a and b, s.v. Macon.

The question, raised by Brantôme, about the inconsistency involved in burning a hundred heretics and at the same time protecting the same heresy's nest, centre, and metropolis, is embarrassing for all those who do not realize that this is one of the commonest scenes in the grand comedy of the World. This is the play that princes have made with Religion at all times, and they are still playing this game today. They persecute at home the faith whose triumph they are promoting abroad to the best of their ability. You must not take this as evidence that these princes are utterly indifferent to Religion. That is not so: they are often religious to the point of bigotry. The truth is that the temporal advantage of their country is still more precious to them than the reign of Jesus Christ. I will not allow that the Pope himself is an exception to this law. I fancy that His Holiness was hardly better pleased than Francis I was at the Emperor's successes against the Protestant League.[1]

It is certain that a union between the Lutherans and the Calvinists would have been achieved long ago if this had depended on nobody but the princes; but, as this affair is at the mercy of the theologians, it has never been able to have success, and never will be able, as far as one can foresee.[2]

(ii) Religious Leaders must be Violent-minded

Innate character is nearly always the first and the principal determinant of the conduct even of those persons who do God's work here below. There are people who maintain that it was necessary for Luther, Calvin, Farel, and some of the others to be hot-tempered, choleric, and full of bile. Without this, so they say, they never could have overcome the resistance [that they encountered].[3]

We may marvel here at one feature in the destiny of Man. His virtues are apt to have consequences that are tainted with a tinge of vice; they have their drawbacks. On the other hand, his bad qualities produce good results in a number of situations. Modesty, moderation, and love of peace create, in the most scholarly minds, a fund of fair-mindedness that renders such minds in some sense luke-warm and irresolute. [By contrast,] pride and spleen may create, in the mind of a great authority, such a passionate conviction that he will not feel the slightest doubt, so that there will be nothing that he will not dare and will not suffer in the cause of promoting his opinions and making them prevail.[4]

It is not in the temporal interest of a religious communion that all

[1] Bayle, P., *Dictionaire*, 3rd ed., ii. 1212 a, s.v. François I.
[2] Ibid., ii. 1519 b, s.v. Hottinger.   [3] Ibid., ii. 1152 b, s.v. Farel.
[4] Ibid., iii. 1965 a and b, s.v. Melanchthon.

its members should be reasonable-minded. The violent spirits, who adhere to it solely out of factiousness, perform for it, humanly speaking, a thousand valuable services. So it is useful that hot-heads of this sort should be found in its ranks; this is a necessary evil.[1]

These turbulent zealots who produce a thousand disorders in a state through their eagerness to exercise dominion over the masses, and who are not sorry to get themselves persecuted, in order that the populace, through its sympathy with them in their punishment, may be led to revolt and so to complete what the zealots' intrigues have begun.[2]

(iii) *Religious Controversialists must be Unfair-minded*

Is it not true that the spirit of ardent partisanship, which usually prevails among journalists (*nouvellistes*), also prevails among most people who have a passionate devotion for their religion?[3]

Extreme zealots are apt to become credulous and suspicious, and are prone to conceive a violent animosity against people who are suspect in their eyes.[4]

Zeal sometimes has the effect of leading people into persuading themselves that a heretic is capable of the most infamous plots; and from this persuasion they easily pass over into another: they imagine that the heretic is actually perpetrating all the machinations of which they have judged him to be capable.[5]

This passion [*Odium Theologicum*], which has long since become proverbial, finds heresies wherever it desires to find them. . . . Injustice is not the only [moral fault] that is displayed by people who are possessed by this passion; duplicity over weights and measures is another of their besetting iniquities. Ask them to censure their agitators and their hounds; make it impossible for them not to see the justice of your cause: they will either turn a deaf ear or else put you off with some kind of patter. These are the occasions on which their charity 'suffereth long' and 'thinketh no evil'.[6]

(iv) *Power breeds Intolerance*

It is worthy to be observed and lamented that the most violent of these defenders of the truth, the opposers of errors, the exclaimers against schism, do hardly ever let loose this their zeal for God, with which they are so warmed and inflamed, unless where they have the civil magistrate on their side. But, as soon as ever court favour has

[1] Bayle, P., *Dictionaire*, 3rd. ed., ii. 1029 a and b, s.v. Drusius.
[2] Ibid., i. 492 b, s.v. Beda.   [3] Ibid., iii. 2221 a, s.v. Pellisson.
[4] Ibid., i. 520 b, s.v. Bérenger.   [5] Ibid., ii. 1089 b, s.v. Episcopius.
[6] Ibid., i. 418 a, s.v. Baius.

given them the better end of the staff, and they begin to feel themselves the stronger, then presently peace and charity are to be laid
aside. Otherwise they are religiously to be observed. Where they
have not the power to carry on persecution and to become masters,
there they desire to live upon fair terms, and preach up toleration.[1]

One finds that, as soon as the Christians were in a position to
persecute, they levelled the same reproach against religious error
that Paganism had once levelled against Christianity. They laid
to Paganism's door the failure of harvests and abnormalities in the
weather. . . . One is bound to say that there are some faults that are
displayed by religious sects, not in consequence of their being systems
of belief, but in consequence of their being in power. This is why the
same religious communions change their spirit and their policy
according as they either gain ascendancy or lose it.[2]

His [Scipio Lentulus's] apologia for the edict that the Grisons
had published against heretics ought not to be held to be surprising
on the ground that he himself had suffered persecution in the past.
There is nothing more common than to find religious refugees
ringing the tocsin against dissenters.[3]

He [? Jurieu] strongly disapproved, when in France, of the
authority of the secular arm being involved; and then, when in
Holland, he strongly disapproves when he is told that it must not be
invoked.[4]

Unhappy advocates of intolerance! Your malady must indeed be
a bizarre one, considering that it is proof against being cured by the
application of the *lex talionis*.[5]

B. INTELLECTUAL DOUBTS

(i) *Human Beings are easily taken in*

In matters of Religion, it is very easy to deceive Mankind, and
very difficult to undeceive them. Man loves his prejudices, and he
can always find leaders who will indulge him in this foible. . . .
These leaders make their business pay in the coin of authority as
well as monetary profit. The more disinterested natures realize,
when the malady has become inveterate, that the remedy would be
worse than the disease. These dare not heal the wound; the others
would not wish to heal it. This is how the abuse perpetuates itself.
Dishonest people protect it; honest people tolerate it.[6]

[1] Locke, John, *A Letter concerning Toleration* (first published in A.D. 1689).
[2] Bayle, op. cit., iv. 2804 b, s.v. Vergerius.
[3] Ibid., ii. 1680, s.v. Lentulus.　　　　　　[4] Ibid., i. 330 a, s.v. Arius.
[5] Ibid., iii. 2069 b, s.v. Navarre (Marguérite de Valois, Reine de, fille
de Henri II).
[6] Ibid., i. 89 b, s.v. Agar.

There are gentry for whom it is a great piece of good fortune that the people never bothers to call them to account on matters of doctrine, and, indeed, is not even capable of doing so.[1]

The peoples show excessive indulgence to gentry who keep dissension going by publications that are violent, vituperative, and full of chicaneries, and who do this under a false pretence of zeal. . . . So long as one finds the people following the party that makes the most noise and the greatest hubbub, one has to take it that the malady is incurable.[2]

A very potent mechanism for mounting great revolutions is to prepare the peoples for them by interpretations of the Apocalypse, uttered with an air of inspiration and enthusiasm. This is what has given the enemies of Protestantism an excuse for saying that all the work on the Apocalypse that has been done by Protestant authors has had no other purpose than to foment a general European war by inspiring princes, who would never have thought of this for themselves, with a desire to profit by the opportunities that wars bring with them. Comenius has not been entirely immune against this suspicion.[3]

There are people who have taken the line that the patrons of these diviners have made an error in their timing, and that an age which is as philosophical as the present one is not a propitious time for bringing these gentry on to the stage. This view has, from some points of view, something to be said for it, but, when all the circumstances are taken into account, their argument turns out not to hold water. There is, I admit, a larger number of private individuals today than in the past who are capable of holding their ground against the flood and putting up a fight against illusions; but, save for this, I maintain that our age is just as easily taken in as its predecessors.[4]

The visionaries and fanatics of the future have nothing to fear. They have merely to utter brazenly whatever comes into their heads, provided that they have sufficient address to accommodate themselves to the passions of the hour. They will not have the laughers on their side; but they will have supporters who will more than outweigh the laughers.[5]

(ii) *The Naïveté of the Zealots*

Each imagines that the truths of his own religion are so clear that the able representatives of another party cannot have failed to see them

[1] Bayle, op. cit., i. 390 b, s.v. Augustin.

[2] Ibid., i. 171 b, s.v. Alting (Jacques) (cp. i. 110 a, s.v. Agrippa).

[3] Ibid., ii. 1018 b, s.v. Drabicius (cp. ii. 1374 a, s.v. Hadrien, and ii. 1484 b, s.v. Hoe).

[4] Ibid., i. 6 a, s.v. Abaris.   [5] Ibid., ii. 1019, s.v. Drabicius.

and can be deterred from making an open confession of this by nothing but considerations of a human order.[1]

Where can one find anyone who does not hold, by force of habit, that the same things are most just when he is inflicting them on someone else and most unjust when they are being inflicted on him? When this spirit is so rife, you need have no fear that the multiplicity of sects will create many sceptics. Everyone, whatever happens, will stick tight to the cause that he has made his own.[2]

(iii) *Christianity must depend on Revelation, since Manichaeism stands to Reason*

There is no system which is exempt from having to satisfy two conditions in order to be accepted as valid. The first condition is that the ideas in it should be clear; the second is that it should be able to account for the facts of experience.... Man alone—Man, who is the masterpiece among all the visible works of creation—is a very great stumbling-block to a belief in the unity of God.... Man is wicked and unhappy: every one of us knows this from what goes on within his own self, as well as from the dealings that he is obliged to have with his neighbour.[3]

Who will not be overcome by astonishment and dismay as he contemplates the destiny of our Reason? Here are the Manichaeans succeeding, on an hypothesis that is patently absurd and self-contradictory, in explaining the facts of experience a hundred times better than these are explained by the orthodox on the postulate of a principle that is infinitely good as well as omnipotent, though this postulate is manifestly just and necessary and alone in accordance with the truth.[4]

The [Christian] dogma that the Manichaeans attack ought to be recorded by the Orthodox as a truth of fact which has been clearly revealed; and, since, after all, we [Christians] should be compelled to agree that we do not at all understand either the causes or the reasons of this [mystery], it is better to admit this from the start, and to be content with that—letting the philosophers' objections run their course like the empty sophistries that they are, and meeting them with no retort but silence behind the shield of the Faith.[5]

It must be admitted that this false doctrine [of two principles, one good and the other bad], which is much older than Mani, and which is untenable as soon as one accepts Holy Scripture either completely or [even] partially, would be rather difficult to refute if it were

[1] Ibid., i. 37 b, s.v. Abulpharage.
[2] Ibid., ii. 1825 a, s.v. Luther.
[3] Ibid., iii. 1899 a and b, s.v. Manichéens.
[4] Ibid., iii. 2205 a, s.v. Pauliciens. [5] Ibid., iii. 2214 a, s.v. Pauliciens.

championed by pagan philosophers who were veteran adepts in the art of disputation. It was lucky that St. Augustine, who was so well acquainted with all the twists and turns of this controversy, should have abandoned Manichaeism; for he would have had the ability to rid it of its grosser errors and to forge the rest into a system which, in his hands, would have been most embarrassing for orthodox [Christians].[1]

The obligation that is incumbent on the Roman Church to respect the system of St. Augustine involves it in an embarrassment that has a decidedly ridiculous side.... The physical predetermination of the Thomists, the necessity of St. Augustine, and the necessity of the Jansenists are all, at bottom, the same thing; and yet the Thomists disown the Jansenists, while both maintain with one accord that it is a calumny to accuse them of teaching the same doctrine as Calvin.[2]

(iv) *If Christian Theology is True, God is a Monster*

The disputes that have raised their heads since the Reformation among Christians in the West have shown so clearly the *impasse* into which Christians bring themselves, when they attempt to solve the difficulties about the origin of evil, that a Manichaean would be [even] more formidable [an antagonist for us] today than he was in the past. Today he would refute us all by playing us off one against the other. You have exhausted, he would say, all the forces of your intelligence. You have invented *Scientia Media* to serve as a *deus ex machinâ* come to clear up your chaos. But this invention is a chimaera.... It does not prevent all Man's sins and sufferings from still being products of the free choice of God. It does not prevent us from being able to compare God (*absit verbo blasphemia*, [see marginal note (50)])[3] to a mother who, knowing for certain that her daughter would sacrifice her maidenhood if, at such and such a place and at such and such an hour, she were to be solicited by such and such a seducer, did nevertheless arrange for the meeting, bring her daughter to the trysting-place, and leave her there after putting her on her honour.[4]

[1] Bayle, op cit., iii. 1897-1900, s.v. Manichéens.
[2] Ibid., i. 390 and 390 b, s.v. Augustin.
[3] 'This comparison has shocked a number of religious-minded people; but I beg them here to take into consideration the fact that I am simply paying the Jesuits and Arminians back in their own coin. These gentlemen draw the most horrible comparisons in the world between the god of the Calvinists, as they are pleased to put it, and Tiberius, Caligula, and so on. It is a good thing to show them that one can meet them in battle with weapons like their own.'
[4] Ibid., iii. 2207 b, s.v. Pauliciens.

Some people say that God has permitted sin because He could not have prevented it without trenching on the free will that He had given to Man—a gift that was the finest of all that He had conferred on him. Those who say this are exposing themselves egregiously. . . . We do not need to have read Seneca's fine treatise *De Beneficiis*; we know by the light of nature that it is of the essence of being a benefactor that he should not bestow graces which he knows that the proposed recipient would abuse so thoroughly that their only effect would be to ruin him. . . . No good mother who had given her daughters permission to go to a dance would fail to cancel this permission if she knew for certain that, if they went, they would be violated and would lose their virginity; and any mother who, knowing for certain that this could not fail to happen, did let them go to the dance all the same, after having contented herself with putting them on their good behaviour and with threatening them with disgrace if they came home other than they had been when they had started out—well, any mother who behaved like that would, at the very least, incur well-deserved censure for having shown no love either for her daughters or for the virtue of chastity.[1]

If you say that God has permitted sin in order to manifest His wisdom, which shines out more clearly in the disorders that human malice produces every day than it would do in a state of innocence, the answer that you will receive is that this is tantamount to comparing the Deity either to the father of a family who would let his children break their legs in order to bring to the notice of a whole town his skill in mending broken bones, or else to a monarch who would let seditions and disorders grow, throughout his dominions, in order to gain the glory of having put them right. . . . Let us imagine to ourselves two princes, one of whom lets his subjects fall into distress in order to extricate them from it when they have wallowed in it sufficiently, while the other prince always conserves his subjects in a state of prosperity. Is not this second prince better than the other? Is not he, in truth, the more kind-hearted of the two?[2]

If Christian theology—at least as interpreted by the Augustinian-Calvinist-Jansenist school—is true, God is a monster! This conclusion from these premises seemed logically inescapable to the Wesleys in the eighteenth century, as it had seemed to Bayle in the seventeenth. But the Methodists' reaction to the paradox was not the same as the ex-Calvinist's.

[1] Ibid., iii. 2206 a, s.v. Pauliciens.
[2] Ibid., iii. 2205 b, s.v. Pauliciens.

Bayle tacitly accepted the conclusion; the Wesleys passionately rejected the premises.

> To damn for falling short
> Of what they could not do,
> For not believing the report
> Of that which was not true.[1]

This is the blasphemy clearly contained *in the horrible decree* of predestination. You represent God as worse than the Devil; more false, more cruel, more unjust. But you say you will prove it by Scripture. Hold! What will you prove by Scripture? That God is worse than the Devil? It cannot be. Whatever that Scripture proves, it never can prove this; whatever its true meaning be, it cannot be this meaning. No Scripture can mean that God is not Love, or that His mercy is not over all His works; that is, whatever it prove beside, no Scripture can prove predestination.[2]

(v) *The Rapier of Ridicule*

They [a Japanese sect] go even farther than Epicurus. They relieve God of the burden of reasoning-power and intelligence. No doubt they are afraid that these qualities might disturb His repose, since they know by their own experience that the exercise of the reason is accompanied by some degree of fatigue.[3]

Since there is no indication that God overrides general laws of Nature except in cases in which the weal of His children requires it, it would be unwarrantable to take for miracles anything that occurs among the Infidels and among the Faithful indiscriminately. . . . Miracles that are still in the future are an object of Faith, and consequently an object that is obscure.[4]

Achilles was not the only worker of miracles on the Island of Leuce: his wife Helen took a hand too. . . . This is a field in which abundance does more damage than scarcity. . . . Credulity is a mother who is smothered to death by her own fecundity sooner or later—in minds, that is, which make some use of their faculty of Reason.[5]

One must not imagine that the other councils of the Church are acquitted of having been vitiated by passions and cabals to any

[1] Wesley, Charles, in *The Poetical Works of John and Charles Wesley*, ed. by Osborn, G. (London 1868-72, Wesleyan Methodist Conference Office, 13 vols.), vol. iii. p. 36.
[2] Wesley, John, in *Wesley Works*, ed. by Jackson, T. (London 1856-7, Mason, 14 vols.), vol. vii, p. 365.
[3] Bayle, P., *Dictionaire*, 3rd ed., ii. 1533, s.v. Japon.
[4] Ibid., i. 923 b, s.v. Constance.   [5] Ibid., i. 62 and 62 b, s.v. Achillea.

lesser degree [than the Council of Ephesus admittedly was], even if one accepts the plea that these other councils were not conducted with the precipitation of which Cyril was guilty at Ephesus. It is indeed necessary that the Holy Spirit should preside at these assemblies; for, but for that, all would be lost. This assistance [of the Holy Spirit]—which is something exceptional and is much more potent than ordinarily—ought to reassure us and to leave us firmly persuaded that the Holy Spirit has accomplished His work in the midst of the pandemonium made by [human] creatures and that, out of the darkness of [human] passions, He has succeeded in bringing forth the light of His truth—not, of course, in all the councils, but in some of them.[1]

One must . . . be careful to observe that there have crept into Christianity a vast number of abuses that are so similar to the disorders of Paganism that it would be impossible to write against the Pagans without providing some zealots with plausible grounds for saying that the Christian Religion has been debauched by the Pagan Religion. Those who give occasion for such reproaches are under a moral obligation to examine, in their own consciences, what their motive has been, and whether their real design has not been to enable their readers to find a portrait of modern abuses in the writers' descriptions of ancient disorders. English Nonconformist Protestants are sometimes accused of having written their vivid descriptions of the corruption of the ancient Roman clergy for no other purpose than to paint pictures calculated to bring odium upon the present state of the [English] Episcopalians.[2]

[1] Ibid., iii. 2078 a, s.v. Nestorius.
[2] Ibid., iii. 2255 a and b, s.v. Periers.

14

THE SEVENTEENTH-CENTURY
SECULARIZATION OF WESTERN LIFE

THE opening of the seventeenth century had found the
Western Christian Wars of Religion in full swing and
Western Christian fanaticism still at its height. Before the close
of the same century, Religion had been replaced by Technology,
applying the findings of Experimental Science, as the paramount interest and pursuit of the leading spirits in the Western
Society. When the century closed, this revolutionary change in
the Western attitude and êthos was, no doubt, still confined to a
minority. Yet it is remarkable that even a minority should
have moved so far in so short a time, and, still more, that they
should have set the rest of Society moving in their wake. In
the course of the quarter of a millennium running from the
beginning of the eighteenth century to A.D. 1956, the leaven of
secularization and the zest for Technology had spread progressively from one stratum of the Western Society to another
till they had permeated the whole mass.

The apotheosis of Technology was not an inevitable consequence of the discrediting of the West's Christian heritage.
This disillusionment did inevitably produce a great moral
and intellectual vacuum that was bound to be filled by some
new set of ideals and ideas; but the substitute for Christianity
in Western hearts and minds need not have been the ideal of
increasing Man's technological mastery over Non-Human
Nature by applying to this practical purpose an experimental
method of scientific research. Before this new ideal captivated
Western imaginations, a now discredited authoritarian Western
Christianity already had a rival in the shape of a no less authoritarian ghost of Hellenism. So the vacuum might have been
filled simply by installing a pre-Christian Hellenic oracle in the
place of a Christian oracle, and thus continuing to live, as
before, under a traditional authority's auspices.

This is what had actually happened in similar circumstances
in contemporary China, where, down to this point, the course

of History had run parallel to its course in the West. At the eastern, as at the western, extremity of the Old World a broken-down and disintegrating civilization had won a reprieve by incorporating itself into an oecumenical empire. When this empire had broken up and the moribund civilization had gone, with it, into dissolution, its castaway crew had found a new spiritual home in an oecumenical church. And, after this church had served as a chrysalis for hatching out a new civilization, the children of this rising society had eventually turned against a religious institution that had come to seem no longer indispensable. In all these successive changes of fortune, the history of the Mahāyāna in China had anticipated the history of the Christian Church in Western Europe; but in China, when a reaction against the Mahāyāna had declared itself, it had been inspired, on each successive occasion, not by a new ideal, but by a nostalgia for the classical civilization of Eastern Asia that had risen and fallen in the pre-Buddhist age of East Asian history. In the fifth, the ninth, and the seventeenth century of the Christian Era, the revolt against the authority of the Mahāyāna had been led by champions of the rival authority embodied in the pre-Buddhist Confucian philosophy and way of life.

In Early Modern Western Christendom, history did take this Chinese course on the plane of Politics. Here an uncritical belief in the divine right of the Apostle at Rome was simply replaced by an equally uncritical belief in the divine right of parochial states which had been the most disastrous of all the superstitions of the Graeco-Roman Society in its pre-Augustan age. These secular polities, which, in Western Christendom, had commanded only a partial and conditional allegiance so long as they had been subordinated to the Papal Respublica Christiana, were now deified there in the Graeco-Roman fashion. France, Portugal, Venice, and Venezuela were thus invested with the aura of the goddesses Belbina, Sparta, Athens, and Rome. In A.D. 1956 this resuscitated Hellenic worship of parochial states constituted the greater part of the religion of the greater part of the population of the Western World, and was accepted by its adherents on authority, just as blindly as Christianity had been accepted in the West in the Middle Ages.

On the economic, technological, and intellectual planes,

on the other hand, the leading spirits in the Western Society had parted company, before the close of the seventeenth century, with the Chinese and also with most of their other contemporaries in rejecting, not merely one previously established authority, but the principle of Authority itself. This was the issue in the Western 'Battle of the Ancients and the Moderns', which was fought in the seventeenth century in the same generation that saw the West repudiate its Christian heritage. The question was whether the West should transfer to an authoritarian Hellenism the allegiance that it was withdrawing from an authoritarian Christianity. In the field of Belles Lettres, the battle was inconclusive; but in the fields of Technology, Science, and Philosophy the Moderns were victorious. This victory was a decision, on behalf of Western Man, that, in these fields, the vacuum left in his heart and mind by the discrediting of a traditional Christianity should be filled, not by some alternative authoritarian system, but by an experimental attitude and a technological bent that were latent in the genius of the Western Civilization and, indeed in Human Nature itself.

These proclivities had been repressed in the soul of Western Man by the genius of Christianity so long as this had been in the ascendant in the West, and they were no less alien from the genius of Hellenism. Their outburst in the seventeenth century was a double victory over the two time-honoured authorities that were then competing for Western Man's allegiance, and the consequent enthronement of Experiment in place of Authority, and of Technology in place of Religion, was a morally as well as intellectually revolutionary act. The antecedents and the consequences of this seventeenth-century apotheosis of Technology are touched upon below in Chapter Seventeen. In the present chapter we may glance at the motives that moved seventeenth-century Western Man thus deliberately to transfer his treasure to Technology from Religion.

The prime motive was a horror at the wickedness and destructiveness of religious fanaticism; and this state of mind in England after the Civil War has been described, in a famous passage, by the Royal Society's first secretary and first historian.

It was . . . some space after the end of the Civil Wars at Oxford, in Dr. Wilkins his lodgings, in Wadham College, which was then the place of resort for vertuous and learnèd men, that the first meetings were made, which laid the foundation of all this that follow'd. The University had, at that time, many members of its own who had begun a free way of reasoning, and was also frequented by some gentlemen, of philosophical minds, whom the misfortunes of the Kingdom, and the security and ease of a retirement amongst gown-men, had drawn thither.

Their first purpose was no more then onely the satisfaction of breathing a free air and of conversing in quiet one with another, without being ingag'd in the passions and madness of that dismal age. . . .

For such a candid and unpassionate company as that was, and for such a gloomy season, what could have been a fitter subject to pitch upon then Natural Philosophy? To have been always tossing about some theological question would have been to have made that their private diversion, the excess of which they themselves dis-lik'd in the publick; to have been eternally musing on civil business, and the distresses of their country, was too melancholy a reflexion: it was Nature alone which could pleasantly entertain them in that estate. The contemplation of *that* draws our minds off from past or present misfortunes, and makes them conquerors over things, in the greatest publick unhappiness. While the consideration of men, and humane affairs, may affect us with a thousand various disquiets, *that* never separates us into mortal factions, *that* gives us room to differ without animosity, and permits us to raise contrary imaginations upon it without any danger of a civil war.[1]

A second motive for the seventeenth-century Western spiritual revolution was a recognition of the psychological truth that Western Man would not be able to emancipate himself from a hitherto obsessive interest in militant con-troversial religion unless he could provide himself with a psychological equivalent of comparable potency, and he turned to Technology to perform this social service for him. The difficulty of driving one nail out without driving another nail in was perceived by Bayle.

We may allow ourselves to deplore the wretched condition of the Human Race. It cannot extricate itself from one evil except by way

[1] Sprat, Tho., *The History of the Royal Society for the Improving of Natural Knowledge* (London 1667, Martyn), pp. 53 and 55-6.

of another. Cure it of ignorance and you will be exposing it to controversies that are shocking in themselves and that sometimes shake and even overthrow the established political order.[1]

Some thirty years before this passage was first published, the cultivation of Natural Philosophy had been recommended by Sprat as a promising antidote to the zeal for religious controversy.

Whatever other hurt or good comes by such holy speculative warrs (of which whether the benefit or mischief overweighs, I will not now examine), yet certainly by this means the knowledge of Nature has been very much retarded. . . . The wit of men has been profusely pour'd out on Religion, which needed not its help, and which was onely thereby made more tempestuous, while it might have been more fruitfully spent on some parts of Philosophy which have been hitherto barren and might soon have been made fertil.[2]

Experimental Philosophy will prevent men's spending the strength of their thoughts about disputes, by turning them to works.[3]

In the eyes of Western Man in the later decades of the seventeenth century, to try to create an Earthly Paradise looked like a more practicable objective than to try to bring a Kingdom of Heaven down to Earth. Recent Western experience had shown that the specifications for a Kingdom of Heaven on Earth were a subject of acrimonious and interminable dispute between rival schools of theologians. On the other hand the differences of opinion between practical technicians or between experimental scientists would be likely to remain at a low emotional temperature and would be certain to be cleared up, before long, by the findings of observation, and of reasoning about the results of observation, on which there would be no disagreement.

The doctrine of right and wrong is perpetually disputed, both by the pen and the sword, whereas the doctrine of lines and figures is not so, because men care not, in that subject, what be truth, as a thing that crosses no man's ambition, profit, or lust. For I doubt not, but if it had been a thing contrary to any man's right of dominion, or to the interest of men that have dominion, that the three angles of

[1] Bayle, P., *Dictionaire*, 3rd ed., iii. 2651 b, s.v. Stancarus.
[2] Sprat, op. cit., pp. 25-6.   [3] Ibid., p. 341.

a triangle should be equall to two angles of a square, that doctrine should have been, if not disputed, yet, by the burning of all books of geometry, suppressed, as far as he whom it concerned was able.[1]

The point here made by Hobbes with characteristic cynicism is taken up by Sprat in a no less characteristically constructive spirit, apropos of the nascent Royal Society's temper and methods of work.

Their principal endeavours have been that they might enjoy the benefits of a mix'd assembly, which are largeness of observation and diversity of judgments, without the mischiefs that usually accompany it, such as confusion, unsteddiness, and the little animosities of divided parties. That they have avoided these dangers for the time past there can be no better proof than their constant practice, wherein they have perpetually preserv'd a singular sobriety of debating, slowness of consenting, and moderation of dissenting. . . . They would not be much exasperated one against another in their disagreements, because they acknowledg that there may be several methods of Nature in producing the same thing, and all equally good; whereas they that contend for truth by talking do commonly suppose that there is but one way of finding it out. The differences which should chance to happen might soon be compos'd, because they could not be grounded on matters of speculation or opinion, but only of sense; which are never wont to administer so powerful occasions of disturbance and contention as the other.[2]

[They cultivate a plain style], bringing all things as near the mathematical plainness as they can, and preferring the language of artisans, countrymen, and merchants before that of wits or scholars.[3]

Nor is it the least commendation the *Royal Society* deserves, that, designing a union of mens hands and reasons, it has proceeded so far in uniting their affections. For there we behold an unusual sight to the English nation, that men of disagreeing parties and ways of life have forgotten to hate, and have met in the unanimous advancement of the same works. There the soldier, the tradesman, the merchant, the scholar, the gentleman, the courtier, the divine, the Presbyterian, the Papist, the Independent, and those of Orthodox Judgment, have laid aside their names of distinction and calmly conspir'd in a mutual agreement of labors and desires—a blessing which seems even to have exceeded that evangelical promise that the

[1] Hobbes, Thomas, *Leviathan*, Part I, chap. 11, first published in A.D. 1651.
[2] Sprat, op. cit., pp. 91-2.   [3] Ibid., pp. 111-13.

lion and the lamb shall ly down together; for here they do not onely endure each others presence without violence or fear, but they work and think in company and confer their help to each others inventions.[1]

On the morrow of the Wars of Religion, the technicians and experimentalists seemed not only amiable by comparison with the theologians but also impotent to do much harm, even if they had been maliciously inclined. In the later decades of the seventeenth century they were mostly people whose hands were remote from the levers of power, both ecclesiastical and political. 'Displaced persons' and disfranchised nonconformists were in force among them.[2] There was no fear of their seizing power in any of the forms in which power was familiar as yet; and, at this stage, there was no realization of the truth that, by their non-controversial inventions, these apparently harmless technicians were creating power of a new kind which would be used eventually by other hands, if not by theirs, to upset the existing balance.

The technological kind of power had been commended for its innocence by Bacon before the theme was taken up by Sprat.

It will perhaps be as well to distinguish three species and degrees

[1] Sprat, op. cit., p. 427.
[2] The evils of religious fanaticism in a seventeenth-century Western Christendom were, naturally, felt the most sharply and detested the most heartily by the people who suffered from them the most severely. These were the religious refugees (especially the Huguenot refugees from France after the revocation in A.D. 1685 of the Edict of Nantes) and the religious minorities which were allowed to remain in their homes at the price of political and social penalization (e.g. the Nonconformists in England after A.D. 1662). The penalty of political disfranchisement forcibly prevented the English Nonconformists from putting any of their treasure into the worship of an idolized parochial state, and so constrained them to put into Economics, Technology, and Science all of their treasure that did not go into their Free Churches. Thus it was no accident that the father of the eighteenth-century Western anti-religious philosophical Enlightenment should have been a seventeenth-century French Huguenot refugee in Holland, Pierre Bayle, or that the pioneers of the nineteenth-century Industrial Revolution in England should have been the eighteenth-century English Nonconformists. This role of 'displaced persons' as innovators in the Late Modern Age of Western history (circa A.D. 1675-1875) had a bearing on the Western Civilization's prospects in the twentieth century, considering how great was the relative, as well as the absolute, number of the 'displaced persons' abroad in the World in A.D. 1956.

of ambition. First, that of men who are anxious to enlarge their own power in their country, which is a vulgar and degenerate kind; next, that of men who strive to enlarge the power and empire of their country over Mankind, which is more dignified but not less covetous; but, if one were to endeavour to renew and enlarge the power and empire of Mankind in general over the Universe, such ambition (if it may be so termed) is both more sound and more noble than the other two. Now the empire of Man over things is founded on the arts and sciences alone, for Nature is only to be commanded by obeying her.[1]

Civil reformation seldom is carried on without violence and confusion, whilst inventions are a blessing and a benefit without injuring or afflicting any.[2]

If . . . our nation shall lay hold of this opportunity to deserve the applause of Mankind, the force of this example will be irresistibly praevalent in all countries round about us; the state of Christendom will soon obtain a new face; while this halcyon knowledge is breeding, all tempests will cease; the opposition and contentious wranglings of Science, falsely so call'd, will soon vanish away; the peaceable calmness of men's judgments will have admirable influence on their manners; the sincerity of their understandings will appear in their actions; their opinions will be less violent and dogmatical, but more certain; they will onely be gods one to another, and not wolves.[3]

[1] Bacon, Francis, *Novum Organum*, Partis Secundae Summa, Aphorismus cxxix: 'Non abs re fuerit tria hominum ambitionis genera et quasi gradus distinguere. Primum eorum qui propriam potentiam in patriâ suâ amplificare cupiunt; quod genus vulgare est et degener. Secundum, eorum qui patriae potentiam et imperium inter Humanum Genus amplificare nituntur; illud plus certe habet dignitatis, cupiditatis haud minus. Quod si quis Humani Generis ipsius potentiam et imperium in rerum universitatem instaurare et amplificare conetur, ea proculdubio ambitio (si modo ita vocanda sit) reliquis et sanior est et augustior. Hominis autem imperium in res in solis artibus et scientiis ponitur. Naturae enim non imperatur nisi parendo.'

[2] Bacon, ibid., 'Statûs emendatio in civilibus non sine vi et perturbatione plerumque procedit; at inventa beant et beneficium deferunt absque alicuius iniuriâ aut tristitiâ.'

[3] Sprat, op. cit., pp. 437-8.

14 ANNEXE

CONTEMPORARY EXPRESSIONS OF THE SEVENTEENTH-CENTURY WEST'S REVOLT AGAINST THE PRINCIPLE OF AUTHORITY AND OF ITS ADOPTION OF THE METHODS OF OBSERVATION AND EXPERIMENT

A. THE REVOLT AGAINST THE PRINCIPLE OF AUTHORITY

Leonardi da Vinci (*vivebat* A.D. 1452-1519) was at least 150 years ahead of the common run of his contemporaries in his intellectual outlook, so no apology need be offered for citing him in the company of seventeenth-century writers of ordinary mental stature.

Anyone who conducts an argument by appealing to Authority is not using his intelligence; he is just using his memory.[1]

'Just' and 'unjust' invariably change character in changing climate. Three degrees of elevation of the Pole upsets the whole corpus of Jurisprudence; a meridian decides what is the truth. . . . A nice kind of justice that can be confined by a river-boundary! Truth on this side of the Pyrenees, error on the other side![2]

It is pitiful to see so many Turks, heretics, and infidels following in their fathers' track, for the sole reason that each has been conditioned to believe that this track is the best. This accident of birth is also what decides everyone's condition in life, making one man a locksmith, another man a soldier, etcetera.[3]

The best account that many can give of their belief, is, that they were bred in it; which indeed is no better, then that which we call, the Woman's Reason. And thousands of them, whom their profession and our charity styles Christians, are driven to their Religion by custom and education, as the Indians are to Baptism; that is, like a drove of Cattle to the water. And, had our Stars determin'd our nativities among the Enemies of the Cross, and theirs under a Christian horoscope, in all likelyhood Antichristianism had not been the object of our aversion, nor Christianity of theirs: But we should

---

[1] Leonardo da Vinci in *The Literary Works of Leonardo da Vinci*, compiled and edited from the original MSS. by J. P. Richter, 2nd edition (Oxford 1939, University Press, 2 vols.), vol. ii, p. 241, No. 1159: 'Chi disputa allegàdo l'autorità, non adopera lo ingiegno, ma piutosto la memoria.'

[2] Pascal, *Pensées*, No. 294 in Léon Brunschvicg's arrangement.

[3] Pascal, op. cit., No. 98.

have exchang'd the Scene of our belief with that of our abode and breeding.[1]

There being but one truth, one way to Heaven, what hope is there that mere men would be led into it if they had no rule but the religion of the court, and were put under the necessity to quit the light of their own reason, and oppose the dictates of their own consciences, and blindly to resign themselves up to the will of their governors, and to the religion which either ignorance, ambition, or superstition had chanced to establish in the countries where they were born? In the variety and contradiction of opinions in Religion, wherein the princes of the World are as much divided as in their secular interests, the narrow way would be much straitened; one country alone would be in the right, and all the rest of the World put under an obligation of following their princes in the ways that lead to destruction; and, that which heightens the absurdity and very ill suits the notion of a Deity, men would owe their eternal happiness or misery to the places of their nativity.[2]

The way of authority necessarily leads individuals to be Mahometans in Turkey, pagans in China, and [, in fact,] everywhere and always [to be adherents] of the national religion.[3]

There is an almost universal complaint that Philosophy is injurious to Theology. Yet, on the other hand, it is certain that Theology is harmful to Philosophy. Here are two faculties that would find some difficulty in agreeing on the delimitation of the frontier between them, if this question were not well and truly settled, as it is, by the way of authority, which is always in favour of the interests of Religion.[4]

They [the Greek and Roman gods] have been disposed of, as soon as one makes the assumption that, sooner or later, age kills false doctrines. Please note, though, that this principle would be capable of serving as valid evidence only on condition that one gives some ruling about what is the minimum length of time that is sufficient for discriminating between errors and truths. If a millennium is sufficient, then any opinion that has ten centuries to its credit will be veritable; but, if you do not enact any statute of limitations, then you will get nowhere by arguing that, because a dogma has lasted for four thousand years, it ought therefore to rank as being indubitably true: in reasoning in this way you will be leaving the future out of account: you cannot tell whether the fifth millennium

---

[1] Glanvill, J., *The Vanity of Dogmatising* (London 1661, Eversden), pp. 127-8.
[2] Locke, John, *A Letter Concerning Toleration* (first published in A.D. 1689).
[3] Bayle, P., *Dictionaire*, 3rd ed., iii. 2396 a, s.v. Puccius.
[4] Ibid., i. 327 a, s.v. Aristote.

may not be the death of a dogma which has held its own against the previous millennia.[1]

The way of authority, which Roman Catholics profess to follow, is the high road to scepticism. Anyone who is in earnest in seeking genuinely to make certain that he ought to submit to the authority of the Church will be obliged to verify that this is ordained by Scripture as well. This at once exposes him to [having to take account of] all the points discussed by Mr. Nicolle, and, besides that, he will have to verify whether the doctrine of the Fathers, and that of all other ages of Christian history, is compatible with that submission to the Church's authority for which he is seeking authorization. He will have to be indefatigable indeed if he does not find himself preferring a complete agnosticism to the prospect of having to embark on such extensive researches as these; and he will be acute indeed if, after having taken all the trouble that this task requires, he does see light at the end of it all.[2]

One cannot say that it [the Aristotelian school] has not had its reverses and its misfortunes, or that in this seventeenth century, above all, it has not been violently shaken; however, the Catholic theologians on one side and the Protestant theologians on the other have rushed to its aid as fast as firemen, and they have obtained such support from the secular arm against the new philosophers that it does not look as if Aristotelianism were going to lose its dominion for a long time to come.[3]

It is not surprising that the Aristotelian philosophy, in the form in which it has been taught for some centuries past, should find so many protectors, or that its interests should be thought to be inseparable from those of [Christian] Theology. Aristotelianism accustoms the mind to assent without evidence. This solidarity of interests ought to afford the Aristotelians a guarantee for the immortality of their school, and ought to give the new philosophers cause to scale down their expectations.[4]

B. THE ADOPTION OF THE METHODS OF OBSERVATION AND EXPERIMENT

Experience, which is the interpreter between artful (?) Nature and the Human Species, teaches us what are this Nature's operations among us mortals. The constraint of necessity makes it impossible for her to work otherwise than Reason, her rudder, teaches her to work.

---

[1] Bayle, P., *Dictionaire*, 3rd ed., ii. 1671 a, s.v. Launoi.
[2] Ibid., iii. 2088 a and b, s.v. Nicolle (cp. iii. 2220 a and b, s.v. Pellisson).
[3] Ibid., i. 321, s.v. Aristote.   [4] Ibid., i. 326-7, s.v. Aristote.

Wisdom is the daughter of Experience.

Truth is the only daughter of Time.

Experience never misleads; what you are misled by is only your judgments, and these mislead you by anticipating results from experience of a kind that is not produced in your experiments.

Instead of making this instance into a general rule, verify it two or three times over, and watch whether these several verifications do produce similar results.[1]

All knowledge is to be got the same way that a language is: by industry, use, and observation.[2]

Such a philosophy they would build, which should first wholly consist of action and intelligence before it be brought into teaching and contemplation.[3]

If we enquire the reason, why the Mathematicks, and Mechanicle Arts, have so much got the start in growth of other Sciences: We shall find it probably resolv'd into this, as one considerable cause: that their progress hath not been retarded by that reverential aw of former discoveries, which hath been so great an hinderance to Theoretical improvements.[4]

There is no certainty in the sciences where there is not a possibility of applying one of the mathematical sciences, or in the case of their not being united with the mathematical sciences.[5]

---

[1] Leonardo da Vinci, in *The Literary Works of Leonardo da Vinci*, compiled and edited from the original MSS. by J. P. Richter, 2nd ed. (Oxford 1939, University Press, 2 vols.), vol. ii, p. 240.

'La speriēza, interprete infra l'artifitiosa natura e la umana spetie, ne insegnia ciò che essa natura infra mortali adopera, da neciesità costretta non altrimēti operarsi possa che la ragiō, suo timone, operare le 'nsegni' (No 1149).
'La sapiētia è figliola della speriētia' (No. 1150).
'La verità fu sola figliola del tempo' (No. 1152).
'La speriēza nō falla mai, ma sol fallano i vostri giuditi, promettendosi di quella efetto tale che ne nostri experimēti causati nō sono' (No. 1153).
'Innanzi che tu facci di questo caso regola generale, pruovalo 2 o tre volte, e guarda se le pruove fanno simili effetti' (No. 1153A).

[2] Sprat, Th., *The History of the Royal Society of London for the Improving of Natural Knowledge* (London 1667, Martyn), p. 97.
[3] Ibid., p. 93.
[4] Glanvill, J., *The Vanity of Dogmatising* (London 1661, Eversden), pp. 139-40.
[5] Leonardo da Vinci, in *The Literary Works of Leonardo da Vinci*, compiled and edited from the original MSS. by J. P. Richter, 2nd ed. (Oxford 1939, University Press, 2 vols.), vol. ii, p. 241, No. 1158:

'Nessuna certezza delle sciētie è, dove nō si può applicare una delle sciētie matematiche over che non sono unite con esse matematiche.'

It cannot be denied that it is rare to find any great religious devotion in people who have once tasted [the enchantment of] the study of mathematics and have made any remarkable progress in this province of Science.[1]

[1] Bayle, P., *Dictionaire*, 3rd ed., iii. 2187 a, s.v. Pascal.

15

THE WORLD'S RECEPTION OF A SECULARIZED LATE MODERN WESTERN CIVILIZATION

THE revolutionary shift of interest from Religion to Technology among the leading spirits of the Western World in the later decades of the seventeenth century had two effects that changed the rest of the World's attitude towards the West. The Late Modern West's concentration of attention and energy on Technology brought to the West an increase in wealth and power that, for scale and speed, was perhaps unprecedented in the previous history of any civilization; and at the same time the Late Modern West's alienation from its own traditional religion brought with it an abatement of the West's traditional religious intolerance.

Intrinsically the West's technological achievements during the last quarter of a millennium are not such great prodigies of human ability as the primary technological discoveries, made by Primitive Man, on which all subsequent technological advances have been based: how to make fire and keep it alight; how to chip a stone into an edged tool; how to navigate a hollowed-out tree-trunk—not to speak of such relatively late and sophisticated inventions as agriculture, the domestication of animals, and the wheel. What has been unprecedented in the last 250 years of Western technological history has been the pace—and in A.D. 1956 this pace had not yet begun perceptibly to slacken. This pace has been the result of an unprecedentedly large investment of human ability and non-human capital in deliberately experimenting in improvements over the whole field of Mankind's apparatus, including domesticated plants and animals.

The change in the West's temper which opened the way for this technological 'drive' showed itself in the West's dealings with people of alien religions. At the beginning of the seventeenth century the temper then prevailing in the West had made it virtually impossible to study in a Western country without having accepted the locally established form of Western Christianity—Catholic or Protestant. The University of Padua, which was under the aegis of the Republic of Venice, had been unique in opening its doors to non-Catholics. The Protestant Englishman Hervey, the discoverer of the circulation of the blood, and the Eastern Orthodox Christian Chiot Alexander Mavrogordato, who wrote a treatise on Hervey's discovery before entering the Ottoman public service, were, both of them, students there. But the University of Padua's liberality had been an exceptional régime which was partly due to Venice's possessing a colonial empire with a mainly Eastern Orthodox Christian population. Other Western universities were slow in waiving their religious tests. The University of Oxford, for instance, continued down to A.D. 1871—a date by which Britain had already lost one empire and acquired a second—to exact a declaration of assent to the Thirty-nine Articles of the Episcopalian Church of England from every candidate for a degree. Before the end of the seventeenth century, however, the West was beginning to create for itself a non-university organization for study and for the exchange of information and ideas in the shape of a 'Republic of Letters' composed of local academies patronized by enlightened monarchs, and here the traditional religious tests were not applied. As the Late Modern Age of Western history ran on, the Paduan rift in the Western veil of compulsory religious uniformity began to widen.

This dawn of religious toleration in the West in the Late Modern Age of Western history made it possible for non-Westerners now to go to school in the West without any longer being compelled to accept the local Western religion as a condition *sine qua non* for being allowed to receive a training in Western technology. Concurrently, the West's technological progress in this age made it imperative for leading spirits in non-Western societies to take advantage of their new access to the fountainhead of Western technique in order to master the new Western technology in the interests of self-defence.

In the Early Modern Age the West had not yet forged so far ahead of other living societies in its military technique as to make it impossible for these societies to master the use of Western military inventions without revolutionizing their own way of life. In the sixteenth century the Ottoman Turks, the Russians, and the Japanese readily mastered the use and manufacture of the Western fire-arms of the day. In the Great Northern War of A.D. 1558-83, Muscovy was able to take the offensive in a first attempt to conquer the Baltic Provinces from the Western World, and was checked with great difficulty by a coalition of Sweden, Denmark, and the United Kingdom of Poland-Lithuania, which stepped into a breach opened by the collapse of the resistance of the Teutonic Order. Japan, which enjoyed the advantage of remoteness, besides that of political unity, was able, as late as A.D. 1637, still to dictate terms to all Western comers. On the other hand, the bout of anarchy in Muscovy during the years A.D. 1603-13 ('The Time of Troubles') showed that even such relatively backward border Western countries as Poland-Lithuania and Sweden had now become decisively stronger than Muscovy in military technique. The Poles were able to occupy Moscow itself during the years A.D. 1610-12; the Swedes were able to conquer Muscovy's only Baltic seaboard, at the head of the Gulf of Finland, in A.D. 1611, and Muscovy had to accept this loss in the peace treaty of A.D. 1617. As between the Ottoman Empire and the West, the turn of the tide was marked by the failure, in A.D. 1683, of the second Ottoman siege of Vienna.

Such experiences as these made it urgent for the West's non-Western neighbours to master Western military technique and to keep abreast of its accelerating progress. This response to the challenge of the West's military ascendancy was made in Russia, after 'the Time of Troubles', by Peter the Great, who came into power *de facto* in A.D. 1689. In Turkey it was made, after the shock of the disastrous Russo-Turkish war of A.D. 1768-74, by Selīm III (*accessit* A.D. 1789). In Japan it was made, after the shock of Commodore Perry's irresistible intrusion in A.D. 1853, by the authors of the Japanese revolution of A.D. 1868. It was fortunate for these non-Western countries that the seventeenth-century Western revolution that had made the West unprecedentedly powerful had also made it unprecedentedly tolerant. This concomitant change in the West's temper made it possible for leading spirits in Russia, the Ottoman Empire, and Japan to learn in a Western school those Western arts that they must now master if they were to have any prospect of holding their own against the preponderance of their Western neighbours.

The most dramatic demonstration of this new possibility was Peter the Great's self-educational tour in the West in A.D. 1697-8. It was an extraordinary piece of good fortune for Russia that, in an age in which she was in dire peril of falling into Western hands, an *anima naturaliter Occidentalis* should have been 'born in the purple' at Moscow. Peter was not merely a born technician of the Late Modern Western type; he was born 100 years before people with his aptitude and outlook began to make their mark in the West itself. He was the coming *homo mechanicus* of whom the fathers of the Royal Society had dreamed, but whom they were never to see in the flesh except in the person of this exotic seventeenth-century Russian forerunner of the eighteenth-century English artificers of the Industrial Revolution. Yet Peter's native bent towards Technology, precocious though it thus was, might not have sufficed, in itself, to enable him to do his life-work in Russia if it had not been open to him in his generation to serve the apprenticeship in Holland and England that he turned to such good account.

More significant, though less sensational, than the welcome given in the maritime Western countries to Peter the Great was the Danubian Hapsburg Monarchy's acceptance—in three successive instruments promulgated in A.D. 1690, 1691, and 1695—of a proposition from insurgent Serb Eastern Orthodox Christian subjects of the Ottoman Empire. These Serbs had offered to transfer their political allegiance to the Hapsburg Monarchy on two conditions. They must be given permanent asylum behind the Hapsburg military lines, and at the same time they must be allowed to retain, as subjects of the Holy Roman *Caesarea Maiestas*, not only their own religion, but the communal autonomy, under the presidency of their own patriarch, which they had enjoyed under the Ottoman régime. Both conditions were accepted; and this *volte face* in the Hapsburg Dynasty's ecclesiastical policy, only forty-two years after the end of the Thirty Years War, was something portentous.

The shock of defeat in the War of A.D. 1682-99 did not move the 'Osmanlis to go to school in the West in person, as Peter had done; but it did move them to take two steps. They now gave responsible positions in the public service to Greek Eastern Orthodox Ottoman subjects who had not been educated in the Sultan's Slave-Household and had not been converted to Islam, but had acquired a Western education on their own private initiative.[1] They also hired Western technicians to come to Turkey in order to train 'Osmanlis in some of the most highly technical branches of the Western art of war, especially in military engineering and in gunnery. These Ottoman essays in the acquisition of Western military technique between A.D. 1699 and A.D. 1768 were, however, fragmentary, spasmodic, and half-hearted.[2] A second shock, administered by a more humiliating defeat in A.D. 1768-74, was needed in order to move Sultan Selīm III to make the first attempt at a thorough-going Westernization of the Ottoman armed forces. This time the 'Osmanlis had been defeated by Russian co-religionists of their despised Eastern Orthodox Christian subjects, in virtue of the process of Westernization through which Russia had been putting herself during the previous eighty years. This triumph of the Western military technique, even in Russian hands, convinced the 'Osmanlis at last of the necessity of acquiring for themselves the same Western talisman.[3]

The Japanese did not begin to substitute nineteenth-century for seventeenth-century Western armaments till after Commodore Perry's descent on Japan in A.D. 1853. By that date the obstacle to the reception of a Western education by a Japanese student in the West was not any Western xenophobia; it was the unfamiliarity of the West to the Japanese after a period of self-seclusion that, by then, had lasted for more than 200 years.

The policy of these pioneer military Westernizers was a negative one. They wanted to take nothing, even of the secular residue of a deconsecrated Western Civilization, except the bare minimum of Western military technique that would be sufficient to secure their countries' survival in warfare with Western or Westernizing Powers. None of the pioneer Westernizers were moved by any positive attraction towards the Western Civilization. Their motive for mastering elements of the Western Civilization was in all cases a wish to acquire the

---

[1] See *A Study of History*, vol. ii, pp. 224-5; vol. viii, pp. 187-8.
[2] See ibid., vol. viii, p. 557, footnote 5.   [3] See ibid., vol. viii, pp. 239-49.

power that this mastery would bring with it. The self-Western-educated Ottoman Greeks and Bengali Hindus who were taken, respectively, into the Ottoman and the British administrative service, saw in their Western education an instrument for getting even with a Muslim 'ascendancy' which was slower than they were to recognize that the key to power was now a mastery of Western technique of one kind or another. Those non-Westerners who, unlike eighteenth-century Greeks and Hindus, were still politically independent now recognized that they would forfeit their independence to Western conquerors if they did not acquire sufficient Western military technique to enable them once again to hold their own against the West in war. But the pioneer Westernizers in these still independent non-Western societies all started with the aim of preserving as much as possible of their traditional non-Western civilization at the price of adopting as little as possible of Western military technique. They wanted to insure against the worst risks only at the cost of a minimum premium. The sequel demonstrated, however, that a selective reception of elements of an alien civilization was impossible in the long run.

This was impossible because every civilization or way of life is a pattern of conduct in which the parts are interdependent. This interdependence is so multiple and so intimate that elements which, at first sight, look as if they could not have any connexion with one another turn out to be indissoluble when a practical experiment is made in replacing some single native element by some single foreign element. The single native element proves impossible to eliminate without also eliminating, or at least modifying, a whole set of other native elements; the single foreign element proves impossible to introduce without also introducing a whole set of other foreign elements.

The introduction of a Late Modern Western military technique in place of a traditional native one proved to be a case in point. The importation of Western weapons was not enough in itself; they were often still inferior to non-Western weapons. The French cavalryman was not so well equipped as the Egyptian mamlūk whom he defeated in A.D. 1798; a British musket did not carry so far as the Afghan jezayl that proved more than a match for it in A.D. 1838. Western military superiority sprang from the use of Western weapons by disciplined troops; and military discipline is the apex of a pyramid of social achievement. It is the fruit of law and order in civil life; for it cannot be established without effective hygiene and without regular pay. Effective hygiene in the armed forces requires a corresponding standard of public health in civil life, maintained by physicians with a Western medical training. The regular payment of troops requires sound public finances. Sound public finances require business ability and a productive economy. And the economy must be productive, not only of agricultural produce for feeding the troops, but of industrial skill for the manufacture of armaments in the Western style. A non-Western army that depended for its armaments entirely on imports from the West, without any plant, or any corps of technicians, for manufacturing them at home, would be in an intolerably precarious position.

For these reasons a World which had rejected the Early Modern Western ecclesiastical civilization found itself constrained in the end to adopt the Late Modern Western secular civilization unreservedly; but the time that it took for would-be minimal Westernizers to learn by experience that their choice was one between all and nothing was very different in different cases. In Turkey, more than 200 years passed between the first experiments in adopting fragments of Western military technique in the early eighteenth century and Mustafā Kemāl Atatürk's wholehearted option for total Westernization in A.D. 1919-28. In China more than half a century passed between the first moves towards Westernization, under the shock of military defeats by Western Powers during the years A.D. 1839-61, and the triumph of the Kuomintang in A.D. 1923-8 with a programme of total Westernization by stages—an enterprise which eventually failed and, in failing, opened a door for the entry of Communism. On the other hand the pioneer Westernizers Peter the Great in Russia, Mehmed 'Alī in Egypt, and the inaugurators of the Meiji Era in Japan all alike perceived that they must Westernize without reservations, and must extend this total revolution to every department of human activity, if they intended to be successful in preserving their societies by mastering Western military technique.

In thus resigning itself, sooner or later, to an unlimited

Westernization in this second encounter with the Modern West, the non-Western World was condemning itself, as we have observed,[1] to be implicated in the spiritual crisis by which a secularized Western Society was to be overtaken within 300 years of the seventeenth-century Western spiritual revolution. In a Late Modern Age of Western history the Western Civilization to which the non-Western World was reluctantly capitulating was more enigmatic than was suspected at the time either by the proselytes or by the native Westerners themselves. In what did this imposing Late Modern Western Civilization consist? That was a question which confronted every Westernizer who came to recognize—as all Westernizers did sooner or later—that the price of self-preservation was nothing less than the adoption of the Western Civilization *in toto*, without reservations. The non-Western men of genius who divined this hard truth, and acted on their insight, were all inclined to take the Late Modern Western Civilization at its technological face-value. They saw it as a cornucopia out of which they could draw techniques that would be of practical use in the military, political, and economic fields.

This superficial view of the contents and character of the Late Modern Western Civilization was a pardonable one at the time, because this was the picture of the Western Civilization that the contemporary Western exponents of it were deliberately presenting. Peter the Great would have been confirmed in his estimate of the West's genius if he had read Sprat's history of the Royal Society. Sprat and his contemporaries were painting their picture of the West in complete good faith. Yet, in the historical perspective given to Posterity by the lapse of 300 years, this narrowly utilitarian seventeenth-century self-portrait looks like an expression of the Late Modern West's reaction against the evils of Western religious fanaticism in the immediately preceding age, and not like an objective self-appraisal; and it was assuredly a misrepresentation, and indeed almost a caricature, of the actual spirit of the Western Civilization either at the close of the seventeenth century or in any subsequent generation.

Thomas Sprat (*vivebat* A.D. 1635-1713) and Joseph Glanvill (*vivebat* A.D. 1636-80) were, both of them, clergymen of the

[1] See Chapter 11, pp. 149-50, above.

Church of England. Sprat ended his ecclesiastical career as a bishop; and he was evidently unconscious of there being any incompatibility between his endeavours as a churchman and his endeavours as the secretary of the Royal Society. In promoting an interest in Technology, he was seeking to provide a psychological substitute, not for Religion, but for religious fanaticism.[1] He deplored the decay of religious belief, which he correctly foreboded.[2] He believed that 'the spiritual vices of this age' were largely responsible for this drift towards scepticism. He was convinced that 'the most efficacious remedy that Man of himself can use is not so much the sublime part of divinity as its intelligible and natural and practicable doctrines'[3] derived from Man's dispassionate study of God's revelation of Himself in Nature. Sprat's outlook was, in fact, the same as Locke's, whose first draft for an essay on Toleration was composed in A.D. 1667, the year in which Sprat's history of the Royal Society was published. In *A Letter concerning Toleration*, which was composed in A.D. 1685-6 and was published in A.D. 1689, Locke did not denounce the spirit of Christianity as being exclusive and intolerant; he deprecated the spirit of exclusiveness and intolerance as being un-Christian.

Whatsoever some people boast of the antiquity of places and names, or of the pomp of their outward worship; others, of the reformation of their discipline; all, of the orthodoxy of their faith—for every one is orthodox to himself—these things, and all others of this nature, are much rather marks of men striving for power and empire over one another than of the church of Christ. Let any one have never so true a claim to all these things, yet, if he be destitute of charity, meekness, and good-will in general towards all Mankind, even to those that are not Christians, he is certainly yet short of being a true Christian himself. . . . The Gospel frequently declares that the true disciples of Christ must suffer persecution; but that the church of Christ should persecute others, and force others by fire and sword to embrace her faith and doctrine, I could never yet find in any of the books of the New Testament. . . . Neither Pagan nor Mahometan nor Jew ought to be excluded from the civil rights of the commonwealth because of his religion. The Gospel commands

[1] See the passage, of *The History of the Royal Society*, quoted in Chapter 14, pp. 183, 184, 185-6, and 187 above.
[2] See the passage quoted in Chapter 11 Annexe, pp. 151-2, above.
[3] Quoted already on p. 152 above.

no such thing. The church which 'judgeth not those that are without' (1 Cor. v. 12-13) wants it not.[1]

Both Locke and Sprat are patently sincere in professing that their aim is, not to undermine Christianity by inciting people to withdraw their treasure from it, but to preserve Christianity by purging it of fanaticism in accordance with Christ's own principles and precepts. Even the French *déraciné* Bayle, who had suffered more severely from seventeenth-century Western Christian intolerance than either of these two English contemporaries of his, and had been carried by the same reaction against fanaticism into reacting against religion itself to some extent, would perhaps have flinched from acknowledging this even in the privacy of his own heart. Bayle's published works give the impression that he was, himself, a victim of the artful ambiguity that was his master-weapon in his assaults upon the rearguard of the seventeenth-century fanatics. The eighteenth century, which saw the Late Modern West's anti-religious mood expressed without ambiguity or reserve by Voltaire, also saw a revived Christian faith preached by Voltaire's contemporary Wesley; and it is significant that this revival should have started in the generation that saw the recession go farthest. The seventeenth-century secularizing movement in the West was bound, as has been suggested in the eleventh chapter of this book, to evoke a counter-movement sooner or later, because Religion is an essential element in Human Life which cannot ever be ignored or repressed for very long at a time.

Thus it would be no exaggeration to say that the twentieth-century spiritual crisis in the West was already implicit in the seventeenth-century spiritual crisis there, and that this coming crisis was working up, under the surface, throughout a Late Modern Age of Western history which was witnessing a progressive reception of the Western Civilization by the rest of the World. This would mean that the Late Modern Western Society was seriously, though unintentionally, deceiving the contemporary Westernizers in giving them the impression that a transient secularizing phase of the Western Civilization was the whole of the Western Civilization as this had been, was, and was to be. It would also mean that the Westernizers, in

[1] Locke, John, *A Letter concerning Toleration.*

their turn, were unintentionally deceiving their simple-minded
non-Western compatriots in taking this deceptive Western
presentation of the West at its face-value.

The Westernizers, however, can hardly be blamed for
having overlooked the unsolved religious problem that, all the
time, was gnawing at the West's vitals, since Religion did not
head the queue of these distracted Westernizers' cares. The
deficiency of which they were conscious in their own societies,
and which they were seeking to make good by drawing on the
resources of the West, was a deficiency, not in their ancestral
religion, but in their traditional technology. Western technology was, for them, the one Western pearl of great price
which they felt themselves constrained to buy even at the cost
of selling all that they had.[1] It did not occur to them that
Western religion was any concern of theirs. So they committed
themselves and their compatriots unreservedly to the secularizing Late Modern phase of the Western Civilization without
realizing that this phase was necessarily ephemeral. Indeed, in
putting themselves through the agonizing ordeal of renouncing
their ancestral ways of life and adopting an alien Western way
instead, they found consolation in the conviction that, at this
grievous price, they were purchasing the privilege of living
happily ever after in a 'Civilization' that was definitive. The
sequel was to show that what they had purchased in fact was
the penalty of being implicated in an imminent Western
spiritual crisis.

15 ANNEXE

CONTEMPORARY EXPRESSIONS OF THE SEVENTEENTH-CENTURY WEST'S REVULSION FROM THE WEST'S TRADITIONAL RELIGIOUS INTOLERANCE

A. PAGANS AND ATHEISTS HAVE BEEN NO WORSE THAN CHRISTIANS

The fear and the love of God are not always the most powerful
motives of human actions. . . . So it ought not to be taken as a
shocking paradox, but ought rather to be accepted as something
quite natural, that people who profess no religion should be impelled towards good conduct by the stimuli of innate character—

[1] Matt. xiii. 46.

accompanied by a love of good repute, and sustained by a fear of discredit—more powerfully than other people are impelled by the voice of conscience. We ought to feel much more deeply shocked when we see so many people who are convinced of the truths of Religion and yet at the same time are plunged in crime. It is even more strange that the idolators of the Pagan World should have performed good actions than it is that atheistic philosophers should have lived good lives. For the idolators ought to have been impelled towards crime by their very religion; they ought to have believed that, in order to fulfil the aim and essence of Religion by achieving the imitation of God, they must be dishonest, envious-hearted, loose-lived, adulterous, addicted to unnatural vice, and so on. From this we may conclude that those idolators who did lead upright lives were governed solely by the ideas of Reason and by the ideals of Uprightness, or else by the desire for good repute or by innate character or by other motives that can all be found in the minds of atheists. Why, then, should one expect to find a higher moral standard under the reign of the idolatry of the Pagan World than under the reign of irreligion? But be careful, if you please, to observe that, in speaking of the good conduct of some atheists, I have certainly not been crediting them with veritable virtues. . . . Their performances were merely 'brilliant sins', *splendida peccata*, as Saint Augustine has characterized all the noble deeds that stand to the Pagans' account.[1]

To speak frankly, it must be said of the Pagans, to their credit, that they certainly did not live in accordance with their principles. It is true that, in the Pagan World, moral corruption did go to extremes; but in that world there were always many people who did not follow the example of their false gods, and who gave the ideals of Uprightness the precedence [even] over an authority so great [as that of their pagan religion]. What is strange is that the Christians, whose system is so pure, are hardly an inch behind the Gentiles in their plunge into vice. It is a serious error to imagine that the moral practice of a religion will correspond with the doctrines in its confession of faith.[2]

People who have had some acquaintance with Spinoza, and the peasants of the villages where he lived in retirement for some time, concur in saying that he was a man of good character socially (*d'un bon commerce*)—affable, honest, consciencious, and extremely strict in his morals. This is strange; yet, at bottom, it ought to give no greater cause for astonishment than the spectacle of people

---

[1] Bayle, P., *Dictionaire*, 3rd ed., iv. 2987, I Éclaircissement.
[2] Ibid., ii. 1602 b, s.v. Jupiter.

leading very bad lives in spite of their being completely persuaded of the truth of the Gospel.[1]

B. MUSLIMS ARE NO WORSE THAN CHRISTIANS—EXCEPT AT THE TRADE OF MAKING INFERNAL MACHINES

How is one to resist conquering armies that come demanding signatures? Ask the French dragoons, who plied this trade in 1685; the answer that you will get from them will be that they will guarantee to make the whole World set its signature to the Alcoran, provided that they are allowed time enough to apply the commandment 'Compel them to come in'. . . . The debt has to be acknowledged: the kings of France resorted to Mahometan methods for establishing Christianity in Frisia and in Saxony, and the same violent means were used to establish it in Scandinavia. . . . The same methods were resorted to for dealing with [Christian] sects that dared to condemn the Pope; and they are going to be resorted to in India as soon as the power to apply them is there.

Now the manifest moral of all these examples of Christian behaviour is that the fact of Mahomet's having propagated his religion by force can no longer be used against Mahomet [by Christians] to Mahomet's prejudice. If you doubt this, consider what Mahomet would be able to say in presenting an *argumentum ad hominem*: 'If force were bad intrinsically, there would never be an occasion on which it would be legitimate to use it. But, now, you Christians have been using force from the fourth century [of your era] down to the present day, and you maintain that, in doing this, you have not been doing anything on which you cannot congratulate yourselves heartily. So you are bound to admit that this method is not bad intrinsically; and consequently I, Mahomet, have been acting legitimately in resorting to force since the first years of my prophetic call. It would be absurd [for you Christians] to maintain that something which would have been gravely criminal in the first century [of your era] becomes right in the fourth though it is not right in the first. One could have maintained this if, in the fourth century, God had laid down new laws; but am I not right in thinking that you rest your case for justifying your conduct from the time of Constantine down to the present day on these words in the Gospel—"Compel them to come in"—and on the [religious] duties of princes? Well, on this showing, you ought, if you had had the power, to have used force from the very morrow of the Ascension.'[2]

[1] Ibid., iii. 2635-6, s.v. Spinoza.
[2] Ibid., iii. 1854 b and 1855 a, s.v. Mahomet.

The Mahometans, according to the principles of their faith, are under an obligation to use violence for the purpose of bringing other religions to ruin; yet, in spite of that, they have been tolerating other religions for some centuries past. The Christians have not been given orders to do anything but preach and instruct; yet, in spite of this, from time immemorial they have been exterminating by fire and sword all those who are not of their religion. . . . We may feel certain that, if the Western Christians, instead of the Saracens and the Turks, had won the dominion over Asia, there would be today not a trace left of the Greek Church, and that they would never have tolerated Mahometanism as the Infidels have tolerated Christianity there.[1]

Once upon a time, people who had the Popes' ear could make the best part of Europe uninhabitable for a man whom they had definitely taken it into their heads to label as a heretic; and this poor wretch could then well apply to them, *mutatis mutandis*, certain passages of Psalm cxxxix. So it is not surprising that Peter Abelard should have wanted to go in search of peace among the Mahometans or the Pagans. His hope was that, at the price of paying tribute, he would enjoy freedom to profess Christianity beyond the sphere of activity of *Odium Theologicum*; and he was afraid that, short of taking this step, he would find himself imprisoned in this sphere for ever.[2]

Some Christian authors give tongue to a very ridiculous story concerning the credulity of the Mahometans on the subject of miracles (QQ).[3] Monsr. Simon has been blamed for some things that he has published which tend to extenuate the infamy of Mahometanism. . . . But, if he is right in essentials, he deserves commendation, for one ought not to foment the hatred of evil by the trick of painting it blacker and more hateful than it is in fact.[4]

I am not suggesting that Christians are laxer morally than Infidels, but I should hesitate to assert that they were less lax. The accounts given by travellers are conflicting.[5]

I do not know whether one ought to venture to expose oneself to being judged on one's culture (*moeurs*); but, if the Infidels were to agree to submit to a competitive examination in which the marks were to be awarded for intelligence, for learning, and for the military

---

[1] Bayle, P., *Dictionaire*, 3rd ed., iii. 1859 b, s.v. Mahomet (cp. iii. 2078 b–2079 b, s.v. Nestorius).

[2] Ibid., i. 140 b, s.v. Alciat (Jean Paul).

[3] QQ. . . . 'Here we can see how one half of the World derides the other half—for it is unlikely that the Mahometans are unaware of all the ridiculous stories that are current about Christian monks.'

[4] Ibid., iii, 1866-7, s.v. Mahomet.   [5] Ibid., iii. 1856 a, s.v. Mahomet.

virtues, we ought to take them at their word; for, on these terms, they would inevitably be beaten at the present day. On all these three points they are far inferior to us Christians. We enjoy the fine advantage of being far better versed than they are in the art of killing, bombarding, and exterminating the Human Race.[1]

[1] Ibid., iii. 1856 a, s.v. Mahomet.

THE RE-ERECTION OF TWO
GRAECO-ROMAN IDOLS

THE secularization of the Western Civilization in the seventeenth century, so far from producing a stable way of life, raised the question: What is going to fill the temporary spiritual vacuum that this deconsecration of Western life has created in Western souls? Alternative attempts to fill this vacuum have constituted the unstable spiritual history of the Western World during the last 250 years. The first new objects of worship that inserted themselves in place of the West's dethroned ancestral Christianity were ghosts from a Graeco-Roman Civilization to which the Western Civilization is affiliated. The first of these Graeco-Roman idols to be resuscitated was the deified parochial community; the second was the deified oecumenical empire.

The re-erection of the first of these two idols in the West was a disaster. The political parochialism of the Modern Western World has been a perhaps inevitable nemesis of the break-up of the western provinces of the Roman Empire into parochial sovereign successor-states in the fifth century of the Christian Era, but this nemesis did not fully overtake Western Christendom until the Renaissance and the Reformation. It is true that, during the intervening millennium, the political break-up of the Roman Empire in the west into a litter of local successor-states had not been repaired. Western Europe had never seen a return of those halcyon days of the Roman Principate, when a civilian could travel from Rome to the Rhine without meeting any soldiers *en route* except one detachment, 1,200 strong, at Lyons. But the untoward political effects of the fall of the Roman Empire in the west had been mitigated at first by the fortunate psychological fact that these post-Roman local states had been regarded as an accident and a pity, and that their subjects had put no more than a minimum of their spiritual treasure in them.

The larger part of this treasure had been transferred from a dead unitary Roman Empire to a living unitary Western Christian Church. The Venerable Bede, for example, had told the stories of the petty English successor-states of the Roman Empire in Britain within the grander framework of an *Ecclesiastical History*; and this concentration of feeling on the Church, instead of on the local states, had been accentuated during the century and a half—*circa* 1050-1200—that had seen the rise and floruit of the Papal Respublica Christiana. Even the ghost of the Roman Empire that had been resuscitated by Charlemagne, feeble though it had always been, had also attracted some loyalty and affection, of which Dante has left a rather academic literary monument in his *De Monarchiâ*. Thus, down to the beginning of the Late Middle Ages, the unity which had been lost, some 800 or 900 years back, on the political plane had still survived to a large extent on the spiritual plane; and its survival here had put local secular rulers under a salutary restraint. This charge of feeling was not liberated from its attachment to the Western Church till the break-up of the Western Respublica Christiana, which had begun in the thirteenth century in the war to the death between the Papacy and Frederick II and which was consummated in the Early Modern Age in the Reformation.

The Reformation found instruments and allies in the parochial sovereign states as against the oecumenical Western Church, and in the parochial vernacular languages as against the oecumenical Latin language; and this movement towards putting treasure in parochial institutions was not confined to countries that went Protestant. Catholic Venice was equally insistent in asserting her local sovereign rights against the Vatican, and even Catholic Spain jealously maintained the patronage of the Crown in ecclesiastical appointments in the new Spanish Empire overseas. Again, in all Western countries, Catholic as well as Protestant, the cultivation of the vernacular languages, which had been started in the twelfth century by the troubadours and had been carried farther in the fourteenth century by Dante and Petrarch, was now extended from the fields of poetry and romance into the fields of administration and law and science. When, in the seventeenth century, French partially replaced Latin as a Western *lingua franca* for diplomatic and literary use, French gained no more than a fragment of what Latin had already lost.

The transfer of allegiance from the Western Christian Church to parochial Western secular states was given a positive form—borrowed from the Graeco-Roman Civilization—by the Renaissance. In our memories of the Western renaissance of Hellenism in the Early Modern Age, its literary and artistic sides loom largest; but really its political side has been by far the most important in subsequent Western history.[1] On the artistic and literary planes the Renaissance proved, as we have noted in Chapter Thirteen, to be no more than a passing infatuation; but on the political plane it is still an obsession in our day. On this political plane the Renaissance revived the Graeco-Roman worship of parochial states as goddesses; and it did this all the more insidiously because it did it unavowedly, out of deference to the West's Christian past (the Greeks had deified Athens and Sparta consciously and frankly). This unavowed worship of parochial states was by far the most prevalent religion in the Western World in A.D. 1956. Even the experience of the rise and fall of Hitler's Europe and the menace of Russian Communism have hardly begun to shake the hold of nation-worship over Western hearts; and the Graeco-Roman inspiration of this Modern Western nationalism is ominous, because we know, from the long since concluded history of the Graeco-Roman Civilization, that this form of idolatry was the main cause of that Civilization's breakdown and disinte ration.

The erosion of the West's traditional common institutions and common outlook by Nationalism has been progressive. The unity of the clergy in Western Christendom was broken by the Reformation. The unity of the Western 'Republic of Letters', as it had existed down to the generation of Erasmus and Saint Thomas More, was broken when Latin was ousted by the local vernacular languages, and it was re-established only very imperfectly when Latin was partially replaced by French in the seventeenth century. The unity of the West European aristocracy—a polyglot social circle knit to ether by inter-marriage—was broken by the French Revolution, by the

---

[1] This point has been put by the writer in *A Study of History*, vol. ix, pp. 3, 6, 7-8.

smothering of the aristocracy in Britain in the nineteenth century in the embrace of a prolific middle class, and by the rise of the United States, where the West European aristocracy had never struck root.

The West European Royal Family had been still more closely knit together by inter-marriage than the West European aristocracy, and, if possible, still better educated in the gift of tongues. But its unity, too, was broken by the French Revolution; by the rise to power of middle-class and working-class parliaments and electorates; and by the political unification of Germany in A.D. 1871. This last event nationalized the royal family in the minor German states, where, up till then, it had remained nationally neutral and therefore eligible for such purposes as the export of West European kinglets to Eastern Orthodox Christian successor-states of the Ottoman Empire. The final stroke was the deposition of a number of dynasties in West European countries defeated in the First and Second World Wars.[1]

The unity of the diplomatic corps was broken by the eclipse of the aristocracy and by the rise of the United States and of the successor-states of the Hapsburg, Hohenzollern, Romanov, and Ottoman Empires—all of which had to draw their diplomats from among *novi homines* who had been born and brought up as nationalists and who had not been taught to speak French as virtually a second mother tongue. The successive liquidation of all these oecumenical families, corporations, and classes has

---

[1] There were, however, indications, by A.D. 1956, that this decimated and politically depotentiated West European Royal Family might be going to have a new lease of life on a new plane. Their decimation in the wars and revolutions of the past century and a half had given the survivors a rarity value; and it was no accident that the few countries in which the institution of Monarchy did survive were those in which it had previously lost its political power. This detachment of the Crown from politics had had the unforeseen result of giving it a new significance as a politically non-controversial symbol of social solidarity transcending the divisions between parties and classes. This new symbolic role had given the Crown a new hold on people's hearts; and in A.D. 1956 it looked as if at least six of the seven monarchies then still in existence in Western Europe were going to become increasingly important as emotional focuses for the sense of unity, not only within the frontiers of their respective countries, but throughout the Western World, including the non-European states members of the British Commonwealth and even the United States. This striking reversal of the historic role of an institution that had formerly bred division and strife was a good augury for the future of the Western Civilization.

meant a progressive removal of the traditional barriers in the Modern Western World to a totalitarian idolatrous worship of parochial states.

As the traditional oecumenical institutions of Western Christendom were liquidated or rejected, one after another, a post-Christian Western Society began to feel the painfulness and dangerousness of the vacuum, and it deliberately set itself to fill the gap with new oecumenical institutions of its own creation. In the seventeenth century the broken Medieval Western fraternity of Latin-learnèd clerks was partially replaced by a more artificial and self-conscious French-cultivated fraternity of *savants* and men of letters.[1] But the increasing self-assertion of the local vernaculars, which had sabotaged the oecumenical use of Latin, has sabotaged the oecumenical use of French too—and this at a rapid pace since the fall of France in A.D. 1940.[2] In the nineteenth century the establishment of the International Red Cross at Geneva provided a secular substitute for the religious restraint once imposed by a common Christianity on the barbarity of War, and also for the aristocratic restraint once imposed on it by chivalry. But the symbol

[1] 'This Republic [of Letters] is a state with an extremely liberal constitution. The only dominion that is recognized here is that of Truth and Reason; and under the auspices of these a bloodless war is waged without respect of persons. Every citizen of this commonwealth is sovereign and is at the same time subject to every other citizen's jurisdiction.'—Bayle, P., *Dictionaire*, 3rd ed., i. 812 a, s.v. Catius.

[2] The consequent fall of France's linguistic and cultural empire had gone far in both South-West Asia and Latin America by A.D. 1956. In both these cultural provinces of a Westernizing World the English language seemed at the moment to be profiting by the French language's loss, but it would have been rash to take it for granted that English would eventually succeed in filling a gap which the fall of Latin had left behind it and which French had never succeeded in filling more than partially. Throughout the 600 years that had run from the conquest of the Achaemenian Empire by Alexander the Great down to the first collapse of the *Pax Romana* in the third century of the Christian Era, a 'Standard Attic Greek' (the *koinê*) had been the *lingua franca* of a Graeco-Roman World which had expanded into India in one direction and into Britain in another. In Saint Paul's generation even a cautious observer might have ventured to commit himself to the prophecy that, whatever else the Future might or might not hold in store, it could now be taken as certain that the Attic *koinê* was going to be the common language of half the World for good and all. The non-fulfilment of this then apparently reasonable expectation was a warning to observers of a Westernizing World in the twentieth century of the Christian Era that, at this date, the prospects of the English language were not certainly assured.

of the Red Cross proclaimed that a secular nineteenth-century Western humanitarianism was living on a dwindling fund of religious capital.

On the technological plane 'the conquest of distance' by mechanical inventions within the last 150 years has provided not only the West itself but the whole of a Westernizing World, over all the habitable and traversable surface of the planet, with the physical apparatus for making one family of all Mankind. Since Technology has replaced Religion as the pursuit in which Western Man has put his treasure in the Late Modern Age, it is natural that he should have expected his new idol to reward him for his worship by enabling him to fill the spiritual vacuum which he had created by discarding his ancestral religion. Yet, so far from easing his difficulties, the physical unification of the World by Technology has aggravated them.

The physical facilities for peaceful intercourse which the progress of Western technology has provided at an ever accelerating pace have suddenly established contact between societies which have hitherto been physically insulated from one another by lack of adequate physical means of communication, and which therefore have developed very different manners and customs and outlooks. Technology can bring strangers physically face to face with one another in an instant, but it may take generations for their minds, and centuries for their hearts, to grow together. Physical proximity, not accompanied by simultaneous mutual understanding and sympathy, is apt to produce antipathy, not affection, and consequently discord, not harmony. Perhaps a subconscious realization of the truth that a sudden conquest of physical distance may be inimical to a union of hearts explains why, in A.D. 1956, the people of the World were putting up so patiently with the administrative obstacles that their governments were putting in the way of physical communications: tariffs and quotas, exchange controls, immigration controls, health controls, and the rest.

In spite of all the tariffs and the quotas, the annihilation of physical distance has made a Westernizing World economically interdependent to a much greater extent than it ever was before the Industrial Revolution. In an age in which local states are dependent on the World outside their frontiers for the supply of staple raw materials and foodstuffs, the political partition of the *Oikoumenê* into sixty or seventy fully self-governing parochial states is becoming more and more burdensome in peacetime and more and more devastating in wartime. In a world that is already economically interdependent but still remains politically disunited, the social disturbance caused by wars is necessarily far greater than it was in a world in which Man's economic operations had no wider a range than his political communities had. Moreover, Technology is a neutral power that lends itself impartially to all purposes, including war. This is a point that needs no elaboration in an atomic age; and we are forced to conclude that Technology has not healed the wound that was inflicted on the Western Civilization in the seventeenth century by its leading spirits when they discarded their ancestral religion. Technology has made the wound worse; and Modern Western Man's rueful recognition that, after all, this master-art of his is no panacea for his social and spiritual maladies has been virtually confessed in his successive attempts to attain a general and lasting peace by creating for himself some new form of oecumenical organization.

The West lost its original oecumenical institutions when in the thirteenth century the Papacy wrecked the Holy Roman Empire and when in the fourteenth century it wrecked itself. Since then there has been a series of attempts to replace these lost oecumenical Western institutions by new ones.

The Conciliar Movement was an attempt to salvage the medieval Respublica Christiana by placing the papal monarchy on a parliamentary representative constitutional basis. This movement was defeated by the Papacy's lust for absolute power, which was the régime of the day in Northern and Central Italy and was the régime of the future in the rest of the Western World. Charles V's Europe was an attempt to give the Western World effective political unity, which the Holy Roman Empire had never been able to give it, by uniting a sufficient number of key parochial states in a network of dynastic marriages. This project was frustrated by the unwillingness of France—the most fertile and populous state in the Western World of the day—to renounce her national ambitions for the sake of a Western common weal. Louis XIV's and Napoleon's

Europe was an attempt to unite the Western World under the hegemony of the militarily strongest parochial Power in it. The military domination of France was alleviated, in both these attempts to impose it, by the cultural gifts which the French armies brought with them in this age. But France's bid for hegemony in the Western World, like Spain's earlier bid and Germany's later bids, was overtrumped by the play of the Balance of Power.

The post-Napoleonic Concert of Europe was an attempt to make the Balance of Power serve a constructive purpose by putting in commission among the Great Powers the hegemony that previously had been denied to Spain and to France in turn. The League of Nations was the Concert of Europe expanded to a world-wide range, provided with a written constitution, and democratized by the inclusion of the middle-sized and small states side by side with the Great Powers, though not on an equality with them. The failure of the Concert of Europe to avert the First World War, followed by the failure of the League of Nations to avert the Second World War, indicated that the Balance of Power was not an effective substitute for the hegemony of a single Power, to which it had repeatedly proved to be an effective obstacle. Its failure as a constructive agency was proclaimed in a revival of the crude alternative method of trying to establish political unity. Hitler's Europe was a fresh attempt to unite not only Europe but, this time, the whole World under the domination of the militarily strongest parochial Power in it. But Hitler's outrage was not mitigated by any Napoleonic gifts from the conquerors to the conquered; and, considering that Napoleon had failed, it would have been surprising if Hitler had succeeded. The total defeat of Hitler's abominable design has given the World one more chance of putting itself in political order by a constructive use of the Balance of Power. The United Nations is an attempt to revive the League of Nations, but this under conditions that are less favourable in a world in which the number of Great Powers has been reduced, by the shattering effects of a Second World War, from seven to no more than two.

Thus our Westernizing World has several good reasons for feeling anxiety. It is armed with atomic weapons. It has already experienced two devastating pre-atomic wars in one lifetime. And its political power is now neither distributed, as it was in the Concert of Europe and in the League of Nations, nor concentrated, as Hitler, Napoleon, and Louis XIV tried to concentrate it, but is polarized between two rival Powers and two only. In these circumstances our anxiety is well warranted. For, while we can foresee that, in an Atomic Age in which physical distance has been 'annihilated', the control of atomic weapons is bound to be unified in the hands of some single authority sooner or later, we cannot foresee whether we shall reach this inevitable goal of world-government without inflicting on ourselves a supreme catastrophe. We can, however, foresee that, when world-government does come, the need for it will have become so desperate that Mankind will not only be ready to accept it even at the most exorbitantly high price in terms of loss of liberty, but will deify it and its human embodiments, as an excruciated Graeco-Roman World once deified Rome and Augustus. The virtual worship that has already been paid to Napoleon, Mussolini, Stalin, Hitler, and Mao indicates the degree of the idolization that would be the reward of an American or a Russian Caesar who did succeed in giving the World a stable peace at any price; and in this baleful light it looks as if the oecumenical welfare state may be the next idol that will be erected in a still discarded Christianity's place.

17

THE IDOLIZATION OF THE INVINCIBLE
TECHNICIAN

A SOCIETY cannot maintain its social cohesion unless a
decisive majority of its members hold in common a number of
guiding ideas and ideals. One of the necessary social ideals is a
symbolic hero to embody, in a personal form, the recognized
goal of the society's endeavours. In Medieval and Early
Modern Western Christendom the West's symbolic ideal figure
was the inspired saint (with the chivalrous knight as a secondary
alternative). In the Late Modern Age the West has transferred its spiritual allegiance from the inspired saint to the
invincible technician, and this change in Western Man's
personal ideal has produced changes in his spirit, outlook, and
aims.

The technician, not 'the natural philosopher', whose theories
the technician translates into practice, was the new hero whom
the West adopted in the later decades of the seventeenth
century. Francis Bacon pronounced that

The real and legitimate goal of the sciences is the endowment
of human life with new inventions and riches.[1]

And Philosophy was defined by Thomas Hobbes as a means
for attaining technological results:

By philosophy is understood the knowledge acquired by reasoning . . . to the end to be able to produce, as far as matter and
humane force permit, such effects as human life requireth.[2]

Sprat, in *The History of the Royal Society*,[3] points out that the
Graeco-Roman philosophy never did anything for Technology,
and he suggests that it was owing to its unpractical, esoteric

[1] Bacon, Francis, *Novum Organum* Partis Secundae Summa, Aphorismus
lxxxi: 'Meta . . . scientiarum vera et legitima non alia est quam ut dotetur
vita humana novis inventis et copiis.'
[2] *Leviathan*, Part IV, chap. 46.   [3] Pp.117-18.

outlook that this Graeco-Roman philosophy foundered in storms which a Graeco-Roman technology survived. He commends the fathers of the Royal Society for having broken away from this supercilious philosophical tradition:

> By turning it [Philosophy] into one of the arts of life, of which men may see there is daily need, they [the Royal Society] have provided that it cannot hereafter be extinguish'd.[1]

Sprat's advice to the natural philosopher is that he should take off his coat and apply his hands to the practical arts.

> What greater privilege have men to boast of then this, that they have the pow'r of using, directing, changing, or advancing all the rest of the creatures? This is the dominion which God has given us over the Works of His hands. . . . It is impossible for us to administer this power aright unless we prefer the light of men of Knowledge to be a constant overseer and director of the industry and works of those that labour. The benefits are vast that will appear upon this conjunction. . . . By this the conceptions of men of knowledge, which are wont to soar too high, will be made to descend into the material world, and the flegmatick imaginations of men of trade, which use to grovell too much on the ground, will be exalted.
>
> It was said of civil government by Plato that then the World will be best rul'd when either philosophers shall be chosen kings or kings shall have philosophical minds. And I will affirm the like of Philosophy. It will then attain to perfection when either the mechanic laborers shall have philosophical heads or the philosophers shall have mechanical hands.[2]

This late-seventeenth-century exaltation of Technology over Pure Science had been anticipated, like so much else in the seventeenth-century spiritual revolution, by the genius of Leonardo da Vinci.

> Mechanics is the paradise of the mathematical sciences, because, with mechanics, we reach the fruit that mathematics can be made to bear.[3]

---

[1] Sprat, op. cit., p. 119. [2] Ibid., pp. 395-7.

[3] 'La meccanica è il paradiso delle sciētie matematiche, perchè cō quella si viene al frutto matematico'—Leonardo da Vinci, in *The Literary Works of Leonardo da Vinci*, compiled and edited from the original MSS. by J. P. Richter, 2nd ed. (Oxford 1939, University Press, 2 vols.), vol. ii, p. 241, No. 1155.

Instrumental, *alias* mechanical, science is most noble and also most useful above all the other sciences, because this one is the means by which all living bodies that have the power of movement perform all their operations.[1]

At the same time Leonardo pointed out, with characteristic vision, that, if Technology were to divorce itself from Pure Science, it would become incapable of achieving its own aims.

Science is the captain and Practice the rank and file. . . . People who fall in love with Practice without Science are like the skipper who boards ship without rudder or compass and who consequently never knows where he is going.[2]

The penetrating point here made by Leonardo seems to have been either overlooked or deliberately ignored by his seventeenth-century successors; but, for the first 250 years after the seventeenth-century exaltation of Technology, the Human Spirit's saving grace of disinterested curiosity prevented Western Man's utilitarianism from blindly frustrating itself.

Long before Technology was thus openly exalted in the West by the leading spirits of the Western Society in the seventeenth century and by their forerunner Leonardo da Vinci, a practical cultivation of Technology had already borne fruit in many different provinces of Western life. The Western Civilization was both Christian and Hellenistic, and Hellenism and Christianity, though at variance in so many ways, were of one mind in setting no store by Technology. So long, therefore, as Western Man remained content to regulate his life by following authority, with these two authorities as the only alternatives within his cultural horizon, his native bent towards Technology was bound to be submerged and suppressed. The persistence of this bent for thirteen centuries in these adverse circumstances is impressive evidence of its strength; and this declared itself

---

[1] 'La scientia strumentale over machinale è nobilissima e sopra tutte l'altre utilissima, cōciosiachè mediante quella tutti li corpi animati, che ànno moto, fanno tutte loro operationi'—ibid., p. 241, No. 1154.

[2] 'La sciētia è il capitano, e la pratica sono i soldati. . . . Quelli che s'inamorā di pratica saza sciētia sō come'l nocchiere che ētra navilio sanza timone e bussola, che mai à certezza dove si vada'—ibid., p. 241, Nos. 1160 and 1161.

when Technology, after long probation in the servants' quarters, was at last given a place of honour among Western Man's activities that corresponded to his hitherto repressed passion for it. It is not surprising that, from the close of the seventeenth century onwards, Technology should have gained in the West a momentum that had no precedent in the history of any other civilization.

The Western bent towards Technology had already declared itself in the western provinces of the Roman Empire in the Western Civilization's pre-natal age. In Gaul after the Roman conquest the extension of agriculture in a thinly populated country had evoked the invention of a reaping-machine which, crude and clumsy though it may have been, was a unique achievement of its kind in Graeco-Roman history.[1] The further depopulation of the western provinces as a result of the barbarian invasions in the third century of the Christian Era produced an acute and continuing local shortage of man-power, and in the fourth century this stimulated a writer, whose name is unknown, to publish a memorial *De Rebus Bellicis* in which he proposes a number of mechanical devices for economizing man-power in warfare.[2] This was a voice crying in the wilderness, and the next century witnessed the collapse which the anonymous fourth-century reformer and inventor had foreseen and had sought, in vain, to avert. Yet the social and political breakdown of the Roman Empire in its western provinces, which left the central and eastern provinces unscathed, did not arrest the now politically derelict western provinces' technological progress. The social nadir of West European life between the close of the fourth century and the close of the seventh saw the spread of the water-mill over the West, where flowing water was abundant, from its place of origin in the Levant, where flowing water was comparatively scarce.[3]

[1] See Plinius Secundus, C., *Historia Naturalis*, Book XVIII, § 296; Palladius, *Agricultura*, Book VII, chap. ii, § 2. A reconstruction of this machine, by Nachtweh, is reproduced in *A Roman Reformer and Inventor* (see the following footnote), fig. XIII.

[2] *A Roman Reformer and Inventor*, being a new text of the treatise *De Rebus Bellicis* with a translation and introduction by E. A. Thompson (Oxford 1952, Clarendon Press).

[3] Thompson, op. cit., pp. 47-8. The watermill had been in use, but not yet in common use, in Italy in the first century of the Christian Era (see Plinius Secundus, C., *Historia Naturalis*, Book XVIII, § 97).

The number of water-mills in use in Western Christendom continued to increase all through the Middle Ages;[1] and in the twelfth century, at the latest, the water-mill was supplemented in the West by the introduction of the windmill. This vigorous practical application, in Ultima Thule, of inventions that had been made in the Middle Eastern heart of Civilization's domain in the Old World was followed up by one native Western invention after another.

The decisive invention, which opened the way for all the rest by producing a margin of wealth beyond what was required for bare subsistence, was the heavy plough with 'a coulter to cut the sod, a mould-board to turn it over, and wheels which enabled a more even furrow to be cut and lightened the work of the ploughman by relieving him of the task of keeping the plough at the proper level.'[2] This improved plough made it possible to cultivate potentially fertile soils whose stiffness had defied the rudimentary plough with which the Romans as well as their predecessors had been content; and the effective new implement had been invented, beyond the pale of the Roman Empire, in Northern Europe and had been introduced into the Empire's former western provinces by their fifth-century northern barbarian conquerors. This one invention would have been enough to justify the anonymous fourth-century Roman inventor's dictum that 'the barbarian peoples . . . are by no means considered strangers to mechanical inventiveness, where Nature comes to their assistance'[3] ('*barbarae nationes . . . minime . . . a rerum inventione, naturâ opitulante, habentur alienae*').[4]

The next technological invention in the West after the heavy plough—next in productivity as well as in date—was the devising in the tenth century, and the subsequent improvement

---

[1] Lilley, S., *Men, Machines, and History* (London 1948, Cobbett Press), pp. 37-8.

[2] Ibid., p. 42.

[3] E. A. Thompson's translation in Thompson, op. cit., p. 107.

[4] In op. cit., pp. 46-7, Thompson points out that this passage in *De Rebus Bellicis* is not the only testimony to the inventiveness of the barbarians in the age in which these were successfully invading the Roman Empire. Procopius mentions the Sabirian Huns' invention of a better battering-ram (*The Wars of Justinian*, VIII, xi, 27); Zosimus (*Historiae*, VIII, xxi, 3) mentions, as an example, the Goth war-lord Gainas's improvisation of rafts for crossing the Bosphorus.

during the next 200 years, of a new harness for donkeys, horses, and mules that at last enabled these draught-animals to put their full power into traction. For not much less than 3,000 years before that, they had not been able to bring into play more than a third, at the most, of their potential traction-power because a harness that had been invented for oxen, and that effectively brought into play the full traction power of an animal of their physique, had been applied unimaginatively to all other animals that had subsequently been broken in. In a branch of Technology which was of such vital importance before the invention of mechanical traction-power, it was only in Western Christendom in its 'Dark Age' that the inertia of tradition was overcome by a conscious, deliberate, and sustained exercise of Reason. What the Western innovators now did was to modify the traditional ox-harness experimentally till they had adapted it to the quite un-ox-like structure of a horse's, mule's, or donkey's body.[1]

This early Western application of Reason to the problem of traction had a contemporary parallel in the province of military equipment. In the eleventh century the West revolutionized a weapon that had been invented in the Later Palaeolithic Age by setting a windlass, instead of the muscles of the human arm, to draw a bow. This device overcame the limits to the stiffness, and hence also to the propulsive power, of the bow that had been set hitherto by the limits of the human arm's muscular strength. The entry of the cross-bow into the field suddenly increased the range and the penetrative power of missile weapons to an unprecedented degree; and this, in its turn, started a race between missile weapons and body armour. The eleventh century, which saw the invention of the cross-bow in the West, also saw the adoption there of the Sarmatian nomad heavy-armed lancer's equipment.[2] This now at last replaced the antiquated Graeco-Roman equipment that, in a cavalry age, had lingered on in the West for nearly six centuries after the fall of the Roman Empire there, though it had been

---

[1] See Lilley, op. cit., pp. 16 and 39. A fuller account will be found in Lefebvre des Noëttes, ct, *L'Attelage, le Cheval de Selle, à travers les Âges* (Paris 1931, Picard, 2 vols., text and illustrations). See especially the text, pp. 3-5, 9-20, 121-35.

[2] For this, see *A Study of History*, vol. iv, pp. 439-45.

designed originally for a foot-soldier and gave only a poor defence to a horseman.

The adoption of the Sarmatian 'cataphract' cavalryman's body-armour[1] was an effective reply to the invention of the cross-bow; but the rationally experimental Western mind was not content to take this superior equipment as it had found it. The Western converts to it immediately began to improve upon it by substituting for the traditional round target a kite-shaped shield which gave the human body the maximum cover with the greatest economy of surface and weight.[2] This, however, was only the beginning of a race in the West between body-armour and missile weapons which gathered momentum from the eleventh century to the fifteenth. As the cross-bow was raised to a higher power and was then supplemented by the long-bow and by the arquebus,[3] the hard-pressed Western armourer first rationalized the helm, as he had rationalized the shield, and then reinforced a suit of chain-mail, which he had stretched to cover limbs and head as well as trunk, by encasing it in plate that gradually followed the chain-mail in extending all over the body. The race then ended in a definitive victory of Western missile-weapons over Western body-armour; for the steel-cased fifteenth-century *gendarme*, hoisted on to the back of a steel-cased Flemish horse, had arrived at the same dead end as the armoured monsters of a pre-human Reptile

[1] We may perhaps hazard the guess that, in eleventh-century France, this was still in use in places whose name Sermaises, *alias* Sermaize, *alias* Salmaise, testifies that their inhabitants were descended from the fifth-century Alan Sarmatian settlers in Gaul.

[2] The kite shape is the rational shape for a shield designed to protect a pear-shaped human body. The round shape would be rational only if the human body were apple-shaped, which it is not. If the whole length of the body, from shoulders to ankles, is to be covered by a round shield, the shield will have to be prohibitively large and heavy, and about half its surface will be superfluous, as it will project far beyond the body on either side. On the other hand, a small light round target, in the style of the original shield in the Sarmatian cataphract's equipment, will protect, at most, the breast and the face.

[3] The simultaneous adoption, in a fourteenth-century Western Christendom, of the long-bow from Wales and of fire-arms from China has a parallel in the simultaneous invention of the clipper ship and the steamship in the nineteenth-century Western World. The gun, like the steamship, was a wholly new departure; the long-bow, like the clipper ship, was an attempt to obtain the increased efficiency, which the new departure promised to yield, by the alternative method of perfecting an instrument that was ancient and familiar.

Age of life on Earth. He had made himself immobile without having succeeded in making himself invulnerable; and in the course of the sixteenth and seventeenth centuries he reluctantly and dilatorily confessed his defeat by the practical gestures of first streamlining his body-armour and finally throwing the remnants of it away.[1]

The *chef d'oeuvre* of Medieval Western Man's technological achievements was the fifteenth-century Western revolution in the build and rig of ships. This, too, was a triumph of the rational application of the findings of prolonged experiments in which elements derived from many quarters were assembled to create something that was new. The fifteenth-century Western shipwrights laid under contribution native builds and rigs of the Mediterranean seaboard and the Atlantic seaboard of Western Europe and equipped this composite vessel with a set of native Western square sails supplemented by lateen sails that had been invented in the Indian Ocean. The navigators furnished this new ship with an Arab astrolabe, a Chinese compass, and a fixed rudder that, in the West, had been substituted for a traditional steering oar as far back as the thirteenth century.[2] This new ship was, as we have seen,[3] the new instrument by which Western Man won for himself a temporary ascendancy over the rest of his fellow-men by gaining a mastery over the Ocean.

These medieval achievements of Western technology indicated what the West was capable of doing in this line if ever it were to give its mind to Technology and its approval to technicians, and these two requisite conditions were fulfilled at last in the seventeenth-century Western spiritual revolution. The authors of this revolution cannot claim credit for having

---

[1] A psychologist might perhaps bring to light a psychological connexion between the abandonment of body-armour in the West in the later decades of the seventeenth century and the simultaneous abandonment of religious intolerance there. Western Man seems to have realized that breastplates were no protection against bullets at the same moment at which he realized that dogmas were no protection against empirically established facts. In Late Modern Western armies, fifteenth-century plate-armour continued, however, to be worn in the trenches by the sappers and miners as late as the time of the Napoleonic Wars. In some Western armies a little crescent-shaped plate, representing a gorget and hung round the neck by an elegant chain, continued until after the First World War to be worn as part of the insignia of an officer.

[2] See Lilley, op. cit., pp. 40-1.   [3] In Chapter 11, pp. 144-5, above.

given the Western Society a technological bent that had declared itself long before their day; but they did liberate and encourage this bent after it had persisted for thirteen centuries in adverse circumstances.

The seventeenth-century change of social climate in the West in Technology's favour is illustrated in the contrast between the careers of two celebrated Western enthusiasts for Technology who were one another's namesakes. Of the two Bacons, Roger was evidently more richly endowed than Francis was with the practical genius in which they both put their treasure; but Roger (*vivebat* A.D. 1214(?)-94) was frustrated by the social climate of his age. The suspicion and disapproval which his work aroused in the minds of the authorities of the Franciscan Order was not counterbalanced by the patronage of Pope Clement IV. Roger Bacon was hindered by disciplinary restraints from freely pursuing his researches; and, even if he had been left free, he would have found himself handicapped by a lack of apparatus and, still more seriously, by a dearth of congenial fellow workers in his field. By contrast, Francis Bacon (*vivebat* A.D. 1561-1626) won the applause of his own generation in the West and became an inspiration to succeeding generations by putting into words the dream of Technology that was floating before their minds too. Yet Francis Bacon did not show Roger Bacon's practical ability, and consequently his words did not provide the blue-print for the acts which Western technicians were afterwards to perform at his instigation. If the two Bacons could have exchanged life-times, Francis might have fallen no farther short of practical achievement in the thirteenth century than he fell in the seventeenth, while Roger in the seventeenth century might have accomplished practical results that in the thirteenth were out of his reach. For, between Roger's actual lifetime and Francis's, the social, as well as the intellectual, climate of the Western World had changed decisively in the technician's favour; and the honour that was paid to Francis Bacon, as a prophet of Technocracy's future, rankled into an idolization of his successors when these had made his prophecy come true.

Bayle satirizes the accentuation of the cult of Our Lady in the Spain of his day in an amusing passage in which he imagines the Holy Trinity officially abdicating in her favour;[1] and this seventeenth-century fantasy may serve a twentieth-century historian as an allegory of what Bayle himself and the other leading spirits in the West in his age were doing unconsciously and unintentionally. Without waiting for God to abdicate they were proclaiming His deposition; and in thus creating a spiritual interregnum they were opening the way for the enthronement of a goddess in God's stead. This goddess whose fortune was made by the discredit and odium that had over-taken the ancestral god of Western Christendom was not Our Lady but was Technology; and this new divinity was effectively enthroned in Western hearts although the fathers of the seventeenth-century Western spiritual revolution had had no wish to replace the deposed god of Christianity by any alter-native object of worship. Technology was deified, not by Western Man's deliberate choice, but because Religion, like Nature, abhors a vacuum. Technology and the Technician thus became the Dea Roma and the Divus Caesar of a Late Modern Western World.

Divus Caesar was far from being the role for which the Late

[1] 'It is surprising that Spain should not yet have produced writers confidently claiming to know, by revelation, that God the Father, having become aware, through long experience, of the infiniteness of the Virgin Mary's ability and the excellence of the use that she had made of the power with which He had invested her, had resolved to abdicate the Empire of the Universe, and that God the Son, believing that He could not find a better example to follow, had concurred in this resolution—with the result that, after the Holy Spirit, who always conforms to the wills of the two persons from whom He proceeds, had given His approval to this admirable proposal, the whole Trinity had delivered the government of the World into the hands of the Virgin Mary, and that the two ceremonies of abdication and of the translation of the Empire had been performed with all due solemnity in the presence of all the Angels; furthermore, that an accurate and authentic minute of the proceedings had been drawn up; that, from that day onwards, God had no longer interfered in anything, but had relied, for everything, upon Mary's vigilance; that orders had been despatched to several angels to notify on Earth this change of government, in order that Mankind might know to whom and in what style they were to address themselves in future in their acts of invocation; and that they were no longer to address themselves to God, since He had declared Himself, by His own act, to be *emeritus* and *rude donatus*, and were not to address them-selves to the Virgin Mary in the capacity of a mediatrix or of a subordinate queen, but were to address themselves to her as the sovereign and absolute empress of all things. It is surprising, I say, that this extravaganza should still be in the womb of the Future.'—Bayle, P., *Dictionaire*, 3rd ed., i. 98 a and b, s.v. Agreda.

Modern Western technician was cast by his seventeenth-century patrons. We have seen[1] that, when they were deliberately substituting Technology for Religion as the paramount interest and pursuit of the Western World, the characteristic merits that they found in the contemporary technician, by contrast with the contemporary politician and the contemporary theologian, were the technician's apparent innocence and, better still, his apparent inability to make mischief even if the temptation were to seize him. In a technician, however, harmlessness is not enough to justify his existence. We have observed already in this chapter that the leading spirits in a seventeenth-century Western World exalted Technology above Pure Science because of the practical benefits that Technology promised to confer on Mankind. By the end of the Age of the Western Wars of Religion, Utilitarianism was in the air. *Some Considerations touching the Usefulness of Experimental Philosophy* was the title of a book of Robert Boyle's which was written in the sixteen-fifties, was sent to press in 1660, 1661, and 1663, and was published in the last of these three years.[2] In *The History of the Royal Society*, which was published in 1667, Sprat observes:[3]

I rather trust to the inclination of the age itself wherein I write; which (if I mistake not) is farr more prepar'd to be perswaded to promote such studies then any other time that has gone before us.

In another passage of the same work,[4] Sprat avers that, since the Restoration, more Acts of Parliament directed to objects of practical public utility have been passed already, by the time of writing, than in the whole course of the previous history of England. Utility was being pursued as an end in itself; but utility is no sooner attained than it generates power, and power is no sooner attained than it invites idolization.

The Christian saint, whom the technician was replacing in the role of serving as Western Man's symbolic hero, could not so easily be made into an object of idolatrous worship, because one of the hallmarks of a saint's authenticity is that he should

---

[1] In Chapter 14, pp. 184-7, above.
[2] See the Author's advertisement. The place of publication was Oxford; the publisher was Hall.
[3] On p. 5. Cp. pp. 152-3.　　　　[4] On p. 78.

feel and should proclaim that his spiritual achievements are due, not to any spiritual prowess of his own, but to the grace of God working through him. When, however, God Himself had been deposed, there was no such spiritual impediment to the idolization of the technician. Indeed the Christian religion had inadvisedly cleared the ground for the deification of Technology and the technician in a post-Christian age, though, so long as it had been in the ascendant, it had been unpropitious to Technology in virtue of its counsel not to put one's treasure in This World. Like its parent religion Judaism and its sister religion Islam, Christianity had taken the traditional divinity out of Non-Human Nature in its zeal for the faith that there was no god but God and that Nature was nothing but God's creature. In consequence, when this almighty transcendent creator God—the god of Judaism, Christianity, and Islam—was deposed in Western Christendom towards the close of the seventeenth century of the Christian Era, Nature was no longer a competitor with Man in the West for the occupation of God's vacant seat. Emptied, long ago, of her traditional divinity, Nature now lay passive and defenceless, waiting to fall a prey to whatever upstart Zeus was going to succeed in usurping the vacant throne of Cronos. Nature was the prize of seventeenth-century Man's self-deification; his establishment of an effective dominion over Nature was the sign that he had exalted himself into a very god; and he gave this demonstration of his assumed divinity by proving himself a past master in Technology—a Greek word which signifies the sleight of hand that subjugates Nature to Man.

A deified creature could not, however, be substituted for a deposed creator as a compelling object of worship unless and until the new divinity could be invested with some appearance of the omnipotence with which God the Creator had formerly been credited; and, in the minds of the seventeenth-century Western advocates of Technology, the dream of a new age of human innocence was already being chevied by the incompatible dream of a new age of human power. 'To endeavour to renew and enlarge the power and empire of Mankind in general over the Universe'[1] was the programme laid down by

---

[1] Bacon, Francis, *Novum Organum*, Partis Secundae Summa, Aphorismus cxxix, quoted in Chapter 14, p. 187, above.

Francis Bacon for himself, for his Western contemporaries, and for Mankind at large from his time onwards.

Only let Mankind regain their rights over Nature, assigned to them by the gift of God, and obtain that power, whose exercise will be governed by right reason and true religion.[1]

This vision of Bacon's grew, in Descartes' mind, to look like a practical possibility:

I perceived it to be possible to arrive at a knowledge highly useful in life; and, in place of the speculative philosophy usually taught in the schools, to discover a practical philosophy, by means of which —knowing the force and action of fire, water, air, the stars, the heavens, and all the other bodies that surround us, as distinctly as we know the various crafts of our artisans—we might also apply them in the same way to all the uses to which they are adapted, and thus make ourselves the lords and possessors of Nature.[2]

By the sixteen-sixties the Western votaries of Technology were looking forward to progressive conquests over Nature that would go on increasing Man's power *ad infinitum*; and these audacious human hopes of scaling Olympus were frankly expressed, in that decade, by two clergymen of the Established Church of England.

That all arts and professions are capable of maturer improvements, cannot be doubted by those who know the least of any. And that there is an America of secrets, and unknown Peru of Nature, whose discovery would richly advance them, is more than conjecture.[3]

An infinit variety of inventions, motions, and operations will succeed in the place of words. The beautiful bosom of Nature will be expos'd to our view: we shall enter into its garden and tast of its fruits, and satisfy ourselves with its plenty—instead of idle talking and wandring under its fruitless shadows, as the Peripatetics

---

[1] Bacon, Francis, *Novum Organum*, Partis Secundae Summa, Aphorismus cxxix: 'Recuperet modo Genus Humanum ius suum in Naturam quod ei ex dotatione divinâ competit, et detur ei copia: usum vero recta ratio et sana religio gubernabit.'

[2] Descartes, René, *Discours de la Méthode*, Part vi.

[3] Glanvill, J., *The Vanity of Dogmatising* (London 1661, Eversden), p. 178.

did in their first institution and their successors have done ever since.[1]

As the progress of Technology gathered momentum in the course of the Late Modern Age of Western history, these seventeenth-century hopes translated themselves into nineteenth-century achievements. Within some 200 years of Sprat's and Glanvill's day, Man's power of making Non-Human Nature serve human purposes had fulfilled these prophets' expectations by coming to seem limitless.

This appearance of omnipotence was common to the Late Modern Western technician and the Late Greek or Roman philosopher; but there was also a significant difference between the two conceptions of a human being's godlike power. The Western technician's omnipotence was conceived of as being active and aggressive: his role was to be an invincible conqueror of Non-Human Nature. The Greek or Roman philosopher's omnipotence was conceived of as being passive and defensive: his role was to achieve a self-sufficiency that would make him invulnerable against the blows of Fate. This difference in the posture of the human idol reflected a difference in the experience of the two societies at the stages in their histories at which a symbolic human figure was deified. A Late Modern Western Society felt that it had shaken off 'Religion and Barbarism' and was making progress that was so substantial, so cumulative, so continuous, and so rapidly accelerating that it must assuredly be beyond all danger of being checked, arrested, or reversed. By contrast, a post-Periclean Greek Society had felt that it was sliding downhill farther and farther from the peak of a past golden age.

As a Late Modern Western Technology went from triumph to triumph faster and faster, and as the religious fanaticism that had held the West in its grip during the Early Modern Age died away progressively *pari passu*, the negative, sophisticated, cynical vein in the late-seventeenth-century Western feeling about Technology gave way more and more to the positive, naïve, credulous vein. By the nineteenth century, this antithetical vein had gained a complete ascendancy. A

[1] Sprat, Tho., *The History of the Royal Society for the Improving of Natural Knowledge* (London 1667, Martyn), p. 327.

Technology that had first won temperate approval in the West as a harmless hobby in which a criminal Human Nature might safely be encouraged to indulge was now fervidly admired as a magic key which was going to unlock the door into an Earthly Paradise by solving all the problems that, in pre-Newtonian 'Days of Ignorance', had either baffled Man or been ignored by him.

In the nineteenth century the West unreservedly recognized and gloried in the vast additions that the technician was making to human power by his continuing and accelerating discoveries. At this stage of Western history it was taken for granted that all additions to human power must be good, because it was assumed that, since the close of the seventeenth century, the wheels of Western Civilization had been set on lines running forward in an endless progress, and that the accelerating train could never come into danger of being derailed. In these supposed circumstances, to give more power to the locomotive could have no other effect than to make the train progress faster. The Wars of Religion were now far enough back in the past for their lesson to have been erased from the Western Society's memory. Western statesmanship had ceased to reckon with the demonic element in Human Nature; for in public Western life—though not, of course, in private—this jinn had been kept battened-down for nearly 200 years by the date of the publication of *The Origin of Species* in A.D. 1859. The twentieth century, however, has seen the Western technician suffer a fall into adversity which has been sensational because it has been unexpected. Since 1945 the Western technician has begun to lose his popularity, his self-confidence, and the intellectual freedom that is an indispensable condition for success in his work.

Though this change of moral and intellectual climate, which has been conspicuous since A.D. 1945, was not foreseen, it can be traced back in retrospect to earlier dates and to more than one cause.

From the late seventeenth century to the early twentieth century, one of the safeguards of Late Modern Western experimental science had been the postulate that its field of investigation should be limited to Non-Human Nature. The founding fathers of the Royal Society, for example, had imposed this self-denying ordinance on themselves.

These two subjects, God and the Soul, being onely forborn, in all the rest they wander at their pleasure . . . and in bringing all these to the uses of human society.[1]

In the seventeenth century, Human Nature was out of bounds for Experimental Science, as being within the province of Theology. It was only on this condition that Experimental Science could obtain toleration from the then still formidable ecclesiastical authorities of the Western World; and it was a condition that the experimental scientists and technicians of the day were willing to accept. They had vast worlds still to conquer in the realm of Non-Human Nature; and, while they felt that the theologians' way of dealing with Human Nature had been intellectually barren and morally and socially pernicious, the experimental scientists, at this early stage of their intellectual conquests, had no method of their own for dealing with Human Nature in their own style. In the nineteenth century, however, Western Science began to extend its conquests from the non-human to the human province of Nature. It began to discover how to deal with Human Nature by the methods that had proved successful in the investigation of Non-Human Nature. Human branches of Science now began to be added to the classical non-human branches: first Political Economy, using data provided by the Industrial Revolution; then Anthropology, using data provided by the West's encounters with primitive societies; then Sociology, applying the standpoint and methods of Anthropology to the Western Society itself; and then, after A.D. 1914, Psychology, using data provided by cases of shell-shock in the First World War.

This eventual invasion of the province of Human Nature by Western experimental science produced several changes in the Late Modern attitude towards Human Nature. It redirected upon Human Nature an attention and interest that had been concentrated on Non-Human Nature since the close of the seventeenth century. Though the ecclesiastical ban upon the free investigation of Human Nature had long since become a dead letter, the rise of the doctrine of Progress had headed

[1] Sprat, Tho., *The History of the Royal Society of London for the Improving of Natural Knowledge* (London 1667, Martyn), p. 83.

Western minds off from this now open field of inquiry by creating the illusion that Human Nature presented no serious problems. It was assumed that, in human affairs, progress was taking place and would continue to take place automatically; and the uncritical acceptance of this unverified doctrine about Human Nature left little or nothing here to discuss. But, when Science began to deal with the spiritual as well as with the non-spiritual universe, the prestige that Science now enjoyed redirected the public's interest and attention to each successive allotment in the Spiritual Universe that Science chose to stake out for itself. And so, under the patronage of Science, one portion of the Spiritual Universe after another began to loom up again in the Western *Weltanschauung* side by side with the Non-Spiritual Universe.

As soon as the Spiritual Universe thus came to be displayed through Science's lens instead of Theology's, Western minds showed themselves ready to take on trust from Science the existence and importance of spiritual problems. Minds that were closed to the conviction of Sin were open to the investigation of psychic complexes, lesions, traumas. But, while the positive discoveries of Science in the human field were as impressive as any of those in the non-human field, the negative discovery of the depth of human ignorance about Human Nature was more impressive still—above all in the field of Psychology. Thus Western science, at this stage in its Odyssey, began to re-instil into Western minds and hearts some of that sense of the mysteriousness of the Universe which it had done so much to banish at the earlier stage at which it had stepped into the place that Theology had previously occupied. This was the background to the discovery and application, in the Second World War, of a technique for releasing and discharging atomic energy.

The release of atomic energy by Western technology in A.D. 1945 has had three effects on the Western technician's position. After having been undeservedly idolized, for a quarter of a millennium, as the good genius of Mankind, he has now suddenly found himself undeservedly execrated as an evil genius who has released from his bottle a jinn that may perhaps destroy human life on Earth. This arbitrary change in the technician's outward fortunes is a severe ordeal, but his loss of popularity has not hit him so hard as his loss of confidence in himself. Till 1945 he believed, without a doubt, that the results of his work were wholly beneficent. Since 1945 he has begun to wonder whether his professional success may not have been a social and a moral disaster. He has realized that the power that he has been capturing from Nature, and bestowing on Mankind, is, in itself, a neutral force, which can be used at will for evil as well as for good. He now sees his latest invention being used to give an impetus to morally evil actions by putting into them an unprecedentedly powerful charge of material energy. He finds himself wondering whether he may now have placed in human hands the power to destroy the Human Race.

At the same moment the technician has lost the intellectual freedom which he enjoyed for the 250 years ending in the year 1945. The intellectual atmosphere in which a Late Modern Western technology won its sensational successes was one of complete freedom for scientific discussion by private investigators, without any ecclesiastical or political censorship, control, or veto. This freedom was lost in an instant when Western technology entered the field of atomic physics; for this new departure enslaved the technician in several different ways at once. The material apparatus now required was so costly that it was beyond the means of private individuals or institutions; it could be financed only by governments; and these governments insisted on concealing the resulting discoveries behind the iron curtain which, from time immemorial, every government has always pulled down over the 'knavish tricks'[1] that governments play on one another. The governments claimed this right because the discoveries had been made with their resources, and could not have been made without them; they exercised the right because the military power generated by these new discoveries was so enormous that they could not bring themselves to share it with potential enemies. Every government looks upon all other governments as being its potential enemies, not excluding those that, at the moment, are its allies against others; and the power in the new discoveries would have become the common property of all governments if these discoveries had been publicly discussed in accordance

[1] These plain-spoken words will be found in the British National Anthem.

with the principle of the freedom of scientific inquiry that had
been in vogue in the Western World since the close of the
seventeenth century.

What are going to be the ulterior effects of this sudden
reversal in the Western Technician's fortunes? In A.D. 1956
several possibilities suggested themselves. It looked as if the
restriction of freedom for scientific discussion in the atomic
field, in the interests of military security, might slow the
advance of atomic science down. It was to be hoped that the
use of atomic energy might be gradually diverted from destructive to constructive purposes. But, whatever might be the
future application of atomic science, it looked as if Experimental
Science and Technology in general might now become less
attractive pursuits than they had been recently for the ablest
minds and the most conscientious spirits. Scientists and
technicians would now find themselves hampered professionally by political controls which would not be quickly relaxed,
even if the international situation improved; and, besides, they
might come to feel that the production of fresh, and still more
potent, lethal weapons for employment by governments against
Mankind was an anti-social activity, even if the governments
assured them that these weapons were unlikely to be used.
This second consideration might influence not only the technicians but their fellow human beings. Indeed, among the
public in a Westernizing World in the later decades of the
twentieth century, there might be a revulsion of feeling against
Science and Technology like the revulsion against Religion in
the later decades of the seventeenth century. Once again, a
mental activity by which the public had been continuously
obsessed over a period of many generations might be repudiated
by its former devotees because it had become known, by its
fruits, to be a shocking vent for Original Sin and a serious
threat to Man's welfare and perhaps even to his existence. If
Voltaire were to cast himself for an avatar in the twentieth
century, perhaps his war-cry, this time, would be: '*La technique,
voilà l'ennemi! Écrasez l'infâme!*'

If the World is going to withdraw its treasure from Technology and from the Experimental Science that is Technology's
life-blood, in what field is this liquid spiritual capital going
to be reinvested? Perhaps the recent opening-up of the

human sciences may give us a clue. If the non-human sciences now lose their temporary freedom of investigation and consequently fall again under an eclipse, perhaps there will be a concentration of interest and energy on the human sciences. And then, when Man's mind has reached the limits of the scientific study of human affairs, perhaps this chastening intellectual experience may re-open an avenue leading to Religion along a new line of approach which, if humbler, will be spiritually more promising.

18

THE RELIGIOUS OUTLOOK IN A
TWENTIETH-CENTURY WORLD

In the last two chapters we have been looking at some of the idols that, in a Late Modern Western World, have been taking the place of Western Man's discarded ancestral religion, Christianity; and our attention has been caught by three idols in particular: Nationalism, Oecumenicalism, and the Technician. We have observed that two of these three idols—the Technician and Nationalism—seem now to be falling. On the other hand, there seems to be a future for an oecumenical state.

In contrast to a parochial state whose rulers' first concern must be to defend it against other parochial states and to promote its interests at the expense of these rivals, an oecumenical state, being relieved, *ex hypothesi*, of all rivals, could afford to concern itself less with its own self-preservation and more with the service of human beings. It could, in fact, be primarily a 'welfare state', and could dedicate itself to promoting the interests of Mankind as a whole. But everything that is of any value has its price. If a Westernizing World in which distance had been 'annihilated' by Late Modern Western technology were ever to enter into an oecumenical state on a literally world-wide scale, this political institution would be bringing to the whole of the Human Race, this time, the boon that had been brought to fractions of it, at other times, by states that had been oecumenical in function and feeling without having embraced the entire habitable and traversable surface of the planet. The boon would be security; and the price of security is a sacrifice of freedom. A world-wide readiness, in a dangerous age, to buy security at the cost of freedom would be the state of mind expressed in a literally world-wide welfare state, if this were ever to be achieved.

In a Westernizing World mid-way through the twentieth century of the Christian Era, there were at least three demands —all of them strong, persistent, and wide-spread—that were militating against freedom and in favour of regulation and regimentation. There was a demand for security, a demand for social justice, and a demand for a higher material standard of living.

The threat to freedom in the name of security came to our attention at the end of the preceding chapter, when we were considering the adversity into which the technician had fallen since the advent of the Atomic Age in A.D. 1945. But the ban upon freedom of discussion to which the atomic technician and experimental scientific researcher were now being subjected by governments was, of course, only one among a number of restrictions on freedom that the demand for security was exacting. Statesmanship might perhaps succeed in reducing to vanishing-point the danger of a world war fought with atomic weapons, and the vast enhancement of Man's material power through atomic science might be applied eventually, not to armaments, but to constructive civil purposes making for an increase in human welfare. But, even then, the sheer potency of Mankind's new equipment would make a stringent public control and regulation of the use of it still necessary, even if and when it was no longer being used for the deliberately destructive purpose of atomic warfare. Already, more than a hundred years back, public safety-regulations to govern the operation of power-driven machinery had been found necessary when the mechanical power at Man's command was still merely the relatively puny force of steam. It was therefore probable that the need for safety-regulations would not be eliminated if atomic power were to be applied exclusively to pacific and beneficent uses. So far from that, the stringency of the necessary safety-regulations would be likely to increase *pari passu* with the increase in Man's command over Physical Nature—and, mid-way through the twentieth century, Man seemed still to be conquering Nature at an accelerating pace.

An epitome and symbol of the abiding need to regulate the use of mechanical power in the interests of security was to be seen, in A.D. 1956, on the roads of a world in which the facilities for communication were becoming more and more important for the well-being, and indeed for the maintenance, of Society. The publicly enforced rules of the road were becoming both more elaborate and more severe as the increase in the speed, mass, and momentum of power-driven vehicles was increasing the seriousness of the effects of accidents. No such measures had been required in the past, when the swiftest vehicles on the road had been stage-coaches and the most ponderous had been carriers' carts. In that antediluvian age, the problem of traffic had not been how to avoid accidents; for these had not been dangerous when the typical accident was a collision between a donkey-cart and a wheelbarrow. The problem in the pre-mechanical age had been how to transport a large enough volume of goods at a high enough speed. The virtual solution of this problem through mechanization had now given rise to the problem of accidents; and accidents could not be avoided without regimentation.

Moreover, security against physical damage or destruction in the factories and on the roads was not the only kind of security that would still be required in a scientifically efficient society that had succeeded in abolishing Man's traditional institution of War. There were, for example, the demands for security against incapacitation both by sickness, during the years of working life, and by old age after the date of retirement. The prolongation of the average expectation of life by an increasingly successful application of preventive medicine was increasing both the individual's need for an old age pension and the burden of this charge upon Society; and the problem could not be solved except by compulsory public insurance financed by levies on employees, employers, 'self-employed' persons, and tax-payers. A high rate of taxation, and a steep grading of the rate as between incomes of different sizes, were required in any case by the demand for social justice. In a twentieth-century Westernizing World, this demand was being met, not merely by a reduction of the difference between rates of remuneration paid to individual earners, but by the public provision of social services financed by a graduated tax. Arrangements for insurance against sickness and old age were only two out of a number of social services that were now being provided by a compulsory redistribution of private incomes by public action; and the reverse side of this policy was an increasing reduction of the quota of an individual's earnings that he was left free to spend or invest as he chose after the tax collector had made his levy.

These restrictions on freedom that were the price of security and of social justice were considerable. Yet they were not so far-reaching as the restrictions that seemed likely to be required by the vocal demand for a rise in the material standard of living, and by the still more exigent tacit demand that the standard should at any rate not be allowed to decline from a level which, in A.D. 1956, was barely above the starvation line for perhaps three-quarters of the living generation of Mankind. Supposing that the threat of a third world war had receded, and that atomic power had been wholly applied to the increase of human welfare, the consequent possibility of raising the standard for the almost destitute majority of the Human Race might still be more than offset by the success of preventive medicine in lowering the death-rate. In Britain, preventive medicine had begun to produce this effect in the seventeen-forties; and, in consequence, the population of Britain had nearly quadrupled within the next 140 years, before the prospect of a return to equilibrium had been opened up, in the eighteen-eighties, by the beginnings of a fall in the birth-rate.

This episode of English social history reveals the formidable length of the time-lag, after an impetus has been given to the growth of population by an advance in preventive medicine, before a brake is eventually put upon this impetus through a change in social habits. An advance in preventive medicine can be achieved very quickly, because this is the work of the Head. Even in a socially backward and conservative-minded country a small personnel, putting the simplest measures of public health into operation, can bring about a rapid fall in the death-rate. On the other hand, the change in social habits that is required if there is to be a lowering of the birth-rate is an affair of the Heart; and even in an advanced and progressive-minded country the Heart cannot easily be moved to go faster than its habitually slow gait. The time-lag of 140 years in Britain between the Head's effect and the Heart's effect upon the movement of population is unlikely to have been longer than the average; and, during the interval, the population of Britain increased nearly fourfold.

Britain was able to maintain this rising population at a rising standard of living, because, within less than a quarter of a century after the improvement of public health in Britain had begun to make itself felt in a rise in the population, Britain initiated the Industrial Revolution and thereby won for herself, for a century, as her reward for having been first in the field, the remunerative role of serving as 'the workshop of the World'. No other country in the World thereafter could tide over the same time-lag by even temporarily winning for itself the same industrial monopoly. Yet Britain had been merely the first of a series of countries whose population was going to increase at approximately the same rate in consequence of the same time-lag between a fall in the death-rate and an eventual countervailing fall in the birth-rate. In China, too the population had begun to rise in the eighteenth century as a consequence, there, of the law and order established by the Manchu imperial régime, working together with the introduction of new food crops from the Americas. In India, the law and order established by the British raj, working together with the extension of irrigation and the improvement in means of communication, had brought about a comparable increase of population in the nineteenth century. The Indian and Chinese figures dwarfed the British figures in their scale; and, in the twentieth century, the growth of population from the same causes was coming to be world-wide.

It could hardly be hoped that the change of social habits, necessary for stabilizing the World's population through a voluntary reduction of the birth-rate, could be achieved before the increase in the World's population would reach the limit of the numbers that could be fed, even if the World's food production were to have been raised to the highest degree that could be attained by the systematic application of science. In that event, Malthus's forecast would have been wrong only in antedating the crisis by a mere 150 years or thereabouts, and the inevitable consequence would be a further restriction of freedom—and this time in a field in which governmental interference had been almost unheard-of hitherto.

The regulation of the movement of population by means of artificial restrictions is not, of course, in itself a new thing in human affairs. At many times and places, population has been regulated by divers expedients. But, when and where this has been done, it has been done almost entirely by the free choice of husbands and wives (or at any rate of husbands), acting at their own private discretion as a law unto themselves. The inner sanctum of family life is a domain into which, in the past, governments have been chary of intruding. The Lycurgean régime at Sparta was exceptional in claiming and exercising the right for a government to refuse to let a baby live, whatever its parents' wishes might be. But, in a world whose population had reached the limit of the numbers that the face of the planet could feed, an oecumenical welfare state would be bound to take responsibility for providing every living person with a minimum food ration, and consequently be bound to assume the Lycurgean prerogative of limiting the number of living mouths.

If, in this world crisis, parents failed to accept, of their own accord, the revolutionary idea that the World had a right to have a say about the number of children that they were to bring into it, then the public authorities would find themselves constrained to impose their quota of births by exercising the coercive powers that states can bring to bear upon their subjects. This Lycurgean use of force would, in fact, be the only alternative to allowing Famine, in a world that had been freed from Pestilence and from War, to do the whole of the barbarous work that, in the past, the three traditional destroying angels had done between them; and Famine could not stalk the World again without soon bringing Pestilence and War back in its train. To allow the World's population once again to be kept down in these irrational and inhuman traditional ways would be a confession of social bankruptcy; and we may guess that, if and when the formidable choice had to be faced, it would seem preferable that the state should restrict the freedom of individuals even in this the most intimate of all hitherto private affairs.

These considerations made it look, in A.D. 1956, as if freedom were likely to be restricted to an unprecedented degree, and that this restriction would be felt eventually in family life, as well as in economics and in politics. At this date, the limitation of the size of families by public policy had not yet become a live issue; but public restrictions on individual freedom in the economic and political spheres had already been multiplying and were still on the increase. In a Westernizing World that was

manifestly moving towards social uniformity, these encroach-
ments on the former preserves of individual freedom were taking
place, at divers rates and to divers degrees, in all countries,
and not only in those that were now under Communist or
semi-socialist régimes. The same tendency could also be discerned in the United States, and here it was particularly impressive. For, of all countries in the world of the day, the
United States was the one in which the material standard of
living was the highest, and in which the demands for social
justice and for security had been met the most adequately
already. The increase in regulation and regimentation in the
United States was thus 'an acid test' of their increase in the
World as a whole. On this test, it looked as if the field for
freedom, which had seemed almost boundless in a nineteenth-
century Western Society, was likely, in a twentieth-century
Westernizing World, to be not only severely limited but
drastically curtailed.

In a world in which Freedom was thus being driven from
pillar to post, what was the sphere of life in which she was going
to find asylum? The question presented itself because Man
cannot live without a minimum of freedom, any more than he
can live without a minimum of security, justice, and food.
There seems to be in human nature an intractable vein—akin
to the temperament of Man's yoke-fellows the camel, mule, and
goat—which insists on being allowed a modicum of freedom
and which knows how to impose its will when it is goaded
beyond endurance. This hard core of obstinacy in Man has
been the bane of tyrants. Even the most long-suffering peoples
revolt at some point, as is witnessed by the record of revolutions
in Russia and in China; and even the most efficiently despotic
governments have found it impossible to suppress freedom in
all spheres simultaneously. Despots who have recklessly sat on
the safety valve have usually been blown sky-high sooner or
later; and the frequency of this mishap has taught the more
prudent practitioners of the hazardous art to leave some vent
open for their subjects.

Naturally the despots look for this vent in some activity that
does not appear to them to affect whatever may be their own
paramount concern. In seventeenth-century Western Christendom, for example, where the paramount concern of despots was

Religion, they were willing, as we have seen,[1] to allow their subjects the apparently harmless vent of applying experimental science to Technology. In the twentieth century, when a scientific technology had placed edged tools in Man's hands, and when the paramount concern of governments was security, the technician was being deprived by governments of the freedom that had been granted to him by these governments' seventeenth-century predecessors. Security against War, against accidents, and against want was an objective that could not be pursued effectively without restricting freedom in the spheres of political, economic, and perhaps eventually even domestic life. In A.D. 1956 the surviving parochial governments were already embarked on that course; and there was no reason for expecting that this tendency in public policy would change if and when these parochial governments were superseded, or, short of that, were subordinated, through the establishment of an oecumenical régime. In these circumstances it might be forecast that, in the next chapter of the World's history, Mankind would seek compensation for the loss of much of its political, economic, and perhaps even domestic freedom by putting more of its treasure into its spiritual freedom, and that the public authorities would tolerate this inclination among their subjects in an age in which Religion had come to seem as harmless as Technology had seemed 300 years back.

This forecast had some support in history; for Religion had in fact been the sphere of activity in which the subjects of past oecumenical empires had been allowed by their rulers to seek and find compensation for their loss of freedom in other fields. This was one of the reasons why so many of the historic higher religions had arisen within the framework of empires that had been oecumenical in the pertinent sense of being world-wide in feeling—as distinct from being world-wide in the literal meaning of the word.

No empire had ever been literally world-wide so far. This had not been a practical possibility until 'the annihilation of distance' had been achieved by Modern Western technology. Yet the limits of the geographical range of the oecumenical empires of the past did not make their experience irrelevant to the problem of the future of freedom in a Westernizing World

[1] In Chapter 14, pp. 184-7, above.

in which world-government, in the literal sense, had now become technically possible. For both the subject's demand for freedom, and the government's policy in dealing with this demand, were matters, not of physical geography, but of human nature; and, in this psychological and political context, an empire that was felt to be all-embracing—in the sense of embracing all lands in which its subjects could feel themselves at home—was as effectively oecumenical as if it had literally had no frontiers. It was oecumenical in the subjective sense of there being nowhere else in the World where its subjects could find a tolerable asylum if life were to become intolerable under this régime; and this subjective sense was the sense in which the Roman Empire was legitimately equated with 'the Inhabited World', and the Chinese Empire with 'All that is under Heaven'. In a society composed of parochial states with a common civilization, an Athenian who found life intolerable at Athens could move to Thurii or Miletus or any one of a number of other Hellenic city-states without exiling himself from the Hellenic Civilization that was his native social element. On the other hand, a subject of the Roman Empire who found life intolerable under this oecumenical Hellenic régime could not emigrate to the Parthian Empire without expatriating himself psychologically as well as politically.

This means that even a less than literally world-wide oecumenical empire differs from any parochial state in the nature of the psychological pressure that it exerts. If it makes itself intolerable to its subjects, an oecumenical empire is apt to breed in them a much more acute claustrophobia than they would have felt in a state which they could have left without having to lose their cultural heritage as the price of changing their domicile. Such acute claustrophobia is an explosive force; and prudent oecumenical governments have generally been anxious not to let the pressure of this force accumulate to a dangerous degree. Their general policy has been to leave open to their subjects some vent for freedom, under their own régime, that would save the subjects from having to make the excruciating choice between intolerable conditions at home and likewise intolerable conditions in exile. The vent which oecumenical governments have usually found the least objectionable has been some measure of freedom in the field of spiritual life, as is witnessed by the fact that a number of oecumenical empires have allowed themselves to be used as mission-fields by higher religions. The Achaemenian Empire, for example, served as a mission-field for Zoroastrianism and for Judaism; the Maurya Empire for Hīnayāna Buddhism; the Kushan Empire and the Han Empire for Mahāyāna Buddhism; the Roman Empire for Isis-worship, Cybele-worship, the cult of Juppiter Dolichenus, Mithraism, and Christianity; the Gupta Empire for post-Buddhaic Hinduism; the Arab Caliphate for Islam.

A striking common feature that comes to light, when these instances are surveyed synoptically, is the comparative for-bearance towards alien, and in some cases aggressive, non-official religions that was shown by oecumenical governments whose general temper was suspicious and their general policy repressive. In the policies of the pre-Christian Roman Empire towards Christianity, and of the Han Empire's avatar, the T'ang Empire, towards the Mahāyāna, the remarkable feature is, not the imperial government's occasional resort to persecu-tion, but its usual tolerance, *de facto*, of a non-official religion that was not only distasteful to it but was officially proscribed by it. Conversely, it is not surprising that Hinduism should have flourished under the Gupta Empire, and Islam under the Arab Caliphate, since, in these two cases, the successful religion was professed and patronized by the imperial govern-ment. What is surprising in these two cases is the fact that the Hindu-minded Gupta emperors did not persecute Buddhism, and that the toleration, explicitly accorded in the Qur'ān to Jews and Christians, so long as they submitted to Muslim rule and paid a surtax, was extended, *de facto*, by the Caliphs to their Zoroastrian subjects, and by successors of the Caliphs to Hindus, though neither Hindus nor Zoroastrians had been men-tioned, in the Qur'ān, in the catalogue of 'People of the Book'.

A rather surprisingly large measure of religious toleration has, in fact, been a conspicuous generic feature of oecumenical empires, and the wisdom of this policy has been demonstrated by the disasters that have been the penalty for departing from it. The Mughal Muslim raj in India was wrecked by Awrang-zib's departure from a policy of tolerating Hinduism that had been taken over by the Mughal dynasty from previous Muslim rulers in India. The Roman Empire, after Constantine's adoption of Catholic Christianity as the imperial government's official religion, brought crippling eventual losses upon itself when Theodosius I abandoned Constantine's prudent policy of toleration for all faiths and replaced this by a militant policy of persecuting all varieties of religion except the now officially established one.

The suppression of Paganism, which was started by Theodosius I and was completed by Justinian I, might, it is true, appear to have been justified by success. By Justinian's day, a Romania which, by then, had become predominantly Christian had, in the process, become partly alien to an obstinate residual minority of unconverted Hellenes. Yet seven discharged professors of Hellenic philosophy, who sought and found asylum in the Persian Empire after Justinian's closure of the University of Athens in A.D. 529, discovered by experiment that the air of an ex-Hellenic oecumenical empire in which they were now forbidden to teach was still the only air that they could breathe. The atmosphere of a Zoroastrian Iran proved to be so much more uncongenial to them than the atmosphere of a Christian Romania that they soon became desperately homesick for the Christendom in which their religion was being stamped out. Their recovery, under the Persian Emperor's aegis, of their freedom to teach was no consolation in a social milieu in which their Hellenic philosophy had no public.

Their exile was indeed a more forlorn one than that of the Nestorian Christians, who had found asylum in the same Persian Empire 100 years before them. The Nestorian Christian refugees from the Syriac-speaking provinces of the Roman Empire had been able to strike new roots on the Persian side of the frontier among an indigenous Syriac-speaking Christian population there whom they soon succeeded in winning over to their own interpretation of the Christian faith. There were no Greek-speaking students of Hellenic philosophy still surviving in the Persian dominions to welcome the seven refugee Hellenic professors a century later. So the professors capitulated and petitioned for repatriation; and their protector the Emperor Chosroes showed understanding for their plight, and magnanimity in coming to their rescue once again. So far from taking

offence at the Hellenic exiles' inability to strike root in his
Iranian World, Chosroes chivalrously wrote into a peace treaty
that he was negotiating with Justinian an article stipulating
that the seven pagan academic refugees should not only be
allowed to return home to Romania but should be exempted
there from the operation of Justinian's anti-pagan penal laws.

When the Nestorians had been driven beyond the bounds of
Romania and when the Hellene exiles had sued for permission
to return on terms that condemned their Hellenic paganism to
die with them, the Theodosian policy of intolerance might
appear to have been vindicated. Yet already, in Justinian's
day, this policy was being defeated by a mass-secession of the
Roman Empire's Coptic-speaking, Syriac-speaking, and Arm-
enian-speaking subjects from the Imperial ('Melchite') Catholic
Church to Monophysitism. The Monophysites were not a
minority that could be expelled like the Nestorians or be
suppressed like the Hellenes. They were in a decisive majority
throughout an area extending from Upper Egypt to the head-
waters of the Tigris and the Euphrates. They could neither be
suppressed nor be expelled; but they could revolt against the
Roman Empire, as they had already revolted against the
Catholic Church, as soon as an opportunity presented itself.
Their chance came when the Muslim Arabs invaded the
Roman Empire little more than half a century after Justinian's
death; and the disaffection of the Monophysites towards the
Empire partly accounts for the rapidity, and the apparent
ease, with which the Arab invaders wrested Syria, Mesopo-
tamia, and Egypt out of Melchite Roman hands.

This disastrous eventual result of a policy of intolerance
inaugurated by Theodosius was a retrospective vindication of
the opposite policy of toleration *de facto* which had been the
usual policy of the Roman Imperial Government before
Diocletian had consented, against his own better judgement,
to put Christianity under a ban. Toleration had been re-
established by Constantine, and now not merely *de facto* but
de jure, when, after his conversion, he had lifted this ban on
Christianity without imposing a ban on Paganism. In the
liberalism of his religious policy, Constantine was not merely
being faithful to the spirit of a pre-Christian Roman régime;
he was taking a line that has been characteristic of oecumenical

empires as a class. Theodosius's ban on Paganism, like Diocletian's ban on Christianity, was an aberration that led to a disaster. These historical precedents suggest that, if a twentieth-century Westernizing World, in its turn, were to purchase security at the price of submitting to the political and economic bondage of some kind of oecumenical government, Religion would be the field, once again, in which human beings would seek the freedom without which they cannot live, and also, once again, the field in which the public authorities would be the least chary of leaving open the necessary vent.

In a regimented world the realm of the spirit may be freedom's citadel. But spiritual freedom cannot be achieved solely by the action of the State. What the State can do to provide for freedom is, no doubt, indispensable when the state has an oecumenical range; but, at the same time, this necessary action on the State's part is, and can be, only negative. The State can and should refrain from either penalizing or favouring any religion that is professed by any of its subjects, and it also can and should 'hold the ring' in the sense of restraining its subjects from combating one another's religions by the use of any means except non-violent missionary activities. But this necessary negative action on the State's part is not enough to make spiritual freedom a reality; for to be real it must also be alive in the hearts of the people themselves. True spiritual freedom is attained when each member of Society has learnt to reconcile a sincere conviction of the truth of his own religious beliefs and the rightness of his own religious practices with a voluntary toleration of the different beliefs and practices of his neighbours. A toleration that is genuinely voluntary is the only kind that has any virtue in it; but the degree of the virtue depends on the motive, and the motives for toleration are various. They can be lower or higher, negative or positive.

The lowest negative motive for toleration is a belief that Religion is of no practical importance, and that therefore it does not matter what religion our neighbours profess. The next lowest negative motive is a belief that Religion is an illusion, and that therefore it is idle to inquire whether this or that form of Religion is true or false or right or wrong. The next lowest negative motive is a prudential one arising from the observation that a resort to force is apt to provoke a resistance which may recoil upon the aggressor. However telling my own unprovoked first blow promises to be, I cannot be sure that the knock-out blow will not be received by me from the neighbour whom I have made my implacable enemy by wantonly assaulting him. The next lowest negative motive arises from the observation that religious conflict is a public nuisance which easily becomes a public danger. It is therefore better for discordant religious sects to resign themselves to living and letting live, without breaking the peace by trying to eliminate one another.

These negative motives for toleration would appear to have been the prevalent motives in the Western World when it opted for toleration in reaction against the evils of the Catholic-Protestant wars of religion;[1] and our current Western experience is now showing us that toleration inspired by such negative motives is precarious. So long as we are not moved by any higher and more positive motives than these, there is no guarantee that intolerance will not raise its head again. If it does not reappear in Religion itself, it may make its appearance in some psychological substitute for Religion in the shape of a secular 'ideology' such as Nationalism, Fascism, or Communism. Happily, higher and more positive motives did also enter into the seventeenth-century Western spiritual revolution,[2] and these are the motives that we need to confirm and strengthen in our own hearts today.

The fundamental positive motive for toleration is a recognition of the truth that religious conflict is not just a nuisance but is a sin. It is sinful because it arouses the wild beast in Human Nature. Religious persecution, too, is sinful because no one has a right to try to stand between another human soul and God. Every soul has a right to commune with God in God's and this soul's way; and the particular way concerns none but God and the particular soul in question. No other human being has a right to intervene by the use of any means except non-violent missionary action. And Violence in this field is not only sinful; it is futile; for religions cannot be inculcated by force. There is no such thing as a belief that is not held voluntarily through a genuinely spontaneous inner conviction. Different

---

[1] See the Annexe to the present chapter, pp. 251-4, below.
[2] See the Annexe to the present chapter, pp. 254-60, below.

people's convictions will differ, because Absolute Reality is a mystery of which no more than a fraction has ever yet been penetrated by—or been revealed to—any human mind. 'The heart of so great a mystery cannot ever be reached by following one road only.'[1] However strong and confident may be my conviction that my own approach to the mystery is a right one, I ought to be aware that my field of spiritual vision is so narrow that I cannot know that there is no virtue in other approaches. In theistic terms this is to say that I cannot know that other people's visions may not also be revelations from God—and these perhaps fuller and more illuminating revelations than the one that I believe that I myself have received from Him.

Moreover, the fact that I and my neighbour are following different roads is something that divides us much less than we are drawn together by the other fact that, in following our different roads, we are both trying to approach the same mystery. All human beings who are seeking to approach the mystery in order to direct their lives in accordance with the nature and spirit of Absolute Reality or, in theistic terms, with the will of God—all these fellow-seekers are engaged in an identical quest. They should recognize that they are spiritually brethren and should feel towards one another, and treat one another, as such. Toleration does not become perfect until it has been transfigured into love.

18 ANNEXE

THE SEVENTEENTH-CENTURY REACTION IN THE WEST AGAINST RELIGIOUS INTOLERANCE

The Pertinence of Seventeenth-century Motives in the Twentieth Century

The Late Modern Western practice of toleration seemed, in A.D. 1956, to be in serious danger of being brought to an end by a resurgence of fanaticism. This time the causes that were evoking this familiar evil spirit were not the conflicting varieties of Western Christianity in whose rival names the sixteenth-century and seventeenth-century Western wars of religion had been fought. They were secular 'ideologies', such as Nationalism, Fascism, and Communism. Yet in these professedly

[1] Quintus Aurelius Symmachus, in a controversy with Saint Ambrose.

new-fangled faiths the fanatical vein in the traditional spirit of Judaism and Christianity, as well as some of the principal motifs of a traditional Jewish and Christian mythology, were clearly discernible and easily traceable to their historical origins. In fact, a spirit that had been suppressed in Western Christendom at the close of the seventeenth century was reviving in the twentieth century. This revival raised the question why it was that the practice of toleration should now once again be in jeopardy in the West after having prevailed there for no less than a quarter of a millennium, and after having been taken for granted, all this time, as an instalment of civilization which, now that it had been achieved at last, was secure against ever being lost. Some light on the answer to this question, which was presenting itself so insistently in A.D. 1956, could perhaps be found by recalling the motives in the minds of the founding fathers of a Late Modern Western Liberalism, when they had inaugurated, about 250 years ago, an era of toleration that was now proving not to be automatically everlasting. Some of these motives are on record in classical works of seventeenth-century pioneer Western liberal literature. They come to light in the following passages, which are here arranged in the order in which the motives themselves have been surveyed in the chapter of this book to which the present annexe attaches.

The two lowest of the negative motives in our catalogue might prove difficult to document from seventeenth-century Western sources. Some of the seventeenth-century advocates of toleration, like Locke, were sincere professors of Christianity. They were moved to plead for toleration largely because they felt that intolerance was unchristian and saw that the practice of intolerance in the name of Christianity was alienating Western hearts from the West's ancestral religion. Others, like Bayle, were at least partially alienated from Christianity already, and even from religion of any kind; but these were well aware that, though faith might be ebbing, in the wake of an ebbing fanaticism, in the Western World of their day, the contemporary climate of Western feeling and opinion was still such as to make it advisable for sceptics to disguise their scepticism, even if the disguise were perfunctory and transparent.

A Resort to Force is apt to provoke a Resistance which may recoil upon the Aggressor

The establishment of this one thing [toleration] would take away all ground of complaints and tumults upon account of conscience; and, these causes of discontents and animosities being once removed, there would remain nothing in these assemblies [vulgarly called, and perhaps having sometimes been, conventicles and nurseries of factions and seditions] that were not more peaceable and less apt to produce disturbance of state than in any other meetings whatsoever. . . .

If men enter into seditious conspiracies, it is not religion inspires them to it in their meetings, but their sufferings and oppressions that make them willing to ease themselves. Just and moderate governments are everywhere quiet, everywhere safe; but oppression raises ferments and makes men struggle to cast off an uneasy and tyrannical yoke. . . . There is only one thing which gathers people into seditious commotions, and that is oppression. . . .

It is not the diversity of opinions (which cannot be avoided), but the refusal of toleration to those that are of different opinion (which might have been granted), that has produced all the bustles and wars that have been in the Christian World upon account of Religion. The heads and leaders of the Church, moved by avarice and insatiable desire of dominion, making use of the immoderate ambition of magistrates and the credulous superstition of the giddy multitude, have incensed and animated them against those that dissent from themselves, by preaching unto them, contrary to the laws of the Gospel and to the precepts of charity, that schismatics and heretics are to be outed of their possessions and destroyed. . . . That magistrates should thus suffer these incendiaries and disturbers of the public peace might justly be wondered at if it did not appear that they have been invited by them unto a participation of the spoil.[1]

It cannot be denied that the fear of the death penalty has a great effect in silencing people who might have doubts to put forward against the dominant religion, and also great effects in maintaining an ecclesiastical unity in externals; but any dogma that sanctions this practice will be condemning itself to what happens with bombs, mines, and other infernal machines employed in war. The people who are the first to use these gain great advantages from them, and, so long as they have the upper hand, they are in clover; but, when they lose the ascendancy, they are hoist with their own petard.[2]

[1] Locke, John, *A Letter Concerning Toleration.*
[2] Bayle, P., *Dictionaire*, 3rd ed., i. 543 b, s.v. Bèze.

Religious Conflict is a Public Nuisance which easily becomes a Public Danger

Religion, which is regarded by everyone as being the firmest of all the supports of political authority, and which would indeed play this role if it were rightly understood and rightly practised, is ordinarily the force that does most to hamstring political authority.[1]

There can be no doubt that the love of [theological] novelties is a plague which, after having set on fire the academies and the synods, shakes and convulses the secular governments and sometimes overthrows them. So no praise could be too high for those professors who recommend their disciples to give a wide berth to this spirit of innovation. . . . The opponents of a new method of teaching display too much passion. . . . They are apt to be just as imprudent as their adversaries: they seem not to have noticed that a new method that is ignored falls to the ground of its own accord, while, on the other hand, if people deliver a frontal attack upon it, it degenerates into a regular sect.[2]

The providence of God, whose ways are always infinitely wise, allowed human frailty to have its part in the great work of the Reformation, in order to arrive, by the play of natural cause and effect, at His [divine] goal, which, as experience teaches us, was to make it impossible for either of the two religions to bring the other to complete ruin.[3]

Religious Conflict is Sinful, because it arouses the Wild Beast in Human Nature

Do not carry disputes beyond the point to which you can push them without disturbing the public peace, and keep quiet as soon as you have practical evidence that you are producing divisions in the family circle or are fomenting the formation of parties. Do not go to the length of re-awaking a thousand evil passions which ought to be kept in chains like so many wild beasts; and on your head be it if you are responsible for these wild beasts' breaking their fetters.[4]

Religious Persecution is Sinful, because No one has a Right to stand between Another Human Soul and God

No man can be a Christian . . . without that faith which works, not by force, but by love. . . .

[1] Bayle, P., *Dictionaire*, 3rd ed., ii. 1585 b, s.v. Junius.
[2] Bayle, op. cit., i. 169 b and 170 b, s.vv. Alting (Henri) and Alting (Jacques).
[3] Bayle, op. cit., i. 100 a, s.v. Agricola (George).
[4] Bayle, op. cit., i. 182 a, s.v. Amyraut.

Although the magistrate's opinion in religion be sound, and the way that he appoints be truly evangelical, yet, if I be not thoroughly persuaded thereof in my own mind, there will be no safety for me in following it. No way whatsoever that I shall walk in against the dictates of my conscience will ever bring me to the mansions of the blessed. . . . I cannot be saved by a religion that I distrust, and by a worship that I abhor. . . . Faith only, and inward sincerity, are the things that procure acceptance with God. . . . Men . . . must be left to their own conscience. . . .

There is absolutely no such thing under the Gospel as a Christian Commonwealth. . . . Christ . . . instituted no commonwealth . . . nor put he the sword into any magistrate's hand, with commission to make use of it in forcing men to forsake their former religion and receive His. . . .

Nobody ought to be compelled in matters of religion either by law or force.[1]

One would be attributing to the Church a power which she does not possess if one were to maintain that she has a right to treat all those who leave her as the kingdoms of This World treat rebels. The Church can have none but voluntary subjects and never has the right to exact an oath that infringes the law of order—a law which rules that, always and everywhere, one should follow the lights of conscience.[2]

To believe that the Church is in need of reformation and to approve of some particular way of reforming it are two very different things. On the other hand, to blame the conduct of the opponents of a reformation and to disapprove of the conduct of the reformers are two things that are entirely compatible. So one can imitate Erasmus without being an apostate or a traitor, without sinning against the Holy Spirit, and without being untrue to the lights of one's conscience.[3]

Koornhert was never tired of saying that Luther, Calvin, and Mennon had made vigorous attacks on a vast number of Roman Catholic errors, but that they had had singularly little success in combating the frightful and impious dogma that it is right to force people's consciences, and that, instead of fighting this dogma well and truly, they had actually strengthened its hold—because each of them had put it into practice, wherever he had managed to make himself the master, and, in fact, each of them had created a new Papacy by the establishment of a schismatic church that condemned all others. . . . As for him, he maintained that it is not right

[1] Locke, op. cit.　　　　[2] Bayle, op. cit., ii. 1304 b, s.v. Grégoire I.
[3] Bayle, op. cit., i. 801 b, s.v. Castellan.

to hate anybody; that all godly people, who by faith in Jesus Christ are doing their best to make themselves imitators of Him, are good Christians; and that the duty of the civil authorities is to regard all peaceable inhabitants of the realm as being good subjects.[1]

These two witnesses [a Protestant minister and a Catholic priest] agree on another point which is rather shocking. Each of them severally admits that, if the Christian princes had not brought the full rigour of the law to bear against the enemies of orthodoxy, the false religions would have inundated the whole Earth. In other words, when our Saviour made His promise to maintain His church against the gates of Hell, this promise will have meant nothing except that He would raise up princes who would quell the enemies of the truth by robbing them of their patrimony, thrusting them into prison, banishing them, sending them to the galleys, having them hanged, and so on. There is no doctrine, however absurd, which could fail, if it resorted to such means as these, to brave all the infernal powers that might desire to do it injury.[2]

People who want to maintain neutrality during civil wars, whether political or religious, . . . are exposed to being insulted by both parties alike. . . . Deplorable fate of Man! Manifest vanity of his Philosophic Reason! . . . 'Blessed are the peacemakers', says the Scripture. . . . And that is true enough with reference to the Other World. In This World, though, they are miserable. They have no desire to be the hammer, and this condemns them continually to serve as the anvil, right and left.[3]

If only the peoples were reasonable, informers and judges of this sort would have reason to dread their wrath. After all, what can we think of that is more frightful, when one looks at it with an unprejudiced eye, than the thought of a human being who is condemned to the flames because he is unwilling to break the faith that he has sworn to keep with the true God?[4]

Religions cannot be inculcated by Force. There is No Such Thing as a Belief that is not held Voluntarily

All the life and power of true religion consist in the inward and full persuasion of the mind; and faith is not faith without believing. . . . And such is the nature of the understanding, that it cannot be compelled to the belief of anything by outward force. . . .

[1] Bayle, op. cit., ii. 1622 b, s.v. Koornhert.
[2] Bayle, op. cit., iii. 2079 a, s.v. Nestorius.
[3] Bayle, op. cit., ii. 1090 b, s.v. Eppendorf (cp. ii. 1403 a, s.v. Heidanus).
[4] Bayle, op. cit., i. 534 b, s.v. Berquin.

Nobody is born a member of any church, . . . but everyone joins himself voluntarily to that society in which he believes he has found that profession and worship which is truly acceptable to God. . . .

No religion which I believe not to be true can be either true or profitable to me. . . .

To believe this or that to be true, does not depend upon our will.[1]

Absolute Reality is a Mystery to which there is more than one Approach

Every church is orthodox to itself; to others, erroneous or heretical. . . . The controversy between these churches about the truth of their doctrines and the purity of their worship is on both sides equal; nor is there any judge . . . on Earth by whose sentence it can be determined. The decision of that question belongs only to the supreme judge of all men. . . .

The truth certainly would do well enough if she were once left to shift for herself. . . .

Those whose doctrine is peaceable and whose manners are pure and blameless ought to be upon equal terms with their fellow-subjects. . . . Neither Pagan nor Mahometan nor Jew ought to be excluded from the civil rights of the commonwealth because of his religion.[2]

It is dishonourable to pass a hard censure on the religions of all other countries: it concerns them to look to the reasonableness of their faith; and it is sufficient for us to be establish'd in the truth of our own.[3]

While the Bishops of Rome did assume an infallibility and a sovereign dominion over our faith, the reform'd churches did not onely justly refuse to grant them that, but some of them thought themselves oblig'd to forbear all communion with them, and would not give them that respect which possibly might belong to so antient and so famous a church, and which might still have been allow'd it without any danger of superstition.[4]

Several people of merit and authority in the other party were reasonable enough to do justice to a Protestant author who argued his case well without trespassing outside the bounds of his subject. Our Mr. Drélincourt is one case in point, and Monsr. Claude is another, for he was held in high esteem in Roman Catholic circles.

[1] Locke, op. cit.   [2] Locke, op. cit.
[3] Sprat, Tho., *The History of the Royal Society of London for the Improving of Natural Knowledge* (London 1667, Martyn), p. 63.
[4] Sprat, op. cit., p. 47.

This makes an exposure of the gross misconception or gross insincerity of certain people who take great credit for being detested like the plague in Catholic, Arminian, Anabaptist, and other circles. If they had done nothing but argue their case well, they would not have become objects of universal detestation. It is their behaviour, their personal invectives, the dishonest statements that they have spread abroad in their publications—it is all this that is responsible for the aversion with which they are regarded.[1]

[The zealots] want everybody to do as they do, that is, to embrace an opinion firmly and to anathematize the opposite one. They would be incapable of understanding that one could be a true adherent of a religion if they saw one retaining all one's sang froid in comparing one's own religion with others, and saw one preserving a large fund of fair-mindedness towards the followers of heresy.[2]

It is shocking beyond words to see the disputes about Grace producing such a venomous cleavage in human souls. Each sect attributes to the other the teaching of horrible impieties and blasphemies and pushes its animosity to the farthest limits; yet, according to all the laws of decency, doctrines of this kind are precisely those on which people ought to be the most ready to practise a mutual toleration. Intolerance would be pardonable in a party that could give a clear demonstration of the truth of its opinions and could make clean-cut, categorical, and convincing answers to the difficulties. But, when people are obliged to say that they have no better solution to offer than [that these are] secrets which are impenetrable to the human intelligence and which are hidden in the infinite treasure-houses of the incomprehensible immensity of God, it seems quite inexcusable that people who find themselves in this intellectual predicament should take a high line, should hurl the thunderbolt of anathema, and should banish and hang their opponents.[3]

The Pilgrims exploring Different Approaches are Fellow-seekers of the Same Goal

That a queen [Marguérite de Valois, Queen of Navarre, the sister of Francis I] should grant her protection to people who were being persecuted for opinions which she believed to be wrong, that she should open to them an asylum in order to preserve them from the flames in which their persecutors wished to put them to death,

[1] Bayle, op. cit., ii. 1020 a and b, s.v. Drélincourt.
[2] Bayle, op. cit., ii. 1028 a, s.v. Drusius.
[3] Bayle, op. cit., iii, 2596 b, s.v. Synergistes.

that she should give them the means of subsistence, that she should alleviate, with a liberal hand, the tedium and discomfort of their exile: this is magnanimity of an heroic order that is almost unexampled. It is the effect of an elevation of mind and genius to which hardly anyone can rise. It implies a capacity for sympathizing with the distress of people who are in error, and for admiring at the same time the fidelity with which they are obeying the voice of their conscience; a capacity to do justice to the goodness of their intentions and to the zeal that they are displaying for truth in principle. It implies a recognition that, while mistaken in their hypothesis, they are being true, in their [fundamental] thesis, to the unalterable and eternal laws of order—laws which command us to love the truth and to sacrifice to this love the temporal goods and amenities of life. In a word, it implies a capacity for distinguishing, in the soul of the same person, between this person's opposition to truths of detail, of which he is ignorant, and his love for truth in principle—a love which he makes conspicuously manifest through the strength of his attachment to the doctrines that he believes to be true. Such was the discernment of which the Queen of Navarre showed herself to be capable.[1]

Someone who is convinced of [the truth of] the fundamental articles of the Christian Faith, but who abstains from communicating, because he regards this act as an indication that one condemns other Christian sects, could be treated as an atheist only in the judgment of an old driveler who had forgotten both the meanings of things and the definitions of words. I go farther and maintain that one could not deny to a man, such as I have described, the name of Christian.[2]

It is certain that there is no accusation that has been so grossly abused as that of Atheism. Innumerable petty-minded creatures or malicious spirits level this accusation against anyone who confines his affirmations to the grand and sublime truths of a solid metaphysic and to the general doctrines of Scripture. They want to compel such people to commit themselves, in addition, to all those articles on points of detail that are customarily propounded to the people a thousand times over. Anyone who ventures to exempt himself from this routine is impious and 'tough-minded', if some of our doctors [of Divinity] are to be believed.[3]

The mind of Man is so made that, at first sight, an attitude of neutrality in the matter of the worship of God is felt to be more

[1] Bayle, op. cit., iii. 2058 a and b, s.v. Navarre (Marguérite de Valois, Reine de, soeur de François I).
[2] Bayle, op. cit., ii. 1325 b, s.v. Grotius.
[3] Bayle, op. cit., ii. 1481 a, s.v. Hobbes.

violently shocking than the worship of false gods. So, when people hear that someone has abandoned the religion of his fathers without having adopted any other, they are more deeply horror-stricken than if they had heard that he had gone over from a better religion to a worse one.[1]

[1] Bayle, op. cit., i. 69 b, s.v. Acosta.

19

THE TASK OF DISENGAGING THE ESSENCE FROM THE NON-ESSENTIALS IN MANKIND'S RELIGIOUS HERITAGE

IN the second half of the twentieth century of the Christian Era a Westernizing World has been overtaken by two historical events which, together, make it now an obviously urgent task for us to try to disengage the essence in Mankind's religious heritage from non-essential accretions.

On the one hand the West's disillusionment with the idols which it took to worshipping in the Late Modern Age of its history has now brought the West back, once more, face to face with its ancestral Christianity. The West cannot avoid this re-encounter, and cannot have the experience without finding itself compelled to reconsider how it stands towards its discarded religious heritage. At the same time 'the annihilation of distance' through the achievements of a Late Modern Western technology has brought all the living higher religions, all over the World, into a much closer contact with one another than before. This closer contact is making the relations between them more intimate. In A.D. 1956 a stage could already be foreseen at which the hereditary adherents of each living religion would have become well enough acquainted with the other living religions to be able to look at their own ancestral religion in the light of its contemporaries; and, in this light, they would have an opportunity of seeing it with new eyes. Within Western Christendom itself, this was already happening as between the different, and once rival and hostile, Western Christian sects. Protestantism and Catholicism were learning from one another; and individual Western Christians, who had been brought up in one or other of the Western Christian churches, were deliberately choosing their church for themselves in after life. This change in the relations between Protestantism and Catholicism, and this new possibility of making an individual choice between the two, were portents of what might be going to happen as between Christianity, Judaism, Islam,

Zoroastrianism, Hinduism, and Buddhism. It looked, in fact, as if the living higher religions of the World would now, once again, have to face the same intense comparative scrutiny that they and their forerunners had formerly faced in those *soi-disant* oecumenical empires that had been foretastes of a literally world-wide society.

Thus, in our society in our time, the task of winnowing the chaff away from the grain in Mankind's religious heritage is being forced upon us by a conjunction of social and spiritual circumstances; but these circumstances are not unique, and the task is not an extraordinary one. It is a perennial task, with which the adherents of every higher religion are confronted all the time. 'The Reformation' is not just a particular past event in the Early Modern chapter of the history of the Western branch of Christianity. It is a perpetual challenge which is being presented at every moment to all higher religions alike, and which none of them can ignore for one moment without betraying its trust.

In the life of all the higher religions, the task of winnowing is a perennial one because their historic harvest is not pure grain. In the heritage of each of the higher religions we are aware of the presence of two kinds of ingredients. There are essential counsels and truths, and there are non-essential practices and propositions.

The essential counsels and truths are valid at all times and places, as far as we can see through the dark glass of Mankind's experience up to date. When we peer into the records of Man's religion as it was before any of the higher religions made their epiphany, we find the light of these counsels and truths already shining there, however dimly. And, if we could imagine to ourselves a future world in which every one of the living higher religions had become extinct, but in which the human race was still surviving, it would be difficult to imagine human life going on without still having these same essential counsels and truths to light its path and guide its steps, as in the past. In fact, the counsels and truths enshrined in the higher religions would appear to have still longer lives than the higher religions themselves. They would seem, indeed, to be coeval with Mankind, in the sense of being intimations of a spiritual presence accompanying us on our pilgrimage as a pillar of cloud by day and a pillar of fire by night[1]—an accompaniment without which Humanity would not be human.

These guesses carry us beyond the narrow limits of our historical knowledge; and this knowledge also does not tell us how the spiritual light reaches, or is reached by, us. Yet, whether it comes to us by discovery or by intuition or by revelation, and whether it is abiding or transitory, it is a matter of indisputable historical fact that it shines in all the higher religions, and it is also clear that this light in them has been the cause of their historic success. The higher religions have had a longer hold on a greater number of minds and hearts than any other institutions known to us up to date; and this hold has been due to the light that they have thrown, for Man, upon his relation to a spiritual presence in the mysterious Universe in which Man finds himself. In this presence, Man is confronted by something spiritually greater than himself which, in contrast to Human Nature and to all other phenomena, is Absolute Reality. And this Absolute Reality of which Man is aware is also an Absolute Good for which he is athirst. Man finds himself needing, not only to be aware of It, but to be in touch with It and in harmony with It. That is the only condition on which he can feel himself at home in the world in which he finds himself in existence.

This is 'the true light which lighteth every man that cometh into the World';[2] and the higher religions are carriers of it. But at the same time these same higher religions are historical institutions; and they have been making a transit through Space-Time in which, at every point-moment in their trajectory, they have been encountering the local and temporary circumstances of human life. While the higher religions have been influencing the older religions and one another and the mundane civilizations, they have also been receiving influences from the mundane civilizations and from one another and from their forerunners, and these influences that they have received have left their mark on them in accretions. This is something that we can verify, because an historian can trace these accretions back to their origins and can show, in many cases, that these origins are alien to the essential truths and counsels enshrined in the higher religion in question. He can show that

---

[1] Ex. xiii. 21-2. [2] John i. 9.

they have attached themselves to the religion, in the course of its history, as a result of historical accidents.

These accidental accretions are the price that the permanently and universally valid essence of a higher religion has to pay for communicating its message to the members of a particular society in a particular stage of this society's history. We can express this in the traditional language of Christianity by saying that the price of redemption is incarnation. Alternatively, we can express it in the current language of a twentieth-century world by saying that, if the eternal voice did not 'tune in' to its present audience's receiving-set, its message would not be picked up. But, in order to be picked up, the message has to be denatured to some extent by a translation of what is permanent and universal into terms of something that is temporary and local. At any rate, the message, if not positively denatured, will be limited by being put into terms of something that is not permanent and universal, and will thus be denatured at least in a negative sense, considering that the message itself is spiritually infinite. If the essence of a higher religion did not compromise with local and temporary circumstances by 'tuning in' to them, it would never reach any audience at all; for, in every human society, the permanent and universal counsels and truths are overlaid by one of those local and temporary culture-patterns with which Adam and Eve have covered their nakedness ever since they first ate of the fruit of the Tree of Knowledge. On the other hand, if a higher religion is unable or unwilling to change its tune when it is carried by the current of History to new theatres of social life in other times and places, its undiscarded adaptation to a past social milieu will put it even more out of tune with the present social milieu than if it had presented itself without any accessories at all.

A case in point is the Western costume in which Christianity has been conveyed to non-Western Christians and non-Christians in a Modern Age in which Western missionaries of Christianity have disembarked on all the shores of all the oceans. Are these Western Christian missionaries to strip Christianity of a local and temporary Western suit of clothes in order to reclothe it in the ancestral dress of the particular people to whom they are preaching? Or are they to present Christianity as part of the paraphernalia of their own ancestral civilization—as, in fact, the tribal religion of Western Man? This question gave rise, in the seventeenth century, to a controversy between the Society of Jesus and the Franciscan and Dominican Orders. The Jesuits in the mission-field had been trying to divest Christianity of its Western accretions in order to make sure that the non-Christian audience to whom they were addressing their message should not be deterred from accepting the essence of Christianity through being required also to accept things whose association with it was merely local, temporary, and accidental. In this seventeenth-century 'Battle of the Rites', the Society of Jesus suffered defeat; but the experience of the following 250 years has been demonstrating, more and more conclusively, that the Jesuits were as right as they were brave in resolutely wielding the winnowing-fan.

If the Jesuit missionaries were acting with uncommon insight and courage in trying to discriminate the essence of Christianity from its Western accidents, the Vatican was not acting in an uncommonly benighted or tyrannical way when it found in favour of the less adventurous of the two policies then in debate among Roman Catholic Western Christian missionaries. It was acting in a way that is characteristic of ecclesiastical authorities. For the distinction between the essence and the accidents in Religion is one which the ecclesiastical authorities, always and everywhere, are reluctant to admit.

This attitude has had disastrous consequences because it is a wrong attitude in itself. We cannot hope to be able to begin to put it right until we have diagnosed its cause; and this cause is not obscure. The evil has nothing to do with Religion itself and it is not peculiar to the religious institutions for which the ecclesiastical authorities are responsible. It is a manifestation of the Original Sin which is another name for self-centredness. This sin is always and everywhere on the look-out for opportunities for asserting itself, and one of its greatest opportunities is offered to it by Man's inability to do without institutions.

Institutions, as we have seen,[1] enable Man to satisfy social needs that cannot be provided for within the narrow range of relations attainable through direct personal intercourse. Yet the tragic experience of human history shows that the possibilities that the invention of institutions have brought within

[1] In Chapter 8, pp. 106-7, above.

Man's reach have been purchased by Man at a high price. The cost of the quantitative gain is a qualitative loss; for, while institutional relations leave personal relations far behind in respect of the number of the souls that they can bring together into society, all human experience testifies that institutional relations at their best cannot compare in spiritual quality with personal relations at their best. The miscarriages of both kinds of relations can be traced to an identical cause in the innate self-centredness of human nature, but a soul that surrenders itself to 'nosism' can deceive itself into imagining that this self-centredness in the first person plural is 'altruism', whereas a soul that surrenders itself to 'egoism' cannot so easily persuade itself that this singular self-centredness is not sinful.

One generic evil of an institution of any kind is that people who have identified themselves with it are prone to make an idol of it. The true purpose of an institution is simply to serve as a means for promoting the welfare of human beings. In truth it is not sacrosanct but is 'expendible'; yet, in the hearts of its devotees, it is apt to become an end in itself, to which the welfare of human beings is subordinated and even sacrificed if this is necessary for the welfare of the institution. The responsible administrators of any institution are particularly prone to fall into the moral error of feeling it to be their paramount duty to preserve the existence of this institution of which they are trustees. Ecclesiastical authorities have been conspicuous sinners in this respect, though ecclesiastics have not been exceptionally sinful persons. Most of them have not fallen below the average level of human sinfulness, but have risen conspicuously far above it. The reason why they have gone rather far in succumbing to the administrator's temptation to mistake means for ends is to be found, not in their character, but in their duties. Churches have been the most long-lived and most widespread of all institutions hitherto known; and their unusual success as institutions has made their institutional aspect loom unusually large in their official administrators' eyes.

The true purpose of a higher religion is to radiate the spiritual counsels and truths that are its essence into as many souls as it can reach, in order that each of these souls may be enabled thereby to fulfil the true end of Man. Man's true end is to glorify God and to enjoy Him for ever: and, if the ecclesiastical authorities were to make this true purpose of their religion the paramount consideration in the determination of their policy, they would be constantly re-tuning their unvarying essential message to different wave-lengths in order to make it audible to different audiences. Instead, they are apt to make the preservation of their church their paramount aim; and this consideration tempts them to insist that their religious heritage must be treated as an indivisible whole, in which the accidental accretions are to be accepted as being not less sacrosanct than the essence itself. They are moved to take this line by two fears. They are afraid of distressing and alienating the weaker brethren,[1] and they are afraid that, if once they admit that any element in the heritage is local and temporary and therefore discardable, they may find themselves unable to draw a line or make a stand anywhere, till the very essence of the religion will have been surrendered.

Such a policy is not only wrong; it is also bad psychology and bad statesmanship. It is bad psychology because it implies that the essence of the religion which the ecclesiastical authorities are seeking to safeguard has not the power to hold hearts and minds if it is stripped bare of accidental accretions and of institutional wrappings. The badness of the statesmanship has been demonstrated repeatedly by the event. The authorities' unwillingness to discriminate has not had the effect of constraining the less weak members of their flock to put up, for the sake of the essence, with accretions that have become unacceptable to them. 'Tacking', as this device is called in parliamentary politics, is a way of trying to apply coercion; and coercion nearly always defeats its own purpose in the long run. It defeats it when applied on the political and economic planes, and on the spiritual plane it is self-defeating *a fortiori*. A flock that is told by its pastors that it may not benefit by what it feels to be the essence of their and its common religion, except at the price of consenting to put up with what it feels to be anachronistic or exotic non-essentials, will, sooner or later, reject the non-essentials even at the cost of having to forgo the essence. It will feel that it cannot truly benefit by the essence if it is being guilty of hypocrisy and insincerity in its

[1] See Rom. xiv; 1 Cor. viii.

attitude towards the non-essentials. Both the nemesis of an ecclesiastical policy of 'totalitarianism' and the rewards of the contrary policy of discrimination can be illustrated from the history of the Western Christian Church.

At the Council of Florence (A.D. 1438-9), which had been convened with the object of negotiating a union between the Eastern Orthodox churches and the Roman See, a statesman-like distinction was boldly drawn by the Western ecclesiastical negotiators. They required, as the conditions for union, an agreement in doctrine with the Western Church and an acceptance of the Roman See's ecclesiastical supremacy; and they insisted on these two conditions being complied with. But at the same time they showed themselves ready to allow to Eastern Orthodox churches that did agree these conditions a very wide liberty in the field of rites. They were to be free, for instance, to retain their own traditional liturgies in their own liturgical languages, and their own traditional customs and practices—as, for example, the custom that parish priests should be married men. This discriminatory policy did not attain its immediate purpose. At the time, the Eastern Orthodox peoples repudiated the signatures of their representatives, and the Greek people opted for political subjection to the Ottoman Empire as, in their eyes, a lesser evil than ecclesiastical sub-mission to the Roman See. But this immediate rebuff did not move the Vatican to revoke the terms for union that it had offered in A.D. 1438-9; and, in the course of the five centuries that have passed since that date, the result of this enlightened liberality has been the reconciliation with Rome of a number of uniate churches recruited not only from Eastern Orthodox Christendom but from the Monothelete and Monophysite and Nestorian communions too.

This episode of ecclesiastical history is significant because in this case the concessions that reaped the rewards were not far-reaching. At Florence in A.D. 1439 the Roman Church was drawing its line, not between the essence of Christianity and non-essentials, but merely between some non-essentials and others. The ecclesiastical supremacy of the Roman See is a non-essential in non-Roman Catholic Christian eyes; and so too, in many eyes, is a great deal of what is traditional Christian doctrine. Thus, in making its dissection, the Roman Church was not coming near to touching the quick. Yet even this modicum of discrimination ultimately reconciled with the Roman Church an appreciable number of dissidents.

There is a melancholy contrast between the Roman Church's measure of discriminating liberalism in its dealings, since the fifteenth century, with the non-Western Christian churches and the 'totalitarian' intransigence displayed by the same Roman Church, and likewise by most of the Protestant Western churches, during the last quarter of a millennium, in the war that they have been waging with a Late Modern Western experimental science. In this war most of the positions that have been contested have had as little to do with the essence of Christianity as the positions that were yielded in A.D. 1439; almost all of them have been accidental accretions with which Western Christianity happened to be encumbered in the seventeenth century, when the scientific movement started. The consequent alienation of many of the leaders of Western thought from the West's ancestral tradition has been the tragedy of the West in its Late Modern Age. When, in the twentieth century, the ideals inspiring the current Western way of life were challenged by Communism, this schism in Western souls proved to be the West's gravest spiritual weakness; and the responsibility of the ecclesiastical authorities for this unhappy and untoward consequence of spiritual discord was perhaps, on the whole, greater than the responsibility of the agnostics and the atheists.

The ecclesiastical authorities' responsibility was perhaps the greater because their true duty is to winnow away the fresh accretions to their religious heritage that are constantly accumulating.

We have observed that what is permanent and universal has always and everywhere to be translated into terms of something temporary and local in order to make it accessible to particular human beings here and now. But we ought never to allow ourselves to forget that every translation of this kind is bound to be a mistranslation to some extent, and that it is therefore also bound to be contingent and provisional.[1] The penalty for neglecting the perpetually urgent task of discarding the current mistranslation is to allow the light radiated by the

[1] See Chapter 9, pp. 121 and 125-7, above.

essence of a religion to be shut off from human souls by an opaque film of accretions.

This will happen because a translation into the language of one social milieu makes the essence of a religion unintelligible in a different social milieu whose mother-tongue is a different vernacular. The point may be illustrated from the use of language in the literal sense as a means of conveying a religion's message. In the first century of the Christian Era the dissemination of the books of the New Testament in the Attic *koinê*—the 'standard Greek' of the day—ensured their finding readers as far afield from Palestine as Britain in one direction and India in another; yet, in our twentieth-century Western World, the words 'it is Greek to me' mean, not that I can understand it, but, on the contrary, that I find it unintelligible. The self-same medium that was pre-eminently conductive there and then has become pre-eminently non-conductive here and now. In terms of visual means of communication, we can put the same point by saying that 'one man's lens is another man's blinker'.

Thus the task of winnowing the chaff away from the grain is always making its demand upon us; and yet the operation is always as hazardous as it is indispensable. It is hazardous for the reason that makes the ecclesiastical authorities so often flinch from their duty of undertaking it. It is certain that any religious heritage, at any stage of its history, will be compounded of essential elements and accidental accretions which differ from one another in their nature, in their value, and in the treatment that they ought to receive from the religion's adherents. But it is at the same time probable that it will prove difficult to make a dissection of this composite body which will be so accurate that it will distinguish the accretions from the essence quite correctly.

In setting about this task, the theologian finds himself in a plight which he shares with the astronomer and with the historian. A human observer is never in a position to take his observations from a fixed point outside the object that he is observing. The astronomer who is trying to survey and comprehend the stellar cosmos has to do his intellectual work from the saddle; for, all the time, he himself is riding at breakneck speed on one of the circling planets of a travelling star in a galaxy that is part and parcel of the phenomena that he is attempting to study. The historian, again, is himself being carried down a lower reach of the time-stream of human history whose upper reaches he is trying to map; and his own motion will make any particular reach on which he is focussing his attention take on, as he gazes at it, a kaleidoscopic succession of different appearances. It is not really passing through any corresponding changes; but the lower reach, down which the historian himself is travelling, is constantly twisting and turning and also constantly varying the rate of its flow, now to a faster and now to a slower pace, and, at each of these changes, is presenting the upper reach to the historian's eyes in a changed perspective. The theologian finds himself in a similar quandary when he seeks to discriminate non-essential accretions from the essence of a religious heritage. In trying to correct the mis-translations of the essence of the religion into the transitory vernacular languages of a succession of past times and places, he must never forget to allow for the fact that the present time and place, which is his unescapable standpoint, is, all the time, forcing him to make a mistranslation of his own. This mis-translation is even more difficult for him to correct than those made by his predecessors are.

Another difficulty with which the theologian has to contend arises from the ambivalence of the character and function of the accretions that he is proposing to scale off from the essence to which they adhere; for we have noticed that an accretion which, for one eye, is a blinker, shutting out the light, may, for another eye, have been a lens letting the light in. Moreover, the transformation of the lens into a blinker is seldom a sudden mutation. It is usually a gradual metamorphosis—so gradual that it may seem arbitrary to try to identify a point-moment at which the change has taken place. This, too, makes the task of trying to distinguish the accretions from the essence a delicate one.

The theological critic's task of discrimination is, indeed, a more hazardous one than the peeling of an onion or the clean-ing of a picture. You might go on peeling an onion till you found that you had peeled away the heart as well as the skin; and you might go on cleaning a picture—stripping off successive coats of varnish and layers of paint—till, with a shock, you found yourself left with nothing but the bare canvas backing. In these two operations you are not likely to go to those disastrous lengths; yet, in every case at every stage, you clean and you peel at your peril. If, however, because of this risk, you refrain from trying to peel your onion, you will never have an onion to eat, and, if you refrain from trying to clean your picture, you will never reveal again, either to your own or to any other human eyes, the work of the old master who painted the now overlaid masterpiece.

In view of the inherent difficulty of Psyche's task, it is audacious to censure the ecclesiastical authorities for their reluctance to take this task in hand. Amends are due; and the most pertinent amends will be for the rash censor to test his thesis at his own peril by making the hazardous attempt to discriminate the accretions from the essence in the principal living higher religions of his own day. The errors into which he is bound to fall will give the theologians an opening for pronouncing, if they choose, that in this field discretion is the better part of valour.

In the twentieth century there are at least seven higher religions to be taken into account by the would-be analyst if he reckons that the Hīnayāna, as well as the Mahāyāna, has now virtually completed its metamorphosis into a religion from the philosophy that it was originally. There are three Buddhaic religions: the Hīnayāna Buddhism of Ceylon and South-East Asia; the Mahāyāna Buddhism of Eastern Asia, Tibet, and Mongolia; and the post-Buddhaic Hinduism of India. There are three Judaic religions: Judaism, Christianity, and Islam. And there is the Zoroastrianism of the Parsee diasporà in South-East Persia and Western India—a religion that is decidedly Judaic in spirit and outlook, whatever may be its historical relation to Judaism on the one hand and to pre-Buddhaic Hinduism on the other. We must keep all these seven religions in view in trying first to identify the essence of the living higher religions and then to scale off some, at least, of the non-essential accretions that are adhering to this essence in our day.

Let us begin with the essential truths and essential counsels that are preached by all seven religions alike.

They all agree that the phenomena of which we are aware do

not explain themselves. These phenomena must be only a fragment of a universe of which the rest remains obscure to us; and the key to the explanation of the whole lies hidden in the part which we do not perceive or understand. So the universe in which we find ourselves is a mysterious one.

In this mysterious universe, there is one thing of which Man can feel certain. Man himself is certainly not the greatest spiritual presence in the Universe. He understands the Universe only partially, he can control it only slightly, and manifestly he did not bring it into existence. His own presence in the Universe is, for him, an accomplished fact which has not come about through any choice or act of his.

There is a presence in the Universe that is spiritually greater than Man himself. This presence is not contained either in some of the phenomena or in the sum total of them.

In human life, knowledge is not an end in itself, but is a means to action. Knowledge of truths is valuable in so far as it serves as a guide to action leading towards the goal of human endeavours. For example, the pre-Buddhaic Indian philosophers saw the truth that 'Thou art That': a human self is identical with Absolute Reality in some sense. But the sense in which this intuitive knowledge is true can be discovered only by taking action. The statement 'Thou art That' is, in truth, not a mere statement but a call to thee to make thyself that which thou knowest that thou canst be. An imperative is implicit in the indicative. The intuition of a truth is the designation of a goal.

Man's goal is to seek communion with the presence behind the phenomena, and to seek it with the aim of bringing his self into harmony with this absolute spiritual reality.

A human self cannot be brought into harmony with Absolute Reality unless it can get rid of its innate self-centredness. This is the hardest task that Man can set himself; but, if he accomplishes it, his reward will be far more than proportionate to the toil and pain of the spiritual struggle. In giving up self-centredness he will have felt as if he were losing his life; but in achieving this act of self-sacrifice he will find that he has really saved his life, because he will have given his life a new centre, and this new centre will be the Absolute Reality that is the spiritual presence behind the phenomena.

Thus far, all seven religions speak with one voice; but at this point we come to a difference of view between the Hīnayāna and the other six in regard to the nature of Absolute Reality. All seven agree with one another in holding that Absolute Reality has an impersonal aspect. For Buddhism this is Nirvāna; for Hinduism it is Brahma; for Zoroastrianism it is Ahuramazda's abstract attributes; for the Judaic religions it is the experience of the mystics. But six out of the seven—all, in fact, except the Hīnayāna—also agree with one another in holding that Absolute Reality has a personal aspect as well. For them, Absolute Reality has a facet which is personal in the sense in which a human self is personal; and, in this manifestation of It, human beings have encounters with It which can be described, without this being misleading, in terms of the encounters that they have with one another. On this issue, Mahāyāna Buddhism parts company with Hīnayāna Buddhism and agrees with the other five religions in practice, though it does not break with the Hīnayāna in theory.[1] In theory the bodhisattvas are not personal aspects of Absolute Reality; they are phenomenal and ephemeral selves that have arrived at the verge of achieving harmony with Absolute Reality by extinguishing themselves and have it in their power at any moment to take the final step. In practice, the bodhisattvas are virtually divinities akin to the gods or God in whom Absolute Reality reveals Itself in Its personal aspect in the view of the other five religions.

The consensus of these five religions with one another and with the Mahāyāna, as against the Hīnayāna, in holding that the greatest spiritual presence known to Man has a personal aspect is a bond of unity which transcends the differences between their views of what the personal aspect is. For the Mahāyāna, this personal aspect of a superhuman presence, manifested in the bodhisattvas, is plural; for Hinduism and Christianity the personal aspect of Absolute Reality is triune; for Zoroastrianism, Islam, and Judaism it is singular. These differences are momentous. All the same, they are perhaps not so significant as the point of agreement which distinguishes

---

[1] In practice, the Hīnayāna, too, like the Mahāyāna, has travelled some distance along the road leading towards a theism that is incompatible with Buddhist theory.

all six religions alike from the Hīnayāna. Their common tenet that Absolute Reality has a personal aspect governs not only their theory but their aim. It determines their interpretation of the common counsel to the Self to strive, with all its might, to get rid of its innate self-centredness. The Hīnayāna interprets this counsel as a call to self-extinction.[1] For the other six religions the attainment of harmony with Absolute Reality means, not self-extinction through the Self's own exclusive exertions, but self-reorientation with God's or a bodhisattva's aid. It means the transfer of the Self's centre of attachment from the Self to a bodhisattva, or to Absolute Reality in Its personal aspect in which It manifests Itself as God. For these six religions, the goal implicit in the pre-Buddhaic Indian philosophers' intuition 'Thou art That' is attained in a communion of selves, human and divine. On this view, human selves realize their potential identity with Absolute Reality, not by dissolving themselves, but by making God's will theirs.[2]

This vision of the Universe as a society of selves raises problems of good-and-evil and right-and-wrong if it is true that two of the attributes of selves, as exemplified in our human selves, are consciousness and will. If we believe that human selves are conscious of the difference between good and evil, and are free to choose between doing right and doing wrong, we must infer that the same faculties are possessed by Absolute Reality in the personal aspect in which It is a self in the sense in which a human being is. In God, however, the consciousness and the will that are familiar to us in Man become mysteries that are beyond our human understanding. Since God is Absolute Reality, His consciousness must be omniscient and His will must be omnipotent. But it looks, at least at first sight, as if an omnipotent God must be the author of all evil as well as all good and be the doer of all wrong as well as all right; and these conclusions are incompatible with the beliefs that God's nature is good and that Man's will is free. Conversely, these beliefs seem, at least at

---

[1] See Chapter 2, p. 16, Chapter 5, pp. 63-5, and Chapter 6, p. 83, above; and Chapter 20, pp. 289-94, below.

[2] This difference in aim between the Hīnayāna and the other six religions is not reflected in any corresponding difference in conduct. In this field the Hinayanian Buddhist peoples compare well, not only with Mahayanian Buddhists, but with the followers of the other five living higher religions.

first sight, to be incompatible with a belief in God's omnipotence. For, in the fragment of the Universe that is within
human ken, evil occurs and human beings do wrong; and, if
God is good, this evil-happening and wrong-doing must
happen in spite of God's will and must be done in defiance of it.

This mystery has confronted the six religions that agree in
holding that Absolute Reality has a personal aspect. Each of
them has tried to find an explanation; and, in this quest,
Hinduism has parted company with the others. Hinduism has
sought to vindicate God's omnipotence by seeing in Him the
author of evil as well as good and the doer of wrong as well as
right. Of the three persons of the Hindu Trinity, Shiva is
maleficent, while Brahmā[1] is 'beyond Good and Evil'. The
Mahāyāna, Zoroastrianism, and the three Judaic religions have
sought to vindicate God's goodness by finding a prime author of
evil and prime doer of wrong in a Devil who is not God and is
not on an equality with God, but who, in spite of being God's
inferior and God's creature, is permitted by God to oppose
and, temporarily at least, to defy, His will. In the Christian
Trinity, all three persons alike are beneficent; and, if the Hindu
Vishnu finds his counterpart in God the Son, the Hindu Shiva
finds his antithesis in God the Holy Spirit. Yet, in excluding
the author of Evil from the Godhead, Christianity cannot
banish him from the Universe and cannot relieve God of
responsibility for the Devil's activity or, indeed, for his existence.
Of the five religions that find in the Devil an explanation of the
mystery, Zoroastrianism is perhaps the frankest in recognizing
the difficulty of reconciling a belief in the existence of the Devil
with a belief in the omnipotence of God. This answer to the
riddle is, in fact, unconvincing to the Head, while the Hindu
answer is repugnant to the Heart. Yet Man cannot have a
vision of Absolute Reality in terms of personality without both
feeling God to be good and also knowing Him to be omnipotent; and our inability to reconcile these two intuitions
indicates, not that there is an inner contradiction in the nature
of God, but that there is a limit to Man's powers of comprehension.

The five religions that vindicate God's, or the bodhisattvas',
goodness as best they can all agree in holding that God's, or the

[1] See Chapter 2, p. 16, footnote 1, above.

bodhisattvas', attitude towards human beings is not one of aloofness or indifference. In virtue of His goodness, God, or a bodhisattva, cares for human beings, loves them, and helps them. As Judaism sees God, 'He delighteth in mercy';[1] as Islam sees Him, He is 'the merciful, the compassionate'; as Zoroastrianism sees Him, He is the leader and champion of the hosts of the good in the age-long war between Good and Evil. This vision of God's attitude towards Man is shared with Judaism, Islam, and Zoroastrianism by Christianity and by the Mahāyāna, but it looks—at least in the eyes of one observer who has grown up in the Christian tradition—as if the Maha-yanian and the Christian vision had also brought to light some-thing else in God's nature and action which, in the vision of the other three religions, is perhaps latent but is not explicit. Both Christianity and the Mahāyāna hold that a superhuman being has demonstrated His love for human beings in action, and this at the cost of the Suffering that is inseparable from being a self. A bodhisattva is a self that is deliberately refraining from entering into Nirvāna for the sake of continuing to help its fellow sufferers at its own cost. Christ is a self that has found itself 'existing in God's form' and 'on an equality with' Him. Yet, instead of 'thinking of this as being a prize to be clutched', Christ has deliberately 'emptied Himself by taking a menial's form—for this is what He did in assimilating Himself to human beings. Exposing Himself thus in human guise, He showed His Humility in His obedience. He was obedient even to the point of submitting to die—and this by a death on the cross.'[2]

In this Christian-Mahayanian vision, Absolute Reality deliberately accepts a consequence of selfhood which follows necessarily from an assumption of selfhood that is genuine. Suffering is as inseparable from selfhood as will and conscious-ness are; and Absolute Reality accepts a self's suffering from a motive which human selves can understand because they too can be moved by it. This motive is a love for other selves which does not shrink from suffering for their sake.

If it is hazardous to try to state the essence of the higher religions, it is even more hazardous to try to discriminate from it the non-essential accretions that can be, and ought to be, discarded. It is perhaps safest to begin by stripping off what

[1] Mic. vii. 18.   [2] Phil. ii. 5-8, quoted in Chapter 6, p. 86, above.

looks like the outermost layer, and then to feel our way cautiously, through one layer after another, towards the quick. But even the outer layers have acquired, by long use and want, a tenacious hold on human feelings; so that these, too, cannot be removed without inflicting pain and arousing resentment and regret.

For example, strong feelings are focussed on local holy places, though these are perhaps the least controversial of all permissible discards. There is a charge of emotion in the very names Heliopolis, Abydos, Delphi, Bethel, Shiloh, Jerusalem, Mount Gerizim, Mecca, Medina, Karbalā, Najaf, Qazimayn, Mashhad, Rome, Compostela, Monte Gargano, Loreto, Lourdes, Bodh Gaya, Benares, Tun Hwang, Wu T'ai Shan, and the rest. Yet, considering that a sense of holiness is a sense of a spiritual presence behind the phenomena, a feeling that one spot on the surface of this planet is holier than another will be a feeling that this particular spot is more redolent of the presence of Absolute Reality than other spots are. This notion is incongruous with the idea of what Absolute Reality is; for it is of the essence of Absolute Reality that It is omnipresent. Moreover, in almost every case, an historian can trace back the hallowing of a particular spot to historical events that have nothing to do with the essence of the religion in whose tradition this spot has acquired a special odour of sanctity. And, since every higher religion holds that God is present everywhere, and also believes its own mission to be to preach the Gospel to all Mankind on all the face of the Earth, every higher religion's ultimate verdict on local holy places must be: 'The hour cometh, when ye shall neither in this mountain, nor yet at Jerusalem, worship the Father'.[1] No doubt, this hour could not come so long as a lack of adequate physical means of communication was still constraining Mankind to go on living in a number of small separate compartments, each a miniature world with its own local centre. But this former physical *raison d'être* of local shrines has vanished in an age in which Technology has 'annihilated distance'. In this age 'the Earth shall be filled with the knowledge of the glory of the Lord, as the waters cover the sea'.[2]

A still higher charge of feeling is accumulated in rituals: the

[1] John iv. 21.   [2] Hab. ii. 14. Cp. Isa. xi. 9.

pilgrimages that are symbolic recognitions of a holy place's
holiness; the kissing of the Black Stone embedded in the
Ka'bah, or the kissing of the toe of a bronze statue of St.
Peter; the Passover; the Muslim's daily round of prayers; the
Christian and the Mahayanian Buddhist liturgies. Acts of
worship tend to become institutionalized when the con-
gregation extends beyond the family circle. Yet God can be
worshipped by human beings, congregationally as well as
individually, at any place and time, and this without formalities.
'God is a spirit, and they that worship Him must worship Him
in spirit and in truth.'[1]

A still higher charge, again, is accumulated in tabus: not to
eat pork ever; not to eat the flesh of mammals on Fridays; not
to work on the Sabbath; to fast partially in Lent and totally
during daylight hours in Ramazan; to circumcise male
children; to eat human corpses, or to expose them to be eaten
by vultures and hyaenas, instead of burning or burying them;[2]
to keep every jot and tittle of the Jewish or the Zoroastrian
Law. Yet 'the Sabbath was made for Man, and not Man for
the Sabbath'.[3]

Particularly violent feelings are aroused by conflicts between
different social conventions: celibacy versus marriage for a
Christian priest according to the Latin as against the Eastern
Orthodox rite; monogamy for a Christian layman versus
polygamy for a Muslim up to a limit of four wives; stringency
versus laxity in the Christian as against the Muslim regulation
of divorce; caste versus the brotherhood of all believers in the
Hindu as against the Islamic or the Sikh community. In this
field, as in those of tabus and rituals, the Roman Church has
set an example of courageous discrimination which we have
cited at an earlier point in this chapter. The uniate churches of
non-Latin rite are so many monuments to the wisdom and
liberality of the Roman See in drawing a distinction between
some non-essential things and others, and in conceding that,
in some non-essentials, the uniates should be free to follow their
own traditional practice so long as they fulfil the two conditions
of recognizing the Roman See's ecclesiastical supremacy and
agreeing with the Roman Church on questions of doctrine.

[1] John iv. 24.   [2] See, for example, Herodotus, Book III, chap. 38.
[3] Mark ii. 27.

Though shrines, rituals, tabus, and social conventions are highly charged with feeling, they do not come so close to the heart of a religion as its myths: the portrayal of death as the seed of life in the figure of Tammuz-Adonis-Osiris-Attis, embodying the fruitfulness of the year that dies to be born again;[1] the portrayal of self-sacrifice for the salvation of fellow-sufferers in the figure of Christ or of a bodhisattva; the portrayal of superhuman spiritual stature in the figure of a hero whose mother is human but whose father is divine (the birth-story that is told of Jesus, Augustus, Alexander, Plato, and every pharaoh of Egypt since, at latest, the beginning of the Fifth Dynasty). Can these myths be discarded without taking the heart out of the faiths whose essence the myths convey? If the Universe is a mystery, and if the key to this mystery is hidden, are not myths an indispensable means for expressing as much as we can express of the ineffable? 'No man hath seen God at any time'[2] and 'Alles Vergängliche ist nur ein Gleichnis';[3] yet 'das Umbeschreibliche, hier ist's getan'.[4] This similitude of Absolute Reality in the World of Time and Change is the nearest approach towards the Beatific Vision that can be attained by human souls; and myths are the instruments through which these farthest flights of the Human Spirit are achieved.[5]

This is true; and it does mean that myths are indispensable to Man for probing a mystery that is beyond his intellectual horizon. Yet no particular myth can be sacrosanct; for myths are woven out of poetic images borrowed from This World's passing scene. The myths that fall least far short of being universal and eternal are those inspired by the primordial experiences of human life. 'Das ewig Weibliche zieht uns hinan.'[6] Man's feelings about the part that Woman plays in his life are rooted in Human Nature itself; and it is no wonder that a myth quarried from this bedrock should keep on reappearing in variations that betray its identity. A primordial element is perhaps to be found in every myth that makes its mark. Yet the stuff of which myths are fashioned is mostly local and ephemeral.

---

[1] John xii. 24; 1 Cor. xv. 35-8.
[2] John iv. 12.
[3] Goethe, *Faust*, l. 12104.
[4] Ibid., ll. 12108-9.
[5] See Chapter 9, pp. 123-4, above.
[6] Goethe, *Faust*, ll, 12110-11.

This is true even of the images taken from agriculture, which, for most of the Human Race, has been Man's staple means of livelihood for the last 7,000 or 8,000 years, and which, by now, has been propagated over almost the whole of the cultivable surface of the planet. The Christian adaptation of the myth and ritual of the agricultural year, which, in Christendom, seems as if it were speaking an oecumenical language, is in truth speaking no more than the regional language of the parochial realm of wheat and the vine. The Western traveller to Japan finds that the alien realm of rice—which is the food of half the Human Race—has no words for bread and wine in its vocabulary. If Christianity had made its first epiphany in Eastern Asia and not in Palestine, its primary symbols would not be the Mediterranean imagery that they are. So even the most expressive symbols prove to have no more than a limited range in Space and Time, and therefore cannot be of the essence of Religion. They can be no more than local and ephemeral indications of a Reality that, in itself, is omnipresent and eternal.

What is true of myths must be true, *a fortiori*, of Theology, if there is any force in the argument of an earlier chapter of this book.[1] It has been argued there that the poetic usage of words, which is their usage in myths, differs from the scientific usage of the same words in feeling, intention, and meaning; and it has been suggested that Theology, in its handling of myths, has been acting under a misapprehension which has condemned it to defeat its own purpose. Theology's purpose is to clarify the meaning of myths, and it seeks to do this by treating their words as if these were being used in their scientific sense. But theologians seem not to have recognized the limitations of the scientific usage. This, too, has a limited field of application, as the poetic usage has; and it is not a more exact usage than the poetic one is. It is not truer to reality intrinsically. It is simply the best notation for describing a fragment of the Universe that is within the Human Intellect's grasp. But the poetic usage is the best for reconnoitring this foreground's mysterious hinterland. Consequently an attempt to take a poetic intuition of the mystery as if it were a scientific analysis does not sharpen our faculties but inhibits them from serving us. The music of the

[1] Chapter 9, pp. 116-27, above.

spheres ceases to be audible when it is transposed into a mathematical scale of numerical ratios.

In the same context we have sought to trace back to their historical origins the accretions of theology with which the mythical expressions of Christianity, Islam, and Hinduism have been overlaid, and we have found these origins in the price that has had to be paid for the conversion of a philosophically educated élite. The 'intellectuals' could not be induced to accept a new religion unless this could be presented to them in terms that would be acceptable to them philosophically; and Theology is thus a monument of an encounter between 'intellectuals' and missionaries.

If it is true that an intellectual operation which once commended a religion to a particular class of potential converts has actually obscured, instead of clarifying, this religion's meaning, intention, and feeling, as these are conveyed in its myths, then, if it is also true that the myths themselves are not of the essence of a religion, it must follow that the theology into which these myths have been transposed cannot be essential either.

The sacrifice of Theology is as desolating for the intellectual minority in a religious community as the sacrifice of current myths is for the community at large; but there is one sacrifice that is even more painful than these, and that is the sacrifice of self-centredness. Since self-centredness is innate in Human Nature, we are all inclined, to some extent, to assume that our own religion is the only true and right religion; that our own vision of Absolute Reality is the only authentic vision; that we alone have received a revelation; that the truth which has been revealed to us is the whole truth; and that, in consequence, we ourselves are 'the Chosen People' and 'the Children of Light', while the rest of the Human Race are gentiles sitting in darkness. Such pride and prejudice are symptoms of Original Sin, and they will therefore be rife in some measure in any human being or community; but the measure varies, and it seems to be a matter of historical fact that, hitherto, the Judaic religions have been considerably more exclusive-minded than the Indian religions have. In a chapter of the World's history in which the adherents of the living higher religions seem likely to enter into much more intimate relations with one another than ever before, the spirit of the Indian religions, blowing where it listeth,[1] may perhaps help to winnow a traditional Pharisaism out of Muslim, Christian, and Jewish hearts. But the help that God gives is given by Him to those who help themselves; and the spiritual struggle in the more exclusive-minded Judaic half of the World to cure ourselves of our family infirmity seems likely to be the most crucial episode in the next chapter of the history of Mankind.

[1] John iii. 8.

20

SELVES, SUFFERING, SELF-CENTREDNESS, AND LOVE

No human soul can pass through This Life without being challenged to grapple with the mystery of the Universe. If the distinctively human impulse of curiosity does not bring us to the point, experience will drive us to it—above all, the experience of Suffering.

In casting about for an approach to the mystery in a Westernizing World mid-way through the twentieth century, we might do well to take a cue from our seventeenth-century Western predecessors, who opened up for us a view that still holds us under its spell today. So far, Mankind has never succeeded in unifying the whole of its experience of the universe in which it finds itself. We can see the Universe from different angles, and from each of these it wears a different aspect. From one angle we see it as a spiritual universe; from another as a physical one; and from either of these two angles we can drive a tunnel into one flank of the great pyramid. But our tunnels driven into it from these two directions have never yet met, and neither of the two approaches, by itself, has enabled us to explore the mystery more than partially: neither of them has revealed its heart.

Mid-way through the twentieth century we Westerners are still exploring the Universe from the mathematico-physical angle that our seventeenth-century predecessors chose for us. In order to choose it, they had to wrench themselves away from the spiritual approach which Christianity had followed since its first epiphany, and which, before that, the Hellenic philosophers had been following since Socrates, and the prophets of Israel since Amos. This radical change of orientation required of the seventeenth-century Western mental pioneers who made it a great effort of will and imagination as well as a great effort of thought, and the spectacle of their prowess should inspire us to follow their example now at their expense. The time has come for us, in our turn, to wrench ourselves out of the seventeenth-century mathematico-physical line of approach which we are still following, and to make a fresh start from the spiritual side. This is now, once again, the more promising approach of the two, if we are right in expecting that, in the atomic age which opened in A.D. 1945, the spiritual field of activity, not the physical one, is going to be the domain of freedom.[1]

In taking this new departure, if we do take it, we shall be courting disappointment and frustration if we do not constantly keep in mind two limiting conditions. We must realize that we shall not penetrate right to the heart of the mystery along any line of approach. We must also realize that we cannot return either to the traditional Christian vision of the spiritual universe or to the post-Socratic Greek philosophers' vision of it after having delved into the mystery from the mathematico-physical angle for a quarter of a millennium. We cannot erase this long chapter in our Western mental history, and we ought not to want to erase it; for it has not only been long: it has been fruitful as well, within its limitations. So our aim should be, not to discard our predecessors' contribution to our cumulative heritage, but to find the due place for it—not giving it more than its due, but also not giving it less. The importance of doing justice to our predecessors is brought home to us by the consequences of their failure to do justice to theirs. Our seventeenth-century predecessors' aim was to jump clear of the strife and controversy of the foregoing age of the Western Wars of Religion, but they allowed themselves to be carried, beyond their aim, into discarding Religion itself as well as religious fanaticism. This was not their deliberate intention, and it was an unfortunate undesigned effect. Our easy wisdom after the event, which has enabled us to recognize their mistake, leaves us no excuse for repeating it.

In the seventeenth century the spiritual approach had led, as we have seen, to barren but bitter conflict springing from Christianity's vein of exclusiveness and fanaticism, and this conflict on the religious plane had been exploited for political purposes. Our seventeenth-century predecessors' withdrawal of their mental treasure from its traditional investment in spiritual values, and their reinvestment of it in the exploration

[1] See Chapter 17, pp. 235-6, and Chapter 18, pp. 243-9, above.

and conquest of Physical Nature, was a testimony to the strength and to the repulsiveness of Original Sin in their day. But Man does not exorcize Original Sin by averting his mind from it; and it still retained all its power over the technologist who was winning credit first for being harmless and then for being useful. For the technologist is a human being, and Original Sin is endemic in Human Nature. The carrier of Original Sin in the Technological Age was not Technology itself; it was Technology's human master. Technology has simply put into human hands an additional charge of physical power which can be used for evil as well as for good; and, since human beings are still as sinful as ever, this has put such a terribly potent drive into sin that we cannot afford to go on ignoring and neglecting the problem of Human Nature any longer. The very intractability of the problem, which makes us shrink from handling it, is a danger-signal; and, on the late-seventeenth-century principle of expediency and utility, 'the proper study of Mankind is Man'[1] for the twentieth-century successors of the seventeenth-century utilitarians.

In fine, we, in our generation, have as good a reason as our late-seventeenth-century predecessors had in theirs for trying to jump clear from a traditional approach to the mystery and for making a new start from a different angle. So, in our generation, let us set our feet on the spiritual path again, but, in making our jump in our turn, let us take care not to fall into our predecessors' mistake. Let us be sure to bring away with us the mental tools that Experimental Science and Technology have been forging during these last 200 or 300 years; for it would be unwise to discard them till we have found out whether they can be adapted for use in striving to reach the spiritual goal which is now again to be our objective.

In the preceding chapter, we have found all the higher religions agreeing that this goal is to seek communion with the presence behind the phenomena, and to seek it with the aim of bringing oneself into harmony with this Absolute Reality. In making a fresh attempt to approach this goal, we may find a promising starting-point in a paradox that has been disclosed in every penetrating analysis of Human Nature, in whatever time and place and social milieu the observation has been taken.

[1] Pope, *An Essay on Man*, Ep. ii, line 2.

I delight in the law of God after the inward man; but I see another law in my members, warring against the law of my mind, and bringing me into captivity to the law of sin which is in my members.[1]

Man's war within, between his Reason and his Passions. . . . If there were nothing but the Reason, and were no Passions. . . . If there were nothing but the Passions, and were no Reason. . . . But, as Man has both, he cannot be free from war, since he cannot be at peace with the one without being at war with the other. So he is always divided, and always his own adversary.[2]

Thus is Man that great and true amphibium, whose nature is disposed to live, not onely like other creatures in divers elements, but in divided and distinguished worlds.[3]

Human Nature is, in truth, a union of opposites that are not only incongruous but are contrary and conflicting: the spiritual and the physical; the divine and the animal; consciousness and subconsciousness; intellectual power and moral and physical weakness; unselfishness and self-centredness; saintliness and sinfulness; unlimited capacities and limited strength and time; in short, greatness and wretchedness: *grandeur et misère*.[4] But the paradox does not end here. The conflicting elements in Human Nature are not only united there; they are inseparable from one another.

The greatness of Man is great because Man knows that he is wretched. A tree does not know that it is wretched.[5] . . . All these miseries are so many proofs of Man's greatness; they are the miseries of a grand seigneur, the miseries of a king who has been dispossessed.[6] . . . One cannot be wretched unless one can feel it. A ruined house is not wretched. Man is the only wretched creature that there is. . . .[7] Man knows that he is wretched, so he is wretched, since this is the fact; but he is also impressively great, because he does know that he is wretched. . . .[8] This ambivalence of Human Nature is so evident that some people have supposed that we have two souls; an undivided personality seems to them incapable of such extreme and abrupt variations, from a boundless presumption

[1] Rom. vii. 22-3.
[2] Pascal, B., *Pensées*, No. 412 in Léon Brunschwicg's arrangement.
[3] Browne, Sir Thomas, *Religio Medici*, Part I, section 34.
[4] Pascal, *Pensées*, Nos. 416 and 443, and, in general, Nos. 397, 423, and 431-3.
[5] Ibid., No. 397.   [6] Ibid., No. 398.
[7] Ibid., No. 399.   [8] Ibid., No. 416.

to a horrible spiritual prostration. . . .[1] If he boasts himself, I humble him; if he humbles himself, I boast him; in fact, I contradict him all the time until I make him understand that he is an incomprehensible monster.[2]

Human Nature is an enigma; but Non-Human Nature is an enigma too; and both must be samples of the nature of the universe in which Man finds himself. It is as reasonable to explore the Universe in terms of the one as it is to explore it in terms of the other. Human Nature will not account for the aspect of the Universe that mathematics and physics reveal; but then these will not account for the aspect that is revealed in Human Nature. There is no ground except caprice or prejudice for treating the mathematico-physical aspect of the Universe as being real in any fuller measure than the spiritual aspect is. The mathematico-physical aspect, like the spiritual aspect, is a datum of human consciousness. Our view of the physical universe is no more objective than our view of ourselves. Our experience of the union of conflicting yet inseparable opposites in Human Nature may explain more things in Heaven and Earth than just Man himself. This ordeal of serving as a battlefield on which opposing spiritual forces meet and struggle with one another may be characteristic of the nature, not only of Man, but of all life on this planet. It might even be characteristic of the nature of God, if we use the traditional name for the personal aspect of an Absolute Reality which must have other facets besides. In any case, a human sample of the Universe is as fair a one to take as any other.

This human sample indicates that the Universe is a society of selves, besides being the set of waves and particles that we see through the lenses of mathematics and physics; and in a society of selves there are bound to be both desires and sufferings. This must be so, because a self cannot be self-contained. It cannot insulate itself, and it cannot embrace within itself the sum total of selves and things. If it were not conscious of things or selves outside itself, it could not be conscious of itself either; and consciousness is one of the hall-marks of selfhood. But, if, for this reason, a self cannot either shut out the rest of the Universe or annex it, then two other hall-marks of a self must

---

[1] Pascal, *Pensées*, No. 417.   [2] Ibid., No. 420.

be the experiences of yearning and of suffering. A self is bound to feel yearnings towards selves or things, outside it, of whose presence or existence it is aware. These yearnings are bound often to be thwarted, since the satisfaction of them lies only partly within the power of the self by which they are being felt; and, where there is frustration, there is pain. The inseparability of desire and suffering from selfhood is attested by the universal experience of Mankind, and all the higher religions agree in taking the fact of this experience for granted. But they differ with one another, as we have seen, over their policies for dealing with a practical problem that arises from the undisputed matter of fact—and this practical problem cannot be evaded. A human being can perhaps avert his mind from the intellectual problem of the mystery of the Universe, but he cannot help yearning and suffering; and a religion that had nothing to say to its adherents about these feelings would ring hollow.

Let us look again at the difference in policy between the Hīnayāna and other higher religions which we have already noticed in the preceding chapter.[1] This difference in policy does not arise from any difference in the diagnosis of the facts. The inseparability of selfhood, desire, and suffering is not in dispute. The difference in policy arises from a difference in the valuation of the facts; for different valuations of the same facts produce different answers to the question: What ought to be Man's paramount objective in the perplexing situation in which he finds himself?

The Hīnayāna arrives at its policy by starting with the value-judgement that the greatest of all evils is Suffering.[2] From this premiss it follows that a release from Suffering must be the greatest of all goods; and from that conclusion it follows, in turn, that a human being's paramount objective ought to be to extinguish Suffering at whatever the price may be. The price turns out to be nothing less than the extinction of the Self; for Suffering cannot be extinguished without the extinction of Desire, and, when Desire is extinguished, the Self is extinguished with it. The opponents of the Hīnayāna do not deny that its prescription for extinguishing Suffering is an effective one. What they deny is that the Hīnayāna's objective is the right

[1] See Chapter 19, pp. 274-7, above.   [2] See Chapter 5, pp. 63-5, above.

one for a human being to take as his paramount aim, and they
deny this because they dispute the Hīnayāna's initial postulate
that Suffering is the greatest evil that there is. As they see it,
the Hīnayāna is wrong in its valuation of the facts of Human
Nature because it has not penetrated deep enough in its
diagnosis.

A religion cannot be true unless it has attained a true knowledge
of our nature. It will have to have attained a knowledge of Man's
greatness and of his pettiness, and a knowledge of the reason for
both these characteristics of his. What religion has attained this
knowledge except Christianity?[1]

It seems unlikely that, when Pascal was thinking this, he will
have had Buddhism, as well as Christianity, in mind. Yet his
thought is at least an unconscious criticism of the Hīnayāna
and commendation of the Mahāyāna as well as a conscious
commendation of Christianity. Christianity and the Mahāyāna
arrive at their policy by starting with a distinction, which the
Hīnayāna does not draw, between desires of two different
kinds and by going on to appraise the two so differently that
they place them at opposite extremes of their scale of values.[2]
According to the Christian-Mahayanian diagnosis, there are
self-centred desires, in which the Self yearns for an object
outside itself simply in order to exploit this object of desire for
the greedy Self's own satisfaction; and, where it is a question
of these self-centred desires, the Christian-Mahayanian and the
Hinayanian policies do not differ. The common counsel is:
'Extinguish them.' The difference in policy arises when
Christianity and the Mahāyāna go on to diagnose another kind
of desire which is not self-centred but, on the contrary, is self-
sacrificing. Self-sacrifice means, not selfishly extinguishing the
Self, but lovingly devoting it to the service of others at the cost
of whatever Suffering this service may bring with it.

When a self is yearning in this self-devoting way, it is treating
the object of its yearning, not as an 'it' which is fair game, but
as a 'thee' who is sacrosanct because this 'thou' is another self.
In feeling a desire of the self-devoting kind, the loving self is
treating the Universe as a society of selves like itself; in feeling a

[1] Pascal, *Pensées*, No. 433.   [2] See Chapter 5, pp. 63-5, above.

desire of the self-centred kind, it is treating everything in the Universe outside itself as a soulless set of waves and particles. It is a fact of experience that every human self can and does have desires of these two different kinds, and that the two are not only different but are at opposite poles of the spiritual gamut. Here we have a further manifestation of the paradoxical union, in Human Nature, of opposites that conflict yet are inseparable. And the unceasing struggle which is an unescapable accompaniment of human life in This World is, in truth, a struggle to extinguish our self-centred desires and to follow the lead of our self-devoting desires at whatever the price may be. The price turns out to be Suffering to an extreme degree. The pain to which we expose ourselves through Love is still greater than the pain to which we expose ourselves through Cupidity. In the judgement of Christianity and the Mahāyāna, even the extremity of Suffering is not too high a price to pay for following Love's lead; for, in their judgement, Selfishness, not Suffering, is the greatest of all evils, and Love, not release from Suffering, is the greatest of all goods.

A synoptic view of the living higher religions thus confronts us with two different policies for the conduct of human life, based on two different diagnoses of the nature of Man and the Universe. Which of the two diagnoses comes the closer to the truth? And which of the two policies will bring us the nearer to the true end of Man?

If a twentieth-century inquirer, brought up in the Christian tradition, found himself called upon to answer these questions as best he could, no doubt he would be likely to declare in favour of Christianity and the Mahāyāna as against the Hīnayāna. On the question of fact he would find the Hīnayāna's diagnosis superficial in its failure to distinguish between self-devoting and self-centred desires. He would find that a superficial diagnosis had led to a wrong valuation and a wrong prescription; and he might go on to argue that the Hīnayāna's policy was also impracticable because, as he saw it, it was self-stultifying. How can a self set itself to extinguish Desire without feeling a desire to extinguish it? On the other hand, how can it succeed in extinguishing Desire so long as the desire to extinguish it remains unextinguished?[1] Has not the candidate for Nirvāna

[1] See Chapter 5, p. 64, above.

embarked on an enterprise in which he is bound to defeat his own purpose? Has he not placed himself in the predicament of a sufferer from insomnia who is making it impossible for himself to fall asleep by longing so anxiously for sleep to overtake him? What he desires is to lose consciousness of himself, and what is thwarting his desire is its self-centredness. This simile brings out the telling point that the Hinayanian arhat's desire for Nirvāna is a desire of the self-centred kind. For the arhat, in his pursuit of detachment, every other self in the Universe is, not a 'thou' to be loved, but an 'it' to be repudiated; and a desire that treats persons as if they were things is self-centred even when its only use for them is to be quit of them.

At this point, the statement of the case against the Hīnayāna might be taken over from the spokesman for Christianity by a spokesman for the Mahāyāna. This Buddhist critic of the Hīnayāna would cite the evidence of the Hinayanian scriptures and would argue from it that the Mahāyāna, not the Hīnayāna, is the Buddha's own school of Buddhism. The Hinayanian scriptures purport to be recording the Buddha's practice as well as His preaching; and, if their record is true, we are bound to conclude from it that the Buddha was not preaching what He was practising. In preaching, if He did preach this, that Man's paramount aim ought to be self-extinction, He was recommending to others a course of action which He had rejected for Himself when the Tempter, after His attainment of Enlightenment, had suggested to Him that He should make His exit into Nirvāna without delay. In choosing, instead, deliberately to postpone His own release from Suffering in order to work for the release of His fellow sentient beings, the Buddha was declaring, in a positive act, that, for Himself, He believed that to suffer in the cause of Love was a better course than to release Himself from Suffering through Self-extinction. But, when it is a question of what is the true end of Man, what is right for oneself must be right in itself and therefore also right for other people. So, in making His choice, the Buddha was preaching by example; and this example that He set by the life that He lived must count for more than the teaching that is attributed to Him. Even if He did recommend in His teaching a self-centred pursuit of self-extinction, He was tacitly countermanding His words by His acts of self-devoting love. These acts, which have inspired the Mahayanian ideal of the bodhisattva, seem also to have had more influence than the Buddha's teaching on the spirit and conduct of everyday life in Hinayanian Buddhist countries. If our Mahayanian critic of the Hīnayāna was candid and charitable, his *coup de grâce* would be this *argumentum ad hominem.*

The picture, painted for us in the Hinayanian scriptures, of the Buddha resisting His temptation has a Christian counterpart in the passage of Saint Paul's Epistle to the Philippians which we have quoted.[1] Here we have a picture of a self which, like the Buddha after His enlightenment, finds itself in the extraordinary position of being completely master of its situation. Like the Buddha Gautama, Christ Jesus now has it in His power to be immune from Suffering for ever. He finds Himself 'existing in God's form' and 'on an equality with' Him; and a self that is in this Godlike state of existence cannot have any unfulfilled desires and therefore cannot be exposed to the pain of being disappointed. Like the Buddha's access to Nirvāna, Christ's apotheosis in Heaven might be taken as 'a prize to be clutched'; but, like the Buddha, Christ resists the temptation. He deliberately chooses the Suffering that is inseparable from Selfhood—and this the extreme Suffering to which a self lays itself open when its ruling passion is not Cupidity but is Love.

In resisting their identical temptation, Christ and the Buddha are each revealing, in action, an identical truth about the Self. A self is a talent which is meant to be used. To withdraw it from circulation by burying it or by melting it down would be contrary to the purpose for which the talent has been issued. This truth is true not only for ordinary selves; it is also true for an enlightened self like the Buddha Gautama's and for a deified self like Jesus Christ's. Selfhood is inseparable from Desire, and therefore also inseparable from Suffering, even for a self that has achieved a perfect union with Absolute Reality and even for Absolute Reality Itself in Its personal aspect as God.

What is God? For a man, God means helping one's fellow-creatures.[2]

---

[1] In Chapter 6, p. 86, and in Chapter 19, p. 277, above.
[2] 'Deus est mortali iuvare mortalem'—An anonymous philosopher, quoted by Pliny the Elder, *Historia Naturalis,* Book II, chap. 7 (5), § 18.

Love is of God. . . . Herein is love, not that we loved God, but that He loved us. . . . If we love one another, God dwelleth in us and His love is perfected in us. . . . God is love, and he that dwelleth in love dwelleth in God, and God in him.[1]

Thus, when a Mahayanian Buddhist or a Christian compares the Hīnayāna with his own faith, he will probably come to the conclusion that his own faith is the better one. It gives, he will probably feel, a deeper insight into the mystery of the Universe; and it holds up a higher ideal of what human beings should try to do with themselves. If this is the Christian's conclusion, what is the consequent action that he ought to take in a world in which the 'annihilation of distance' by Technology is now bringing all the higher religions into ever closer relations with one another? His first impulse might be to act like 'certain which trusted in themselves that they were righteous, and despised others';[2] and he would find many precedents for this in the histories of Judaism and Islam, as well as Christianity. Yet these precedents would also be warnings. For Pharisaism has been the besetting sin of the religions of the Judaic family, and this sin has brought retribution on itself in a tragic series of atrocities and catastrophes. The fruit of Pharisaism is intolerance; the fruit of intolerance is violence; and the wages of sin is death. The sinfulness and deadliness of the Catholic-Protestant Wars of Religion in Western Christendom was the evil that moved our seventeenth-century Western predecessors to establish religious toleration in the name of Christian charity. In our lifetime we have seen an apparently settled habit of toleration, which we have inherited from our seventeenth-century predecessors, being undermined by secular ideologies which have retained nothing of the Western religious tradition except its pharisaical exclusiveness and fanaticism.

If we find ourselves, nevertheless, still tempted to drop back into a traditional pharisaic rut, we can fortify ourselves against this temptation by recollecting several truths which are so many counsels of charity.

The touchstone of a religion is its comparative success or failure, not merely in divining the truths and interpreting the

---

[1] 1 John iv. 7, 10, 12, 16.   [2] Luke xviii. 9.

counsels, but also in helping human souls to take these truths to
heart and to put these counsels into action. So the last word
has not been said about a religion when we have accepted or
rejected its definitions of the nature of Reality and of the true
end of Man. We have also to look into the daily lives of its
adherents and to see how far, in practice, their religion is
helping them to overcome Man's Original Sin of self-centredness. This is a question which every religion has to abide.
And a Christian who rejects the Hīnayāna's vision of Absolute
Reality and its policy for coping with human life will condemn the Hīnayāna at his peril if his adverse abstract judgement has not been confirmed by personal experience of the
spiritual climate of the Hinayanian Buddhist World. If he has
not been convinced, by direct observation, that human beings
are leading less good lives under the Hinayanian dispensation
than under the Christian, it will be unwarrantable for him to
pronounce his own religion to be the higher of the two.

We believe that our own religion is the way and the truth,[1]
and this belief may be justified, as far as it goes. But it does not
go very far; for we do not know either the whole truth or nothing but the truth. 'We know in part' and 'we see through a
glass, darkly'.[2] When the light has shone out into the darkness,
the Universe still remains a mystery.[3]

'The heart of so great a mystery cannot ever be reached by
following one road only.'[4] Even if it should prove to be true
that the other higher religions have less of the truth in them than
ours has, this would not mean that they have in them no truth
at all; and the truth that they have may be truth that our own
religion lacks. Symmachus's argument for tolerance has never
been answered by his Christian opponents. The forcible
suppression of his ancestral religion by the secular arm of a
Christian Roman Government was no answer at all. And he has
not even been silenced; for, though Symmachus's ancestral
religion is long since extinct, Hinduism lives to speak for
Symmachus today.

In the world in which we now find ourselves, the adherents
of the different living religions ought to be the readier to
tolerate, respect, and revere one another's religious heritages

---

[1] John xiv. 6. [2] 1 Cor. xiii. 9 and 11. [3] John i.
[4] Symmachus, quoted in Chapter 18, p. 251, above.

because, in our generation, there is not anyone alive who is effectively in a position to judge between his own religion and his neighbour's. An effective judgement is impossible when one is comparing a religion which has been familiar to one in one's home since one's childhood with a religion which one has learnt to know from outside in later years. One's ancestral religion is bound to have so much the stronger hold upon one's feelings that one's judgement between this and any other religion cannot be objective. Our impulse to pass judgement between the different living religions ought therefore to be restrained by us till the physical 'annihilation of distance' has had time to produce the psychological effects that may be expected from it. A time may come when the local heritages of the different historic nations, civilizations, and religions will have coalesced into a common heritage of the whole human family. If that time does come, an effective judgement between the different religions may then at last begin to be possible. We are perhaps within sight of this possibility, but we are certainly not within reach of it yet.

Meanwhile, all the living religions are going to be put to a searching practical test. 'By their fruits ye shall know them.'[1] The practical test of a religion, always and everywhere, is its success or failure in helping human souls to respond to the challenges of Suffering and Sin. In the chapter of the World's history on which we are now entering, it looks as if the continuing progress of Technology were going to make our sufferings more acute than ever before, and our sins more devastating in their practical consequences. This is going to be a testing-time, and, if we are wise, we shall await its verdict.

If we do not feel that we can afford to wait for Time to do its discriminating work, we are confessing to a lack of faith in the truth and value of the religion that happens to be ours. On the other hand, if we do have faith in it, we shall have no fear that it will fail to play its full part in helping human souls to enter into communion with the presence behind the phenomena and to bring themselves into harmony with this Absolute Reality. The missions of the higher religions are not competitive; they are complementary. We can believe in our own religion without having to feel that it is the sole repository of truth. We can

[1] Matt. vii. 20.

love it without having to feel that it is the sole means of salvation. We can take Symmachus's words to heart without being disloyal to Christianity. We cannot harden our hearts against Symmachus without hardening them against Christ. For what Symmachus is preaching is Christian charity.

Charity never faileth; but, whether there be prophecies, they shall fail; whether there be tongues, they shall cease; whether there be knowledge, it shall vanish away.[1]

[1] 1 Cor. xiii. 8.

APPENDIX

Gropings in the Dark

Toynbee finished this essay in September 1973, under a year before the onset of his fatal illness. It was the last piece of any length that he wrote, and represents his final thoughts on the great mysteries of love, death, and existence. A discussion of some of the points raised in this essay is contained in Veronica Toynbee's Preface to the Second Edition at the beginning of the book.

I. SELF

IN setting out to feel my way in the dark, I have to find my starting-point in the conscious 'layer' (a metaphor) of my self, for my consciousness is my only instrument for exploration. By now, I have been conscious for about 82 years, and I am one of the living inhabitants of the biosphere enveloping the planet Earth. This planet is an infinitesimally small mote in the stellar physical cosmos; 82 years is an infinitesimally small span of the age, to date, of human consciousness in the biosphere, of life in the biosphere, of the biosphere itself, and of this planet. We do not know the age of the stellar cosmos; astronomers at present seem to hold conflicting views, but, as far as I understand these, no astronomer holds that physical matter has come into existence out of something that is non-material. No present school of physicists believes in the creation of matter—or of the electricity that masquerades as matter— *ex nihilo.*

My consciousness's location/date in space/time—i.e. the biosphere A.D. 1891–1973—is certainly not the centre/'axis age' of the phenomena of which my consciousness is aware. I do not know whether the three orders of phenomena within my ken do have either separate centres/'axis ages' or a common one. Anyway, these terms are only metaphorical except in their application to the material order of existence. The fact that my consciousness does have a centre/'axis age' is not evidence that I am the focus and *raison d'être* of the phenomena apprehended by my consciousness; so far from that, my inescapable egocentricity is evidence that the 'I' of which I am conscious is unimportant and ephemeral. I am in a weak position for both observing and acting; my limitations suggest that my observations are likely to be to a large extent erroneous, and my actions to a large extent ineffective or bad or both. Yet, being what I am, I am bound to observe and to take action as long as the matter of which my body is composed is a vehicle for life, and as long as my life is a vehicle for consciousness.

The phenomena of which I am aware include physical sensations (e.g. of malaise or of well-being) which are signs of life; emotions (e.g. love and hate, exhilaration and depression, self-confidence and anxiety); things and people apparently external to myself (e.g. inanimate matter, including the visible parts of the material cosmos outside the biosphere, and the inanimate and animate constituents of the biosphere, including non-human and human living beings). I am aware that I myself have been one of these living human beings since 1889; I am also aware of possible choices open to me, between different courses of action; of the distinction and opposition between good and evil; of the ethical nature of some of my choices (i.e. choices between good and evil); of ethical judgments, made by me and by other people, on my own and other people's conduct and on the operation of non-human nature; I am aware of a conscience which compels me consciously to pass judgement on my own actions in the ethical field. In some cases my conscience condemns what I have done, and I respond, *nolens volens*, by feeling contrition and remorse; in other cases my conscience acquits me, and then I am in danger of being ethically self-satisfied.

I am both a spectator and a participant. Within my life-time, Rutherford and his successors have shown that we cannot observe the structure/undulation of the atom except by taking action that disintegrates it; and Einstein has shown that an observation is a space/time interaction between the observer and the object that he is observing.

I am a participant in human society in the biosphere; human society is a network of relations—spiritual, animate, physical—

between human beings, alive, dead, and still unborn. I am a participant in life in the biosphere; in this respect, I am one specimen of one species of living beings. But I am also a participant in a spiritual order of existence. I am aware of a spiritual presence 'behind' and 'beyond' the phenomena. Twice in my life, to date, each time at a moment of spiritual crisis, I have had what seemed to be a direct confrontation with this spiritual presence. Thus I am conscious of participating simultaneously in three orders of existence. I am alive in a physical body, and I am a soul associated at present with a live human being.

If I were a Hindu of my present age, 84, probably I should already have discarded material possessions, mundane activities, and perhaps even relations with other human beings. I should have focussed my attention and effort on my relations with the spiritual presence 'behind' and 'beyond' the phenomena. But I have been born into the Western Society in its modern age, in which this society has pressed its participants to direct their attention and their action to the mundane plane of life. In me, as in many of my Western contemporaries, 'the care of this World, and the deceitfulness of riches, choke the Word'.

Ever since I can remember, I have been conscious of being anxious; my anxiety has prompted much of my action, including many of my creative acts. My anxiety has two causes; I am anxious to play a good and useful part in the society in which I am a participant; but I am also anxious for fear that, if I am not preoccupied by mundane activities, I shall find myself spiritually naked and unscreened in the presence of the Ultimate Spiritual Reality that I have encountered, so far, only in two brief experiences. I am taking refuge from a recurrence of these experiences when I immerse myself in work; and this is just as cowardly, and just as frivolous, as turning on the television (a form of escapism which I arrogantly despise). Here I am confessing my agreement that 'it is a fearful thing to fall into the hands of the living God'. This is strange, because, when I am thinking rationally, I am a religious agnostic. I do not know whether there *is* a living God, and, on the whole, I think this is improbable, if the word 'God' implies a human-like personality.

I know that I ought to welcome, and to seek, spiritual leisure as an opportunity which is the *raison d'être* of being human; actually, if I find myself spiritually unpreoccupied, my impulse is, as I have said, to take refuge from contemplation in action, as I am now doing in writing this paper.

I know that I shy away from communion with the Ultimate Spiritual Reality because my two experiences of this communion have taught me that this requires changes in myself; and these changes that I must make will be determined, not by me, but by the reality that is 'behind' and 'beyond' the phenomenon 'I'.

'I' am incarnate in a live animal. From time to time I have seen a corpse, i.e. the physical component of the now dead psychosomatic vehicle of a human soul. The soul has disappeared at death—sometimes it has faded out, before physical death, into a state of coma or senility. We know what happens to the corpse. After physical death, it is re-absorbed into the inanimate component of the biosphere. The scientists have ascertained that a surprisingly large part of the biosphere consists of ex-organic matter.

What is going to happen to my soul when I die? Will it be extinguished, as my life will be? Or will it be re-absorbed into a supra-personal spiritual reality? Or will my soul survive my death as the consciousness that I am so long as I am alive and am *compos mentis*? The rational expectation seems to me to be that my soul, like my corpse, will be re-absorbed. This expectation distresses me, because it implies that, at death, I shall be cut off from communion with the human beings that I love and, indeed, from communion with the Spiritual Reality itself. If absorption is my soul's destiny, it seems to be tantamount to annihilation, since it will put an end to love, and I believe that love is a human soul's *raison d'être*. (This is a leap into an unverifiable act of faith.)

'From Him we come, and to Him we return.' Muhammad believed that this was a message from Ultimate Reality, conveyed to him by the Archangel Gabriel. But the meaning is ambiguous. The preposition 'to' ('*ilay*') might signify either a re-absorption into reality or a communion with it that will be continuous and intimate. Muhammad certainly understood the message in the second of these two alternative possible senses; for he believed that the Ultimate Spiritual Reality is a person; a god who is a person is, in this respect, a being of the same kind as a human being. The essence of personality is individuality; so two or more persons can commune with each other but cannot fuse with each other. I should be happy if there were evidence that the message received by Muhammad gives authentic information about the nature of the Ultimate Spiritual Reality; but I cannot make the leap into this further act of faith. I do not know whether the nature of the Ultimate Reality is personal or is supra-personal; so I do not know what is going to happen to my soul at death.

This ignorance does not make me fear death or resent it. I am content to die at any moment, and, when I die, I shall depart 'like a satiated participant in a feast' ('*satur ut conviva*'). I hope that my *karma*-account in my passage through life in the biosphere will close with a credit balance, but I shall not know the final state of my account, and, if other people try to ascertain it, their conclusions will be largely guess-work.

'Shall not God search this out? For he knoweth the secrets of the heart.' But is the Ultimate Reality a person who reads these secrets and feels a concern about me? My fellow human beings do not know them, and I know little more of them myself; for these secrets are hidden in the subconscious depths of my psyche. On the two occasions that I have mentioned, the Ultimate Spiritual Reality did appear to me as a person: on the first occasion as a rescuer like Saint George, on the second as a merciful and compassionate judge. These images were natural for someone who was brought up as a Christian, as I was. After I grew up, I was never a believing Christian, but I am steeped in the Christian tradition. Those appearances make me believe that the spiritual presence is real and that it is also always 'close at hand' (another metaphor), but, considering my Christian heritage, I do not find in these appearances any cogent evidence that the presence is a person. If I can communicate with the presence, and can interact with it, this certainly implies that the presence has a personal facet, but, though this facet may be the important one for a human being who is seeking to enter into communion, it does not follow that this is the essence of the Spiritual Reality. I do not know what Reality's essential nature is.

II. EXISTENCE

THE Christians inherited the Jews' explanation of the Phenomena (alias, the data of experience). According to this account,
the sum total of the Phenomena, embracing the several different
orders of reality, has been created by the 'fiat' of a unique god.

This explanation, if found convincing, accounts for the
diversity from each other of the orders of reality, matter, life,
and consciousness, consciousness being, for Man, the enabling
condition for purpose, design, and execution; and for the
diversity within each order, including the diversity of the
species of living beings.

In the Book of Genesis, God is conceived of as having created
the Universe in the way in which a human being builds a
house. The stages of the work are successive, not simultaneous;
but, once the work has been completed, it has been finished,
unless and until the creator chooses to demolish his own work.

To ex-Christian minds, this traditional Jewish–Christian–
Muslim explanation of the phenomena is unconvincing for the
following reasons:

It is anthropomorphic. The hypothetical creator-god's way
of working is imagined on the analogy of the procedure of a
human being who has constructed a house or some other piece
of human apparatus. But mankind is one of the items in the
sum total of the phenomena that we are seeking to explain. It
is improbable that the Universe, including mankind, has been
created by a god who has made things in a human-like way.

The, to this extent, human-like creator-god has also, incongruously, to be credited with super-human powers and with
inhuman conduct. God is deemed to have made the Universe
out of nothing except his own will-power. A human being wills
the execution of his purposes, and he can make things that are
genuinely new, but he cannot create these things unless he can
find and shape and assemble indispensable raw materials,
whereas the creator-god is held to have created the Universe
without having had any pre-existing raw materials. A human
creator's raw materials consist partly of inanimate matter (e.g.
the potter's clay), partly of non-human living beings that he
has domesticated (e.g. the breeder's sheep, horse, dog), and
partly of thoughts and words (the poet's raw materials); but so

far no human being has ever created either matter or life or the consciousness, the power of choice, and the will that are the indispensable pre-existing resources for human works of creation. The creator-god is credited, not only with super-human power, but with omnipotence; but, if he exists and is omnipotent, he must be a monster in a human being's ethical judgement (and a recognition of the distinction and the contrast between good and evil, right and wrong, virtuousness and wickedness, is one of the built-in specific modes of human consciousness, whether or not this distinction and this contrast are valid at the level of Ultimate Reality). In the phenomenal Universe, life entails suffering as well as satisfaction, and human consciousness entails wickedness as well as virtuousness. If the hypothetical creator-god is omnipotent, he must be the responsible author of suffering and wickedness as well as of satisfaction and virtuousness. He must be morally compre-hensive and therefore morally ambivalent: both beneficent and malevolent, both a creator and a destroyer. The Hindus have faced and recognized this moral implication of omnipotence in their conception of Shiva, and a Shiva-like malignity is attributed to the creator-god in the final petition in the Lord's Prayer. Yet the Judaic god is conceived of as being good, or at least as being unimpeachable. Unlike Shiva, Yahweh is not a self-consistent figure. Omnipotence (if the word is not meaning-less) is incompatible with goodness, considering what the Universe is like in our human experience.

The concept of a once-for-all act of creation is inadequate as an account of human creative activity, in terms of which the hypothetical divine creativity is imagined. Besides creating apparatus out of inanimate matter, human beings breed new varieties of plants and animals by a repeated and cumulative selection of specimens that best suit the human breeder's purpose. A new variety of a domesticated living being is bred gradually by taking advantage of the spontaneous variability of the specific type. This human feat of creation through selection is not attributed to the Judaic creator-god. (Yahweh *is* supposed to have selected a 'chosen people' to serve the purpose that Yahweh has in mind for mankind as a whole, but the 'chosen people', being human, and therefore wilful, has not always been amenable to Yahweh's will.)

This combination of objections to the account of the creation of the phenomenal Universe in the Book of Genesis is decisive for ex-Jewish and ex-Christian minds. They cannot believe in this traditional account; but also they cannot simply reject it and thus leave the phenomena unexplained. Human minds demand explanations. Can science find an alternative explanation that is more convincing than the traditional one?

The ex-Christian men of science have had two objectives: to provide a convincing comprehensive account that dispenses with the hypothesis that purpose, design, and the achievement of objectives have played any part in the production of the phenomena that are the data of human experience.

In the traditional account, the sole bond between the several orders of reality—namely matter, life, and consciousness—is that they are deemed to be, all alike, the creations of the same unique creator. When this bond is removed, the orders fall apart, and, so far, the ex-Christian men of science have not succeeded in re-uniting them by discovering an alternative link between them.

To date, alleged cases of inanimate matter generating life have been proved by scientific investigation to be spurious. Invariably, life has been found to have been generated by pre-existing life. Nor has any human being succeeded, so far, in transforming inanimate matter into live matter in a laboratory. Moreover, if this was eventually to be achieved, it would be with the operation of a living agent, though, in this event, the living agent would be a manufacturer, not a progenitor. Already, life reproduces itself in two different ways: by fission and by sexual coitus. The manufacture of living creatures by human action would merely be a third way in which life would have succeeded in reproducing itself.

Also, no scientist, so far, has observed a non-conscious living creature becoming a conscious one. We infer, from material pieces of evidence, that mankind is descended from some species of primate that was not yet conscious. We may guess, from the scraps of material evidence, that our ancestors became conscious at least 500,000 years ago, but we have no inkling of the process by which, or of the reason why, at this conjectural date, they came to acquire consciousness—or came to be possessed by consciousness (perhaps a more apposite form of words to indicate what happened to our ancestors at this stage). We do not know whether the dawn of consciousness in the primate which thereby became Man was gradual or sudden. We cannot see any bridge between consciousness and non-consciousness, any more than we can see any between life and non-life.

The belief in the unitariness of reality is a corollary of the belief in a unique creator, and, if this antecedent belief has ceased to be convincing, there is no compelling reason for the belief in the unitariness of the sum total of the phenomena to be retained. All the same, the loss of the belief in a unique creator raises a question about the relations of the different orders of reality to each other. We have no experience of life unaccompanied by matter. This invariable association with each other of different orders of reality that seem to have nothing else in common becomes enigmatic if we have ceased to believe that they have a common author in a creator-god—at least in that province of his creation that is accessible to human perception and understanding. The ex-Christian men of science have not yet found an alternative link between the different orders of reality to replace the link provided traditionally by the belief in a single creator.

Nor have the ex-Christian men of science met, more than partially, the demand for a non-teleological explanation of all the phenomena except purposive human action.

The ex-Christian astronomers and physicists debate whether the material cosmos has always been multiple, as it is now, or whether it has expanded in the course of time from a single hydrogen atom to its present magnitude and complexity; but they have not been able to explain how matter itself can have come into existence. If it was not brought into existence by the fiat of a creator-god, the flow of matter through the medium of time/space can be conceived of only as having had no beginning and as never going to come to an end. The men of science can strip down the solid, liquid, and gaseous data of the senses into their chemical elements, dissect the elements into atoms, and split the atoms into particles, some of which can present themselves alternatively, though never simultaneously, as waves; they can reduce all the material phenomena to electricity; but electricity is still a material phenomenon; it is not a form of life or of consciousness or of some unknown other order of reality which, unlike consciousness and life and matter, is beyond the range of human experience.

In their investigation of life, the men of science have been successful in finding a convincing non-teleological explanation of the present diversification of the phenomena. Taking as their clue a human husbandman's proven ability to produce new varieties of domesticated plants and animals the scientists have shown that the non-purposive action of the environment on a particular species may give rise to the formation of an entirely new species, through a 'natural selection' of heritable mutations in the former's genes.

Mutations in the arrangement, form, and composition of any specific set of genes are rare events, and, when mutations do occur, they are likely to be unfavourable to the survival of the specimens in which they occur, since the reason why a species has survived is presumably because it has become adapted to its present environment. However, a mutation that is a present risk may turn out, if its carrier does survive, to be an insurance against the future risk of a change in the environment—and no species has ever found an environment that has been permanently stable. Of course, the next change in the environment may prove equally lethal to the species' non-mutated and to its mutated specimens, but at any rate the mutation will have doubled the chance that the species may survive the change in its environment. The chance is slight, but the number of the mutations has been immense, for the immensity of the time during which life has been present in the biosphere has given the non-purposive agency of 'natural selection' sufficient scope, against enormous odds, for differentiating all the known species, extant or fossil.

The discovery of the operation of 'natural selection' has demonstrated that the multifarious species of living beings have come into existence, in the course of time, through a vastly long series of non-purposive differential innovations. (Differential innovation is what the scientists mean by their term 'evolution', though this is a misnomer, since the word means 'unfolding', and the unfolding of something that already exists is not the same process as the production of something that is new.) All species may perhaps be descended from a single unicellular common ancestor, just as all galaxies may perhaps be derived from a single hydrogen atom. The scientists' discoveries leave the origin of life, as well as the origin of matter, unexplained, but at least the scientists have traced the history of both matter and life back to a possible primary form.

However, the differential innovations that have resulted in the multiplicity and multifariousness of extant and extinct species could not have occurred if life itself had not existed and persisted; and, when we are confronted with these two major aspects of life, the non-teleological approach is not practicable. When we have discarded the unconvincing hypothesis of the existence and activity of a creator-god, the origin of life is inexplicable, and the persistence of life is explicable only if we attribute to life the human-like purposefulness that we no longer attribute to God.

It has been noted already that scientific investigation suggests that mutations in the specific genes of a species are rare events. The implication of this finding is that normally a species reproduces itself true to type. This feature of life has been familiar to mankind since an early date in the history of the acquisition of knowledge and understanding by our human consciousness, but it is only within the last two or three centuries that scientific investigation has brought to light the intricacy and efficiency of the composition and organization of the matter in which life normally succeeds in reproducing itself true to type.

All forms of life, from unicellular organisms to multicellular species that reproduce themselves by sexual coitus, display one common feature that appears to be of life's essence, and this can be described only in the human-like purposive terms that have been used traditionally in describing the activity of a hypothetical creator-god. Life is 'determined' to maintain itself in its embodiments in some of the matter composing the biosphere that envelops the planet Earth, and, in its 'pursuit' of this 'objective', life has planned and executed a consummately efficient 'organization' of matter for the 'achievement' of the 'objective' that is life's obsessive 'aim'. In the multicellular, sexually reproductive species, this 'organization' takes the form of an arrangement of gene-cells in ribbon-like chromosomes, and, through sexual coitus, the genetic chromosomes of feminine and masculine specimens of a species interact with each other in the successive processes that have been labelled 'mitosis' and 'meiosis'.

In the differential elaboration of the process of reproduction, the role of 'natural selection' is confined to its effect in occasionally eliminating those specimens of a species whose gene-cells have not undergone any 'lucky' mutations, and sparing the specimens in which some 'lucky' mutation has occurred, but this non-purposive play of 'natural selection' is manifestly a minor factor in the history of life. The major factor is life's 'determination' to maintain itself in its embodiments in matter.

Here we find ourselves in the presence of a normal 'success' and a series of occasional 'failures' to accomplish a constant purpose. If life were not purposive and did not also occasionally fail to achieve its purpose, the non-purposive play of 'natural selection' would have no opening for coming into operation. In the history of life, purpose is prior to non-purposive occurrences both logically and chronologically; and, besides being the prior factor, purpose is by far the more important of the two. The discovery of the role of 'natural selection' in the differentiation of species is a brilliant intellectual achievement, but it has succeeded only to a minor extent in explaining the data of human experience other than purposive human action without having still to resort to the concept of purposiveness.

The discoveries made by the ex-Christian men of science confirm the Buddha's identification of life with 'grasping' (a teleological concept). Every specimen of every species of living being is striving all the time with all its might to set itself up as a centre, a *raison d'être*, and an exploiter of the sum of things. In the pursuit of self-perpetutation both a unicellular living organism and the gene-cells of a multicellular living organism annex ruthlessly, to the utmost extent of their power, whatever they need from their environment in order to keep themselves in existence. Their field of exploitation is not confined to the contents of the biosphere enveloping the planet Earth; they also draw upon the solar and the cosmic radiation that is constantly bombarding the biosphere. The field of action of even the simplest unicellular living organism is co-extensive with the entire sum of things. Whereas the scientific analysis of matter reduces it to electricity without being able to present it in non-material terms, the scientific analysis of life reduces life to purpose without being able to present it in non-purposive terms—or in non-animate terms; for 'life' and 'purpose' are two names for one and the same phenomenon.

Thus, so far, we have not succeeded in filling more than a fraction of the explanatory vacuum that has been produced by the rejection of the traditional hypothesis of the existence and activity of a creator-god. Our account of the phenomena has not been able to dispense with the concept of purpose in all those phenomena that do not fall within the field of human conscious choice. We have merely replaced a hypothetical purposive agent, the supposed omnipotent creator-god, by another agent, life, which is not hypothetical, but is a datum of experience.

A clue to the appearance, first of unconscious life, and then of consciousness in the biosphere seems to me to be given by the biologists' current endeavours to manufacture life and consciousness. If the biologists succeed in this enterprise, the result will not be that life has 'come out of' unconscious live matter. Actually, life will have been 'put into' inanimate matter, and consciousness into live matter, by purposive efforts to attain these objectives. The biologists will have seized successfully on an opportunity to extend the realms of life and consciousness. This opportunity will have been given to them by the progress, to date, of human science and technology.

The biologists' current endeavour suggests to me that it is illuminating and legitimate to look for a teleological explanation of the origins of life and of consciousness in the biosphere. Perhaps life seized the opportunity to materialize itself in a rudimentary form in a biosphere that offered a rudimentary habitat for it. When once life had materialized in the biosphere, it certainly interacted with the biosphere's inanimate constituents, and this interaction made the biosphere habitable for life in 'higher' forms. Eventually perhaps, consciousness seized the opportunity to incarnate itself in a primate that already had a relatively large and elaborately organized brain and was also on the way to becoming a biped with pincer-like hands. Consciousness certainly fostered and expedited the incipient changes in the brain, stance, and hands of the primate in which consciousness had incarnated itself until hominids, and finally human beings, had been added to the population of the biosphere.

The 'embodiment' of life and the 'incarnation' of consciousness seem to me to be more convincing descriptions of what has happened than the 'evolution' of them. I do not believe that life has 'evolved' out of inanimate matter, or consciousness out of non-conscious life, if the word 'evolution' is used in the sense of a spontaneous transmutation of one order of existence into another. I believe that life and consciousness have successively 'invaded' the biosphere. I believe that a non-purposive process of differential innovation through the 'natural selection' of mutations does account for the origin of species, but I do not believe that this also accounts for the epiphany in the biosphere of life and then of consciousness.

In the field of science I am a layman, and I speak with diffidence and with humility. I am aware that a scientist may be able to show that I speak as a fool. Nevertheless, at my peril, I do venture to speak. I venture because the problems of existence concern all human beings, not only the scientifically competent minority.

III. EVIL

THE awareness of the distinction and opposition between good and evil is one of the consequences of consciousness. Therefore, there cannot have been any conscious and deliberate good or bad deeds in the biosphere before the appearance here of Man. We do not know whether consciousness and conscience are, or ever have been, present anywhere else in the material cosmos outside the narrow physical limits of the biosphere that now envelops our own planet.

Human beings pass moral judgements on their own and on other people's acts, past and present. We also distinguish between what is good and what is evil for us in the non-human components of our habitat. In contrast to our condemnation of human evil-doing, we do not condemn, as being wicked, the evils that are not caused by human action.

The evils here in question are, in the first place, sickness, senescence, and death. In our human judgement, these are in every case deplorable afflictions. We now know that many forms of sickness are caused by bacteria, and we see as being evil all predators—for instance, sharks and tigers—and also all damage done to life, both human and non-human, and to human work and human property, by devastating inanimate forces: earthquakes, eruptions of volcanoes, floods, droughts, storms. We conclude that the biosphere, and the Universe as a whole, is partly good and partly evil for any form of life.

The good and the evil that we find in the biosphere, including the biosphere's human component, display themselves respectively in action in the forms of harmony and strife. We feel harmony to be unquestionably good, and strife to be unquestionably bad. For instance, we reckon among the good things the social cooperation between human beings, the cooperation between plants and animals in exchanging gases, and the cooperation between bees and flowers in which the bees convey pollen and the flowers provide honey. We reckon among the bad things all kinds of predacity, ranging from human warfare to the ravages of bacteria.

How has evil come to pass? The evil inflicted on life by inanimate forces is accounted for if we believe that the biosphere in which life has lodged itself was not fashioned by a god for the express purpose of harbouring life. If we reject the hypothesis of an omnipotent divine creator, we shall see life's lodgment in matter as a *tour de force* which has been achieved only imperfectly. This will also account for strife. The conduct of the various species of living beings that have installed themselves in the biosphere is like the conduct of the war-bands of barbarians that invaded the Chinese and the Roman Empires. Each band was fighting in its own particular interest, and, while some bands found it advantageous to cooperate with each other, others preferred to fight each other over the division of the spoils. This seems to be a convincing account of the cause of both cooperation and strife among human beings, as well as among the biosphere's non-human fauna and flora.

In the biosphere, life has found for itself a habitable but inhospitable setting, and life's reaction has been graspingness and greediness. The Buddha held that grasping (*tanha*) is the root cause of suffering. All the higher religions call, with one voice, for renunciation. But renunciation is a still greater *tour de force* than the self-assertion that has been life's original response to the inhospitality of the biosphere.

IV. ULTIMATE REALITY

IF the nature of Ultimate Reality is reflected in the data of human experience, it must include both good and evil. If we see Ultimate Reality as being unitary as well as all-inclusive, we shall see it in the form of a Janus-faced omnipotent god who is both a creator and a destroyer, who inflicts evil on his creatures besides doing them good.

This vision of God has been given particularly potent expressions in India and in Meso-America. Its classic Indian expression is Shiva, but the same picture of Ultimate Reality is also latent in Vishnu, a god who repeatedly becomes incarnate in order to serve as a saviour. When one of Vishnu's incarnations, Krishna, displays to Arjuna the incarnate god's divine reality, the vision is so terrible that Arjuna cannot bear it. Even the Great Mother becomes sinister when she is made the symbol of the sum total of our human experience of reality. Kali in India, Cybele in Asia Minor, and Hecate in Greece victimize their male consorts and children, and Catullus ends his poem on the plight of Cybele's victim Attis by requesting the goddess not to extend her malign and disastrous attentions to the poet himself.

Man has been at the mercy of Nature for most of his existence to date. Consequently, the evil aspect of the vision of a unitary and omnipotent all-inclusive God has, in the past, been expressed in terms of non-human predators and of devastating inanimate forces. Vishnu, when he drops his Krishna mask, displays himself mangling men and beasts with gnashing teeth and engulfing their dismembered bodies in a ravenous maw. Yahweh and Zeus are thunderers, Poseidon is an earth-shaker, Tlaloc withholds rain at least as often as he brings it; for drought and flood are more telling manifestations of his power than the gift of rain to human beings whose livelihood depends on the harvesting of their crops. In the Pharisees' and

Jesus' vision, Yahweh has been transfigured from any angry thunderer into a living father; yet this transfigured Yahweh is still held to be omnipotent. In the final petition in the Lord's Prayer, it is admitted that, besides being the father, Yahweh is also the devil. In fact, the Lord's Prayer ends on the same note as Catullus's poem.

Within the last 70,000/40,000 years, and decisively within the last 200 years, Man has succeeded in reversing his original relation to the non-human components of the biosphere. Yahweh's and Zeus's thunder was proved to be no match for modern Man's hydrogen bomb dropped from an aeroplane. Today, Man is the master. But a present-day vision of a unitary and omnipotent god would be still more hideous than the vision that Krishna-Vishnu displayed to Arjuna. In the present age of Man's dominance in the biosphere, one of Janus's faces would be Gandhi's; the other face would be Hitler's or Stalin's, and ninety-nine of his hundred whirling arms would be devastating the biosphere by the scientific application of human technology.

This up-to-date vision of a god who is both unitary and all-inclusive has not yet been faced by dominant Man. Dominant Man's impotent ancestor did face the vision. But this vision begs a question; it assumes that Ultimate Reality is unitary, besides being inclusive of both good and evil. Reality's inclusiveness is a datum of experience, but its unitariness is an unverified hypothesis. It is also conceivable that, in reality, good and evil are not monstrously united; Reality may be an arena in which the good is striving to overcome and eliminate the evil, and, if this is the truth, neither party in this contest can be omnipotent.

Egyptians and Iranians pictured present reality as being a battle between a good and an evil god—Horus versus Seth, Ahuramazda versus Angra Mainyush—and Ultimate Reality as being a state of righteousness and happiness in which the good god will have triumphed and the evil god will have been defeated. The same picture is implied in the first petition of the Lord's Prayer, with the difference that here the ultimate victory of the good god is not taken as being a foregone conclusion. 'Thy Kingdom come, thy will be done, on Earth as it is in Heaven.' This is not a prediction: it is a prayer for the fulfilment of a hope. The logical implication of this opening passage in the Lord's Prayer is made explicit in the Marcionite version of Christianity. As Marcion saw it, the good god is not identical with the creator, nor is he omnipotent. Marcion's good god is a stranger who has voluntarily entered a world for whose imperfection he is not responsible in order to redeem it at his own peril.

What has moved this 'stranger god' to embark on an enterprise which may perhaps end tragically for him? The answer is given by the intuition that 'God is love'. This god is certainly a stranger in the biosphere, but he is not the only one. We have guessed that life and consciousness each seized on an opportunity to invade the biosphere. Life seized on the makings of a biosphere; consciousness seized on the makings of a human being. May not another 'invader', love, likewise have found and seized on an opportunity? An opportunity was offered to love by life's progression from the method of perpetuating itself by fission to the method of procreation. In the relation of parents to each other and to their offspring, love found an opening for entry before the 'invasion' of consciousness. Love had implanted itself already in a number of pre-human sexual species of living beings, in birds and in non-human animals.

In our experience of love, both human and non-human, in the biosphere, love is never certain to be victorious. Love has not the power to impose itself, for it is not omnipotent. But, when it is opposed by force, love does not surrender; it persists at the cost of sacrificing itself; and, through self-sacrifice, it defeats force by winning hearts.

For Christians the exemplar of self-sacrificing love is Jesus; for Mahayanian Buddhists the exemplars are the *boddhisattvas*.

I believe that Jesus was a man who authentically lived and died; but, in the Christian Scriptures that are our sole source of information about him, he is already presented as being superhuman. He is said not to have had a human father, to have come to life again after having died, like the corn-spirit and the vine-spirit, and to have ascended bodily into Heaven. Within the lifetime of Saint Paul, Jesus's death was being commemorated in a rite that had already become formalized. If we try to extricate the authentic history of Jesus from the posthumous myth, it is impossible to be sure that his authentic history has been reconstructed correctly.

There is evidence in the Gospels that Jesus was an orthodox Jew; that he believed that Yahweh was both good and omnipotent; that he did not believe that he himself was divine, but did believe that Yahweh had adopted him as his son. We do not know in what sense Jesus thought of himself as being Yahweh's son by adoption, but evidently he believed that he had been commissioned to announce the coming of Yahweh's kingdom. When Jesus came to Jerusalem, he allowed himself to be greeted there as the Messiah, i.e. as the human king of the heavenly kingdom that Yahweh was going to establish on Earth. Jesus did not expect or intend to fight for the establishment of Yahweh's kingdom. Like the Pharisees, and unlike the Zealots, he was non-militant. He must have expected that Yahweh was going to establish his kingdom on Earth by some miraculous exercise of omnipotence. When he found that, instead, he himself was going to be arrested and probably put to death, he was distraught. As he saw it, Yahweh was bringing upon him a fate for which he was not prepared. Should he submit? Or should he fight, as previous claimants to Messiahship had fought? Jesus decided to submit, and he was crucified. On the cross, Jesus reproached Yahweh for having forsaken him. This reproach was wrung from Jesus by his misapprehension that Yahweh was omnipotent.

The turning-point in Jesus's career was his decision not to fight, and we may guess that his motive was the same as the Sanhedrin's motive for asking the Roman governor to put Jesus to death. If Jesus had fought, there would have been a Jewish insurrection in support of him, and many of the insurgents would have been killed in battle with the Roman troops, even in the unlikely event of the insurrection's being successful. It was better that 'one man should die for the people'.

According to this interpretation of Jesus's career, his beliefs—the traditional Jewish beliefs—were refuted by his experience, but his action—which was his own personal choice—transformed a defeat that cost him his life into a posthumous victory. His decision to submit was prompted by love. He chose to accept crucifixion for himself rather than become the cause of a catastrophe for his fellow human beings. The immediate effect of this decision was to shatter his adherents' mundane hopes; the posthumous effect was to win their hearts and to inspire them with an invincible confidence.

This account of Jesus's life and death and posthumous triumph will probably be challenged by many of the people who hold, as I do, that Jesus was simply a human being, and that the supernatural events narrated in the Gospels are un-historical. According to my interpretation, Jesus's victory was won on Good Friday, not on Easter Day. The posthumous devotion to Jesus has been evoked, I believe, by his decision to submit to suffering for the sake of love. Other interpreters may perhaps judge that Jesus's hold on the hearts of posterity has been gained by the legend of his supernatural power— above all, by the story of his resurrection.

However, there are some indisputable cases in which devotion has been evoked by a story of self-sacrificing love without the anti-climax of 'a happy ending'. One historical case is the martyrdom of the two Russian royal saints, Boris and Gleb, who submitted to being put to death rather than fight for their right to the crown. Two mythical cases are the sorrows of the goddesses Isis and Demeter. These two myths do have 'happy endings', but in each case the *dénouement* was preceded by an agonizing ordeal. Isis's love for her husband Osiris and Demeter's love for her daughter Persephone cost each goddess poignant pain and grief, and it was this that moved the hearts of their worshippers. Love that proves its sincerity through voluntary suffering has an irresistible appeal, and I believe that this is the appeal that the story of Jesus has made.

In our experience of love, life, and consciousness, these three forms of reality are incarnated in material bodies domiciled in the biosphere. But I have suggested that both life and consciousness are 'invaders' of the biosphere, and Marcion saw in Jesus an emissary of a god who was a 'stranger' in the phenomenal Universe. The word 'invasion' has a spatial connotation, but of course I am using the word metaphorically in this context. I mean to imply that the incarnations of life and love and consciousness in the biosphere are not the only modes in which these three realities exist, though they are the only modes of them that are within human ken. My belief that these are also transcendental and eternal realities is an act of faith. Thus, rather to my surprise, I find that I am not in the camp of the sceptics.

At the same time, I am aware that I am not an orthodox adherent of any of the traditional religions and philosophies. Perhaps I am not far from being a Quaker or a Taoist, but I should probably be disowned by the adherents of even these least dogmatic of the traditional faiths. I am in limbo. This is a lonely location; but I stand here because I cannot honestly stand anywhere else.

I believe in the reality, but not in the omnipotence, of the Holy Spirit. I believe that this Zoroastrian vision of Spiritual Reality is identical with the Taoist philosophers' concept of the Tao ('The Way'). I believe that both the Holy Spirit and the Tao are synonyms for love. I believe that love has a transcendental existence, and that, if the biosphere and its human inhabitants were to be annihilated, love would still be in existence and be at work.

I see that the biosphere is imperfect. Life has imported suffering into it, and consciousness has imported sin. I do not know whether the biosphere and the rest of the phenomena in the flow of time/space have had a beginning, or whether this phenomenal Universe has always been in existence. If it had a beginning, it must have had a 'prime mover' or a 'creator', but this need not have been a super-human omnipotent person, and 'he' or 'it' need not have been wicked; in the history of the biosphere, there seems to me to have been clear evidence of some incompetence at every stage, but no evidence of wickedness in the biosphere's pre-human age. Therefore I do not believe in the reality of an evil creator-god who is at war with the good god, love. Love does not, and cannot, go to war. Love's mode of operation is a stillness that is motion, and a passivity that is action. This motion and action is not earthquake or thunder or lightning; it is 'a still small voice', and love works to redeem the suffering and sinful World by 'reconciling the World' to love itself.

The author of the *Tao Tê Ch'ing* says:

Tao, though it covers the ten thousand things like a garment,
Makes no claim to be master over them
And asks for nothing from them.

The Chinese philosopher, like St. John the Evangelist, holds that the Spirit is also the creator.

> The ten thousand creatures owe their existence to it, and it does not disown them;
> Yet, having produced them, it does not take possession of them.

But the author of the *Tao Tê Ch'ing* goes on to say:

> The ten thousand things obey it,
> Though they know not that they have a master.

The author of the Fourth Gospel says of the Word:

> He was in the World, and the World was made by him, and the World knew him not,

Up to this point, the Taoist and the Christian author agree with each other, but the Christian does not share the Taoist's confident belief that the un-masterful Spirit is master of the situation. According to the Christian author, the Word 'came unto his own and his own received him not. But as many as received him, to them gave he power to become the sons of God.'

The Fourth Gospel seems to me to describe the findings of human experience more accurately than the *Tao Tê Ch'ing*. Many human hearts, perhaps a majority, have not opened themselves to the Holy Spirit's appeal, but this visitant has been received by at least a minority; every human being has encountered love as one of the facts of life. Love has lodged itself in the World manifestly, and this gives us grounds for hope that love's realm may expand. It also gives each of us a motive for trying to help to extend love's realm by opening his own heart to love and by letting love inspire his conduct towards other people.

To pray is one of Man's impulses. Perhaps it is one of his needs. But there is a difference between 'praying to' and 'praying for'. A human being can only 'pray to' a god whom he believes to possess the power to impose his will if he so chooses. Therefore I cannot pray 'to' love; but I can pray 'for' love, that its realm may expand; I can pray for myself and my fellow living beings that we may help to expand love's realm by our own action.

I believe that love is the supreme Spiritual Reality, but that the Ultimate Reality is beyond the horizon of normal human experience, confined within the flow of time/space. Yet even I have had three mystical experiences. In the earliest of these my normal consciousness of a distinction between myself and the rest of time/space was momentarily in abeyance, and I was aware of time/space flowing through me, and was aware of myself only as an undifferentiated part of the flow. I have mentioned my two later mystical experiences elsewhere. In each of these, I found myself in the presence of love, not incarnate, but transcendent and at the same time close, with the implication that this transcendent presence is always close, though most human beings are rarely conscious of it.

I am groping in the dark. My human capacity for loving and for understanding is feeble. But I hope I shall go on trying to love and to understand for so long as my consciousness survives.

INDEX

Buddha—*cont.*

Indian thinkers, 63; inconsistency of his practice and his preaching, 64, 72, 73, 76-7, 84, 292, 293; identifies life with 'grasping' (*tanha*), 310, 313; love and pity felt by, 72; metaphysical speculation discouraged by, 62, 63, 124; social milieu of, 76; super-divinity of, according to Mahāyāna, 133; temptation of, 72, 76, 292, 293; voluntary postponement of his exit into Nirvana, 64, 66, 72, 76, 84, 292; voluntary uprooting of, 76-7; Yogis scandalized by, 72

Buddhism:

Hīnayāna: conduct of adherents, 275n., 293, 295; date of foundation of, 133; essential truths of, 83-4, 272-3, 289-90; 'Four Holy Truths', 64; human saviour, its need of, 17; impersonal aspect of its approach to Reality, 16, 274; intellect and will, rôles of, 2, 22, 63; metamorphosis into a religion, 272; Oecumenical Council of, 68; practice, emphasis on, 22, 62, 124; propagation of, 90, 246; satisfaction of Man's spiritual needs by, 67-8, 73; scriptures of, 292, 293; self-centredness of desire for self-extinction, 292; self-extinction as goal of, 2, 17, 62, 64, 65, 68, 72, 84, 87, 289-92; serenity induced by, 68; superficial and impracticable in Christian eyes, 291-2; superiority of, to Stoicism, 70; survival power of, 136

Mahāyāna: art, visual, of, 143; as chrysalis of Far Eastern Civilization, 181; avatars, series of, 133; bodhisattvas—character of, 17, 82, 274, 277;—self-sacrifice of, 84, 280, 317; Christianity, common ground with 84-7, 89-90, 125, 155, 274-7, 290, 291; competing religions in Central Asia, triumph over, 98n.; essential truths of, 272-4, 291; exploitation of, for political purposes, 109; genesis of, 72, 77, 292, 293; Hīnayāna, relation to, 65, 118-19, 291ff.; liturgy of, 155, 279; Nature-worship in

relation to, 19; persecution of, 89-90, 101, 246, propagation of, 68, 77, 109, 246; Tantric version of, 112; Zen version of, 21

Superiority of, to Islam and Hinduism, 113

See also under HINDUISM; REALITY

Bull, the, as primordial image, 20-1

Burkitt, F. C., quoted, on Johanan b. Zakkai, 80-1

Byzantine Empire, the, 44

CAESAR-WORSHIP, 46ff., 94, 107, 108, 216

Cain and Abel, 30

Calf, golden, worship of the, 34

'Caligula', Roman Emperor, 47, 50, 176n.

Calvin, Jean, 171, 176, 255

Calvinism, 171, 176n., 177

Canaan: human sacrifice in, 37-40; nature-worship in, 24, 25; religions of, 26, 28, 39, 86n.

Canaanite, Civilization, the, 143

Carthage, 39-40

Carthalon, priest of Melqart, 38

Cassander, Macedonian war-lord, 70

Castilian language, the, 157

Cataphract, the, 222-3

Catullus, 314, 315

Chamulas, the, 159-60

Chance, concept of, 13

Charity, Christian, 297

Charlemagne, 44, 209

Charles V Hapsburg, Holy Roman Emperor, 214

Charles IX, King of France, 170

Chemosh, worship of, 26, 39, 86n.

Ch'ien Lung, Manchu Emperor, 69

Children, sacrifice of, 24, 26, 37-40

China: Christian missions in, 156, 158, 159, 164; population of, 241; religions co-existing in, 28; renaissances in, 43-4, 180-1; revolutions in, 243; westernization of, 199; *see also* CHU; COMMUNISM; CONFUCIANISM; HAN EMPIRE; MANCHU EMPIRE; T'ANG EMPIRE; TS'I; TS'IN EMPIRE

Chivalry, 217

Chosroes (Khusrū) I, Sasanian Emperor, 247-8

Christ: apotheosis of, 293; ascension of,

Churchill, Winston S., 7

Civilizations: chrysales of, 145; encounters between, 112-13, 143ff., —military technique first alien element to be received, 161, 194ff.; —selective reception of elements of an alien civilization, question of, 160-1, 198ff.; expansion of, phenomenon of, 143; social ideals in relation to, 217; *see also* ARABIC CIVILIZATION; FAR EASTERN CIVILIZATION; GRAECO-ROMAN CIVILIZATION; HINDU CIVILIZATION; ISLAMIC CIVILIZATION; MAYAN CIVILIZATION; WESTERN CIVILIZATION

Claudius, Emperor, 47

Clement IV, Pope, 225

Clement of Alexandria, 156

Clement of Rome, 98

Cleomenes III, King of Sparta, 69, 78

Cleon, the slave-king, 80

Clovis I, the Merovingian, 43

Clusium, 44

Coercion, self-defeat of, 267

Comenius, 174

Commodus, Roman Emperor, 47, 50

Communism: challenge of, to traditional Western ideals, 269; Christian texts, possibility of using for propaganda, 92; fanaticism of, 251; in China, 199; menace of, 210

Concert of Europe, the, 215, 216

Conciliar Movement, the, 166-7, 214

Confucianism, 22, 28, 66, 67, 68, 124, 136, 156, 158, 181

Confucius, 15, 66, 69, 76, 124

consciousness, 299-302, 306-7, 311-12, 316

Constantine I the Great, Roman Emperor; adoption of Christianity as official religion, 247; religious policy of, 54-5, 107-8, 110, 118, 248; repeal of proscription of Christianity, 91; Sol Invictus, worship of, 107, 108

Constantius Chlorus, Roman Emperor, 107

Coptic Monophysite Christian Church, the, 112

Corn, worship of, 28, 31

Cortés, Hernan, 53

Council of Europe, the, 150

creation of the Universe, 299, 304-6

Creature, living, definition of, 2

Credulity, 173-4, 178

Croce, Benedetto, 6 and *n*.

Cross-bow, the, 222, 223

Curiosity: as motive of historians, 4-6; as a general human characteristic, 5, 219, 284

Cybele, worship of, 24, 97, 136, 246, victimizes Attis, 314

Cyrus II the Great, Achaemenian Emperor, 43, 54

DANTE ALIGHIERI, 209

Darius I, Achaemenian Emperor, 43, 54, 78, 89

Dasius, Christian martyr, 103

Death-rate, lowering of the, 240, 241

Demeter, worship of, 25, 31

Denmark, 195

Déracinés, 76ff., 186 and *n*.

Descartes, René, on subjugation of Nature, 229

Detachment, 63ff., 105, 292-3

Devil, the, 276

Diasporás, 81-2, 86*n*., 111-12, 138, 139, 143

Diego, Juan, 53

Dîn Ilãhi, the, 55

Diocletian, Roman Emperor, 107, 112, 167, 248, 249

Dion, Proconsul of Roman Province of Africa Proconsularis, 102

Dionysius II, tyrant of Syracuse, 69

Dionysus, worship of, 31

Displaced persons, *see* DÉRACINÉS

Distance, annihilation of, 36, 92, 138, 213, 216, 237, 244, 261, 278, 294, 296

Dominican Order, the, 156, 265

Donatists, the, 115

'Drive', 149, 193, 228ff., 286

Druses, the, 55

Durga, worship of, 24

EAST ASIAN CIVILIZATION, *see* FAR EASTERN CIVILIZATION

East Roman Empire, the, 110, 111, 112

Egypt: alien conquerors' régimes in, 112; artificial religions, attempts to manufacture, 51-2; Middle Empire of, 45, 48; militarism in, 59; New Empire of, 6, 7, 45, 48;

Religions, higher—*cont.*
  all call for renunciation, 313
  as chrysales of civilizations, 145, 181
  as different roads to the heart of the mystery, 251
  avatars, successive, doctrine of, 133
  changes in outward forms, probability of future, 141
  choice of faith, increasing opportunities for, 139
  complementary missions of different religions, 295, 296-7
  co-existence of: claims to uniqueness in relation to, 135-6; means of communication in relation to, 137-9, 261; probable continuance of, 136, 138-9, 261-2; psychological types in relation to, 138-9, conduct the test of validity, 295
  déracinés as seed of, 76ff.
  difficulty of conversion from one to another, 159
  epiphanies of, 35, 74-88, 104; as new departure in history, 139; social milieux of, 75ff., 129, 130, 137
  essential elements of, 155, 261-77
  exploitation of: for cultural purposes, 112; for political purposes, 104-15; resistance to, 113-15
  extinct, 136
  founders of: apotheosis of, 128, 129; authority deemed to have been bequeathed by, 130
  geneses of, 244
  gospel of, 104, 113, 125, 140-1, 286
  historic success of, 263
  holy places, part played by, 278
  institutional aspect of, 263; *see also* CHURCHES
  intermingling of adherents, probable increase in, 139, 261-2, 282-3, 294
  myths, rôle of, 280-1
  objective judgment in making comparisons impossible at present, 296
  persecution of, 89, 101, 105-6; *see also under* BUDDHISM: Mahayana; CHRISTIANITY
  philosophies, encounters with, 116-27
  presentation of, in local and temporary terms, 112, 116ff., 124, 126-7, 156, 158, 168-9, 264-5, 267, 269ff., 282
  propagation of, 246ff.

  reformation as a perpetual challenge, 262
  regional limits of, in the past, 138
  rituals, part played by, 278-9
  rivalry between, 146
  social conventions in relation to, 279
  staying-power of, 136
  subversive effects of, 91-2
  tabus, rôle of, 279
  toleration, motives for, 249ff.
  uniqueness, claim to: challenges to, 131-3; competing claimants, 135ff.; decisive events in relation to, 139-40; passions aroused by, 139; peak in Time-Space, question of, 133-4; sociological and psychological explanations of, 137ff.; sinfulness of, 128, 135, 141, 282-3; *see also above under* co-existence
  whole-hearted response to, dangers of, 113

  see also BUDDHISM; CHRISTIANITY; HINDUISM; GOD; ISLAM; JUDAISM; REALITY; ZOROASTRIANISM

Renaissance, the Italian, 168, 180, 208, 210
'Republic of Letters', the, 194, 210, 212*n*.
Road, rules of the, 238-9
Roman Catholic Church, the: as heir of Roman Empire, 109, 209; ecclesiastical supremacy, question of, 268; heretics, treatment of, 205, 206; liberal and illiberal trends in, 156-9, 268ff., 279; liturgy of, 155, 159, 268; missionary work of, 155-61; Orthodox Christian Churches, Eastern, relations with, 268, 279; priests—celibacy of, 279;—position of, 130; Protestant Churches, relations with, in twentieth century, 261; religious orders, 166; science, attitude towards, 269; scripture, attitude towards, 131; States, relation to, 111, 114; *see also* PAPACY
Roman Empire, the:
  Antonines, age of, 7, 42, 117
  Arab invasion of, 248
  Army: Christians in, 101-3; code of conduct of, 95-6, 99; recruitment of, 93, 94, 99